FUSION

A MODERN 'HOW-TO' GUIDE FOR INTEGRATED MARKETING STRATEGY
(FROM CREATIVE SPARK TO SYNERGISTIC EXPLOSION)

JAMES A. MOUREY, Ph.D.

DEDICATION

To my Odyssey of the Mind family around the world—especially Joanne and Bob Rompel, the Micklus Family, and my competition and judging team members—thanks for helping me nurture my creative soul, release my wildly absurd ideas, and bring laughter and inspiration to others.

To Mom and Dad—my Odyssey of the Mind coaches—thanks for all the crayons, paper, colored pencils, keyboards, instruments, craft projects, computer games, summer day camps, books, movies, video games, and VHS tapes so I could record *Saturday Night Live* and *American Gladiators*.

This explains my obsession with comedy and fitness.

Now, about the long-term effects of *Dirty Dancing*...

CONTENTS

ACKNOWLEDGMENTS

'Insomnia.' If we are going to be honest about who or, in this case *what*, is responsible for this book, I imagine we should really start with insomnia. Insomnia usually gets a bum rap, but there is something to be said for having the ability to collect your thoughts, focus, and write in the wee hours of the morning while also having the soothing sounds of infomercials and phone sex advertisements as your background music.

'Having Strong Opinions' is probably a close second, followed by 'Creativity,' 'Commitment," and, 'Craziness,' in no particular order. It turns out that, given my professional and educational experiences, I had some thoughts about marketing campaign creation that really needed to be released. I honestly thought it was just gas at first. I was mistaken.

Just under three years ago I embarked on my first writing adventure: *Urge*, a fun textbook about Consumer Behavior. Since then I have written research articles, an academic book chapter, and two children's books, but not another full-length adult book (…er, book for adults–the other phrasing sounds like erotic fiction, which I do *not* write…anymore). Now that I have completed book number two, I think there may be *one* more book left in me…someday…but I may need a vacation first.

There are more people to thank for my existence (and weirdness) than there is room in this book, or any book, to list. However, I will do my best to thank as many people as I can with the understanding that 1) there are more of you out there, and 2) I love you just as much.

First, I want to thank my family–Sherry (mom), Jim, Sr. (dad), Chad (brother), Kim and Kelly (sisters), and Mocha (dog and life coach). These people are the most responsible for the person I am today, so really anything I write, create, build, dream, or do starts with this team. There's no secret to happiness and success in this world: a loving, supportive family is all you need. What is extra special is that my in-laws–Heather, Declan, and Bill–are just as amazing, as are my nephews–Caleb, Cooper, and Liam–and my soon-to-be niece! These kiddos laugh at all my jokes, *want* to draw with me (for fun!), and love all the crazy gifts I buy them…not to mention the fact that they are super smart, insanely creative, and all-around great kids. I hope they never grow up.

Also, thanks to my just-as-loving extended family members, who have always been supportive of my crazy endeavors and who provide plenty of hilarity that fuel my comedy sketches and remind me never to take life *too* seriously. I am finishing this book on my grandma's first birthday since her passing this past year, so, "Happy Birthday, grandma! I got you this book!" Seriously, though, my grandmother's wit and sense of humor largely shaped mine growing up, so I am confident some of the zingers and silliness in this book were heaven sent. The same can be said of the positive spiritual juju sent from Coco Maria Chanel, Chihuahua extraordinaire, who often parked herself on my lap to nap while I worked on creative endeavors for hours at a time. If reincarnation is a thing, I hope to be the dog of someone who loves me as much as I have loved my dogs. They are the best.

Thanks to my colleagues at DePaul University–Melissa, Rich, Steve K. #1, Steve K. #2, Nina, Sue, Zafar, Joel, Lawrence, Al, Deirdre, Leslie, Jack, Marina, Tommy, Petr, Andrew, Bruce, Geoff, Roger B., Roger L., Luis, Dan, Jurate, Kate, and more. It is always refreshing to look forward to being in the office and leaving my door open to chat. Yes, it probably cuts into productivity, but when we are 80 and looking back on life, I bet we will appreciate our conversations, our laughter, and our commitment to great research *and* great teaching (*and* great advising, to boot) that truly changes the lives of our students. That said, thanks also to my undergraduate and MBA students for being so passionate about learning, as well as my incredibly talented student members of the DePaul Marketing Consulting Group, the Modern Marketing Lab, the *It's a Brand New Day* podcast, and *Street Walkers* YouTube series. I don't know that I did it intentionally, but I sure hope I am passing on the creative fire that fuels my spirit each day via the work we do together.

Thanks to my marketing mentors and heroes–Del Schwinke and Sara (Story) Krenski–with whom even conversations about "dayparts" can become absolutely magical. Thanks also to the amazing advising team at WashU–Konnie, Lanna, Steve, Dean Hochberg–for being so great at your jobs but, more important, for being such great friends and remarkable people. Thank you to Dr. John Branch and Dr. Amar Cheema for getting me into this mess and Dr. Carolyn Yoon and Dr. Fred Feinberg for keeping me in it. Thanks also to my colleagues at Northwestern University, particularly Dr. Aparna Labroo and Dr. Angela Lee, for being so welcoming, friendly, and fun (in life and at work).

Professionally, I owe a great deal of gratitude and appreciation to the rockstar team in St. Louis that survived in the trenches together: Kelly McMahon, Becky Reichardt, Sarah Thompson, Lisa Robinson, and Karin Moody. Equally as important to (and loved by) me are my colleagues from Los Angeles: Keith, Jim, Dwayne, Josie, Genia, Dawn, Conor, Diana, Sara, April, Jeff, Jordan, Ben, and Adam. FerrazziGreenlight also brought Stan Lim, Mark Goulston, and Julie Ede into my life, and I am forever grateful for their warm, brilliant souls.

Internationally, I want to say, "Danke," to my German family–Stefan, Martin, Christian and Alex, Carola, Kumari, Marie, Juliane, Daniel, Basti, Sabine, and everyone–as well as my dear friends and 'family' spread around the world: Jeanne, Cindy, Melanie, Larissa, Ingrid, and so many others. Culture enriches life, so to be able to share in so many different cultures, perspectives, and experiences with so many great people has really increased my life's taxable income...I need more Swiss friends.

To my Los Angeles family–Luke, Vogel, Dwayne, Frenchie, Ben, EMC–thanks for making me feel like Los Angeles remains my second home. I know I have been promising it for years, but I really am trying to figure out a way so I can split my time between Chicago and LA, and not even because of the weather but because I love all of you *that* much!

Thanks to my Chicagoan friends and family. From the Uptones a cappella group to the 9th Grade Physical Education team at Second City, as well as friends from iO, I am glad we all have each other with whom we can express our creative selves and live the spirit of, "Yes, and..." every day. To Jamee, Jess, Deepti, Kyle, Ilya, Stefan, Tyler, Andrew, Joe, Beth, Stephanie, Steve, Joanne, Lauren, Justin, Javier, Linda, Ed, and all the friends I do not get to see nearly as much as I would like, are you free for brunch this Sunday around noon?

To my Michigan family–thanks to Linda, Joe, and Laura for being the warmest, kindest, and funniest extended family members a guy could ever want! Kelsey, for being my partner-in-crime and Starbucks therapy buddy for so many years (reality show soon to come). Leena, Lisa, Jason, Dana, and Jon for being work, life, laugh, and love partners…but in, like, a totally platonic way. The CEOhs, Cara, Jen, Matt, Jack, Irina, Anna Marie, and co., for singing our hearts out and confusing international students who thought the CEOhs was a club for budding C-suite executives. To Kate for making beautiful music with me (that sounds odd) and so much more; we still have an album to record. To Dr. Alexis Toulouse for confusing every waiter we ever had with your name and joining me for extended work sessions at every coffee house in Ann Arbor so we did not have to feel so lame doing work all the time. To my fellow Ph.D. cohort for surviving the experience (and enjoying it somehow). And especially to my brain *and* heart soul mates, Zach and Jung Robin (and Jae!), for laughter, love, and life advice every magical minute we get to spend together.

To my academic family (a.k.a., LOBES), thanks to Keisha, Adriana, Eugenia, Stephen, Kelly, Lin, and my brother-from-another-mother, Ryan, for being the highlight of every work trip, of this career, and of life, in general (as well as your growing families!). Thank you to Robin Soster, karaoke queen, who introduced me to the wonderful group at IÉSEG that served as the impetus for making this book happen at long last. My collaborators–Jenny, Daphna, Andy, Lawrence, Ben–for working with me and my crazy schedule to still produce world-class research even though I email you back 4:00am.

To Ms. Erin Joy Haigh, few people know that you singlehandedly kept me studying business at WashU when I was thinking about leaving to go study education elsewhere. From our first phone call (you had me at, "Danish") to our GChats, random phone calls, and occasional reunions, I am thankful for every second we get to spend chatting in our busy lives because you have made such a huge difference in mine. Here's to many more years of playing phone tag and enjoying the inevitable reunions when they happen. You see, I would not have written this book if it weren't for you; instead, I would likely be doing improv on cruise ships.

To Mr. James Curtis Pomeroy, thank you for putting up with me while I penned this book. I imagine you are probably the person who is the second-happiest that I have finally finished this tome (although there is a chance you might be even happier than I am because now you don't have to hear me say, "I really need to work on the book, but I don't have any time!" every five seconds). Thanks for the iced coffees in the morning, the turkey chili in the evenings, and the suggestion "go get donuts" at Do-Rite each and every single time. Here's to many more adventures (and many more donuts, especially donuts on the beach)! Now that the book is finished, I think it is time to start planning for Parson!

Thank you Berenice Varela for serving as my editor for both *Urge* and now *Fusion*. No matter how hard we try we can never seem to catch our own mistakes, so thank you so much for taking the time to read the book so carefully and to correct my silly typos, random words, and unclear points. Your opinion is worth its weight in gold!

And, finally, thanks to the Odyssey of the Mind family–starting with Dr. Sam and Carole, Sammy and Cheryl (and Katarina and William), Stephanie and the entire team at CCI, and all the volunteers, coaches, and team members from around the world who live *the* most creative lives every single day. I love my team members just like family–Krystal, Mo, Erin, Brandy, Ben, Kari, Andrew–past and present–Stefan, Marci, Rob and Kathy, Jimmy, Michael, Marie, Allen, Lynda, Lindsey, Kristin, Tracy, Matt, and so many more–because we *are* a creative family. It is up to us to share our passion for creativity, our love of the world, and our love of our friends around the world to ensure a better future for these generations and the generations to follow.

Okay, just one more round of thanks: Harney & Sons Cinnamon Spice Tea, Honest Cinnamon Sunrise Herbal Tea, Boom Chicka Puff Sweet & Salty, Terra Sweet Potato Chips, and Starbucks (...everything about Starbucks). Oh, and supportive phone calls from Mom and Dad! The brain needs energy to be creative, but the heart and soul appreciate some attention, too. ☺

JAMES A. MOUREY

Focus

PROSPECTIVE AUDIENCE (PA)

Desired Objective (DO)	My Customers	Others' Customers	Hot-Off-The-Press Customers	Wandering Customers
Multiply Purchases				
Open Up More Options				
Rally the Troops				
Educate				

Understanding

Lifestyle — Demographics, Personality, Media Habits, who are these people in relatable terms?

Education — How much do customers know/not know about your brand, product, industry?

Attitudes — Thoughts & feelings re: brand, product, etc. — perceptual and preference maps.

Reflection — How do customers see themselves? How do others see them? What do they aspire to be?

Needs — Are needs fully addressed? Do needs exist that are not being addressed?

Synthesize

Focus Objectives → [FROM] **CREATIVE SPARK** [TO AN IDEA YOU] **LOVE** ← Understanding Insights

Logical idea logically connects our focus goals with our understanding of the core consumer.

One-of-a-Kind idea is new and could actually be applied to another brand!

Valuable idea is a thematic idea that has creative "legs" and works across media.

Emotional idea is emotionally evocative or otherwise engaging.

Ideation

PARTNERSHIPS
- Sponsorships and Endorsements
- Public Relations and Press Releases
- Sales/Customer Service
- Bundling/Cross-Promotional Activities
- Promotions
- Sampling
- Philanthropic Initiatives
- Product Placement

OUTLANDISH
- Guerilla Marketing
- Content Marketing
- Experiential Marketing

REVOLUTIONARY
- Product Innovation
- Packaging Redesign
- Pricing Shift
- Pricing Shift
- Alternative Access
- Promotional Strategy

TRADITIONAL MEDIA
- Television
- Radio
- Outdoor
- Indoor
- Internet/Website
- Print
- Mobile
- Direct Marketing
- Tradeshows/Events

SOCIAL MEDIA
- Social Networks (e.g., Facebook, Instagram, Twitter)
- Word-of-Mouth
- Forums and Message Boards
- Blogs and Tumblrs

Operation

RESPONSE — Anticipating competitive responses to your integrated marketing campaign and adjusting the campaign accordingly.

EDITING — Reviewing the campaign in its entirety, locating holes, eliminating redundancy, and striving for the most elegant campaign.

AFTERMATH — Considering the lull between campaigns or the transition from your current campaign to the next integrated marketing campaign.

COUNTERATTACKS — Preparing for provocations or reactions from competitors that affect our company, product/service, and/or campaign.

TIMELINE — Reviewing the campaign over its proposed timeline to determine the most efficient media spend, execution amount, and synergy.

TEST — Awareness, Liking, Purchase Intentions, Knowledge, Willingness-to-Pay.

Net Effect

Affect — Changes inc:
- Feeling Type
- Feeling Strength
- Emotional Connection
- Preferences

Behavior — Changes inc:
- Purchasing frequency
- Portfolio purchases
- Premium purchases
- Referrals

Cognition — Changes inc:
- Thoughts
- Awareness
- Attitude Importance
- Knowledge

[To Focus]

(Upon reviewing the campaign's effectiveness with respect to the focus goals and objectives, begin the cycle again...)

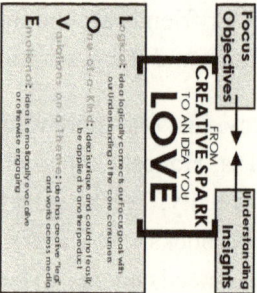

fu·sion (fyo͞oZHən) *n.*
A nuclear reaction in which atomic nuclei combine to form more massive nuclei with the simultaneous release of energy.[1]

[1] American Heritage® Dictionary of the English Language, Fifth Edition. Copyright © 2011 by Houghton Mifflin Harcourt Publishing Company.

PREFACE | My Creative Odyssey

I once caught an international thief.

No really, it's true! Benny the Balsa Breaker, the leader of a notorious global crime ring, had been traveling around the world stealing famous international landmarks from the Eiffel Tower to the Great Wall of China, Big Ben to the Great Pyramid of Giza. After picking up on subtle, cryptic clues–like a picture of an "eye" that was "full" of a "tower" (get it?)–I finally caught up with Benny, made the arrest, and stopped his evildoings. The best part? I was only in fourth grade at the time.

Before you start thinking you accidentally picked up the wrong book written by a crazy person, I will explain this madness. Benny the Balsa Breaker was a character in a skit I helped write for a school activity I had recently joined: Odyssey of the Mind. Odyssey of the Mind is an international school program that has challenged gifted and talented youth everywhere to solve problems using creativity and divergent (v. convergent) thinking for over 40 years. Each year five "problems" are released and students around the world set out to solve those problems, a process that involves writing skits, building backdrops, designing costumes, constructing vehicles and weight-bearing structures made of light-weight balsa wood, and more. Think of it as "Hollywood Club" – where kids learn writing, producing, costume design, acting, singing, set construction, and directing!

Sounds cool, right? Well, let's be clear: before fourth grade, I was a fairly nerdy kid...let's be honest: I am *still* a huge nerd. As a kid, I would spend my free time writing comedy sketches, moving furniture around to make a "stage," and forcing my siblings to perform shows with me while my very loving (and very patient) parents pretended we were funny (...or maybe we *were* actually funny, but when the only remaining evidence of our work from this era consists of a rap we wrote about the breakfast cereal "Fruity Pebbles," our comedic talent must be called into question). Whereas most kids in kindergarten said they wanted to be policemen or firemen or veterinarians, my response was usually something like, "I want to be on *Saturday Night Live*." A kid can dream, right?

Beyond tormenting my parents with jokes that could only be funny to children, I would sit at the table for *hours* and draw Disney characters, caricatures of famous people, architectural blueprints for the massive mansion I planned to own one day (each wing of the mansion populated by my favorite dog breeds...I clearly didn't think through the logistics, or smell, of that). I would write poetry that later became songs. I would sit at my mom's electric organ, the one she used to take lessons on growing up, to teach myself how to play piano using her old song books. As a result, most of my earliest songs were the hits of the 1960s and 1970s, like Petula Clark's

"Downtown" and the 5th Dimension's "Aquarius/Let the Sunshine In." If you are not realizing my level of "cool" just yet, it's about to get real…

Personal computers were just becoming a "thing" when I was a kid, a time pre-Internet when families first began getting a "family computer" for the house. That's right, young'uns, *one* computer for the *entire* house. I remember our family's first computer purchase like it was yesterday. My father bought the computer, as well as a massive computer desk/cabinet with a nice faux wood finish, and we were instructed not to play around the computer as if it were a holy relic to be revered but never touched like a Kardashian face or something. Now, my family was not destitute, but we were also not living like the Romneys or Donald Trump, either. A computer was a big deal, not to mention the accompanying printer and the paper that had the holes on either side and connected each sheet with a perforated edge (remember that?). This all seems so ancient and foreign now, but for years this was the world of computers, and I *loved* it. I would sit at the computer for hours and design CD album covers in Microsoft Paint. I would write short stories, poems, and sketches in word processing programs that predated Microsoft Word (I was a pioneer). I would teach myself programming in DOS. The computer was another outlet for me to *create*, and I found that I had a penchant for creating.

However, my absolute *favorite* thing to do on the computer was to play computer games. From the *King's Quest* series to *Jeopardy!*, *SimCity* to a surgery game called *Life and Death* (spoiler alert: my patients died *every* time, perhaps cementing the idea that a career in medicine was not in the cards for me). I would sit for hours and be taken away to the kingdom of Daventry, the valley of esoteric and arguably useless knowledge (i.e., *Jeopardy!*), and the basement morgue of the hospital (where I was consistently berated for accidentally killing my patients–I still don't understand why they let me come back time after time). Still, no game measured up to one in particular, the computer game of all computer games: *Where in the World is Carmen Sandiego?*

If you are unfamiliar, the Carmen Sandiego series is rooted in the genre of international spy/thief-chaser stories. You work as a detective for the ACME Detective Agency, and your goal in life is to catch this sly criminal mastermind, Carmen Sandiego, famous for her bright red trench coat, oversized hat, and cunning ability to evade capture by the world's best detectives. In the original game, you chase Carmen and her henchmen (who have clever names like "Ken Hartley Reed" and "Heidi Gosikh") as they steal famous artifacts from around the world, chasing them from international city to international city based on historical facts and clues about each destination. In other words, it is really an *educational* game that just so happens to be a lot of fun. To this day, I know an obscene amount about other countries, cultures, international flags, and history thanks largely to the Carmen Sandiego games. You also now know where that sketch idea about Benny the Balsa Breaker came from: it was a parody of the Carmen Sandiego game series.

This brings us back to Odyssey of the Mind. In fourth grade, my gifted and talented teacher, Joanne Rompel (one of my all-time favorite people), told my parents she thought I might be good for this program called Odyssey of the Mind. I had no idea what it was, and I was happy enough keeping to myself and channeling my creativity through dances my siblings and I choreographed to *Sister Act* songs and romantic comedies starring my superhero toy figurines (you wouldn't guess it based on his icy exterior, but Batman is *such* a romantic). No, I did not need to do some weird program with some long name like "Odyssey of the Mind."

"But it's *international*," I remember my brother telling me. I remember my mom being on the phone with Mrs. Rompel while Chad, my brother, was talking to me about how I would get to meet people from France and Germany and [insert country of choice here...except maybe not North Korea]. Chad, who later went on to become a lawyer, was already quite adept at using his skills of rhetoric and persuasion. Knowing that Carmen Sandiego had piqued my interest about the world and its many cultures and languages, Chad sold me on the idea that I might get to meet *foreign* people! You have to understand how cool this sounded to a middle-class kid from rural southern Illinois whose only "international travel" experience up to that point was the World Showcase at Epcot (a place I *still* love to this day) and who, in high school, would be cast as Mowgli in a production of *The Jungle Book* due largely in part to his tan skin and the general lack of diversity in my hometown (I like to think my acting skills helped, too...side note: for the first ¼ of the play, the younger version of Mowgli was played by my friend Tralaena Williams, a dark-skinned African-American female...I can only imagine how confused the children in the audience were when I replaced Tralaena later in the show).

So it was really the potential to meet other people from around the world that finally pushed me over the edge. I found myself participating in Odyssey of the Mind, the first year of what has become a 23-year journey. In over two decades, I have made dear friends (family, really) from Germany to India, Singapore to Poland, Mexico to Moldova, and all over the United States. I have traveled around the world to visit these special people over the years. The funny thing is that they all think I came to see them when, in reality, I'm still just looking for Carmen Sandiego.

The first Odyssey of the Mind problem my team and I opted to solve back in 1993 was titled "Which End is Up?" The problem required us to build a balsa wood structure with specific size, shape, and weight requirements. Our structure would be "tested" by supporting as much weight as possible, so our challenge was to design a structure using what little we knew of architectural strength. In addition, we were to present a skit to accompany our structure's weight testing, so we opted to incorporate a "Which End is Up?" theme throughout our performance in which our props and backdrops took on different meaning depending on whether they were upright or flipped over. Taking this theme to the extreme, we also decided to engage in some gender-bending fun by having the main male role of the skit be played by a female (my friend, Maureen) and the main female role of the skit being played by a male (yours truly). For 1992, we were so progressive.

Lest you think this was the first time I had been dressed as a female, let me set the record straight: the year prior, in third grade, my mom found out that my teacher, Mrs. Marvich (another one of my all-time favorite people), was dressing as Mickey Mouse for Halloween. "What is Mickey without Minnie?" thought my loving mother. So, yes, yours truly was ~~encouraged~~ forced to go to school dressed as Minnie Mouse. Insult to injury, when I stayed after school to help clean up, my friend Amanda Hoffman thought it would be funny to push me off a desk I was standing on to take down decorations hanging from the lights. Little did Amanda know that I had been simultaneously holding in a major fart while reaching for that hanging bat decoration. In what seemed like the longest, slow-motion fall ever, upon hitting the ground I let out *the* loudest fart ever, seismic inducing, whilst dressed as Minnie Mouse...in a skirt. You're welcome for that visual.

I competed in Odyssey of the Mind for ten years and then switched to a judging and volunteer role, which I continue to this day. I have had the honor of hosting the awards ceremony for the program's World Finals for almost a decade now, an event that culminates with 15,000 people from around the world in an arena celebrating creativity and young people. I imagine there are few events in the world that evoke more hope for the future than Odyssey of the Mind's World Finals.

When I reflect on my life up to this point, I realize that Odyssey was *the* critical program that opened the floodgates to my creativity and my creative expression. I had dabbled in creative projects for years–from creating a cityscape on an Etch A Sketch in first grade to writing and recording commercial parodies during my summers in elementary school–with no true focus and no real outlet for my creative expression. Finally, with Odyssey of the Mind, not only did I have a channel for my creativity, I also had nerdy friends who were equally as creative who were also looking for an outlet. Odyssey of the Mind made me comfortable in my own skin and taught me skills that made me feel comfortable on stage, at ease in front of large audiences, confident when singing, playing instruments, improvising, working with teams, telling CEOs three times my age what to do, and so much more. To say a single program was instrumental in changing your life is a bold statement, but I mean it, I believe it, and I see it happen every day to children around the world who participate in the program now.

So why do I share this story about Odyssey of the Mind? Two reasons: 1) it's a cool program, so you, your children, or children you know should be involved, and 2) Odyssey of the Mind is what led me to marketing. Let me frame it differently: Odyssey of the Mind *is* marketing. You see, each Odyssey of the Mind "problem" presents a problem that needs to be solved, a list of requirements/limitations any solution must consider, a budget, a time limit, a scoring rubric, and an element of style that encourages you to put a personal flair in the work. This solution will be judged officially by trained judges, experts on the problem, as well as unofficially by an audience, whose applause and laughter will serve as metrics of the solution's success. This is marketing.

Every marketing campaign addresses a problem: a need to increase sales, to generate awareness, to educate. Every marketing campaign is given a budget. Every marketing campaign has constraints and limitations about what can and cannot be done. Every marketing campaign operates on a timeline with specific deadlines. Every marketing campaign has (or should have) specific metrics used to measure success. Highly knowledgeable people—executives, brand managers, colleagues—will have an opinion about how wonderful/terrible your campaign is. A broader audience, customers, will also weigh in by changing their purchasing behavior, commenting on your campaign, or (in the worst case) completely ignoring it (which is also "saying something" without *saying* anything). Although it was completely unintentional and not at all planned, I spent all of my childhood and young adulthood creating mini-marketing campaigns designed to impress audiences of hundreds using humor, music, backdrops, props, and costumes transformed from trash into masterpieces all within a set timeframe and within a tight budget.

Now, I went on to hone my marketing education formally while in undergrad at Washington University in St. Louis and then again when completing my Ph.D. at the University of Michigan. Few people know that I actually began business school as a finance/accounting major with a goal of being an investment banker upon graduating. You see, as a first generation college student, I really had *zero* idea of what I was actually getting into. As an example, when my buddy Alex Latushkin once asked me about my IRA in our early days at b-school, I replied with, "Oh, my dad handles all my taxes." I was off to a great start.

Although I began with a focus on finance and accounting, and I was both good at and enjoyed these classes, something just didn't feel right. The joke I often tell is that I was a creative guy who had spent his entire life doing creative things trying to pursue a career in finance or accounting…and we all know what happens to "creative accountants."

As time went on, I found myself gravitating toward marketing and then embracing it fully when I had the epiphany that I had already been doing marketing my entire life. Furthermore, I noticed that my approach to solving business problems, to creating presentations, to pitching business ideas were *different* from most of my peers. I became known, early on, for having creative, interactive presentations and aesthetically-pleasing deliverables that were as artistic as they were effective, approaches that were clearly inspired by my experiences in Odyssey.

During and just after undergrad, I worked at a marketing agency that helped internationalize local brands (e.g., Bissinger's chocolates), helped localize marketing for international brands (e.g., Ritz-Carlton, Tiffany & Co.), and worked on event-related marketing for arts clients (e.g., the Contemporary Art Museum of St. Louis). This was a nice, natural progression from the independent consulting and branding projects I had done during college, and that progression continued to a C-suite marketing and management consulting position in Los Angeles. My position, the Executive Director of Research, essentially had me integrating science into new modules our consultants used with clients, as well as penning books and developing intellectual property with the head honcho. It was a nice life that I sometimes question leaving behind (especially when it's winter in Chicago), but I had plans to complete my Ph.D. I still do a fair bit of public speaking and consulting projects for clients ranging from private equity firms to startups, apparel companies to educational/non-profit organizations when I am not in the classroom or the lab (yes, labs exist outside of chemistry!), which allows me to keep one foot in the "real world" and one foot in the "academic world."

In each of these positions in which I was tasked to solve or help solve the problems facing real companies, I noticed elements of Odyssey of the Mind peeking through. My approach to problems. My brainstorming process. My obsession with knowing upon what metrics a campaign was to be evaluated and focusing the limited resources as efficiently as possible according to those metrics. These were not skills I learned in business school; they were skills I learned as a child and spent a lifetime honing.

I realize that you probably now know a lot more about my life than you ever thought you would (or maybe even wanted to know), but I provide this background for a reason: to assure you that you are in good hands. I am a lucky, lucky guy. I have been fortunate enough to receive a formal education at some of the world's best business schools (Olin Business School at Washington University in St. Louis and the Ross School of Business at the University of Michigan), so I understand business as a science. I have been able to work in positions that involved complete marketing campaign development from beginning to end, consulting chief executives of Fortune 500 companies, and giving talks to people representing a variety of industries (e.g., finance, tech, media, etc.), so I understand business as a practice. My passion lies in the creative and performing arts, which I have done my *entire* life and continue to this day: singing, improvising, speaking, podcasting, etc.

This brings me to today; it brings me to you. A lot of people I have met assume that I must have known what I wanted to do since birth, that I was simply "born to do marketing" and charted out a course that would steer my ship to its current port. This could not be any further from the truth. In reality, my obsession with a nerdy computer game led to a love of culture, that love of culture led me to do a nerdy school program, that nerdy school program led me to a passion for creative problem solving, that passion for creative problem solving led me to marketing, and that love of all-things marketing led me to where I am today: a professor of marketing who teaches the eager minds of tomorrow about the discipline I have spent an entire life perfecting. I like to remind my students of this when they come to my office as little lost birds unsure of where to fly or how to even leave the nest in the first place. I am a big believer that everything *does* happen for a reason and that any path, no matter how circuitous, has its lessons that will lead you to the right place.

My path has taken me many interesting places–from the very creative places of writing songs for children's television shows, authoring and illustrating children's books, and developing a Pixar-styled animated short to the far less creative, far more analytic places of research, data collection, and complex statistical modeling (#Sexy). Usually, these are two worlds that could not be more opposite; yet, for me, I sit at this weird intersection of creativity and calculation that informs how I view the development of effective, efficient marketing campaigns that also just so happen to be aesthetically pleasing, aurally arousing, and emotionally evocative. I am lucky because I get to engage in the best of both worlds on a daily basis.

And everything, every last piece, stems directly from Odyssey of the Mind: developing creative, hilarious, and memorable solutions while also solving a problem, scoring points, and doing it all as efficiently as possible. Thus, it should be no surprise that I believe a great marketing campaign is one that 1) meets important business objectives, and 2) creates a memorable, unique, artistic, sensory experience in the minds of consumers and *transforms* them. This, friends, is what *Fusion* is all about, and as someone who eats, breathes, and dreams marketing each and every single day of my life, I have a few tips I would like to share.

So let's get started on this creative odyssey, shall we?

OVERVIEW | The FUSION Framework

Marketing is evil.

In fact, some even say that marketing led to the downfall of mankind…okay, maybe that is a *bit* dramatic, but if you are familiar with the classic Biblical story of Adam and Eve then you likely remember that a sneaky serpent slithered into to the garden, beckoned Eve over to the tree of knowledge, and was like, "Hey, girl, you hungry? You gotta try this fruit! It is *delicious*!"

Eve contemplated this proposal for a second remembering that, just moments before, a booming voice in the sky told her and Adam they were welcome to indulge in *any* of the fruits, animals, and vegetation in the replete garden, a true food-lover's paradise, *except* for this one piece of fruit hanging on the Tree of Knowledge.

As an aside, this part of the Creation story also shows God's sense of humor: the Tree of Knowledge was placed right in the center of the garden. He could have easily placed the fruit in some shaded corner in some difficult-to-access part of the garden, but no, He thought it would be fun to put the tree right in the middle of the garden so Adam and Eve would have to see the fruit no matter which direction they were facing. This same sense of humor also explains why God gave us Kanye West and *The Real Housewives* series. He's such a kidder.

So Eve responded to the serpent after some deliberation with a very considerate, very well-thought-through reply: "Umm, no."

The serpent, ne'er one to be deterred, replied, "What?! Why not?! It's delicious – this tree has like five stars on Yelp! That fruit was in the Oprah's Favorite Things issue of *O* magazine!" (Oprah has been around since the beginning).

"But the booming voice in the sky told us not to!" Eve probably said, "Now leave me alone so I can sit here and do my sudoku in peace."

I like to imagine the serpent and Eve then engaged in a bit of a back and forth, cartoon-like scene where the serpent leaves and comes back to the garden in different disguises each time–like a barbershop hat, a fake mustache, a bow tie, and a cane he uses to point to charts discussing the merits of eating the forbidden fruit, each reason increasingly more elaborate than the next (e.g., "It's low on the glycemic index and fits your Weight Watchers plan!" – "It's red, and red is this season's color! It was all over runways in Paris!" – "It's an apple and in a few millennia there's going to be this great company called Apple that has more money than any other company; don't you want to get in on the ground floor of that investment?!" – fun fact of the day: nowhere in Genesis is the fruit actually referred to as an apple but because it fits that final joke we will continue to perpetuate this misconception).

Finally, Eve caves. She takes a bite of the delicious fruit and immediately is flooded with the knowledge of what is good and what is bad. This is likely the moment that Jewish/Catholic/insert-religion-of-choice guilt began (thanks a lot, Eve), but that was not the end of the story. You remember Adam, right? He was still in the garden despite briefly taking a "supporting actor" role while the serpent and Eve had their scene.

So Adam strolls back in (he couldn't be too far – it is *one* garden, remember), sees Eve eating the fruit, and says something like, "Oh hey, Eve! What are you eating there?" to which Eve replies, "Oh, you know, it's just that delicious piece of fruit, the *one thing* that the mysterious booming voice told us not to eat. I'm just, well, you know, I'm just eating it." Eve then offers Adam a piece of the fruit, and almost as easily as the serpent was able to convince Eve to take a bite, Adam also indulges in the fruit. If convincing customers to buy your product/service were as simple as telling someone, "Oh, Bob told me to buy it, so I did; you should, too," we would all be billionaires.

In just mere moments, all of mankind was permanently tainted thanks entirely to a sneaky snake peddling a piece of fruit onto the poor, unsuspecting, Adam and Eve. Adam and Eve, now possessing the knowledge of good and evil, became immediately aware of their nudity, which filled them with shame and led them to hide naked in the garden until they were ultimately banished from the garden–kind of like my grandma was that one time she snuck into our neighbor's garden naked to steal some fruit.

And with that, the Biblical story of Creation forever tells a tale in which two people, convinced they should consume a product they neither needed nor wanted, wind up consuming said product and ruining *everything* for the rest of us. The icing on the cake, of course, is that this story is just one of many (e.g., Pandora's Box) in which the actions of a single woman ruined the world for everyone (thanks for the misogyny, history).

However, beyond the sexist implications of the tale, the story also casts persuasion, consumption, and indulgence in a negative light, as well. The serpent's efforts to persuade are positioned as self-serving, not altruistic. This could be true, as the serpent is often thought (but never explicitly said) to represent the devil himself, but how do we know it wasn't just some snake trying to be friendly? Second, although the garden was replete with food of every kind, it is natural for humans to want the one thing they are told they cannot have. We use this kind of exclusivity in marketing all the time. If getting to consume the *one* thing they were told they could not eat brought more joy and value to Adam and Eve than eating ten of the fruits they were told they *could* eat, why should this be a bad thing? And, finally, who is to say it is wrong to let people indulge in the products they deem appropriate for their personal consumption? If Adam and Eve *knew* the risks associated with eating the forbidden fruit but chose to partake anyway, isn't that on them and not the serpent?

And this is where we return to marketing leading to the fall of mankind. Marketing, it seems, was doomed from the beginning of time to be thought of as an evil process, an exercise in deceit, a zero-sum game with clear winners (the serpent) and clear losers (Adam and Eve), a game perfected by the devil himself.

Of course, that is *one* way to look at it, but it doesn't have to be that way…

*   *   *

Marketing *can* be evil, but, far more often than not, marketing is good.

As marketers, entrepreneurs, businesspeople, and as people, in general, we must always ask ourselves one simple question: when we are attempting to persuade someone to think, feel, or behave a certain way, what value does this bring to *them*? Companies rarely spend marketing dollars unless there is some strategic goal: generating awareness, increasing sales, building customer loyalty, etc. Thus, most marketing campaigns begin with a company's goals in mind, are measured for success based on how well they help the company reach its goals, and include incentives for employees that pertain, almost exclusively, to achieving the company's goals. Somewhere in this process we lost sight of the customer.

Thinking back to Adam, Eve, and that sneaky serpent, the snake had no regard for the needs of Eve or Adam or their protests that they were told not to eat the forbidden fruit. Instead, he was focused on his own selfish, manipulative needs, which may have led to the immediate gratification provided by a delicious bite of fruit but that quickly devolved into chaos, sadness, and disappointment. Super uplifting, I know. This is why snakes are not to be trusted (neither, incidentally, are cats, which it turns out are really just fur-covered snakes).

To a degree, each of us chooses how we see the world. We interpret actions, we attribute responsibility, we create narratives in our minds in the absence of external explanations. You are about to read a book that essentially teaches you how to persuade entire groups of people to think a certain way, to believe a particular idea, to purchase a specific product or service, to *trust* you, your company, and your promises. Marketing is built on a solid philosophical foundation, one positing that humans have needs, humans can create, and–the magical main idea–humans help one another fulfill their needs through their creations. The tools in a marketer's toolkit– persuasion, communication, emotional evocation, reasoning–are extremely powerful. When used correctly, these tools can result in immeasurable joy, happiness, and satisfaction, like a child opening that *one* toy they wanted more than any other at Christmas. Few experiences are as magical as that. When used incorrectly, however, these tools can still be just as effective but result in far starker consequences (see, for example, the work of Joseph Goebbels during World War II).

Thus, before we dive into the *how-to* of creating a successful marketing campaign, it is imperative to begin with the *why*. Why are we trying to change the thoughts, attitudes, and/or behavior of other people in the first place? The foundation of the FUSION framework is, and will always be, *changing the world for the better*, so before we build the model, before we get into the details of each component of the model, let us first begin by laying the foundation.

The Foundation of Marketing: Bringing Value to the Customer

As someone who chose a career in marketing, I have spent the better part of my life defending the discipline I love. Very few professions, except for maybe law and politics, receive as much criticism as marketing. "Oh, so you're in marketing?" they say, "So you make people buy things they don't need? Things that *kill* people? Things that *ruin people's lives?*" Yes, that's exactly how I chose my major in undergrad: I went into my undergraduate advisor's office and asked, "What can I do that will ruin people's lives?" Marketing popped up, and I just *knew* that had to be my major. I should pause here and remind people that it was finance, and not marketing, that led to the global economic collapse of 2008, an unprecedented scandal that ruined countless lives, but I digress.

As someone who eats, sleeps, and breathes marketing every day of his life, I tend to see the good side of marketing more than the bad. This is particularly true in the world of academic marketing where our focus is on uncovering the psychological processes behind how and why consumers make the choices they do so that we can improve decision-making while also minimizing behaviors that lead to harmful consequences. However, as someone immersed in the marketing world, I am also not naïve to the fact that there *are* many, many deceptive people who use marketing as a means for their deception, but I should point out that this is more a characteristic describing the *individual* than the discipline itself. These same people would likely be just as horrible and as deceptive if they worked in finance, accounting, medicine, or law; it's likely just easier to pin it on marketing because marketing is arguably more pervasive in everyone's daily life than any of these other disciplines. Not a day goes by where each one of us is not consuming *something*.

So let me begin by sharing my simple definition of marketing: **Marketing** is the bringing together of those who produce (i.e., suppliers) with those who consume (i.e., buyers) and *every* facet of that relationship, pre- and post-interaction, as well as during the interaction itself. I often tell my students to think of "marketing" as an umbrella term under which you can list concepts like advertising, customer support, sales, sponsorship, new product development, operations and logistics, promotion, research, and much, much more. At the end of the day, marketing is about helping individuals obtain what they want or need, all the while ensuring that they receive complete, honest, and accurate information so that they can make a choice that is right for them. That last part is often where the challenge arises.

To return to our earlier example, if the serpent in Eden would have been honest about his intentions or would have at least acknowledged Eve's protests per the booming voice in the sky's instructions, it is likely that Eve might not have eaten the fruit. Similarly, if tobacco companies had been honest about the fact that their cigarettes contained cancer-causing, addictive ingredients, society probably would not be as critical of them and their business practices as we are now. Most of us likely agree that individuals have a right to consume or not to consume the products and/or services they choose, but companies bear an obligation and a responsibility to be as transparent as possible about the content, production of, and ensuing impact their products/services could have on individuals, society, and the environment. If you know that cigarettes are addictive, contain harmful toxins, and lead to breathing problems but still choose to smoke, that is your decision–as long as you do not do it in my airspace (this is what we call a "negative externality").

A relatively recent philosophy emerged within the past two decades that is often referred to as the **Triple Bottom Line** (a.k.a., **TBL** or **3BL**). The "bottom line" in business lingo refers to the final line of a financial statement of revenues and expenses that indicates whether a company is profitable or experiencing a loss. Because so much is tied to this all-important number–stock prices, company valuation, corporate bonuses, etc.–there has always been an incentive for corporate decision-makers to do *whatever it takes* to ensure that a company's bottom line looks good. Business 101 tells us that in order to boost the bottom line we must increase revenues, decrease costs, or some combination of both. This means charging more for a product, selling more of a product, finding cheaper raw ingredients or materials to make the product, cutting labor costs, and any other number of actions that will pad the bottom line.

Obviously, you can see how this quest for a better bottom line could be slightly problematic. Consider, for example, the scandal plaguing the Michigan city of Flint as I write this book. An appointed (not elected) "emergency manager" in charge of getting the city's finances back in order opted to cut costs by switching the city's main water supply from the Detroit water system to the local Flint River, a move that was expected to save the city $1 million a year. Normally, this would not be a problem and might even be heralded as a smart, efficient business move. However, unlike the relatively safe water that was sourced from the Detroit supply, water from the Flint River was far more contaminated, possessing high levels of chloride, chloride that corroded the iron in the old pipes through which water would travel from the Flint River into the homes of the residents of Flint. As a result, the residents of Flint were exposed to toxic levels of lead in their drinking water for over a year. Now, despite switching the source of the water back to the Detroit supply, lead levels remain far above the accepted level of safety. Replacing the pipes in Flint will likely cost over $60 million, which far outweighs the planned savings for switching in the first place. Even worse news is that the effects of lead poisoning, including cognitive impairments and antisocial behavior, are believed to be irreversible. According to Flint's latest census numbers, nearly 9,000 children under the age of six may have been exposed to the toxic levels of lead simply by drinking water that was supposed to be safe.

Enter the Triple Bottom Line. The Triple Bottom Line includes a version of "economic" profit (the "revenues – costs" profit we think of most readily) that also accounts for any capital tied up as a cost (i.e., **"Economic Costs"**). However, even more significant is the inclusion of Social Costs and Environmental Costs. **Social Costs** include fair labor practices, acceptable wages, and prosocial efforts designed to improve the lives of society and the community in which a business operates. **Environmental Costs** include issues of sustainability, production processes, the ecological footprint of the organization, all the way from the initial growth and development of the rawest of raw materials going into a company's product or service to the post-use disposal of the product by the final end consumer. To say that these costs are comprehensive would be an understatement. In fact, the main idea of the Triple Bottom Line is to force a company to think holistically about how it operates, what it is in the business of doing, and how it can go about bringing value to customers in a way that minimizes the negative impact or costs on society, the environment, and the people and products/services in the company, itself.

To return to our Flint example, the emergency manager who made the catastrophic decision to switch the water supply was operating under an old school, accounting version of a bottom line, as many managers do, which led to extremely grave consequences for the people of Flint. If, instead, this emergency manager had been operating under the Triple Bottom Line philosophy, it is likely more questions would have been asked regarding the proposed switch's potential outcomes for society, the people of Flint, the environment, and other areas affected by the decision. While this is all merely speculative and water under the bridge (or, in this case, water in the corroded lead pipes) at this point, it is reasonable to wonder whether the catastrophe could have been prevented by a simple shift in thinking of what it means to be "profitable."

Now, there *are* some people who believe there should be no restrictions on the resources companies use, that firms have zero obligation to society or the environment and, instead, only need to answer to their shareholders by delivering cold, hard economic profit. This, of course, is absurd. Deforestation, the use of fossil fuels, and the exploitation of limited resources have irreversible consequences for all of society, even those of us not consuming the products made using these exploitative methods. While there may be certain advantages obtained in the *short-term* using this archaic approach, the ensuing costs in the *long-term* may stymie future profits in ways companies may not even realize. This is why governments sometimes get involved: to rein in the potential for companies to put economic profit (and selfish goals) before societal and environmental concerns. As a result, practices like testing cosmetics on monkeys in laboratories, a practice that could have negative physiological or psychological consequences for the monkeys, is strictly prohibited, which makes everyone feel better (…except for maybe the monkeys who were just about to go to a prom or a Glamour Shots photo shoot and now must improvise how to glam up without lipstick, mascara, and blush).

Because we are good, ethical people, we are going to agree, right now, to consider the Economic, Social, and Environmental bottom lines for *everything* that we do from this point on in the book (and in life). The foundation of the FUSION framework is that the value to consumers must never come at a cost so great to society that there is no *true* profit, all things considered. As you will see throughout the book, these additional "constraints" or "requirements" can actually result in *increased* creativity, *cleverer* ideas, and even *greater* profitability than if we were to ignore them. Thus, even when you feel confined or limited, this very perception of limitation can actually be more beneficial than absolute freedom to do what you want. And if anyone tries to argue that environmental regulations, societal protections, or living wages limit corporate "success" or "stunt growth," you can simply tell them that while you can acknowledge their shortsighted, path-of-least-resistance, easy-way-out approach, you are more sophisticated, more interested in long-term success, and more concerned about making sure everyone makes it to the top of the mountain together. Sure, those other people may make it to the top of the mountain and may even get there faster, but it's going to be pretty lonely at the top.

It may seem odd to talk at length about ethics, values, and the Triple Bottom Line before getting into the heart of this book, but the FUSION model is *built* on the belief that our job, as marketers, is to bring healthy, helpful value to consumers and producers. If you create a marketing campaign that can do this, you will be able to sleep much more easily at night (…some people also try wine, others try Ambien, just don't try both – that's dangerous). Plus, as society continues to expect ethical behavior and makes consumption choices that factor in this notion of corporate social responsibility, companies that fail to base their operations on sound ethical principles will be ignored and replaced by those that do.

FUSION: One Approach to Creating a Marketing Campaign

Fusion is a book about the art and science of marketing. Having spent the better part of my life immersed in a world of creativity and numbers, I have a few tips, insights, and techniques I want to share with the world. Now, chances are you picked up this book because 1) you are taking my class (most likely), 2) you work in marketing and want to learn a few tricks or ideas, 3) you made a mistake and were actually hoping to learn about the scientific process of nuclear fusion. Regardless of who you are–student, marketing practitioner, non-marketing person who just thought the book sounded interesting, drunk traveler stumbling through an airport bookstore looking for a distraction–my hope is that you can take some valuable ideas from this book and use them in your work or life.

I also hope that the book is an "easy" or "fun" read: it's definitely not your typical textbook. You *will* learn a lot, and my hope is that you enjoy reading about the real-world examples and personal stories that help teach and reinforce the ideas. My philosophy is that learning can be fun, so I will do my very best in this book to provide you with a framework you can use to develop a successful marketing campaign, but I promise to do so in a way that won't feel overly preachy, sleep inducing, or absolute. These are just some ideas I have that I hope make your life, your job, or your worldview a little bit better.

The FUSION framework is divided into six parts: Focus, Understand, Synthesize, Ideation, Operation, and Net Effect. Within each section, I will provide real-world examples, specific "how-to" steps and considerations, creative anecdotes from my personal and professional experiences, and thought experiments to help you apply the concepts to your unique situation. The sections can be summarized as follows:

> **Focus.** The first step involves considering the core business goal responsible for triggering or initiating a marketing campaign in the first place. Why are we going to spend time, money, and resources on a campaign? Whom are we trying to reach, and what do we want those people to do?

> **Understanding.** The second step involves collecting marketing research that will help us make informed decisions. We want to *learn* about our consumer: what is their lifestyle; how educated are they about our company and our products/services; what are their attitudes about us and our products/services; when reflecting on themselves, how content are they with themselves and their current

status; do they have needs that are not completely satisfied?

Synthesize. The third step involves literally *synthesizing* the goals from Focus with the research insights from Understanding to make sparks fly. Imagine a match striking a box, flint striking steel, or two beautiful young people crossing each other's path for the first time in a Nicholas Sparks book: sparks fly. Whether or not that spark turns into a fire and continues the "fusion" process depends on whether it is an idea we can *love*. We'll explore what it means to "love" a Big Idea, which then opens the floodgates to all-things creative.

Ideation. The fourth step involves the fun, creative, and challenging process of dreaming up various ways to execute a Big Idea across a variety of media. Just as important as the creation process is the destruction process or, put more delicately, a "healthy dose of editing" that produces the most efficient, elegant, and effective campaign possible.

Operation. The fifth step is the tactical war plan of an integrated campaign. Great ideas don't simply launch in a vacuum and obtain success overnight. As such, Operation involves the nitty gritty of Gestalten media planning and buying, ongoing market testing, potential Plan Bs, anticipating and dealing with competitive responses, and more.

Net Effect. The final step in the process is to measure the effectiveness of the campaign, not just in terms of revenues and, as is often the case, not using revenue at all! Indeed, if the goal of a campaign was to generate increased awareness within a certain audience, the metric under consideration would be one that captures changes in awareness. Net Effect provides insights regarding our campaign's effectiveness and hints about what we will need to do going forward.

My goal is to help you dream up marketing campaigns that are as memorable and creative as they are effective and efficient at achieving your specific business goals. As I outlined in the preface of this book, my entire life has been spent straddling the creative and corporate worlds. The great thing about the FUSION model is that it blends calculus with creativity, hard data with intangible ideas, analysis with artistry. If a model ever attempted to capture the "best of both worlds," well, this is that model.

Rest assured, this is not my first rodeo. Two years ago, I penned my first book, *Urge*, in two weeks while camped out at a Starbucks in my new city of Chicago. I have roughly the same amount of time to write this book, as I will be using *Fusion* as the textbook for a course on Integrated Marketing Strategy I will be teaching in Paris in just one month. Crazy, perhaps, but as you will learn in the chapter on creativity, constraints and limitations (including time constraints) often enhance our performance. There's nothing like a tight deadline to make people extremely productive. Let's sure hope that is true in this case. ☺

If you read *Urge*, I have a few points I want to make. First, thank you for reading the book! Second, whereas *Urge* was very theory-driven and covered a wide variety of topics pertaining to consumer behavior, *Fusion* is deliberately written to be more practical. *Urge* provides a "how-to" guide with respect to simplifying, understanding, and applying concepts from psychology in marketing practice. *Fusion* is more of a "how-to" guide regarding the marketing campaign creation process itself. This book relies more on research, data, and (most importantly) the *translation* of data into aesthetically-pleasing, yet bottom-line-effective, creative executions. *Fusion* is, at times, as much about how to be creative as it is about how to be successful as a marketer. People who read both books will find that they have a more solid grasp on how to put together a campaign, from beginning to end, and how to ice that campaign cake with psychological concepts that appeal to the many factors that drive human thought and behavior. Stated differently, *Fusion* provides the roadmap and step-by-step directions for driving from New York to Los Angeles while *Urge* suggests fun activities to do along the way.

And so, here I am again, sitting at a Starbucks across from my place in Chicago (it's a new location since *Urge* – a lot can happen in two years!) on a chilly winter day, pouring my brain and my heart out to you. I sincerely hope that you will find some good in this book and your life will be better, funnier, more creative, more productive, more efficient, or any combination thereof because of this book.

One final point before we dive in...

I want to make one thing clear: the FUSION model is simply *one* way of looking at the world. It is not the *only* way. It is not the one *right* way. It is simply *one* way. It would be arrogant to insist upon having one right method in a discipline that is as much an art as it is a science. That said, I firmly believe that the FUSION model streamlines the integrated marketing campaign development process in a way that is 1) easy to understand, 2) easy to remember, 3) easy to apply, and 4) fun. The model provides a path to follow when often no such path exists. Can you stray from the path? Of course! Straying from the path makes life interesting! I love the FUSION model, which is why I am so excited to share it with you, but I never want you to think that it is the *only* right way to do marketing. It isn't. However,

I do hope the model challenges you and stretches your brain in wonderful ways; ways that inspire more ideas for you, ideas that help you make better decisions, and, ultimately, ideas that help you create *exactly* the marketing campaign *you* need.

So, if you're ready, I suppose it's time to fire up the reactors...

Chapter 1 | What is Integrated Marketing?

Ice, ice, baby.

In the scorching summer of 2014, the hottest on record up to that point (spoiler: 2015 was even hotter...#GlobalWarming), people around the world were cooling themselves not by taking a dip in a swimming pool nor wading out into the ocean but, instead, by sitting around patiently, eyes closed, fists clenched, waiting for someone to dump an oversized bucket of water...and ice...onto their head. Sounds nice, right?

In what became known as the "ALS Ice Bucket Challenge," millions of people around the world grabbed a camera, a friend, some ice, some water, and just a little bit of courage to participate in what became one of the most successful viral marketing campaigns in recent history. The rules of the challenge were simple:

1. State your name.
2. State the name of the person who challenged you.
3. Explicitly state that you are agreeing to the "ALS Ice Bucket Challenge."
4. Name three other people that you are challenging to do the same.
5. Mention that these people must either accept the challenge or donate $100.
6. Mention the ALS website (www.alsa.org).
7. Have ice and water dumped over your head while trying to look cool.
8. Freeze.
9. Post video to social media. Tag the friends you have challenged.
10. Include a link to the ALS donation page in your post and #hashtags.

The goal of the campaign was to generate awareness about, and financial donations for, ALS (amyotrophic lateral sclerosis or "motor neuron disease"), a poorly understood disease in which motor neurons die and, in doing so, inhibit voluntary movement. Because the disease is progressively degenerative, the lack of muscle control eventual results in the inability to eat, talk, or even breathe. Although 5-10% of ALS cases can be identified through genetic, familial links, the other 90-95% of ALS cases can strike anyone, anywhere, at anytime.

The success of the campaign is indisputable: at a cost of virtually *nothing*, the ALS Association (ALSA) managed to generate over $220 million globally (according to ALSA CEO Barbara Newhouse) and to inspire over 90 million Google searches related to ALS, more ALS-related Google searches than the previous ten years combined. That kind of return on investment is typically unheard of and yet, equipped with just a bucket of ice water and mostly phone cameras, regular people around the world made it happen.

Still, for all its supposed success, not *everyone* found the ice bucket challenge particularly heartwarming. Indeed, critics were quite cold in their assessment of the campaign's limitations, typically citing how most people failed to learn much, if anything, about the disease, how people failed to mention the website in their recordings (which could have led others to learn more about ALS), and how participants (and non-participants) failed to follow through on contributing money to the campaign. People who were challenged but did not complete the task were supposed to provide $100 to ALSA (good luck enforcing that), and even those who *did* complete the challenge were encouraged to contribute.

Other critics took aim at the activity itself, specifically that people could "get out of donating" by simply dumping water on themselves. This "donation evasion" hardly seemed charitable, not to mention the fact that gallons of water were being wasted in a time when safe drinking water is considered a luxury to the over 600 million people worldwide who lack safe drinking water...yes, people were even complaining about the water being wasted...talk about a buzzkill.

Even *more* complaints arose regarding the campaign's appeal to vanity, with some people contending that the ALS Ice Bucket Challenge was merely an exercise in self-promotion or "showmanship without substance." One could argue that even if this *were* true, it might not have been a terrible idea to play on the very typical human behavior of self-promotion in a time of selfies and Facebook "likes." Or, stated differently, why not exploit behaviors people are going to do anyway (i.e., online self-promotion) for a good cause?

Regardless of one's opinion regarding the ALS Ice Bucket Challenge and its perceived effectiveness, one thing is indisputable: the campaign exemplified a paradigm shift in modern marketing. Whereas traditional campaigns typically involved having a "Big Idea" and translating that idea across traditional media channels like television, print advertising, and billboards, modern marketing campaigns are a new beast. No longer does the almighty television advertisement anchor the heart of a marketing campaign. No longer is it necessary for millions of dollars to be spent promoting a product, brand, or company. No longer does a creative agency have to be involved with the ideation process. Traditional marketing is experiencing a meltdown.

So whether you participated in the ALS Ice Bucket Challenge or not, whether you donated or *pretended* to donate so your friends and family wouldn't think less of you, whether you appreciated the campaign and watched video after video of your friends, family, and celebrities (like Oprah, Bill Gates, and even Kermit the Frog) getting freezing cold water dumped on their head or simply rolled your eyes at the silliness of people around the world engaging in a more elaborate version of a selfie, if you have witnessed the ALS Ice Bucket Challenge in some way then you have witnessed the transformation of marketing.

But this, my friends, is just the tip of the iceberg…er…ice bucket…

*   *   *

Once upon a time, marketing was a relatively simple discipline: find out what people want, make what people want, communicate that what people want is available for purchase, and then sell people what they want. The end. This process was *so* simple and *so* straightforward that when most people thought of "marketing," they tended to think of "advertising" alone–simply telling consumers about a product or service via a fancy television commercial or an eye-catching magazine print ad was all it took–no need for research or market testing or media buying. This simplicity might explain why the advertising executives depicted in the show *Mad Men* had so much free time to smoke cigarettes, drink martinis, and engage in general misogyny as a sport. Perhaps we should all be thankful times have changed.

Nowadays, the glitz and glamour of the classic Madison Avenue advertising lifestyle is exactly that: a ghost of the past. Television commercials are *not* where modern consumers get information anymore. In fact, television is not even the medium through which most of us initially get *any* information, just as newspapers are quickly become the *last* place we actually get our news. In a time when our attention is spread so thin across an exponentially increasing number of sources, even getting us to focus becomes extremely…wow, there's a great sale happening at Banana Republic right now…extremely challenging.

These shifts in information searching, attention, and general human behavior–for example, how people now spend more time looking at their phones than each other–have led to seismic shakeups in the advertising industry. Case in point, in summer 2013 two of the world's largest advertising-focused companies, the Paris-based Publicis Groupe and the New York-based Omnicom Group, announced plans to merge into a single organization: Publicis Omnicom Group. The merger would have created the world's largest advertising organization, a behemoth entity overseeing countless agencies working on some of the world's most valuable brands. However, the motivation to merge was *not* so much to share the advertising tips and trade secrets that had long been at the forefront of marketing work. Instead, Publicis and Omnicom were teaming up to take on an increasingly problematic threat to their creative world: the rise of Big Data and relevant companies like Facebook and Google, who continue to steal marketing dollars from both organizations' once-loyal clients. When customers are more likely to search Google for product information or to ask Facebook friends for advice about a potential purchase than to watch a television commercial for that product, well, that's a real problem for ad agencies.

Having spent decades perfecting the artistic aesthetic of a beautiful print advertisement, the emotional imagery of a well-shot television commercial, and the articulate, efficient wording of ad copy, Publicis and Omnicom were becoming increasingly aware that technology, social media, data analytics, and online marketing were not in their wheelhouse. They also were not the organizations collecting vast amounts of data. While both companies (and the firms in their portfolios) had certainly explored and evolved into the digital world, few people predicted the paradigm shift Big Data would bring to the realm of marketing.

However, the leap to digital marketing and Big Data has not been without some resistance: traditional advertising (e.g., television, print) *still* receives the majority of most companies' "marketing spend." According to *Strategy Analytics*, the estimated marketing spend in the U.S. market for 2015 placed traditional television advertising on top (42%), digital came in second (28%), followed by print (15%), radio (10%), and outdoor (8.7%). However, a more revealing insight to the direction marketing is taking is the estimated *percentage change* by media type: digital increased the most (13%), while television increased only slightly (1.7%), and print actually decreased (-7.9%).[2] Year after year, spend on digital marketing is increasing as it becomes crystal clear that consumers, zipping and zapping their way through recorded television, are focusing their time and attention elsewhere.

This paradigm shift to all-things online and Big Data has not just increased the emphasis placed on understanding and exploring new media, the shift has also increased the emphasis placed on numbers and metrics, in general. The "Return on Marketing Investment" (ROMI, as it is often called) has been somewhat of an elusive number in the past few decades, as attempts to quantify concepts like "brand equity" and "awareness" can seem arbitrary, subjective, and somewhat abstract. Now companies have access to just about everything customers do online: how long you spend on a website, how many times you click before you purchase, where you move the cursor on the page, whether placing a button here or there significantly increases your likelihood of making a purchase, etc. When the amount of data available to companies increases exponentially, so, too, does the *expectation* that marketing decisions will be rooted in, inspired by, and evaluated on cold, hard *data*.

When YouTube sensations like PewDiePie (who got his start by posting videos of himself playing videogames) and DisneyCollectorBR (an anonymous Brazilian woman who records herself opening Disney toys and playing with them) can track, in real time, the number of viewers watching their videos, use this information to dream up future popular videos their audiences will love, and laugh all the way to the bank carrying gobs of money,

---

[2] *Strategy Analytics Advertising Forecast, 2015*

well, the power of modern marketing makes itself abundantly clear: the *dawn* of digital is behind us; digital now rules the *day*.

In spite of this inevitable shift to digital marketing and data-focused decisions, traditional advertising still exists. Companies are still hiring agencies to film commercials. Print ads still pop out in magazines as beautifully as they have for decades. The difference is that the traditional tactics long-used as the *foundation* of any great marketing campaign are beginning to take a supporting role to newer forms of media, newer approaches to marketing, and newer ways of persuading consumers. Just as television trumped the once-pervasive radio, so, too, has technology dethroned the ever-popular traditional media that ruled for the better part of the 20th century.

Integrated Marketing Strategy: The Whole > Sum of the Parts

It is worth noting that, up to this point in the conversation, for all my talk of "paradigm shifts" and drastic changes in the realm of marketing, I have *not* said anything about the "termination of television" or the "passing of print ads." These approaches are not dead nor are they really "dying" despite sensational media and pop press books (usually trying to sell you on internet-based marketing) suggesting otherwise.

The truth is this: marketing provides several tools, each with its own strengths and limitations, that facilitate the eventual transaction between those who produce and those who consume. Television advertisements are great for reinforcing awareness but not so great at predicting consumer needs. Internet searches and web surfing data are often great at predicting consumer needs but not altogether great at entertaining or capturing consumer attention. Similarly, product placements are a nice, subtle way to gently reinforce a brand or to link a product with a certain emotion, personality, or status, while a sponsored promotion is an explicit, direct way to have consumers engage with a brand or product. No one approach is better than any other approach across the board. In fact, more often than not, a variety of tactics will (or should) be used to increase the effectiveness of a marketing campaign.

Integrated Marketing Strategy (also referred to as Integrated Marketing Communications) refers to a marketing campaign in which several marketing tactics–television ads to print ads, sponsorships to service experiences, trade shows to Twitter tweets–are coordinated together, in harmony, to produce an experience that is more engaging, more enticing, and more effective than any singular tactic would be on its own. By recruiting different tactics that each have unique strengths, a limitation of one approach can be offset by the strength of another. Approaches that appeal more to one's cognition and rational thought processes can be reinforced by approaches that engage one's emotions. Thus, IMS is truly *the* Gestalten approach to marketing, an approach in which the *whole* of all the tactics used in a campaign is truly greater than the *sum* of the campaign's individual parts.

Consider, for example, the famous energy drink Red Bull. Red Bull has a bit of an exotic origin story in that its formulation derives from an energy drink that was popular in Thailand long before it found its way into its now-famous blue and silver cans, into the hands of awkward teen boys trying to cope with puberty acne, and into the alcoholic drinks of twenty-something year-old singles looking for a cheap way to get wasted but stay alert. Sold by the Austrian company Red Bull GmbH, Red Bull is now the world's bestselling energy drink, having achieved global sales of almost 6 *billion* cans in 2015 (up 6% from 2014)–that's almost one for every person on the planet. This, of course, makes Red Bull only the second-worst thing to come out of Austria and take over part of the world (...third if you count Arnold Schwarzenegger).

Red Bull's early commercials were based on the company's motto: "Red Bull gives you wings" (which, admittedly, is an odd slogan for a product whose critics often allege heart palpitations and other adverse health effects). Featuring simplistic line drawings on a white background and basic animation, one commercial from this early period shows a bird flying in the sky and pooping on a nerdy, older, bald gentleman wearing glasses and walking with a newspaper under one arm and a briefcase in hand. The gentleman pulls a Red Bull out if his bag, chugs it, and then grows wings, wings that allow the man to fly up in the sky above the bird, unbuckle his pants, and presumably poop on the bird (...this part is not shown, but we can use our imaginations). These simple animated television commercials based on the "gives you wings" Big Idea essentially *were* the marketing campaign for Red Bull in its early days of internationalization.

However, in its ongoing quest to make our hearts explode out of our chests, Red Bull began to shift away from the cute and clever animations to something a bit more extreme. Well, a *lot* more extreme, actually: extreme sports. Red Bull's most recent campaign has involved several different components that, together, reinforce the brand as *the* high energy drink of choice over and above any of the brand's previous marketing efforts. Venturing beyond traditional television commercials, Red Bull began focusing its marketing efforts on sponsoring extreme sports and producing up to 60-minute extreme sport movies viewable for free online. From a motocross movie to an intense short film featuring the Red Bull Air Force's death-defying aerial stunts, Pro4 trucks racing in the snow to "epic wipeouts" of surfers riding "totally massive waves, dude," Red Bull has become as much an extreme movie production company as it has a beverage company.

Consistent with these online videos is Red Bull's commitment to sponsoring extreme athletes. From skier Lindsey Vonn to skydiver Jon DeVore, surfer Jamie O'Brien to skateboarder Ryan Sheckler, Red Bull reinforces its bad-ass branding by sponsoring some of the sporting world's most extreme athletes. Not one to stop there, Red Bull has also sponsored some of the most extreme stunts in recent history including the Red Bull Stratos jump in which Austrian skydiver Felix Baumgartner jumped from the edge of space back to the Earth. Baumgartner descended so quickly that he became the first human being to break the sound barrier without the use of an engine of any kind. The PR buzz generated by this death defying leap garnered 8 million concurrent viewers on the live YouTube stream of the event, the most of any live stream up to that point in time.

Beyond the sponsorship of extreme athletes and production of extreme sport movies, Red Bull has also collaborated with video games like *Destiny*, a futuristic, planet-hopping "save the world" action game, and has hosted international breakdancing competitions and its own major concerts featuring electronic artists (among others) to engage its core customers. To top it all off, Red Bull has its own in-house social media group, Red Bull Media House, that reinforces this extreme action, sports, stunts positioning across every major social media platform: Facebook, Instagram, Twitter, Foursquare, and even Google+ (for the three people still using Google+).

And lest you think Red Bull divested itself of its classic animated commercials, fear not: the company still produces the simple animations but with a slight twist. Rather than focus on Red Bull actually giving characters wings in comical situations, now the emphasis is less about *literal* wings and more about how drinking Red Bull ups your action and awesome factor. Although these spots are not as well integrated into the extreme sports branding as the rest of Red Bull's current executions, the spots share the same strategic approach as the online movies, events, and sponsorships: Red Bull is not a product, it is a *lifestyle*. Red Bull is not just an energy drink, it is a *lifestyle choice*. People who drink Red Bull are not just tapping into energy, they are tapping into *adventure*.

Red Bull's marketing has been *so* effective at changing perceptions that if you ask people to guess which has more caffeine, a can of Red Bull or a cup of coffee, most people guess Red Bull despite the fact that both servings have roughly 80 mg of caffeine. Of course, sometimes marketing can be *too* successful at affecting perceptions. In 2014, Red Bull settled a lawsuit in which a plaintiff sued the beverage company because the energy drink did not "give him wings" as promised. Well, to clarify, he was not suing because he didn't get *actual* wings but because of the fact that a can of Red Bull offered no more energy than a simple cup of coffee. This proved three things: 1) marketing is powerful, 2) ethical marketing is the way to go, and 3) Americans will sue for just about anything.

The Red Bull example illustrates how a company went from a rather straightforward, old-school marketing approach (i.e., television advertising) to a more modern, more powerful integrated marketing approach. Just about *every* touch point that Red Bull has with its consumers reinforces its extreme, high energy, adventurous positioning. As a result, the product transcends its reality as a combination of caffeine, taurine, B-vitamins, sucrose, glucose, and water ingredients and becomes something more: a conduit to a more exciting, higher intensity, ultra-engaging lifestyle. *That* is the power of integrated marketing.

What is worth pointing out is the way that different media are capable of engaging consumers in different ways. The "live," suspenseful, and community aspect of the Stratos live stream, the aspirational tug of the famous sponsored athletes, the exciting party atmosphere of the music, concerts, and breakdancing events, the interactive components of the social media posts, the pairing of Red Bull's ability to provide energy with the ultra high energy of events like motocross and extreme surfing—each of these efforts reinforces the others in a way that highlights how no single execution could pull off all these accomplishments in one fell swoop. Again, *that* is the power of integrated marketing.

Before we get *too* swept up in all-things integrated marketing and start dreaming up how to convert a Big Idea across every possible medium, there is an important caveat: not *every* IMS campaign needs to use *every* tool. When you build a table from IKEA, you don't get *every* tool out of your toolbox unless you have absolutely no idea what you are doing. Instead, you just grab the tools that you need to build the table as efficiently as possible. The same is true for an IMS campaign: you need not use all the tools available in the IMS toolbox; you should just use the tools that are relevant for what you are trying to accomplish. As we continue throughout this book it is important to keep this efficiency in mind. The most effective campaigns are also the most elegant, and elegance is the art of making a lasting impression as simply as possible.

Create, Rate, and Captivate: The Rise of DIY Marketing
The ALS Ice Bucket Challenge and Red Bull examples highlight another important idea with respect to modern marketing, which is the fact that we now live in a DIY (do-it-yourself) era. Whether watching HGTV or clicking around on Pinterest, at no other time in history have we been as inundated with tips, tricks, techniques, and tutorials for creating our own crafts, furniture, food, or [fill in the blank here]. Because of this, it is not surprising that **DIY Marketing** –or the ability to create your own marketing executions (e.g., video commercials, print ads, promotions, etc.) independent of a hired agency or contracted labor–is a reality. When photo editing apps, video editing apps, graphic design programs, and other creative instruments are available for free, phones come equipped with hi-definition cameras, and just about any creative project can be outsourced online to anyone in the world

willing to do work (especially talented students looking to build portfolios), well, there are few things we *cannot* do ourselves these days.

The ability to create your own marketing executions is only part of the battle, as even the coolest video would do you little good if you have no one with whom you can share said video. However, in addition to our ability to create, we also live in a time when we have never been more connected to each other (virtually, anyway) thanks to Facebook, Instagram, LinkedIn, Twitter, YouTube, SoundCloud, and our own personal websites. That is, we are able to *captivate*. Clever creatives can dream up a new song idea, a new funny video, or a new meme that goes viral within minutes of being posted. This kind of reach and awareness, unheard of in the realm of television advertising, is the new reality for the socially networked world in which we now exist.

The third piece of this puzzle involves yet another difference of our modern era that has forever changed the way we think about marketing: Big Data. Thanks to technology companies and social networks being obsessive about tracking every little thing we do online, we now live in a world where unimaginable amounts of data are being captured about our every search, thought, feeling, and behavior. From the loyalty cards we mindlessly swipe at the grocery store, the corner convenience store, or the major department store to the keywords we enter into a search, the pages we surf online, and the content we post in our status updates, just about *everything* is being recorded, collected, and mined for meaningful patterns and predictive power. It is about now that you should start worrying about that time you may or may not have taken a picture of your "business" on Snap Chat. All those "business" photos, like aliens, are out there...somewhere.

Modern data collection methods are *so* pervasive, that some sites–like YouTube–can even capture *real time* viewership. While television still relies on the relatively outdated and archaic Nielsen ratings complete with its "Nielsen families" (who are these people, by the way? In my three decades on this planet, I have never met a Nielsen family, so how in the world can they represent the rest of us?!), modern marketing eschews the old ways of thinking and replaces it with the new, constantly on, constantly monitoring mindset that includes the internet, mobile phones, and even biometric measures, like those of our Apple Watches and Fitbits. Restaurants can time their promotions to coincide with when you are more likely to be hungry (e.g., low blood sugar levels), which increases the likelihood of you paying attention to the timed advertisement on which they spent money. You are happy because you get discounted food and/or drinks when you are hungry. The restaurant is happy because they get your business (and your money). And the intermediary device's company is happy because they brought value to both a consumer and a producer in a way that reinforces the intermediary's value to both.

Some components of IMS are easier to create than others (e.g., shooting and editing a professional-looking commercial may not be as easy as creating a high-quality print advertisement...although filming a deliberately amateur video could be). Some IMS components, like social media posts and webpages, are easier to collect data on than others (e.g., how many people saw your billboard). And some IMS components are more captivating, such as an engaging live concert, than others (e.g., a sad, old-school newspaper ad). The solution for how to be a good marketer in today's modern world is not to simply shift more money into digital and online because it seems trendy or is the latest, coolest thing to do. The solution is to look at all the possible tactics available to you, separately and together, and to consider each avenue's strengths/weaknesses and potential to reinforce or complement the other tactics to create the most effective, engaging, and efficient marketing campaign possible.

The FUSION Framework as a Guide to Integrated Marketing

Now that you have a solid grasp of what Integrated Marketing Strategy is and how it can transform good marketing campaigns into exceptional marketing campaigns, we can get into the nitty-gritty details of *how* to actually create such a campaign. "It's about time," you're probably thinking, but patience, patience, grasshopper...we needed to cover the basics before we can get to the sexy stuff!

I noticed something annoying when I looked at the existing books on integrated marketing. The existing books are either *too* top-level, bird's-eye view in their approach or *too* mired in the details. Stated differently, the existing books either see a forest off in the distance and comment about said forest *or* are so far into the forest that they are describing the bark on a single tree. In my opinion, neither approach is particularly useful.

While it is nice to have some theory behind different marketing ideas (the bird's-eye view approach) or to be provided step-by-step instructions on writing a creative brief (the mired in the details approach), I think the best approach is actually somewhere in between, a sweet, Goldilocks spot where we can talk about both business and creative ideas in a way that does not swing the pendulum too far in either direction. The existing books are almost barely readable, dropping words like "pica" and "typeface" like they are hot or concepts like "SWOT" and "ROMI" like everyone automatically knows what they stand for. Not this book, friends, not at all! The goal of the chapters that follow is to provide you with different ways of thinking, novel approaches to classic problems, practical tactics, and, perhaps most important of all, a framework that can get you from Point A to Point B in a field where that path can often be quite elusive. So now that we have all the introductory stuff out of the way, let's start where *every* amazing, artistic,

42

memorable, entertaining, successful marketing campaign *should* begin: at the very end–the bottom line.

Let's get down to *business...*

WHAT IF... *ALS Ice Bucket Challenge 2.0*

Although the ALS Ice Bucket Challenge remains the envy of most non-profit organizations attempting to generate awareness of their cause and donations for their bank accounts, the campaign was not without its critics. Some of the concerns raised involved the lack of actual education, the missed opportunity to earn *more* money, and the vast amount of water wasted in the process. Furthermore, as feared, 2015 came and went without an ALS Ice Bucket Challenge Part II or ALS Ice Bucket Challenge 2.0 in spite of the ALS Association's explicit attempt to recreate the magic (even launching a separate, dedicated website for the new year).

What if it were possible to tweak the ALS Ice Bucket Challenge ever so slightly to renew interest in the campaign? Picture it: there are *two* buckets with some ice and water. In this challenge, two people go head to head in a competition to see *who can keep his/her hand submerged in the freezing cold ice water the longest.* Here's the fun part: prior to putting their hand in the buckets, bystanders are asked to place bets on which of the two contestants they think will win the challenge. Then the countdown begins. Three…two…one…go! The contestants submerge their hands into the freezing cold water while a third person, a bystander, uses an ALSA-created app or the ALSA website to ask trivia questions related to ALS. "What percentage of ALS cases are attributed to genetic causes?" "How many people are diagnosed with ALS each year?" "Name three symptoms of ALS." "What does the word amyotrophic mean?" and other questions. Here's the catch: each time someone misses a question more ice is added to his/her bucket. This continues until one of the two contestants finally cannot take the cold any longer and removes his/her hand from the bucket. Then, two more people from the group of bystanders take the challenge using the same buckets of ice and water. The challenge continues until everyone who wants to compete has competed, with each pair challenging someone they know to engage in this new version of the challenge.

How is this approach an improvement of what came before? First, because money is collected on the spot *and* from everyone, even people simply viewing the challenge, the follow-through on donation behavior should improve. Donations may be in increments smaller than $100, but the volume of those donations may increase. Second, the introduction of the trivia game *during* the challenge permits an education about ALS that was absent from the original challenge. This should increase both awareness *and* understanding of the disease, its symptoms, and how donations are being used to fight the battle. Third, the use of the same buckets of ice and water for several pairs of people minimizes the amount of water wasted (it may not be the most sanitary approach, but people can wash their hands before and after the challenge). Fourth, the focus on the education, the good-natured competition, the group-donation aspect (perhaps even competing teams in the same series of videos) minimizes the self-indulgent, self-serving criticism that plagued the original challenge. This approach, reinforced across IMS channels, would be nICE, indeed. ☺

FOCUS

Chapter 2 | Prospective Audience

In 2015, Ronald McDonald was a sad, sad clown.

Somewhere in some tacky, plastic kitchen, Ronald sat slumped over in his chair at an uncomfortable table, wearing his big red shoes and trademark yellow jumper, crying his sugar-coated clown tears into a supersized soft drink while nibbling on mushy, cold fries...the worst kind of fries...and poking at a flattened Big Mac. As he sat in silence pondering his woes, Ronald simply could not help wonder why his Happy Meal was no longer as happy as it used to be.

For decades McDonald's held the honor of being *the* exemplar in the fast food industry. As the "gold(en arches) standard" to which every other fast food restaurant compared itself, McDonald's enjoyed its position as burger "king of the hill" while others, like the actual Burger King and Wendy's, merely fought to come in second place behind the certain first place champion. The surprising part? This dominant position is what ultimately led to McDonald's downward spiral of doom.

Although being "top of mind" in a product category (i.e., the brand that most people think of *first* when they think of an industry – like McDonald's is for fast food or Starbucks is for coffee) is *typically* a good thing, this top-of-mind awareness can become a burden if consumer sentiments regarding your industry, in general, become negative. In the past decade, American consumers' dieting trends have shifted toward healthier eating, which has been a godsend for companies like Whole Foods and Panera but has been nail after nail in the coffin for companies like McDonald's. Indeed, customers began straying from places like McDonald's to dine at what became known as "fast casual" dining options like Panera, Chipotle, and Le Pain Quotidien. These "fast casual" restaurants feature more relaxed atmospheres, menu items *perceived* to be healthier (key word being "perceived" – check the sodium content of your next Chipotle burrito), and added extras like free WiFi.

Now, the folks at McDonald's are no fools (well, except for Ronald McDonald, but he's a clown, so that's sort of his job). Taking notice of the rise in "fast casual" dining, McDonald's started making changes to prevent its customers from straying and to entice fast food diners that might otherwise go to Panera. While McDonald's had offered pay-as-you-go WiFi in the mid-2000s, the company added free WiFi service at most of its locations in 2010. Similarly, seeing the popularity of Starbucks and other coffee chains as a potential threat, McDonald's pushed its McCafé concept in the United States (a concept that had actually been around internationally for several years). The company even renovated several locations to get rid of the cheap, plastic-looking bright red and yellow décor and transformed its locations into modern-looking restaurants featuring faux-wood, muted colors, and more architecturally-pleasing exteriors. In this regard, McDonald's did a swell job imitating its competitors but a far less exceptional job innovating as the first mover.

With respect to its menu, McDonald's also attempted to shed the negative perception that it was contributing to the obesity problem in America. The company quietly phased out its Super Sizing options in which you could eat a bucket full of fries to accompany your tub-sized Coca-Cola. In what probably stirred up the most controversy, McDonald's made changes to its longstanding holy grail: the Happy Meal. Consumer advocacy groups had long argued that McDonald's contributed to the childhood obesity problem sweeping (or, more accurately, crawling slowly and out-of-breath) across America by luring children to the fast food chain with the promise of toys and surprises awaiting them in their Happy Meal and then force feeding them unhealthy Chicken McNuggets and fries upon arrival. In its defense, most McDonald's locations also include a play area for kids to burn off calories, so we should probably just blame the kids for not exercising instead of McDonald's (…just kidding).

McDonald's decided it would remedy this perception of unhealthiness by jumping on the healthy bandwagon, adding salads, wraps, and yogurt parfaits for adults and fresh apple slices and yogurt for Happy Meals. This was a nice gesture, of course, until it was pointed out that some of the salads added to the menu, when selected with the crispy chicken and dressing options, actually contained *more* calories than some of the burgers and sandwiches on the menu. Similarly, although the addition of yogurt and apples to the Happy Meals were nice touches, these options did not change the fact the kids were still eating burgers, Chicken McNuggets, and fries (according to the company's website, the apples and yogurt are interchangeable options for one another). Worse, because McDonald's still maintains top-of-mind awareness as *the* fast food destination, any effort to brand its menu offerings as "healthier" or "healthy" was a steep uphill battle.

Adding in-salt to injury (see what I did there?), the criticism involving McDonald's food extended beyond the effects on obesity and went straight to the source of the food itself. Rumors of "pink slime" and inedible chicken parts showing up in Chicken McNuggets circulated online, and in an era of photoshopped images, social media, and a general acceptance of random statements as facts (…did you know that 78% of all statements purported as factual statements are actually untrue or inaccurate? …actually, I just made that number up, but if you believed it for a second, that's my point), these rumors, regardless of their (in)accuracy were also damaging McDonald's reputation.

With its ever-increasing slide into this unhealthiness oblivion, McDonald's launched an initiative in early 2015 that many on the insider were *convinced* would help turn around the company's declining sales. In a campaign entitled "Our Food, Your Questions," McDonald's hired Grant Imahara who was famous for starring in the show *MythBusters* on which common myths are tested and sometimes debunked. The goal of the campaign was to educate consumers about the source of McDonald's ingredients and menu items. Common questions included, "Is there pink slime in the meat?" and, "Why are the burger patties frozen?" and, "If Golden Arches fall in the forest but no one is around to hear it, do they make a sound?" (…okay, not that last question, but you get the point). Each video was about two minutes in length and featured Imahara interviewing McDonald's executives, farmers, customers, and various people along the supply chain from farm to fast food feast.

The reaction to the videos was not what McDonald's was likely hoping for. Each video, about two minutes in length, has *several* million views but ratings that are split 50/50 with respect to likes/dislikes, not to mention *scores* of negative comments. Commenters were convinced that every part of the commercials was scripted, including Grant Imahara's questions and reactions to McDonald's executives and suppliers answering questions about the source of the ingredients.

In spite of its super-sized efforts, McDonald's same-store sales in the United States market showed a steady decline for two years as the company simply could not figure out a way to stop or slow the freefall. As a result, after almost three years in the position, CEO Don Thompson was ousted in January 2015 (although, officially, he "resigned") and replaced with former Chief Brand Officer, Steve Easterbrook. Easterbrook was charged with the enigmatic task of "turning the brand around" in an effort to curb the declining sales numbers, but what could be done that had not already been tried? In the face of changing consumer preferences, was there anything that could even save the fast food giant or was it just time to accept the inevitable?

One of Easterbrook's first solutions: stop reporting monthly same-store sales numbers. The logic behind this, of course, is that public shaming of McDonald's stemming from the reporting of its declining same-store sales numbers is a self-fulfilling prophecy: the more consumers hear about how no one is eating at McDonald's anymore, the less they are likely to eat at McDonald's, too. But it was another one of Easterbrook's initiatives that turned things around for the struggling company: all-day breakfast.

Although the proposal to do all-day breakfast sounded absurd to many industry analysts at first–after all, people already were not coming to eat because of the perceptions of unhealthiness, how would extending the hours of equally unhealthy menu options save things?–but this seemingly counterintuitive proposal tapped into an insight that, up to that point, had eluded McDonald's executives.

To understand, consider this simple thought experiment. Think of the healthiest person you know; this could be you, it could be a friend, it could be a sworn enemy. That person has likely, at some point in time, eaten at McDonald's. Now, of course, that person would not be caught dead in a McDonald's because it is *so* unhealthy and so far removed from their everyday nutritious diet. These people may occasionally eat out at Panera, or Freshii, or some salad chain when they aren't simply nibbling on lettuce leaves like a rodent, but they are not likely to eat any offerings from McDonald's no matter how healthy they are purported to be. *This* is why the "Our Food, Your Questions" campaign did not work: the focus was on persuading consumers who would *never ever* again eat at McDonald's to eat at McDonald's. The implicit goal of the campaign was to steal back customers from Panera and Chipotle. "We have healthy food, too!" said McDonald's despite having never been known or really *valued* for healthy food options. In hindsight, this was a silly, silly move.

Throughout its many struggles and declining same-store sales, McDonald's still maintained both the largest domestic *and* international market share in the fast food category. Not only that, but industry-wide, same-store sales at Burger King and Arby's actually *increased* 6-8% during the same timeframe that McDonald's sales were declining in spite of the fact that these fast food competitors had menus no healthier than McD's (unless you count "chicken fries" as part of a healthy, balanced diet). People were still eating fast food…just not at McDonald's. Thus, the real challenge facing McDonald's was not the lofty, darn-near-impossible task of convincing healthy diners that all their dreams of healthy eating could be achieved at McDonald's. Instead, the challenge was to lure in the folks who *do* eat fast food on occasion, maybe just not at McDonald's, and to generate excitement among its longtime loyal McDonald's enthusiasts, two audiences that the previous campaign almost completely ignored.

On October 6, 2015, McDonald's locations began offering all-day breakfast in an attempt to lure back customers and to excite its core base of consumers. The breakfast stunt gave once-loyal consumers a fun reason to return while also providing regulars with more menu options. Also spicing up the menu were the additions of a Maple Dijon Bacon Burger and Pico Guacamole Burger, as well as a Buttermilk Crispy Chicken Sandwich. Rather than venture into some uncharted healthy territory with a menu consisting of kale burgers and diet air nuggets, McDonald's menu reflected a classier version of what it was good at: burgers. The menu additions are rumored to be just the beginning of an effort to allow more customized burgers similar to the customization options experienced when walking through the line at Chipotle. The more sophisticated burger options also better position McDonald's against new fast-casual burger joints like Five Guys, but by keeping the original burger options on the menu, McDonald's has not shifted upward in the market to the point of alienating its loyal fans.

The result of these changes? McDonald's reported its first domestic same-store sales growth of almost 1% in the third quarter of 2015 and then almost 6% in the fourth quarter of 2015. Just when people were starting to fear that the Golden Arches had fallen forever, it turns out that the Golden Arches are now shining a bit brighter. Happy Meals just got a bit happier. And if Ronald McDonald is crying now, his tears are tears of joy…or obesity-induced sweat…either way, he's happy.

* * *

When it comes to creating a marketing campaign, most people get *really* excited about what I refer to as the "fun part"—coming up with a Big Idea, picking color schemes, and dreaming up how to make it entertaining…you know, the same thing that high school kids get excited about when planning a prom. Nobody ever wants to talk budget, anticipated revenues, whether Jenny deserves to be Prom Queen (I suppose that's only applicable for the prom), or why you are even staging the event in the first place.

But at the heart of *any* marketing campaign is (or at least *should* be) a fundamental business objective. We tend to think that the business goal of a marketing campaign is to increase sales. "Buy more of our stuff!" is essentially the message of most marketing campaigns. Although increasing sales is always nice—I mean, who *doesn't* want more money?—not every marketing campaign exists to generate more sales. Marketing campaigns can have any number of other goals, including simply educating consumers or generating buzz and excitement among consumers. While these actions may lead to more sales…eventually…the focal goal of the campaign may not be increasing sales directly, and that's totally okay.

However, just about *every* marketing campaign is designed to change people's thoughts, feelings, beliefs, or behaviors. A marketing campaign for Tide laundry detergent may strive to change the kind of detergent you use to clean your clothes. A campaign for a political candidate may attempt to change your thoughts about a competing candidate. A public service announcement denouncing cocaine may attempt to educate you on the dangers of using drugs to prevent you from ever trying substances. Thus, although not every campaign is designed to *sell* you something, every campaign is designed to shift our thoughts, feelings, and/or behaviors.

But whose thoughts, feelings, and/or behaviors are we trying to influence? Everyone's? A small niche's? Does it make sense for a company to try to influence as many people as possible with no regard to who those people might be or whether they are even likely to purchase our product or service in the first place? Of course not, and anyone who has taken an introductory marketing course can probably tell you all about the concepts of segmentation, targeting, and positioning (STP).

"Gee, that's it, Jim?" you savvy marketers are wondering, "This just comes down to segmenting, targeting, and positioning?" to which I'd say, "Calm down!" and then I'd lean in close and whisper, "What if I told you I have a secret?" You'd probably get a little creeped out but still be curious, so I'd continue, "Before you even think about segmenting the market, there's something you should do first, something no one has ever told you before. The secret is…" then my voice would mysteriously trail off, and you would have to move on to the next section…

The Prospective Audience: The First Ingredient of an IMS Foundation

Once upon a time, the wise, old sages of Marketing–white-haired, bearded men in long, flowing robes–lived like wizards in the ivory towers of academia's castles and decreed that one fundamental idea of their discipline would be this: thou shalt not attempt to sell your product or service to *everyone*. The logic behind this idea is rather straightforward. First, not everyone wants what you are selling. Second, even if everyone *did* want what you were selling, the cost of selling to an endless number of people could be prohibitive or detract from the quality of the experience or the level of service you could provide if you focused on a smaller audience.

Because of this age-old edict, marketers the world over have avoided selling blindly to the masses in favor of a "more efficient" method: STP. The long story short on STP is this: rather than attempt to sell your product to a heterogeneous world, you should first segment the world into smaller, homogeneous groups, and then pick one of those groups to target. The logic of STP comes directly from the old-school way of thinking: it is too expensive and too inefficient to market to *everyone*, so focus on a smaller group, preferably a group of people whose members are all very similar, and spend your resources only on those potential customers. How you segment the market is up to you–demographics, psychological factors or values, past behaviors–but the idea behind STP is, and always has been, to break the world down into smaller, more manageable pieces–kind of like how you cut up food for a baby.

STP is still useful and does have value (I still teach it to my students), but our world is very different from the early 1900s and its now outdated notions of assembly-line mass-marketing and even the more recent approach of "mass customization" that has dominated modern marketing. The cost of "reaching out" to audiences in modern times via social media and the internet is virtually nothing. The "commonality" of various segments need not be forced as now we capture enough data to see where any two people overlap and how they differ. This is not to say that segmenting, targeting, and positioning are not useful–they are–but how we go about STP in today's world is rather different than it was ten or twenty years ago. Whereas traditional notions of STP could be somewhat limiting and constraining based on lack of data or inability to communicate with multiple audiences efficiently, the modern world of Big Data and social networks changes the game. Because of this, we can dream bigger and set our sights on a more ambitious goal: selecting a Prospective Audience.

The **Prospective Audience** refers to the focal group we plan to target with our integrated marketing campaign in hopes of changing the way they think, what they believe, and/or how they behave. Simply put, all customers fall into one of four possible categories: our loyal customers, customers loyal to our competitors, customers loyal to no one but who have been in the market for awhile, and customers who are brand new to the market. There are also those people who will *never* buy what we have to offer no matter what we do; we don't call those people "customers" because they are not and most likely never will be "customers" in our market, so we aren't going to waste our time or energy on them. There is a *chance* those non-customers could be in the market *someday* (at which point they would fall into the "customers brand new to the market" group), but right now the effort it would take to lure them into the market could probably be spent more efficiently on customers much closer to purchasing what we are offering. Instead, we focus on one of these Prospective Audiences to begin thinking about the fundamental business motivation for having a campaign in the first place.

The name "Prospective Audience" includes the word "prospective" for a reason…well, for two reasons: first, prospective denotes the future and our expectations for the future; second, the notion of "prospecting," in the context of searching for gold or other mineral deposits, denotes searching out specific areas for the possibility of "striking it rich." We are considering specific audiences that have the potential to be valuable in the future.

To help keep things simple, we can assign names to the four consumer types I just delineated: 1) Wandering Customers, 2) Hot-Off-the-Press Customers, 3) Others' Customers, 4) My Customers. I'm up to something here…because I'm a Marketing guy and I like using memorable mnemonics, an easy way to remember whom your campaign will focus on is to remember **WHOM** your Prospective Audience is (W = Wandering Customers, H = Hot-Off-the-Press Customers, O = Others' Customers, M = My Customers). There are a lot more mnemonics on the way, so hold on to your hat.

Let's explore each of the Prospective Audience types in more detail…

Wandering Customers: Not All Who Wander Are Lost

Wandering Customers are the "hippies" of the consumer world. Free spirits guided by the winds, Wandering Customers simply do what feels right in the moment. "Brand X is on sale this week? Great, I'll buy that," the

Wandering Customer thinks, "Brand Z has a new flavor? Wonderful. I'll try that," they say. The thing about Wandering Customers is that they have virtually *no* loyalty to any one brand in particular. They may have a default brand that they purchase when nothing sexy or new is happening among the other brand choices, but when something bright and shiny happens that catches their attention, these customers will abandon their default brand with little regret, concern, or worry in favor of the brightness and shininess of whatever brand is all gussied up that week.

Lest you think Wandering Customers are simply the kind of folks always looking for the "next best thing," there are many reasons for the nomadic tendencies of these people. Some are simply cost conscious and place a premium on savings over any loyalty or quality of a product. Others are simply less engaged in the actual process of shopping and, as such, just follow the path of least resistance. On the other end of the spectrum are customers who actually enjoy trying out different companies' products and services as a means of comparison in some attempt to figure out which product will become the "preferred" or "default" product of choice. Whatever the reason, the single tie that binds all Wandering Customers together is an apparent lack of loyalty to any particular brand.

When choosing the Wandering Customers group as the Prospective Audience, the goal is not only to convince them that your product is superior to competing products but, perhaps more importantly, to convince them that sticking around has its perks. Thus, it should not be surprising that one effective route to take with Wandering Customers in an integrated marketing campaign is the development of a loyalty program with loyalty points, cards, or other incentives to keep them coming back to you. It is much easier to sell Wandering Customers on a loyalty program than it is to do the same thing for Others' Customers (that's a far bigger hurdle to jump, as we will discuss shortly).

A good example of this in practice is my own experience going to cafés. As I write these words, I am sitting at a Starbucks just across the street from my place in Chicago. In my building there is an Intelligentsia café where I used to spend a *lot* of time working and writing. I don't even have to go outside to get to Intelligentsia, which in Chicago during winter is an absolute treat. However, despite the convenience and ease of going downstairs to Intelligentsia, I find myself bundling up, trekking across the street, grabbing coffee, and doing work at Starbucks. The price is not different enough to justify one location over the other. Both cafés are convenient with plenty of seating, a nice ambiance, and enough outlets and good Wi-Fi (which, let's be honest, are two of the most important things we look for in cafés these days). So what made me switch? Loyalty points. I can accrue points on my Starbucks app every time I grab coffee or food at Starbucks, which I cannot do at Intelligentsia. It is a very subtle difference, but for someone with zero loyalty to either Intelligentsia or Starbucks, the introduction of a loyalty program was *just enough* to tip the scales in favor of the latter.

Wandering Customers can be fickle, however. They're sort of like those people who date several other people at the same time (you know the kind – my European friends call this style of dating "American dating"). You hear from them one day but don't hear from them again for days. Jerks. But therein lies the challenge: you have to figure out a way not just to make yourself seem unique and better than your potential boo's other options but also to show all the extras he/she will get if they spend *more* time with you. That is the way to appeal to Wandering Customers (…and also the way to snag yourself a future lover. You're welcome.).

Hot-Off-the-Press Customers: Newbie, Newbie, New

Like Wandering Customers, Hot-Off-the-Press Customers have zero loyalty to any particular company, brand, or product/service. However, unlike the Wandering Customers, Hot-Off-the-Press Customers lack loyalty not because they go after any bright and shiny object that appears but, instead, because they have zero knowledge or experience within the market. These people are brand new, "newbies," people who have yet to make up their mind about what they like, what they don't like, what's important to them, what they're indifferent to, etc. Hot-Off-the-Press Customers are like the new kid who just moved to town and is trying to figure out which clique he/she belongs to at the new school.

Hot-Off-the-Press customers are innocent and open minded. In many ways they are a blank slate, a group of people who have not formed any strong opinions or feelings about the options in the market. In the next chapter when we talk about objectives (or ways in which we want our Prospective Audience to "change"), it will be clear that there exists a strong correlation between choosing to focus your campaign on Hot-Off-the-Press Customers and an objective to simply *educate* them. These customers know next-to-nothing about their options, the competition, and, in some instances, their own needs and how those needs could potentially be fulfilled.

Because of their newbie naïveté, Hot-Off-the-Press Customers are extremely sensitive to *sincere* appeals or feeling like they are being taken care of truthfully and honestly. They know they are fresh meat and, as such, are sometimes apprehensive and cautious. To help illustrate with an example, let's draw upon the work of the brilliant Tina Fey and her movie *Mean Girls*. Think of the Hot-Off-the-Press customer to be like Cady Heron, the new girl in school played by pre-crazy Lindsay Lohan. Cady comes to North Shore High School knowing no one. Once there, she meets several people but grows to have two core groups of friends: The Plastics—Gretchen, Karen, and the evil Regina George (boo!), and the Artsy Misfits—Janis and Damien. Cady takes a liking to the latter duo because of the genuine concern they seem to have for her: enlightening her about the cafeteria cliques, explaining the social order of North Shore High School, painting a picture of their trio that won a prize. The Plastics, on the other hand, are sneaky, backstabbing, and three-way-calling calculated. Janis and Damien's sincerity and hand-holding guidance cements their friendship loyalty throughout Cady's first turbulent year at North Shore High and it is with this group to which she ultimately bonds for the long-term. See, friends? *Mean Girls* is not just entertaining, it's educational.

Several companies extend this kind of compassion to Hot-Off-the-Press Customers. Cable companies do it with introductory offers for first-time customers (…then they become Satan and steal everything you own). Disney does it by giving first-time visitors to its theme parks large buttons that say "1st Time," which then prompts *every* cast member in the park to go out of his/her way to welcome the first-timer. Even restaurants do this when they ask, "Have you eaten with us before?" If you say, "No," the waiter or waitress will welcome you and then usually go into some memorized routine that includes instructions on how to order, what some preferred menu options are, and the invitation to ask questions if you should need any help deciding. It seems so basic, but this expression of sincere, genuine care and compassion is *exactly* what the Hot-Off-the-Press Customer is looking for. Keep in mind, these customers are strangers to a new world. In addition to wanting a good product or service, these customers also want to feel like they belong, that people are not taking advantage of them, and that they are making a good investment.

As a company, it is in your best interest to provide a genuinely caring, welcoming experience to Hot-Off-the-Press Customers if you hope to have long-term gains from the relationship. You could woo them with a charming, one-night-stand approach, which many companies do (e.g., cable companies); however, while this may work well for short-term gains, it all but kills you on long-term gains and overall satisfaction (e.g., have you ever met *anyone* who is happy with his/her cable company?). Hot-Off-the-Press customers simply appreciate a bit of hand-holding, someone guiding them down an unfamiliar path, which, if done correctly, will create a loyalty that switches them from "newbies" to some of your most loyal customers.

Others' Customers: Turf Wars and Rival Gangs

Competition is one of the most fundamental aspects of Capitalism: great companies live or die by how competitive they are in the marketplace, their ability to squash the competition, the evolutionary fundamentals of "eat or be eaten." Competition stimulates creativity, change, and innovation. These, of course, are all positive consequences of competition. However, there is a dark side (cue *Star Wars* theme song here).

Just like people choose sides at sporting events or in politics, so, too, do people choose preferred companies, brands, or products in the marketplace. The crazy thing about choosing a side is that it is often arbitrary or based on some questionable logic like, "Well, we've just always used [Brand X]," which is like saying, "Well, we've just always voted Democrat/Republican." Heaven forbid we look at the attributes or abilities of a product (or a presidential candidate for that matter) before making a decision. Still, once people have hammered a stake into the ground, they will defend their choice no matter how silly, illogical, or refutable their argument may be.

Others' Customers are simply customers who have, for whatever foolish reason, hitched their wagon to someone else's caravan. These customers can vary in their opinion toward you, from completely neutral to downright spiteful, but regardless of this opinion, their default option is *not* you, your product/service, or anything to do with you.

The reason customers are loyal to another company can vary. Perhaps they simply tried your competitor's product first and felt their product fulfilled their needs well enough. Maybe they used to be your customer but you goofed and they vowed never to return to you (…like a scorned lover). Whatever the reason, Others' Customers are *easily* the most difficult to appeal to and represent the highest hurdle to jump. Why? Well, not only do you have the already difficult job of getting these customers to *like* you, you have an equally challenging task of getting these customers to *unlike* someone else.

So why in the world would you *ever* go after someone else's loyal customers when it seems like a Herculean task? Sometimes, it's the only thing you *can* do.

Consider, for example, the soft drink market. Two industry giants, Coca-Cola and Pepsi, make up about 75% of the soft-drink market. My personal favorite, Dr. Pepper, makes up about another 15% of the market. If you're adding along at home that means that 90% of the market is dominated by just three players: Coca-Cola, Pepsi, and Dr. Pepper. So let's say you are a budding entrepreneur who just invented a great-tasting new soft-drink you named Mr. Bubbles (which is like Dr. Pepper just with fewer years of formal education). If you plan on being successful in a very saturated, established market where most people have loyalty to one of the three dominating brands, well, you are going to have to put your gloves on and prepare for a fight. Your customers aren't going to appear out of thin air – they are going to be wrenched away from the claws of Coca-Cola, Pepsi, or Dr. Pepper, and don't expect for those industry behemoths to sit around idly while you pounce on their prey.

Thus, selecting Others' Customers as your Prospective Audience tends to happen in situations when you really have no other choice. In fact, the only time choosing Others' Customers as your Prospective Audience makes good sense is when you have a "secret weapon" of sorts.

Consider, for example, the case of Whole Foods. Most customers are loyal to a particular grocery store, often grocery stores so local that listing their name would be useless (e.g., you've probably never heard of Schnucks, Dierbergs, or Shop 'n Save unless you were raised in the St. Louis metropolitan area like I was). Over time, national chains like Kroger and expanded stores, like Wal-Mart Supercenter and Super Target, began to infringe on the market of the smaller, local grocery stores. To say this market was saturated would be an understatement because in addition to full-sized grocery stores were smaller convenience and corner stores selling many of the same products as the larger stores just on a smaller scale (not to mention the growth of member-based wholesale companies like Costco and Sam's Club). Now, Whole Foods has been around since the 1980s, where it achieved success in the Austin, Texas, area. The company could have stayed put and enjoyed local success in perpetuity, but thanks to changing consumer trends in food and health, Whole Foods found itself equipped with a "secret weapon" that allowed it to begin expanding and stealing customers in the very saturated grocery store market. What was the "secret weapon?" Organic food. Whole Foods' organic positioning differentiated it from traditional grocery stores (and the Wal-Mart/Target equivalents) during a time when consumer tastes also shifted toward "healthier," organic foods. The expansion was slow at first–it took almost 20 years for the chain to reach 100 stores–as societal trends toward healthy eating and organic food did not really take off just yet. However, once "eating healthy" became a societal norm, Whole Food managed to grow another 331% by 2015. Customers suddenly did not mind paying a premium for their groceries because of the perception that they were making healthier food choices, which now mattered more to them.

Keep in mind that just about every Whole Foods store opened in an area already saturated with competing grocery stores. That's sort of how food and humans work: the latter really don't enjoy being too far away from the former. But in such a saturated industry, Whole Foods really had no choice but to enter the scene and hope, with its very distinct point of differentiation (i.e., healthier, organic food), that shoppers would switch their loyalty from local grocery stores or options like Target or Costco in favor of Whole Foods. It's sort of like when Cinderella enters the ball scene and captures the prince's attention despite a ballroom full of eligible bachelorettes; she's so captivatingly beautiful, thanks to the magic of her fairy godmother, that she immediately stands out in a crowded room.

Of course, Whole Foods is *not* the dominant player in grocery. It has achieved success, for sure, but the funny thing about competition is that your competitors aren't just going to sit around and ignore you while you are stealing their customers right out from under their nose. It reminds me of the old Tom and Jerry cartoons where Jerry (the mouse) would steal cheese, cake, and other delicious treats right in front of Tom (the cat). Tom, irked at Jerry's brazen attempt to steal the food, did not just sit around and let the mouse steal all the good food. Instead, Tom concocted clever traps and revenge plots to stop Jerry and get his goodies back. Of course, these revenge plots never worked because Tom was an idiot, but *most* companies are smarter than a cartoon cat…most companies, anyway. Indeed, now most local grocery stores, as well as broader regional and national grocery chains, have rather robust organic food aisles and fresh salad bars to counter the popularity of Whole Foods. "I'll see your kale chips and quinoa balls, Whole Foods, and raise you one slab of vegan tofu meat!"

The takeaway? If you are going to attempt to enter a highly saturated market then you better 1) be prepared to fight for Others' Customers, 2) have a clear differentiator that makes you stand out, 3) protect yourself from the industry leaders simply copying your style (they probably have more resources than you do), and 4) sleep with one eye open at night because you will most certainly have a target on your back. Just like Jerry in the *Tom and Jerry* cartoons, brute force probably is not an option (he was a tiny mouse; Tom was a big cat). Instead, fighting for Others' Customers often involves cunning wit, cleverness, and creativity, especially when you're just a small player in the market.

Another time you might select Others' Customers as a Prospective Audience is if a company *clearly* drops the ball. Consider the world of cellular phone carriers and the very impassioned, sometimes crass CEO of T-Mobile, John Legere. T-Mobile used to be a sure fourth-place player in the American market, with Sprint in a solid third, and AT&T and Verizon splitting the lion's share of the market. However, in recent years, T-Mobile has caught up to Sprint as the rowdy Legere publicly points out the shortcomings of the big dogs, specifically how the major carriers are failing their customers, and explains how T-Mobile is better. On November 18, 2015, Legere tweeted a series of tweets bashing Sprint (e.g., "@TMobile customers don't have activation fees. @Sprint charges $36 per line! #SprintCountdown #halfoffthetruth"). At the end of 2016, Legere posted his "What's Next in Wireless: My 2016 Predictions" on the T-Mobile website in which he sinks his fangs into the competitions' shortcomings and explicitly highlights T-Mobile's strengths. The approach may not be for the faint of heart, but when you are the little guy in a crowded room already full of too many people, you keep your eye on the prize and seize any opportunity that comes your way especially when your competitors drop the ball. When it comes to Others' Customers as a Prospective Audience, this is war.

My Customers: I Will Always Love You

If choosing Others' Customers is the intense, thrilling action movie that leaves your heart racing, then choosing My Customers as your Prospective

Audience is your rated-G, family-friendly, Disney fairytale movie that lets you sleep easily at night and dream nice dreams of puffy marshmallow clouds and dancing unicorns. The best thing about your customers is that they are *your* customers! They already love you or at least like you well enough to have some loyalty toward you. They are like your cute puppy that pays attention when you call its name, comes when you say to come, fetches when you say to fetch, and only sometimes pees on the floor (but only when they are very, very excited).

In all seriousness, choosing My Customers' as the Prospective Audience is really choosing the lowest hanging fruit. These people already like what you have to offer, at least on some level, and are more likely to pay attention to you by default than any of the other Prospective Audiences as a result. Having this kind of loyalty is great and what most companies strive for if they hope to be around for awhile, but it is worth pointing out that your current customer base is not *always* the best place to look for growth. Let's consider an example...

Meet Julie. Julie is a busy mom who works a full-time job, has four kids (five if you count her lazy husband Joe), and does her best to do business by day and dinner by night. The marketing folks over at Kraft know moms like Julie fairly well. They know Julie wants to feed her kids something they will be happy to eat that she can feel good about without requiring her to be a Michelin-starred chef. Julie has consistently purchased Kraft Deluxe Mac & Cheese (which is, incidentally, one of the most delicious things you will ever put in your mouth) and is fairly happy with the product and is loyal to Kraft.

If Julie is already *super* satisfied with her current product choice and the frequency with which she purchases the product, then giving her coupons or encouraging her to purchase more frequently may not be super effective for Kraft's bottom line. Similarly, encouraging Julie to switch to a different mac and cheese product, one that features *Star Wars*-shaped pasta this month, is not going to be very effective: she already knows what she wants and does not have the time or motivation to switch it up. In other words, Kraft cannot fix what isn't broken and probably should not attempt to do so. The company is already addressing Julie's needs well and should simply focus on nurturing and sustaining *that* relationship.

On the other hand, sometimes your most loyal customers *can* become more profitable. You can get them to purchase more frequently. You can get them to buy premium products within your portfolio or new products within your product mix. Even better, you can get your loyal customers to become your marketers for you! They can generate the kind of buzz and excitement that motivates people to buy more of your product or service and they are the best possible salesperson outside of your company's marketing team to educate other consumers about your product. It is in these latter ways that the My Customers audience is unique among the four Prospective

Audience types: they know a lot about you and your products and, as such, can be great allies with respect to speaking on your behalf.

Let's be clear: your most loyal customers are an *extremely* valuable audience, perhaps the most valuable. But when it comes to *growing* value, this audience may not always be the one from which you can extract the most *growth*. With the My Customers audience you often have the best information available about what they want/need, how satisfied they are, and what they would like more of. The lines of communication are much stronger for this audience than any of the others. So the real focus for the My Customers audience is making sure they feel heard, nurtured, and tended to. If the preferences of your core customers change, so, too, should the attributes of your core product or service to reflect those preferences or else those once-loyal customers are going to seek out alternatives. You may have enough information that suggests you need to innovate and create a new offering that will serve the changing needs of these customers, which is *definitely* a growth opportunity. And remember: your My Customers audience is your competitors' Others' Customers audience. If you drop the ball, even if only once, rest assured your competitors will be there waiting to pick up that ball and run.

Thus, if you choose to focus on My Customers' as your Prospective Audience, treat it like a long-term relationship in real life: show you are committed, maintain trust, keep the lines of communication as open as possible in both directions, and constantly reinforce that you and your customers are better off with each other than without (i.e., you both bring each other value).

Efficiency and STP: Reconciling Modern Ideas with Old Standards

I am often asked, "Jim, when I'm selecting a Prospective Audience, can I only pick just *one*?" The short answer is, "It depends." The long answer is, "You should try to be as efficient and as realistic as possible. Ideally you would focus on *one* audience, but if your campaign motivates people outside that focal audience, well, so be it. Two birds…"

Throughout my formal marketing education, I have heard several different opinions regarding how specific and exclusive one needs to be when setting strategy. In the most extreme cases marketers were only supposed to choose *one* target market or *one* "share stealing" or "demand stimulating" strategy; never two or three target markets or both stealing share and stimulating demand. In theory this seems nice. In practice, however, this always felt a bit silly. There are few, if any products or services that do not appeal to more than one consumer segment no matter how you go about segmenting the broader market. Granted, I completely understand and agree with the strategy underlying the "must choose one" approach: it is simpler, more efficient, and more focused, which are all great things to be. However, in practice, this approach often feels over-simplified, surprisingly inefficient, and almost *too* focused.

My suggestion would be this: carefully consider the four Prospective Audience categories with respect to your company, the market in which you operate, your product/service, your history, current customer satisfaction, and your current resources. That, alone, should guide you to a Prospective Audience that stands out among the four as being *the* one on which to focus your campaign. If another comes in a close second, don't lose sleep over it or worry that you are missing out on a market opportunity. That's the kind of agony the "single strategy" approach from above thrusts upon you. Instead, keep that secondary audience in mind, what their needs are, how they might potentially overlap in some ways with your primary Prospective Audience. It could very well turn out that your campaign, although focused on the core needs of your Prospective Audience, still speaks to the folks in your secondary audience (and maybe even somewhat to the other two remaining audiences). This is not an all-or-nothing game with clean boundaries and black-and-white outcomes. Do your absolute best to create a campaign that really reels in your selected Prospective Audience and appreciate whatever other stowaways hop on for the ride. The opposite strategy, deliberately trying to appeal to *every* Prospective Audience simultaneously, is usually just foolish and wasteful. Unless you are Apple or some other tech giant with billions of dollars of cash just lying around, you may want to avoid this "I'll take everything" strategy because, chances are, you will wind up with nothing.

Another "classic" idea we should pause and reconcile with the Prospective Audience philosophy is the traditional STP approach. The good news is that these concepts are *not* mutually exclusive and can, in fact, actually reinforce one another. The Prospective Audience comes first because STP, although useful and specific, is almost *too* specific in today's world. Beginning with STP sort of narrows our potential audience too early, which, in turn, may unnecessarily limit the success of our campaign.

By selecting the Prospective Audience first, what we are actually doing is framing an implicit message we plan to deliver to whomever we target more specifically in the STP step. If we choose Wandering Customers, the message will involve the value of sticking with us. If we choose Hot-Off-the-Press Customers, the message must be sincere, welcoming, and educational. If we choose Others' Customers, the message will involve why it makes sense to abandon your current company of choice. If we choose My Customers, the message should reinforce the established bond, loyalty, and communication between you and those customers: you're both better off by being together.

Following the selection of a Prospective Audience (and sometimes simultaneously), engaging in STP helps the compass needle point more accurately to an option that can ensure a campaign's success. In other words, whereas the Prospective Audience gives us the "gist" of whom we are going after on a philosophical and big-picture level, STP gets us into the details of specific groups of people our campaign could target while featuring that message inspired by our Prospective Audience focus.

Because I like to illustrate concepts with tangible examples (it's the professor in me), let's consider how this relationship between a Prospective Audience and STP works. Consider Samsung and its Galaxy line of mobile phones. In the U.S. market, only a handful of major players exist in the market: Apple, Samsung, HTC, Motorola, LG, Nokia, and Blackberry. In today's world, most people already own phones, so short of encouraging people to buy a secondary, backup phone or encouraging lonely cat owners to buy Fluffy and Mr. Mittens their own touch-screen phones on which the kittens can play games (you laugh, but I bet it has happened), the only way you're going to increase your sales is to steal customers from your competitors. Yep, that's right: it's the oft-feared Others' Customers Prospective Audience situation! Right away, we know that Samsung would have to send a message in which they bring down their competitors while also highlighting why signing up with Samsung would be beneficial and why sticking with Samsung would be even better. Upon engaging in STP, Samsung realized that they had an "in" with young consumers, primarily young men into technology at that right age where being unique is preferred to "fitting in," which is what led to a clever campaign that directly attacked the common phenomenon of people lining up outside Apple stores on major phone launch days. The messaging? All the amazing, cool ways the Galaxy S3 was different (read: better) than a phone uncool people were foolishly waiting in line for like lemmings.

Had Samsung *only* engaged in an STP exercise, they may have narrowed their market to the same young male market, but the tone of the message could have been very different. Instead of mentioning Apple at all, perhaps the campaign would have focused on educating these consumers (…but they already know technology). Rather than emphasizing how their product and its features are superior to any other phone on the market, Samsung could have emphasized the relationship it had with this target, the open line of communication and feedback (…but this young target market doesn't consist of loyal Samsung users only). You probably see where this is going? By taking just one extra step prior to engaging in STP, we can hone in on the broader business objective we are trying to achieve, which allows us to engage in STP with *focus*.

Continuing the example, let's say another potential segment includes business customers or companies buying mobile phones for an entire fleet of employees. BlackBerry used to dominate the business mobile phone market but has since faded into obscurity. If Samsung identified businesses unhappy with their current mobile phone selection, the company could use the same "uncool" and "outdated" positioning to potentially tap into both the young male segment *and* this business enterprise opportunity. Granted, this campaign would look slightly different from one focusing exclusively on young men–maybe a little more professional, a little less informal–but with the right creative hand striking a good balance, it could easily be done. Thus, again, we see the power of how selecting a Prospective Audience can guide our messaging, which, together with STP, can spark creative ideas and even *better* campaigns than either could hope to do alone.

*   *   *

A great marketing campaign means *nothing* if it does not achieve a *business objective*. The introduction of the Prospective Audience construct roots our marketing campaign development firmly in the foundation of beginning with a business objective in mind. At its core, the Prospective Audience forces us to ask ourselves, "From whom will value come?" and, in the most basic business terms, the answer to that question must be one of four groups: our current customers, brand new customers, our competitors' customers, and the customers lacking loyalty to any particular company. The reason the Prospective Audience is such a critical idea is that, depending on the audience selected, your marketing campaign can *and should* have very different goals and objectives. For example, it is a lot easier to get your current customers to try a new product in your portfolio than it is to get a competitor's loyal customers to do the same. As another example, a campaign targeting customers who are brand new to the market should involve a lot more basic education than a campaign focusing on loyal customers already in that same market. No matter what campaign you are launching, you should *always* start by asking whom the Prospective includes. The Focus of the campaign depends on it.

Although we will not get into discussing specific metrics of success until much later in the book, it is also worth pointing out that the concept of the Prospective Audience directs our attention to where we expect (and hope) to see quantifiable changes. If we are focusing on Wandering Customers, we should be measuring something about those customers' thoughts, beliefs, and/or behaviors prior to launching the campaign, during the campaign, and again after the campaign to see if our strategy is working. While we can certainly capture data on other customers, we *know* we must be capturing data on this selected audience because that is the audience our campaign is designed to influence. And because Prospective Audiences are, by design, tied to valuable outcomes, success in shifting their thoughts, beliefs, and/or behaviors are likely to translate to success in shifting our bottom line.

Revisiting the McDonald's story that began the current chapter, the introduction of the Prospective Audience as a construct helps clarify an otherwise mystifying marketing problem facing the company. From its beginning, the "Our Food, Your Questions" campaign was focused on convincing customers loyal to competitors like Panera and Chipotle to come back to McDonald's. In other words: Others' Customers. Rather than fight this nearly impossible fight, this insurmountable inertia likely to keep those customers right where they are, why not focus on extracting more value from your *current* consumers (i.e., My Customers) or maybe even folks who still dine at McDonald's every so often (i.e., Wandering Customers)? Enter the All-Day Breakfast campaign. During Super Bowl 2016, McDonald's commercial was entitled *Good Morning*, and reminded millions of viewers watching at home that you could now get your favorite hash browns or Egg McMuffins all day, every day. That message is unlikely to sway your picky Panera eater or your choosy Chipotle diner, but for people already open to the idea of eating at McDonald's, well, they just might be ba da ba ba ba…lovin' it.

Don't forget, however: all-day breakfast was only *part* of McDonald's plan. The media certainly picked up on the buzz and excitement of customers no longer having to worry about being denied breakfast for showing up just one minute after breakfast had "stopped," but there was more to the story: McDonald's had also (rather quietly) added new burgers to its menu. Part I of the strategy was getting certain customers to come back to the restaurant, but Part II involved figuring out what customers needed to *do* once they arrived. In the FUSION model, Focus comprises both the audience most likely to create value and what that audience can *do* to create value, which is addressed in detail in the next chapter.

After decades of being everyone's favorite fast food destination, falling to an all-time low, and then resurging, the new-and-improved McDonald's is bringing customers back for the first time in years. Now, the question of what it plans to have those customers *do* has raised expectations and left the company with big shoes to fill…I suppose it's a good thing their mascot is a clown.

What if... *Making McMemories That Last*

Although McDonald's has achieved some success with its All-Day Breakfast initiative, success can be fleeting, particularly as other fast food companies step up their efforts to remind customers they *also* offer breakfast all day. So what can McDonald's so if it hopes to remain relevant in a tough competitive landscape?

Let me ask you a simple question: do you remember going to McDonald's as a child? I do. I have a vivid memory of my mom taking me to McDonald's on Saturday mornings before I attended these cool (translation: nerdy) classes where I studied acting, French, and how to draw cartoons (...not at the same time, but this totally seems like something artsy the French would do). I remember these mornings so clearly because I remember looking forward to each Saturday because of this special time with my mom. I would always get a hash brown (my favorite McDonald's breakfast food), and although I *rarely* eat McDonald's today, my mom can still convince me (without much persuasion) that hot, fresh McDonald's fries are always a good idea.

Let me ask you another question: what was your favorite Happy Meal toy from childhood? I can remember rainy days as a kid when I would have my superhero figurines mixed in with toys I had received in my McDonald's Happy Meals–like the Mac Tonight Moon Man on a motorcycle, a French Fry-box Transformer, and Fraggle Rock characters in rolling cars–dreaming up crazy storylines and plots with my sisters for hours.

And still, one more question: do you remember the joy you experienced as a child finding out your parents were surprising you with McDonald's? I remember that excitement from warm summer nights, having spent an entire day outside swimming and playing, upon finding out that my dad was bringing home McDonald's for dinner. For the record, my mom almost always cooked dinner for our family, but every now and then McDonald's was a special treat, one that my siblings and I surely did get excited about.

Now, as someone who is super into fitness, I would be lying if I said I thought McDonald's were a healthy or altogether appropriate meal to give to children on a regular basis. It isn't. However, I mention these memories and ask you for yours because one secret to McDonald's salvation is *nostalgia*: reminding young parents of the joys *they* experienced under those Golden Arches, the happy memories of bonding with their parents and siblings, the positive emotions that getting a "treat" from McDonald's can provide. This kind of joy is unique to McDonald's–neither Panera nor Whole Foods can provide that kind of memorable experience–McDonald's is able to use its long history to its advantage rather than to its disadvantage with a campaign based on nostalgia. Better yet, this nostalgia-based positioning speaks directly to McDonald's loyal customers and Wandering Customers who still keep McDonald's in their consideration set.

At the heart of a nostalgic "Making McMemories" campaign is the idea that young parents should bring their children to McDonald's both to relive the magic and memories they had as children and also to create *new* memories with their children. However, this also gives McDonald's the opportunity to talk about how it has changed particularly with respect to better ingredients, healthier options, and other features more aligned with the shifted societal preferences.

The television spots could consist of footage of parents taking their kids to McDonald's in the 1970s, 1980s, and 1990s cleverly interwoven with footage of a parent taking his/her child to McDonald's in the present time. The end of the commercial might reveal that the parent in the modern-day version is the kid from the 1980's version. Another commercial in the campaign might show a parent taking his/her child to McDonald's decades ago and then that same parent, now a grandparent, taking his/her grandchildren to the same McDonald's. The tagline might read, "Same great tastes. Same great memories. Healthier ingredients." and include a call to action for people to share their McMemories online, which incorporates a social media component that increases engagement.

Accompanying print and outdoor ads could be a split screen of a McDonald's from decades ago with the same McDonald's today. The copy might read, "Some things never change. Some things do." and feature the campaign tagline, "Same great tastes. Same great memories. Healthier ingredients." to underscore that the food still tastes as delicious and as indulgent as we remember, Happy Meals still have toys that bring joy to children, but that the ingredients and nutritional quality of the food have improved (even if only a slight improvement). McDonald's could play with the McMemories theme by temporarily changing the product packaging to packaging designs used decades ago. Similarly, the company could bring back limited-time menu items that are throwbacks to classic favorites or even include modern versions of classic Happy Meal toys in its Happy Meals. Anything that would tap into the strong, positive, and nostalgic feelings so many of us share for McDonald's would be fair game. In an ironic twist, McDonald's top-of-mind awareness that had so negatively affected its success when consumer tastes shifted could now rely on this nostalgic positioning to evoke strong, positive emotions competitors cannot emulate.

The McMemories campaign would speak directly to McDonald's loyal customers and Wandering Customers, evoking strong memories and tugging on heartstrings. Although inspired by nostalgia and past memories, this positioning also gives McDonald's the opportunity to emphasize the *new* memory making, which could include its new menu offerings, its new experiences (e.g., Wi-Fi – working with an iced coffee while your kids play safely nearby), and its shift to match modern trends in food consumption and fast-casual dining without sacrificing that special place McDonald's holds in people's minds and hearts (even if they feel like they cannot publicly admit it without seeming horribly unhealthy). By relying on its strong and storied past, McDonald's could propel itself into the future allowing you to have your Big Mac…and your kale fries, too.

You: Psst. Hey, Jim...why is this page blank?

Me: For notes, yo! The title of this book includes the words "How-To" because my hope is that each chapter sparks some ideas specific to your particular marketing need. Rather than forget the ideas or think you'll remember them in the morning or when your plane lands (...this never works), you can go ahead and take notes here and on the other blank pages I've included in the book!

You: Wait, you mean I am *supposed* to write in this book?!

Me: Yep.

You: Whaaaaat?! You're so crazy, Jim!

Me: No, YOU are! ☺

[end scene...now go brainstorm and doodle your ideas below!]

Chapter 3 | Desired Objective

"Kiss today goodbye, and point me toward tomorrow."
-"What I Did For Love," *A Chorus Line*

Broadway is a tradition as American as apple pie, baseball, and gun ownership. The "Great White Way," Broadway's theatre district, is rooted firmly in the heart of New York City between 42nd Street and 53rd Street, with various side-street branches housing countless theatres featuring the latest and greatest musicals and plays, as well as classic favorites.

For a tradition so steeped in American culture and history, it is probably surprising to learn that the opening song of *Jersey Boys*, the 2006 Tony Award-winner for Best Musical about the history of the very successful American pop group Frankie Valli and the Four Seasons, is not performed in English. No, mes amis, it is performed in the language of love: French.

Oh là là!

Lest you think the entire show was performed in French, you should know that the reason the first song was in French was central to the group's story, particularly the ability for the group's songs to stay so popular and relevant decades after they first achieved fame. The song, "Ces Soirées-Là," was actually an updated version of another French song, "Cette Année Là," which was a French version of the Frankie Valli and the Four Seasons hit song, "December, 1963 (Oh, What A Night)."...phew. That's a lot to follow.

The original "Ces Soirées-Là" was released in March 2000 by singer and rapper Yannick, was ranked #1 in France for 15 consecutive weeks, and spent almost one full year in the Top 100. As such, the song earned the distinction of being one of the best-selling singles of all time, 25 years after the original song on which it was based was released by Frankie Valli and the Four Seasons. As a result, an entirely new generation of listeners half a world away were dancing to a version of a song their parents and even their grandparents once danced to.

This approach of "making something old new again" is not unique to Broadway. Certain clothing styles that were once out of fashion often become trendy again (e.g., leather jackets, flare jeans, trucker hats, etc.). Furniture styles, like mid-century modern furniture, reappear in designer showrooms. And, of course, movie after movie has been remade in the ever-original, ever-creative Hollywood (e.g., *Ocean's 11*, *Planet of the Apes*, *The Karate Kid*). Yet Broadway has a particular knack of making the old new again in rather inspired ways. Whether simply staging a "revival" of a show that previously closed its curtains years before or creating a brand new show built entirely around non-Broadway tunes, musicals have become an amazing avenue for introducing theatregoers to entire worlds of characters, histories, music, movies, biographies, and so much more.

Here is just a sample of recent musicals and plays that have graced the stages of Broadway and their respective inspirations:

- *Beautiful*: based on the music and life of Carole King
- *Cats*: a stage musical inspired by a T.S. Eliot book of poetry
- *Dirty Dancing: The Musical*: stage musical version of the hit 1980s film
- *Les Misérables*: based on the Victor Hugo novel of the same name
- *The Lion King, Beauty and the Beast, Aladdin, Mary Poppins*: Disney musicals
- *Mamma Mia!*: fictitious story based on the songs of ABBA
- *Movin' Out*: fictitious story set to the music of Billy Joel
- *My Fair Lady*: stage musical version of George Bernard Shaw's *Pygmalion*
- *On Your Feet!*: true story based on the life and music of Gloria Estefan
- *Rent*: pop musical based on the opera *La Bohème*
- *Rock of Ages*: fictitious story featuring 1980s rock ballad anthems
- *Sunny Afternoon*: true story based on the history and music of The Kinks
- *Waitress*: musical version of the 2007 movie
- *We Will Rock You*: inspired by the history and music of the group Queen
- *Wicked*: based on a novel that reimagined the classic *Wizard of Oz* story

...and that's just a few.

Although original productions like *In the Heights*, *Book of Mormon*, and *Avenue Q* pop up from time to time, many Broadway shows are simply revivals, retellings, reimaginings, or reworked tales from existing books, movies, or (non-Broadway) music...and people complain Hollywood is out of good ideas.

But does this seeming "lack of originality" actually mean Broadway is out of good ideas? Is it any less creative to take a hodgepodge of songs from the 1980s, develop a story that links them together, and then package and sell that as a show named *Rock of Ages*? Flipping that approach on its head, is it any less incredible that singer-songwriter Sara Bareilles took a non-musical film from 2007, wrote a musical's worth of original songs capturing the emotion of the movie, and even released her own preview album featuring the new music to spark interest in the musical prior to its debut?

In some instances, the inspiration for these musicals is simply a retelling of a classic story. No more, no less. But in other instances, the inspiration for the show is less about simply retelling a story and more about expanding a portfolio of products (...uh oh, here come those fancy business words again!).

Broadway lovers might start tensing up right about now. "Jim, these producers create these shows for the *art* not the *business*," they are thinking. True. Sort of. While there is no doubt that Broadway shows incorporate art in the form of music, dance, style, set design, and so much more, a Broadway show that does not perform well financially is not going to be around for very long. However, as of late, Broadway shows have not just become a way to make money, they have also become a way to introduce stories, songs, and entire franchises to brand new audiences.

Consider shows like *Rock of Ages, Movin' Out*, and *Mamma Mia!* In each of these instances, each musical is shining the spotlight not on itself but, instead, on the music that inspired each show. ABBA, a common favorite of people who grew up dancing in discotheques in the 1970s and early 1980s, is a group that was less known (if known at all) by people born in the 1980s and after. When *Mamma Mia!* debuted in 1999, ABBA loyalists around the world rejoiced: their favorite music was now a part of a fun, humorous stage show. You can rest assured that these longtime fans of the group were among the very first to see the production. Some actually see the touring show every time it comes through their town! However, there were also people in the audience who had never heard of ABBA or at least only knew songs like "Dancing Queen." The popularity of the musical introduced these new fans to almost *three* decades of music and content from the group, from their early albums to *Chess* (another musical written by the two guys in ABBA), the A*Teens (a teen pop tribute to ABBA's music) to *Muriel's Wedding*, an Australian film in which the main character lives her life like it's an ABBA song. As a result, you are just as likely to see children posing with the life-sized cutouts of the members of ABBA at the ABBA museum in Stockholm than you are to see those children's grandparents doing the same!

From a business perspective, Broadway has allowed creative properties the opportunity to expand their portfolio. In doing so, musicals are able extract more value from loyal consumers (remember My Customers?), as well as value from brand new consumers (remember Hot-Off-the-Press Customers?). Of course, it is not uncommon for creative properties to develop clever ways to expand its portfolio of offerings. Perhaps the most extreme example of this in recent years is the *Harry Potter* franchise. What began as a beloved book series morphed into films, toys, and even multiple theme park lands at Universal Studios' many parks. The most recent announcement, that a stage show inspired by Harry Potter entitled *Harry Potter and the Cursed Child* would debut in London's West End (i.e., England's analog to Broadway), sent Potter fans through the roof! Rest assured that the show will be one of the bestselling theatrical productions in history, both in London and then again when it makes its debut in Broadway, as loyal fans of the franchise have yet another way to enjoy their beloved Harry Potter and friends.

To be sure, turning a famous property into a Broadway show does not *always* ensure success. Case in point: *Spiderman: Turn Off the Dark*. The show, which holds the record of being the most expensive Broadway show to date thanks largely to special effects and acrobatics never before seen on Broadway, was inspired by the famous superhero and featured music penned by Bono and The Edge of the famous band U2. Expectations for the show were high, which is not always a good thing, especially when the show went on to have the *longest* preview run in the history of Broadway due to several production challenges (and several extremely negative critiques). When the show finally debuted after much tweaking, the reviews were better, but not much better, and the show closed less than three years after its debut. The show managed to attain some box office success during its limited run, as you can imagine the comic book crowd could not wait to see Spidey tingle his senses on stage (…that sounds wrong), it is not clear whether non-Spiderman fans immediately started reading his comics or seeing the films following a show that several critics rated among the worst that had ever been on Broadway. There's no ambiguity about it, Spiderman – that bites.

The musical retelling of classic stories, of famous people's lives, of animated Disney films is unlikely to slow down anytime soon. In fact, as I write this book, musical versions of the hit Disney film *Frozen*, the beautiful French film *Amélie*, and the Tina Fey comedy *Mean Girls* are currently in development. Fans of the originals are certain to fill the seats upon these shows' respective debuts, and for the theatregoers who find themselves introduced to Anna and Elsa singing "Let It Go" for the first time (is that even possible?), reflecting on life and love with Amélie, or laughing along with the woes of American high school life, new audiences and new generations are introduced to beloved characters, compelling storylines, and entire business franchises they may never even knew existed.

Just remember that even though you think the show might be over…there is usually an encore.

*   *   *

In the previous chapter, I introduced the idea of the Prospective Market. It turns out that *any* customer who is actually in the market for a product or service falls into one of four general categories: Wandering Customers, Hot-Off-the-Press Customers, Others' Customers, or My Customers. Just like all great marketing tenets, the Prospective Audience *begins with the customers in mind.*

However, when it comes to establishing Focus, the Prospective Audience is only half the story. Identifying the right audience is critically important for a campaign, but in addition to identifying that audience we also must identify what we want that audience to *do*. Together, the Prospective Audience and what I call the Desired Objective determine the Focus of a campaign–they set up the foundation of a campaign by answering a very simple (but a very important) question: "What do we hope to accomplish in the first place?"

In this chapter, I will introduce the concept of the Desired Objective and then explain each of the four possible objectives in greater detail, as well as provide examples of each. The opening motivating story, regarding Broadway and its recent spate of shows inspired by existing creative properties, suggests that one way to extract value from customers is to encourage them to purchase a new product within a portfolio of products. This strategy is not the only one, however, and you will soon see that sometimes the objective of our campaign is not even to get customers to purchase anything at all! Sounds ludicrous, right? Well, let's dive in a bit deeper to understand why that might be the case.

Desired Objective: What do we want our Prospective Audience to *DO*?

Throughout this book I have consistently reminded you that any great marketing campaign should change the way people think, what they believe, and/or how they behave. If your campaign is successful, you should observe *some* measurable difference in your intended audience's perceptions, attitudes, knowledge, and/or purchasing behavior. That's our goal. What else would we be doing all this work for if not to leave the world in some different, better place than which we found it?

To that end, whereas Prospective Audience is half of our Focus goal, its partner in crime is what I refer to as the **Desired Objective (DO)**. The name "Desired Objective" is based on my nickname from college (...kidding). The Desired Objective is simply what we want our selected Prospective Audience to *do*. Because I am all about the mnemonics, it is easy to remember the Desired Objective because we are simply asking ourselves, "What do we want our selected Prospective Audience to *DO*?" It gets better. As I mentioned, in any campaign we always want our audience to do MORE of something (i.e., buy more, feel more, believe more). By now, you know how much I love memory aids, so we can actually use MORE as an acronym for the four basic business objectives any marketing campaign should incorporate: **M**ultiply purchases, **O**pen up more options, **R**ally the troops, and **E**ducate. Each of these four possible Desired Objectives are explained in the sections that follow.

Multiply Purchases: One is Never Enough

One way to add value to the bottom line simply involves getting customers to purchase *more* of your product or service, whether that means purchasing more each trip or increasing the frequency with which those consumers buy the product or service. Thus, **Multiply Purchases** refers to the Desired Objective in which we encourage customers to purchase products or services they are *already* purchasing in greater number (i.e., increase volume) or more frequently (i.e., increase frequency).

Say, for example, I work for the Italian company Ferrero, creators of the indulgent delicacy that we all know and love: Nutella. For many years, Nutella was known for its use as a delicious chocolate hazelnut spread in crêpes accompanying fresh strawberries or bananas (or, if you are me, both strawberries *and* bananas). Consumers in the U.S. tended to associate Nutella with crêpes and, sadly, not much else. However, several years ago, Ferrero USA launched a campaign in which a busy mother discussed Nutella's merits as a healthy, wholesome part of a normal breakfast that kids would love to eat. She highlighted the fact that Nutella consisted of "simple, quality ingredients like hazelnuts, skim milk, and a hint of cocoa" while text appeared across the screen informing viewers that Nutella had "no artificial colors or preservatives."

With respect to the Multiply Purchases objective, this approach was genius: suddenly Nutella was no longer just for use in desserts and crêpes, now it can and should be a part of every wholesome breakfast! Instead of purchasing Nutella every so often when crêpes were on the menu (which is not as often as it should be in the U.S.), moms should consider buying Nutella every time they go to the grocery store just as they do for staples like peanut butter and jelly. By linking Nutella with breakfast and its potential use as a breakfast spread, Ferrero increased the occasions for which Nutella might be used, thereby increasing the frequency with which the product should be purchased in the minds of consumers; a classic Multiply Purchases maneuver.

Although this is, indeed, a spot on marketing strategy, you should know that it did not last very long. Why? Well, in America, people can sue for anything. A mom in California who has too much time on her hands (and who apparently hates fun) decided to sue Ferrero for false advertising, claiming that its included statements regarding Nutella's "simple, quality ingredients" led her to believe the product was a healthy choice for her four-year-old daughter when, in reality, the product contained over 20 grams of sugar, over 10 grams of fat, and 200 calories per serving. She contended that Nutella was hardly wholesome and, as such, should not be advertised as being part of a "wholesome" breakfast.

While the mom may have a point that Ferrero took liberties with its definition of "wholesome," it should be noted that each bottle of Nutella also bears a nutrition facts label that we are all capable of reading. Regardless, the courts ruled in favor of this meddling mom, which meant that Ferrero had to stop talking about Nutella's wholesomeness, thereby thwarting an otherwise solid Multiply Purchases Desired Objective. An easy fix to this legal limitation that would still encourage repeat purchase of Nutella would be to simply market it as an indulgence or "guilty pleasure" that, although not necessarily "wholesome," makes breakfast more fun to eat. Alternatively, Ferrero could have launched a site or social media page dedicated to recipes calling for Nutella–from desserts to dips, spreads to smoothies–thereby increasing the various ways Nutella could be used outside of crêpes. Thanks to sites like Pinterest, Ferrero has loyal Nutella consumers already doing this for them.

As the Nutella example illustrates, the point of a Multiple Purchase Desired Objective is to get people buying *more* of the same product or buying the same product *more often*. In other words, the goal of a Multiple Purchase objective is to increase the volume or frequency with which customers are buying your product or service. Other clever ways to do this include launching timed promotions in which customers have only a limited time to come back to your store or buy-one-get-one (BOGO) promotions in which you encourage customers to buy several of a product or service by luring them with the offer of a free bonus for doing so. So instead of just buying one t-shirt at Banana Republic, people will buy two because they get a third one for "free." Multiply Purchase objective: achieved.

Open Up More Options: You Buy X, But Do You Know About Y & Z?

Another way to increase value from consumers is to expand the products or services within your portfolio that consumers are interested in purchasing. **Open Up More Options** refers to the Desired Objective in which we encourage customers to considering purchasing products or services we offer that they are not yet buying, which includes both lateral shifts (i.e., trying a different product or service within our portfolio) and vertical shifts (i.e., trying a premium or discount version of a product/service within our portfolio).

Uber, the oft-revered, oft-reviled car service company that is the go-to example when discussing the modern "sharing economy," began as a simple way for people to hail a car using an app on their phone. The convenience of not having to wait outside for a taxi, particularly if no taxi is driving down the street, was beneficial, as well as the ability to have all charges (tip included) billed through the app so all you have to do is hop out of the cab at your destination and go about your day. As the company grew in both size and popularity additional levels of service were offered: UberX, UberTaxi, UberSelect, and Black Car (note: the names change city to city for various reasons, but the stratification remains the same). UberX, the lowest level, is the cheapest of the four options and involves Uber-hired drivers using their personal cars (also required to undergo an inspection by the company) to shuttle people around. The UberTaxi connects travelers with actual certified taxi/cab drivers with the app simply making it easier to secure a ride than flailing your arms in the air like a crazy person on the street. UberSelect is the snooty cousin to UberX, as this option is more expensive and fancier. Uber explicitly articulates which cars can be considered for UberSelect (e.g., as of this book's writing, Chicago UberSelect cars must be from 2007 or after, have only leather or vegan leather only, and can only be Mercedes, Lexus,

BMW, Jaguar, Audi, Maserati, Rolls Royce, or Bentley…to name a few). I pity the fool who accidentally orders a Rolls Royce to be dropped off at the grocery store on a rainy day. Finally, Black Car takes the exquisiteness even one step further, permitting only cars from 2015 and beyond (so less than one year old) and an even more limited list of brands. Oh, and the car *must* be black.

With respect to an Open Up More Options objective, by adding on these additional levels of service, Uber created value for its customers and, in doing so, created value for itself. Prior to the different levels of service all customers simply had *one* option: a car-on-demand service. Adding the cheaper option, UberX, likely *increased* the number of times Uber customers would consider taking an Uber as they now had a cheaper alternative. Thus, introducing a cheaper option is one way to engage customers even more; it is likely that customers switch between UberTaxi and UberX often, with the introduction of the latter increasing the frequency with which customers engage with the service. Adding premium options like UberSelect and Black Car relies less on *frequency* and more on the *premium* value provided. For example, business people trying to impress a client or first-time daters trying to make a good impression may splurge a bit on UberSelect to get a fancy car for their trip as opposed to a typical taxi cab or someone's Honda Accord (not that there's anything wrong with a Honda Accord…it's just not a Rolls Royce). The introduction of these higher-end options also make the traditional Uber option seem more affordable in comparison, which may increase the frequency with which one purchases regular Uber trips (as the cost is then justified in one's mind). The introduction of options like UberPool (you share your ride with strangers also going to nearby places) creates yet another, cheaper option for riders. I'm still waiting for UberGold where you get to ride in a golden carriage pulled by flying unicorns with endless ice cream and cookies for the ride…a man can dream.

The prior examples all represent *vertical* shifts in the realm of Uber. That is, the actual service–a trip from point A to point B–is the *exact same* among those options. Uber simply modifies the same experience slightly to provide more value (either by premium features or price) to customers. However, the Open Up More Options objective also refers to *lateral* shifts or the possibility for customers to enjoy *different* products or services in a company's portfolio. Given that Uber is presently valued at $50 billion (…yes, that's right: $50 billion), it should not be too surprising that their portfolio also includes services that represent lateral shifts, as well, some of which might be quite surprising to you.

First, somewhat unsurprising, Uber permits food delivery as a service in some of the cities in which the car sharing service operates. This makes sense, right? You have a bunch of people in cars driving around a city picking up people and taking them from point A to point B. There are going to be busy times–the morning work commute, lunchtime, the evening commute, weekend nights–and the not-so-busy times. Why not take advantage of that commuting downtime to help fulfill one of mankind's primal needs: eating. Uber customers can use the same app they use to hail a car to scroll through menu options and have food delivered directly to their doorstep, office, or even a park bench on a nice spring day. But the excitement does not stop there, friends! Uber engages in seasonal services that range from delivering ice cream in summer to delivering Christmas trees in winter, perfect for carless city dwellers who would otherwise have to lug their Christmas plant through harsh snowy weather. Never again! Now you can just sit at home by the fireplace wearing your robe and drinking hot chocolate, which was probably also delivered by an Uber driver.

My personal favorite service, however, was an initiative Uber launched in coordination with the famed Puppy Bowl event that coincides with the Super Bowl each year. Working with local animal shelters in each participating city, Uber gave customers the option to have puppies delivered on demand to homes or offices for 15-20 minutes of cuddle, play, and rowdy time (…which is funny, because that is also the tagline of Uber's next expansion: UberSex …just kidding…I hope – but I actually wouldn't be surprised if UberPot starts operating in Colorado soon). Say what you will about Uber and its policies, a company that offers playtime with puppies cannot be *entirely* evil.

These services that expand beyond the realm of a car sharing service that gets you from point A to point B all represent examples of lateral shifts. Uber customers primarily use the company for transportation, but encouraging them to have their food delivered, to order ice cream on a hot summer day, and to spend time with an adorable puppy or two to relieve some stress are all ways to bring these customers additional value in line with the Open Up More Options objective. Thus, whether shifting people *vertically* (e.g., UberX, Black Car) or *laterally* (e.g., tree delivery, puppy time), Uber is a great example of how a company can increase customer engagement, loyalty, and, as a result, value.

Rally the Troops: Let's Give Them Something to Talk About

Sometimes the goal of our marketing campaign is to get customers to buy more of our products or services as quickly as possible. When tapping into the Multiply Purchases objective or the Open Up More Options objective, we tend to be focused on increasing sales in the relatively immediate future. However, there is another objective–the **Rally the Troops** objective–that we can pursue whose goal is *not* necessarily increasing immediate sales but, instead, involves engaging customers, themselves, to spark conversations, ideas, and excitement about our products and services. In a world of Facebook, Pinterest, Instagram, and [insert social medium of choice here], the Rally the Troops objective has become increasingly important as customer power has reached heights never before seen. For better or worse, the internet has allowed consumers to air every grievance, rate every interaction with a company, record every customer service call (those are super entertaining), and, thankfully, rave about beloved product or service experiences.

It is often the case that the Rally the Troops objective works well when we select My Customers' as our Prospective Audience. Indeed, companies often lose sight of one of their most important assets: their loyal customers. Not only are these people valuable in that they consistently give you their hard-earned money, they are also likely your biggest fans, your most vocal supporters, and your best possible brand ambassadors. However, we can just as easily excite other Prospective Audiences that are not yet among our most loyal customers.

One domain in which we often see "companies" Rallying the Troops is social media. I say "companies" because the companies in this case are not really companies as we typically imagine them; they are *people*. As of this very moment, the top 10 Instagram accounts consist of a truly remarkable group of people (author's note: heavy sarcasm implied): Kim Kardashian, Kylie Jenner, Kendall Jenner, Nicki Minaj, Justin Bieber, Ariana Grande, Selena Gomez, Beyoncé, and Taylor Swift. In fact, Taylor Swift is *the* most-followed account on Instagram behind Instagram's own @instagram account (which is #1). Now, each of these individuals sell products–from music albums to makeup to sex tapes (sorry, Kim, I went there)–so they obviously have a vested interest in attracting the attention of the largest possible audience of people who can then purchase their products. However, these people are just as much in the business of selling themselves as they are in the business of selling their products. Part of being famous and holding on to that fame involves keeping your loyal followers excited and energized on your behalf, and few tools permit that as easily as Instagram, Twitter, and Facebook. A sensational or unnecessarily sexualized picture on Instagram (i.e., anything someone from the Kardashian family posts) or a shade-throwing Twitter war (i.e., anything Nicki Minaj posts) are often carefully considered and crafted communications from people who cannot really rely on talent or ability alone to keep people interested (i.e., see any nonsensical social media rant from Kanye West...there are several). These posts do not sell lipstick, concert tickets, or music downloads directly, but they do get people talking, particularly the loyalist of the loyal. Posts get shared, tweets get re-tweeted, and conversations get started that soon gain the attention of popular media, which is why we see Kardashian headline after Kardashian headline on American "news" sites: people click on them. Perhaps one of the saddest days of my life was when *USAToday* featured an entire section of "Kardashian News" next to sections like "World News" and "US News." The end times are nigh.

In today's media world, individuals and companies have never been better connected with the audiences they are trying to reach. The Rally the Troops objective helps companies stay top-of-mind, relevant to, and interactive with customers in a way that perpetuates word-of-mouth marketing, buzz marketing, and the kind of once-difficult-to-obtain objectivity that comes from hearing about a celebrity (…or company, or product, or service) through a friend as opposed to the celebrity him/herself. Indeed, some of the most engaging and interactive components of a social media post by a celebrity or company comes not from the one post by the celebrity/company but rather from the hundreds to *thousands* of posts from people just like you and me all around the world. It's a different world.

The Rally the Troops objective can also come in handy to tide us over during any lull in the company. We are not always launching new products or services. There is not always some event coming up to which we can hitch our wagon and launch a campaign. In those times, it is often useful just to excite our audience and get them talking about our company and/or its products however we can just to remind them, "Hey, we are still in this relationship together!" and to get them to express their love for you in return.

Of course, another way the Rally the Troops objective can be used is to encourage customers to create their own genius ways of using your products and/or services. Consider, for example, Pinterest and the ability for people to share recipes, pictures of their completed dishes, craft projects incorporating your products, and any other number of customer-led creation. Whether you are the Just Born company encouraging customers to dream up funny, creative Peep Dioramas that incorporate the company's famous Peeps candy each Easter or Nestlé encouraging cookers, bakers, and delicacy-makers to post their original, creative recipes incorporating your products, a *lot* of value comes from rallying customers. Thankfully, we live in a time when reaching those customers has never been easier.

Educate: Those Who Can't Do Teach

Just as the goal of the Rally the Troops objective may not involve increasing purchases immediately, another Desired Objective has an outcome that may or may not evoke purchasing behavior from customers. The **Educate** objective simply has the goal to educate, enlighten, and inform customers so that they possess additional knowledge upon engaging with the campaign that they did *not* have prior to the campaign.

Classic examples of campaigns with a Desired Objective to Educate include PSAs (public service announcements) like the "truth" anti-smoking campaign and, ironically, Smokey the Bear, the bear who reminds us all to be careful in forests because, "Only you can prevent forest fires!" Of course, these campaigns do have end goals–choosing not to smoke, choosing not to set a forest on fire (…seems like an obvious one)–but the focus is on educating people with knowledge and information: the harmful effects of smoking, the different risks of using fire at forest campsites, and more. Per these campaigns, smoking a cigarette in a dry forest would be the worst possible idea ever.

In the United States, the Ad Council is one non-profit organization known for producing PSAs like the famous Smokey the Bear wildfire prevention campaign, the crying Native American anti-littering campaign, and, more recently, anti-bullying campaigns. The Ad Council's campaigns tend to include facts, details, statistics, and other information designed to educate viewers with the hope that equipping people with this new knowledge will change their thoughts, attitudes, and/or behaviors. Lest you think that campaigns produced by a non-profit that are designed to educate are less interesting or popular than campaigns designed by big, powerful companies, you should know that the third most-watched advertisement of *every* advertisement on YouTube was a clever PSA designed and produced by our friends at the Ad Council. The campaign, Love Has No Labels, was a part of the Ad Council's focus on Diversity and Inclusion. The commercial begins with a view of the ocean and the words Valentine's Day 2015. We then see a large screen placed along a street showing the x-ray image of two people behind the screen. An audience of bystanders has collected in front of the screen to watch the x-ray skeletons dance, hug, kiss, and generally have a great time. We often see two skeletons at a time, sometimes three (with a smaller skeleton, presumably a child, with two adults), with each group engaging in the same kind of frivolity, love, and silliness behind the screen. Then, each pair or group emerges from behind the screen–a lesbian couple, a mixed-race couple, two sisters (one with Down Syndrome), a visually-impaired man and his wife, two fathers and their son, an elderly couple, two little girls of mixed-race, a rabbi and an imam, and more. After each pair emerges, the screen displays a statement: "love has no gender," "love has no race," "love has no disability," "love has no age," and "love has no religion" along with the website www.lovehasnolabels.com. The website contains information on bias, an interactive quiz, tips, stories, and a social gallery, as well as links to associated social media pages for the campaign in a rather well-designed and marvelously executed integrated marketing campaign. If you can watch the video without crying, well, congratulations: you have a heart made of steel.

The great part about the Love Has No Labels campaign is that it is not selling *anything*, it is *educating*. We could argue that the campaign is selling ideas or a way of thinking, but at end of the day the purpose of the campaign is to communicate the idea that the definition of love does not limit the feeling based on gender, race, religion, ability, or age. People of every type can love. What it means to "love" someone is a *universal* feeling. Now, whether viewers of this then take that information and change their perspective on how they view or engage with people of different sexual orientations, people of different religious beliefs, people with disabilities, or even people much older or younger than they are is really up to the person, but the campaign achieved its goal: conveying the fact that love, by definition, does not exclude.

Beyond social awareness and public service campaigns, another use for the Educate objective is to announce major changes to products or services that might affect customer experience. For example, in mid-2015 Kraft announced that it would be dropping artificial preservatives and coloring from its famous macaroni and cheese. This announcement came following an online petition started by a food blogger known as "The Food Babe" that garnered over 350,000 signatures. Although Kraft never explicitly mentioned the petition, one can be sure that the decision to remove the preservatives and dyes was inspired, at least partly, by the petition along with increasing competition from organic mac and cheese brands like Annie's Organic and Natural Mac and Cheese. Lest you think that Kraft tried to keep this change in its core product off the radar, the company deliberately included the information about the change on the front cover of the product's packaging. A box of *Star Wars*-shaped Kraft Macaroni and Cheese included what appeared to be a posted note that read, "Good Stuff! No Artificial Flavors, Preservatives, or Synthetic Colors." Thus, while this shift may result in increased sales of mac and cheese, the goal of the campaign was to educate consumers about the change in the product's ingredients. Importantly, central to Kraft's approach to educating consumers was the assurance that the same great taste would remain in spite of the ingredient change. In other words, customers would be getting the same macaroni and cheese they love but a healthier, less artificial version of it.

Keep in mind, Kraft could have said nothing, could have downplayed any information regarding the change, or could have launched a campaign focused on increasing sales without educating (i.e., a Multiply Purchases objective), but given shifting consumer sentiments, it made more sense for Kraft to send out a press release and subsequently include messages about the change on product packaging. That way, customers who might be tempted to shift to Annie's while riding the current wave of health-conscious food would now have a reason to remain loyal to Kraft. Thus, Education-oriented campaigns can exist for the sole purpose of persuading or shifting attitudes with the hope being that those changed attitudes translate to increased purchases at some point.

And with that, we have rounded out the four Desired Objectives. Could there be others? Certainly. Are there risks inherent in following a certain strategy instead of another? Sure. Rallying the Troops puts a lot of faith and control into the hands of consumers and, as such, we have to be aware of this as marketers so that we can nudge them in the right direction in a way that is effective but not too forceful. Still, these four objectives provide a simple way of thinking about what our campaign should *do*, which will help us craft creative ideas, relevant messages, and metrics appropriate for measuring the campaign's success.

Obtaining Focus: Integrating Prospective Audiences and Desired Objectives

Now that we have a working definition of the Prospective Audience and the Desired Objective, the obvious next question is, "How do we choose?!" The answer to this depends on a few factors: what's your budget, how new is your industry, how competitive is your industry, what share of the market belongs to you, what is the company's broader strategic goal for the short-term, for the long-term, etc. In short, there are a lot of questions to consider before deciding.

However, there are some general themes or ideas that will help guide the selection of a particular audience and objective and please, please, please keep in mind that there is rarely ever *one* right answer. Some solutions certainly make more sense than others, but in the world of marketing rare is it the case that there is only *one* right solution. With that in mind, consider a few of the following tips and tricks to help shape your perspective of how one could go about determining a prospective audience and desired objective.

The first consideration is *how soon you need results*. The "lowest hanging fruit" approach typically involves targeting your current loyal customers and enticing them to buy more of the products they already buy or other products within your product portfolio. You already have their attention, so that's one less thing you have to do. And because these customers are loyal to you, they are more likely to believe what you have to tell them and more willing to try something new as long as it has your brand name on it. Educating these customers usually is not necessary unless you are launching a brand new product; they are already smart when it comes to you and your products. Rallying this group is sometimes a great objective when you want a sustained viral campaign, but if the goal is a quick uptick in sales in the short term, it makes more sense to focus on multiplying product purchases or opening the door to new products and services. A simple promotion in which you give them a coupon to try another product or to purchase more of your product within a certain timeframe is an easy way to do this.

Another consideration is the *age of the industry/market in which you operate*. If a market is brand new, like the currently emerging market for self-driving vehicles, there are no customers to steal, no wandering customers, and no customers currently loyal to you because the market is brand new (unless you are Apple or another established brand who could easily tap into its brand-loyal customers to foray into this new market, something Apple is quite adept at doing). Instead, everyone will be fighting for the Hot-Off-the-Press customers because *all* customers are essentially hot off the press. While each company may want customers to purchase their new car, the desired objectives in such a novel market would most likely involve educating. Before customers can buy they must first have some sense of what it is they are buying exactly.

If a market is mature (i.e., like grandma or grandpa, it has been around for awhile), then a new entrant to that market would probably have to focus on Wandering Customers or Hot-Off-The-Press Customers new to that mature market, as the new entrant almost certainly lacks a solid, loyal customer base at such an early stage. Attempting to go after a competitor's loyal customers in a long-established market would be an uphill battle, as you would have to fight the customers' inertia for switching along with your competition's certain retaliation. That's usually a recipe for disaster.

The right strategy is simply *having* a strategy. You see, regardless of what Prospective Audience you choose or Desired Objective you select, the simple act of even *considering* these important elements in the first place already puts you ahead. Why? By clearly articulating whom you plan to target (and, specifically, audience options directly tied to real value for a company) and what you plan to have them do as a result of experiencing your campaign, you now have a foundation on which 1) your creative plan, and 2) your metrics of success/progress are based. There's no more guessing. There's no wandering through the forest and *hoping* you find your way out. No, a path has been set, and we can now move forward. There's no turning back at this point. We have our Desired Objective, now it's time to make it happen…or, as our friends at Nike would say, it's time to "Just *DO* it."

*　　*　　*

Well-written lyrics can *move* people; emotionally, cognitively, philosophically. As the lyrics that begin this chapter state, "Kiss today goodbye, and point me toward tomorrow." Every marketing campaign should motivate consumers to *do* something: to think differently, to feel differently, to behave differently. Selecting a Desired Objective requires thinking about what you believe customers should *do* differently that will make them better off, that will bring them value.

New Broadway shows will come, classic Broadway shows will close their curtains, and revivals of those classic shows will bring new life into the once dormant spectacles. As long as audiences keep coming to the Great White Way, Broadway will remain the American tradition it has been for so long. Whether offering the chance to buy discounted tickets at a TKTS booth so tourists can see multiple shows during their vacation (Multiply Purchases), encouraging young talents with big dreams the chance to take vocal lessons or dance classes with Broadway stars (Open Up More Options), producing a new show incorporating new songs by an internationally successful band with a loyal fan base like One Direction (Rally the Troops), or offering free study guides, classroom lessons, and interactive activities to teachers around the country using theatre to teach lessons about history, language, skills and more (Educate) like the resources provided by Broadway Educators, like a truly memorable Broadway show, audiences leave as different people than when they came in.

I often liken marketing to theatre, especially improvisational theatre. You must know your audience. You must captivate your audience. You need to capture their attention and keep it–know when that attention is waning and do everything you can to get that attention back. You have the power of creativity. You have the power of words. You have the gift of storytelling, the gift of painting a scene. You have the magic of engaging the senses: sight, smell, sound, touch, and feeling. You have the power to *change* people, to *transform* them, to *bring more value* into their lives. This kind of power can be daunting at first and dizzying even with experience. As someone who has been in this business for awhile, even I still get the excitement butterflies in my stomach at the onset of a new marketing campaign just as seasoned actors and actresses still get butterflies before stepping out from the darkness of the wings into the bright lights of the stage. So in the words of our song from *A Chorus Line*, "Wish me luck…the same to you."

What if... *Hamilton: Theatre as Edutainment*

If you ask most Americans who Alexander Hamilton was, what do you think they would say? I'll tell you what they would say because I actually surveyed 200 average Americans and found that most of them (43% to be exact) thought Hamilton was the 4th President of the United States. Wrong. Thankfully, 32% correctly identified Hamilton as the former Secretary of the Treasury, but that still means only one-third of the sample was correct. Other guesses? Secretary of State (10%), the first Vice President (5%), and, my favorite, the President of the Confederate States during the Civil War (10%)...and these people vote.

Alexander Hamilton's obscurity may be short-lived with the success of the Broadway musical bearing his name: *Hamilton*. The show, completely written by (music, lyrics, and book) and starring the Broadway phenom Lin-Manuel Miranda (creator of the Tony Award-winning musical *In the Heights*), has become one of the hottest shows on Broadway *of all time*, breaking records for advance ticket sales left and right. The musical also won the Grammy Award for Best Musical Theatre Album and is expected to be a sure bet for several Tony Award nominations including Best Musical. *Hamilton* will also begin touring nationally in 2016, so maybe more Americans will answer correctly when I ask them who Hamilton was.

Speaking of education, in late 2015, the creative team behind *Hamilton*, NYC Public Schools, and the Rockefeller Foundation announced a $1.46 million grant that would provide 20,000 NYC public school students the opportunity to see the show, as well as develop classroom material designed specifically to educate students about the Founding Fathers and American history. This initiative, a wonderful idea and an amazing way to integrate Broadway into the classroom, is awesome for NYC students, but what about everyone else?

Imagine if the same partners developed an integrated marketing campaign designed to encourage the use of song, dance, and theatre to teach history. Relying on free hosting by YouTube, the creative team behind *Hamilton* (and other shows) could give tips and pointers about writing songs, choreographic dance, and writing dialogue that students around the country could use in developing their original pieces. Once created, the original songs or performances could be shared via a dedicated social media site, a website, and/or an app for the program. A promotional element could be added to the mix, as well, with the winning student(s) being flown to New York to attend a viewing of *Hamilton* and to perform their winning piece on Broadway to a full audience. The voters? People around the world who, by watching the videos, learn something about history while also gaining an appreciation for how theatre can be used as a tool for education (which may boost school efforts to raise funds for underfunded theatre programs). Whether "Sew Much Love To Give" from *Betsy Ross: The Musical*, "Keep Dreaming" from *MLK*, or "Bright Idea" from *Edison*, learning *could* become a lot more fun with *smart* songs. It's not just Broadway for your ears, anymore...it's Broadway for your *brain*.

UNDERSTANDING

JAMES A. MOUREY

Chapter 4 | Marketing Research: LEARN

Plumbers typically do not save princesses.

However, in 1985, a short, stout plumber with a red cap named Mario joined his brother, Luigi, on a quest to save Princess Toadstool (a.k.a. Princess Peach) who had been kidnapped by the evil Bowser, King of the Koopas…sounds crazy, right?

It doesn't end there.

On an adventure that involved eating mushrooms to grow larger, throwing fireballs after eating fire flowers, and exploring mysterious underground lands after traveling through big green pipes, our heroic brothers searched castle after castle to find the princess only to be told, "Sorry, but our princess is in *another* castle," by a little man named Toad wearing a mushroom hat…sounds *really* crazy, right?

It doesn't end there either.

Now, over 30 years later, Mario, Luigi, Princess Peach, Toad, Bowser, Wario, Waluigi, Yoshi, and a host of other characters have starred in over nineteen "Super Mario" games, eight "Mario Kart" games, ten "Mario Party" games, and over 100 other games featuring one or more of the characters. They very well may be the hardest working cast in video games, and in a time when even real-world celebrities' careers are increasingly more fleeting, Mario and friends have defied the odds.

Part of the Mario crew's success stems from an ultra-loyal customer: the video gamer. The "typical gamer" has several key characteristics that likely come to mind. Picture a "typical gamer" in your mind. What does the gamer look like? What sort of lifestyle does the gamer have? What is his personality? What is his fashion like? What posters are on the walls of his room? What kind of music does he listen to? What kind of movies does he go see? What sorts of things does he care about? How old is he? What does he do for fun? What does he think of himself? What are his social skills like? What motivates him? What does he secretly need that he doesn't talk about? What is his name?

At this point, you probably have a very vivid picture in your mind–maybe it is someone you actually know or some caricature of a gamer–but I bet you are definitely imagining someone. I will even go as far as to make another bet: that gamer you have imagined is most likely *not* a woman.

Okay, okay, you could say, "Well, you kept saying things like, 'What does *he* do for fun?' and, 'What is *his* name?'" True, but I bet at no point during that line of questioning did you think it was weird for a gamer to be described using only male pronouns. Even if the same exercise were repeated using gender-neutral pronouns, chances are that you would still have imagined a young, teenage or early-20s male.

Lest anyone feel guilty or misogynistic for automatically excluding women during that thought exercise, there is a reason most people think of the typical gamer as being a young male: marketing. In modern times, most video game marketing has focused on games like *Halo* and *Call of Duty*, shoot 'em up games that are very clearly marketed toward young men. As such, the campaigns for those games are focused on and, as such, feature young men almost exclusively. However, this phenomenon of depicting gamers as young men is not a recent shift: the earliest commercials for gaming consoles, including Mario's original Nintendo Entertainment System, focus entirely on young men.

In the commercials from the 1980s and early 1990s women rarely, if ever, appeared in the television commercials or print advertisements for Nintendo. If women *did* appear in the campaigns they typically played one role: eager mother excitedly watching her son and his friends playing a video game as if to say, "My only job here is to buy my son a video game and then watch him play it! Wait, what am I saying?! I have mom duties, a house to clean, food to cook in a kitchen, and a hardworking husband to please [who is not pictured because *he's* clearly at work]!" Talk about a freaky flashback to the 1950s.

Nowhere to be found: little girls. This is not to say that Nintendo did not make *some* attempts to court girl gamers. Indeed, there were some Barbie games and a Hello Kitty game on the NES, and subsequent handheld versions of the Nintendo included games for girls like "Girls' Fashion Shoot," "Barbie Dreamhouse Party," "Squinkies 2: Adventure Mall Surprize" (with a "z"), and "Girls Life: Makeover." You probably get the picture: nearly every attempt to focus on young female video gamers came much later in lifespan of any gaming console and tended to reinforce stereotypical gender roles—babysitting, fashion designing, figure skating, shopping. That is not to say that young girls do not enjoy these activities—many do—but girls enjoy many other activities, as well, not to mention the fact that boys can also enjoy babysitting, fashion design, figure skating, and shopping.

Nintendo, in positioning its console and games toward a young male demographic, faced a self-created problem that any product or service focusing exclusively on one gender faces: excluding 50% of the possible market from the very start. From tanning to skin treatments, manicures/pedicures to waxing, services long thought to be female-focused now enjoy male clients, which has increased revenues and expanded opportunities simply by opening up the market and not restricting customers based on a gender-based positioning.

Of course, Nintendo was not completely oblivious to the fact that women and female gamers were being underserved and that its prior attempts to reach these customers—a mix of gender stereotypical games and licensed female toy-themed games—were not particularly successful. Riding the social fitness trend of the time, Nintendo released the Wii Fit, a hybrid fitness game and peripheral (the Wii Balance Board), in 2008. The game became an instant hit with women thanks to its ability to provide at-home yoga (an exercise category still dominated by women at that time), aerobics, and other fitness opportunities. Of course, one must take the good with the bad: the Wii Fit received some negative press when it labeled a 10-year-old girl as "fat" based on her height and weight combination for her age (…oops). Still, the Wii Fit reminded the entire gaming industry that there was a sizable market whose needs had gone long unaddressed by their consoles and games.

However, it was not until 2013 that Nintendo hit a home run with a predominately female audience with a game that, for the most part, did not pander to shopping malls, makeup, or raising babies. The game, *Animal Crossing: New Leaf*, turned over a…wait for it…new leaf (sorry)…in the gaming industry: a game whose development team was composed of many women. Now, the team did not consist *mostly* of women or even *halfway* of women, but the fact that there was more than one woman on the development team was, in fact, groundbreaking in an industry whose development teams are *always* all-male or male-dominated. Although the game proved popular with gamers of both genders, Nintendo's sales numbers noticed something rather remarkable: although 70% of the Nintendo DS consoles sold were purchased by men, about 56% of purchases of *Animal Crossing: New Leaf* were made by women for personal use (i.e., they were not buying the game for a man in their life). Plus, the game's plot did not involve shopping at a mall, designing a wedding dress, or coming up with a list of ways to be a good housewife, so that was also a win.

Any success Nintendo gained with this breakthrough in gender-equal game development was vastly overshadowed by the far more negative story regarding the status of its Wii U gaming console. In 2016, using sales numbers released directly from Nintendo, *Tech Insider* pointed out that the Wii U console (Nintendo's most recent major console as of this publication), released in 2012, had only managed to sell 1/10 of the number of units its predecessor, the Nintendo Wii, had managed to sell during its lifetime. The worst selling Nintendo console prior to the Wii U, the Nintendo GameCube, had sold roughly 22 million units during its lifetime, which was still over *twice* as many units as the Wii U. Even the greats make mistakes.

Where is Mario when we need him? Wait a minute – who needs Mario? Where's Princess Peach when we need *her*? It turns out that Nintendo's salvation rests not in men or male gamers but in the very gamer that the company had ignored for so long: women.

In 2011, women represented 49% of the gaming market, which, although surprising to most people, is actually a statistic representative of the broader population (which is more or less a 50/50 split). Nintendo, noticing this trend, aggressively marketed its handheld Nintendo DS console to women, which proved to be a very lucrative strategy. Of course, the advent of mobile app gaming and the popularity of games like *Candy Crush Saga*, *Words with Friends*, and *Angry Birds* took gaming to a new place, a world where men and women were equally attractive targets but also a world in which purchasing consoles like the Wii or the DS was quickly becoming unnecessary. Furthermore, data from a study conducted by the Internet Advertising Bureau in 2014 revealed that women now represent 52% of the gaming market. Stated differently, women now make up the *majority* of modern gamers.

The surging market of female gamers and the new dominance of mobile gaming compared to traditional console-based games (even mobile consoles like the DS) presented a challenge and opportunity to Nintendo. The challenge: how could the company continue competing with fun, addicting games that were free or available for only $.99 on an app store and played on a console everyone already had (i.e., their phone) with its $40/game and $199/3DS console model? The opportunity: Nintendo could enter the mobile app game market with its beloved characters.

Thus, perhaps it should be no surprise that in 2015 Nintendo made an important announcement: as of 2016, Mario would be going mobile. After 30 years of saving the damsel in distress, it seems Mario's princess is in yet *another* castle, but this time she just might be saving *him*.

*   *   *

I never considered myself a "data-driven" person. Companies often tout their data-driven solutions, but, more often than not, statements like this are merely lip service. Companies either are not actually collecting data and making decisions based on that data or, as we will discuss in the next chapter, they *are* collecting data but are analyzing it incorrectly and making decisions based on faulty analyses.

Nintendo's story is a fascinating one because even though the company has achieved a level of international success of which most companies can only dream, the company has not been without its business challenges especially in recent time. The surprising part? The solutions to Nintendo's business challenges have been hidden in plain sight for years: data. Not only did females represent half the market, in general (almost by definition) for decades, the more recent data on female gamers, mobile gaming trends, and market-level shifts away from console-based gaming to internet- and mobile-based gaming was essentially spotlighting *exactly* what Nintendo needed to do: move into mobile gaming.

Market research, despite being among the most useful asset a company could ever want, is not exactly sexy work. Most of us have seen people conducting surveys on the street or have received phone calls from companies wanting to know if we have some time to answer "just a few questions" for marketing research purposes. As such, we have all become quite good at averting our eyes away from those street survey stalkers and saying something like, "Oh, sorry, I'm running late to this meeting," while pointing to the watch not on our wrists (because most people just use their phones to tell time today). Then, when they say something like, "It will only take a minute," we pretend like we don't hear them or just shrug awkwardly, walk faster, or maybe even start to jog a bit to get away. Telephone surveys are a lot easier: we just hang up the phone. Email surveys are just as simple: delete, delete, delete.

Therein lies the challenge: the very data that can be so useful and so helpful to improving the options, experiences, and satisfaction of consumers is almost impossible to extract from those same consumers. It's as if we can't even help customers help themselves!

Consumers have good reason to be averse to completing surveys. For starters, they are usually boring. Second, the questions are often poorly worded. For example, I recently saw a survey where a company asked its customers, "How happy were you with the delivery experience?" on a scale from 1 = Happy to 5 = Extremely happy. Hmm, I suppose no one was allowed to be unhappy. Third, researchers make it inconvenient for customers to complete surveys. How many times have you called because something is *wrong* with a product or service experience only to be told by the customer service representative, "If you stay on the line at the end of the call you will be asked to complete a survey." Because, you know, the *one* thing you want to do after calling to complain about a product or service and waiting to talk to someone is stay on the line even *longer* to do a survey. Furthermore, why would companies want *these* customers providing feedback? Sure, it's useful to know what is going wrong, but it is also equally as helpful to know what is going *right*. Another problem is that surveys are too long, so although some people start filling out the survey, those people do not complete the survey or their answers start becoming less helpful/accurate due to "survey fatigue." Finally, in a list that is certainly not exhaustive, customers rarely see immediate gains for completing a survey. Promise me 5% off my next purchase and I assure you that I am *much* more likely to complete the survey you want me to fill out. Yes, this approach has potential to lead to a positive bias for the survey, but I bet the completion rates increase, which can provide us with helpful, useful data in a world where some data is preferable to no data at all.

The purpose of the current chapter is to make marketing research more interesting and to highlight how helpful good marketing research can be. Most people do not know where to begin when it comes to picking the right questions to ask or to predicting the insights one hopes to gain (and, as such, the questions one should ask that might lead to those insights). As such, the purpose of this chapter is to provide you with useful marketing research tools regardless of your level of experience, your interest in marketing research, or the industry/business in which you operate. Stated otherwise, the purpose of this chapter is to make data delightful. This, of course, is no easy task, but given that the next chapter involves making statistics sexy, I am willing to try.

To Interview or To Rate 1 or 2: Qualitative and Quantitative Research

In general, research can be broken down into two broad categories: **Qualitative** and **Quantitative Research.** Qualitative research consists of interviews, observational studies, focus groups, and other forms of research in which the data collected tend to come from conversations and are recorded verbally. Quantitative research, on the other hand, consists of surveys, experimental data, recorded sales data, and other forms of information typically recorded numerically.

Qualitative and quantitative research tend to work best together, with many researchers relying on qualitative data for exploratory purposes (i.e., to get a general sense of an idea or theory) and following up on those ideas or theories with quantitative data for the purpose of statistical testing and support. In other words, qualitative data often help inspire ideas or creative thinking about how the world works while quantitative data let us test those ideas.

Note that I did not say that quantitative data help us prove a theory or an idea. That's not how science works. Science is not about *proving* anything; science is about supporting a theory. Now, a theory can be supported for many, many years without being displaced, but it is often the case that modern science presents us with a new theory that explains the world a bit better than a theory it displaces. That is the scientific process. So, if anyone ever tells you that science *proves* something, you should immediately be skeptical.

Another note on qualitative and quantitative data: one type of research is no better than the other. As I mentioned, qualitative and quantitative data often work in tandem. I once got into a friendly debate with a colleague at the consultancy in LA who argued that qualitative research was far superior to quantitative data. I disagreed. I did my best to explain the merits of both kinds of research, how they work well together, and how some research questions may rely more heavily on one type than the other, but he was not hearing it. In the end, we agreed to disagree…and then I shut my door to get back to work, work that involved designing training modules our consultants (including this colleague) would use with clients that integrated data from interviews and scientific experiments or, you know, qualitative *and* quantitative data.

There are countless ways to capture data and equally countless ways to ask a question to obtain a particular insight. This, of course, can be overwhelming to people, so to make your life easier, I have come up with a template that will help you capture critical research that will help inspire your integrated marketing campaign, a survey that I explain in detail next.

The FUSIONLearn™ Survey: A Template for Capturing Critical Data

I know from experience that marketing research is often people's *least* favorite aspect about doing *any* marketing project. Heck, if marketers themselves don't like collecting marketing research, who does?!

One reason people do not enjoy collecting marketing research is because designing and creating a survey is a real pain in the "ask" ...which questions to ask, how to ask, what not to ask, which order to ask, how many questions to ask, etc.

To help eliminate or reduce any pain in the "ask" you currently feel, I have created what I refer to as the FUSIONLearn™ survey, which is available (for free) on my website (www.jimmourey.com). The FUSIONLearn™ survey is not meant to be the only survey or the best survey one can use to capture marketing data. Instead, it is meant to be a template that you can use, customize, edit, or tweak to your specific needs that will help you start with *something* instead of *nothing*. For those of you who hate conducting research and would rather just use a premade survey, well, congratulations! This survey is for you. For those of you who are nerds (like me) and enjoy conducting research, well, congratulations! This survey is *also* for you except you will probably spend a bit more time making the survey your own, which is 100% okay and welcomed!

Here's the big picture, bird's-eye view of the FUSIONLearn™ survey: LEARN is an acronym (are you surprised?) for Lifestyle, Education, Attitude, Reflection, and Needs. At the very minimum, we want to know *who* our prospective customers are on these five dimensions. With respect to Lifestyle, we want to know these individuals' personalities, passions, hobbies, media practices, and demographics. Education concerns these individuals' knowledge about our company, our product/service, and our industry, in general, including how they obtain(ed) this knowledge. Attitude brings in subjective thoughts, feelings, and points of view on our company, brand, and product/service, as well as those of our competitors. Reflection turns the spotlight back on the customers as they reflect on who they are and who they want to be, identifying the overlap or disconnect between the two. Finally, Needs provides an opportunity to recognize how what we have to offer helps satisfy fundamental needs of individuals and/or any opportunities to fulfill needs not currently being fulfilled satisfactorily.

Are there other categories of questions we could ask? Sure. Are there questions we could add to the survey that would help provide even more helpful insight to our market situation? You bet. The FUSIONLearn™ survey is not meant to be exhaustive; the survey is meant to be helpful. So here's a play-by-play for each section of the survey that will highlight its usefulness, its helpfulness, and even its potential limitations that should spark some ideas on how you might be able to use it for your particular situation.

Lifestyle. Some of the greatest actors and actresses make it a habit to "get into character" by understanding the deeper motivations, psychology, and entire make-up of the characters they play. Some performers even go as far as living among people sharing characteristics of the person that will be played (e.g., living among magicians and illusionists if playing Harry Houdini in a biopic – an aside: many people have tried to capture Houdini's unique character but, for whatever reason, his character always escapes them...).

At one point during my early days in marketing I had a realization: some of the best marketers have an acting background. My theory for this is that as an actor you often have to put yourself in other people's shoes, people with whom you may have absolutely *nothing* in common. One of the biggest challenges marketers face is getting out of their own head and into the minds of the consumers they are targeting with a campaign. If I am creating a campaign for Kind bars, which are delicious and made from "ingredients you can see and pronounce" (in their words), life is easy: I love Kind bars and eat them (far too) often. If, however, I am tasked with creating a campaign for Hostess Cupcakes, well, we have a problem. I haven't eaten Hostess Cupcakes since I was a child, and the thought of eating a snack whose first ingredient is sugar followed by a bunch of other junk and chemicals I don't quite understand is not very appealing. While I can try to think back to what made Hostess Cupcakes so alluring as a child, it would require a great deal of role playing to try and figure out what (if anything) is valuable to a consumer about eating something like a Hostess Cupcake. To some people the cupcakes taste good whereas my body rejects the cupcakes like an unholy exorcism.

Thus, the way to think about the Lifestyle component of the FUSIONLearn™ survey is to imagine you are getting into character for a theatrical production and are doing your due diligence with respect to understanding *who* exactly these people are. From general descriptive information (like gender, age, etc.) to deeper psychological thoughts, perspectives, and preferences, the Lifestyle research should provide you enough information that, if tasked with playing this person in a stage production or in a movie, would give you enough useful material to create your character.

The **demographic** information captured in the Lifestyle section includes basics like age, gender, race/ethnicity, sexual orientation, marital status, family size, socioeconomic status, location, highest level of education, current career, and political leaning. Even if we obtained no other information, this basic demographic information already reveals a lot about whom the target customer is. Based on variables like age, marital status, and family size we can get a sense for where people are in the typical life cycle. Young, single people with no kids have very different needs and behaviors than slightly older married people with a few children. The motivations and decisions of these two different groups vary in rather predictable ways (hint: children are costly and take up so much of your time that you sometimes wonder why you made the mistake of having them in the first place – it is said they are rewarding, but the jury is still out). Similarly, capturing information about income level, career position, and education informs the customer's socioeconomic status. It could be the case that an individual educated at the very best universities and who has worked at some of the most successful non-profit or political organizations reports a lower-than-expected income. Does that mean this customer is not valuable or does not have the potential to become valuable? No. In fact, that customer may have more potential value than someone reporting a higher income but less career experience and fewer years of completed education. All in all, the demographic information paints a fairly general picture of the customer–it is not a complete picture, but some information is always better than no information.

Because cake is more delicious with icing, let us add some icing to the demographic layer of the Lifestyle cake (…that was a sentence I never thought I would say). Beyond general demographic questions, the Lifestyle section also includes questions pertaining to **identity**. Like it or not, all of us have a personal identity that informs how we perceive ourselves. In fact, most of us have *multiple* identities that inform how we perceive ourselves. Before you panic and worry you have multiple personality disorder, let me explain. Having multiple identities just means that we have different roles we see ourselves fulfilling each with its own set of norms, rules, and expectations. For example, you are most likely someone's child. That's an identity. If you have siblings, well, you are a sibling. That's another identity. If you are currently a student, that's another identity. If you are an employee somewhere, you guessed it: another identity. Thus, as you can see, most of us have several identities because we play different roles throughout our daily lives.

As such, one place to start with respect to understanding identity involves simply asking people, "What identities do you possess?" While the responses to this question are certainly interesting and informative, what is even more interesting is the *number* of identities that individuals list. Throughout my research I consistently find that people who list one or very *few* identities tend to be rather stubborn and less easily persuaded by marketing than people who list several identities. The exact reason for this is unclear but it could be the case that someone who sees him/herself in *one* particular way (e.g., I am old-fashioned, I am a man, I am a parent) plants his/her flag firmly in the ground of that identity and cannot be shaken. If, alternatively, an individual sees him/herself as fulfilling several roles and, as such, being a bit more flexible, it could very well be the case that these people, okay with having multiple identities, are equally as okay with trying new things. I am partially convinced that this may have something to do with why some otherwise reasonable people are recruited to join terrorist organizations (which, frankly, makes no sense – why would you *ever* sign up to kill yourself, kill other people, and live in filth and squalor as terrorists do? Stupid.). Most of these recruits have nothing going for them–they have few identities if even more than one, and that one identity tends to involve their religious identity. Perhaps one solution to mitigating or reducing terror recruitment is introducing these young people to other identities beyond their limited, shortsighted, fundamentalist religious identity.

Identity also incorporates social comparison, as whether we like it or not we are always comparing ourselves to other people. By asking people whether they see themselves as being better/worse off than others, how willing they are to try new things compared to others, and how easy/difficult it is for them to make a decision compared to most people, we can start placing these individuals within a social hierarchy. People who believe they are better off than most people, are more set in their ways, and believe it is easy for them to make decisions may be more difficult to persuade but could very well be the opinion leaders that would be efficient to target with a campaign. Conversely, people who believe they are worse off than most people, are more flexible in what they believe, and have a hard time making decisions might be low-hanging fruit with respect to persuasion. If you were a cult leader, those would be the people to target (…which is why cults often prey on people who have had some dramatic life event that triggers a great deal of self-doubt) and is the same reason why, as a marketer, we must be careful to make sure that we are truly helping people make choices that help them to live *better* lives.

Another component of the Lifestyle questions involves queries that help us better understand an individual's **media consumption** and day-to-day experiences. Questions pertaining to favorite movies, sports, music, etc., allow us to know which specific genres capture this person's attention (which is useful for endorsements, sponsorships, and media buying/placements that will come later). It is also important to understand *how* these individuals obtain their media–are they watching television, reading magazines, surfing the web, using social media? Which channels do they watch? Which websites do they visit? How often do they check their social media accounts? During what time of the day? Are they using media primarily for news, entertainment, sports information, social connection?

Rounding out the Lifestyle questions are questions pertaining to thoughts and behaviors relating to the acting of **shopping** itself. This allows us to capture favorite brands, how people typically go about shopping (e.g., propensity to search for a deal, which items they prefer buying online v. in store, etc.), how much people like shopping, in general, and other shopping-related questions. Knowing whether people base a shopping decision on price, quality, brand, loyalty, popularity, or some other attribute can help inform the messaging of our campaign. Say, for example, Starbucks is attempting to reach out to Wandering Customers with an Open Up More Options objective and we find out one segment of these consumers shops based on price while another segment shops based on quality, well, depending on the segment we choose to target our campaign takes on a *very* different positioning strategy (either emphasizing value or the taste/ingredients, respectively). See how it all fits together?

As an important aside, remember that everything we do in the FUSION model is tied to creating value for consumers but also for society and the environment, as well. Thus, included in the Lifestyle questions are queries related to the charities these customers value and societal issues about which they are concerned. The responses to these questions can inspire pro-social initiatives we can explore as a way to capture the attention of this audience while also creating value for society and/or the environment more broadly.

By the end of the Lifestyle line of questioning, you should have such a clear mental picture of whom that person is so that if you were asked to cast an actor or actress to play that individual in a made-for-television movie about his/her life, you could do it easily. If you are afraid that this casting decision would still be tough, don't worry: one of the questions in the Lifestyle section actually asks the individual to cast the celebrity that would play him/her in a movie about his/her life. I told you: this survey leaves no stone unturned. I'm looking out for you.

Education. The education portion of the FUSIONLearn™ survey has *nothing* to do with formal education (that's captured in the Lifestyle section) and *everything* to do with how knowledgeable individuals are about you, your company, your product(s)/service(s), and the industry or market in which you operate. Let's face it: some customers are a lot smarter and educated about products than others. Some people know that Keebler, the largest cookie and cracker manufacturer in the United States, is a brand owned by the Kellogg Company whereas others believe that Keebler is a company owned and operated by magical elves that live and bake cookies in trees (…to be fair, that latter group is mostly children, but you never know).

The point is that people have varying levels of **knowledge** about you, your competitors, the product and service options in the market and, as such, have different needs when it comes to an integrated marketing campaign's messaging. Audiences that lack knowledge or familiarity with your offerings need a much more instructive campaign than consumers that possess a great deal of knowledge. Also captured in this section of the survey is *how* people **acquire information** about companies, products, and services in a particular market. Do they check out information online? Do they prefer buying/interacting with the product in person? Do they pay attention to advertisements and, if so, where (e.g., on television, in magazines)? Do they talk with friends?

In today's world people have more access to what other customers think and how other customers feel about companies, products/services, and experiences than *ever* before. This is good and bad. The good, of course, has to do with the transparency with which information can be shared among consumers. This sort of transparency makes it difficult for bad or unethical companies to hide. On the other hand, we know that the people most likely to engage in online ratings are people who either really *loved* their experience or, as is often the case, people who really *hated* their experience. A quick glance at just about any online rating will reveal some awful rants in which people do not hold back. Again, while it can be helpful to get an honest review of a product or service for a consumer, one less-than-stellar customer interaction can be fatal for a company.

Also captured in the Education section are preferences with respect to the **source** of new information. Decades of academic research have found that individuals tend to counter-argue ideas presented in advertisements almost by default. That is, if people know they are the target of persuasive information (as is often the case with advertising), they tend to develop reasons that counter the claims in the advertisement automatically. This, of course, does not serve us well as marketers. However, we also know that people are less likely to develop counter-arguments to information that comes from news stories, friends, or people who remind them of themselves. This, friends, is why companies have PR folks who help generate positive news stories that read like authentic pieces of journalism when they are, in fact, company-initiated fluff stories designed to persuade the masses. Indeed, there were times during my days at the marketing agency in undergrad where stories I wrote on behalf of our clients, companies paying us to do their marketing, were reprinted in reputable news and magazine publications *word-for-word* with the only thing added being the name of the "journalist" or "author" of the article. In fact, the world of PR largely consists of contacting editors and journalists with stories to pitch for their publication. The lessons: 1) good journalism is increasingly difficult to find, 2) don't believe *anything* you read or, at the very least, question whether the information you are reading is truly objective or is possibly the work of some nerdy kid working in PR getting paid to write a sexy story that a lazy journalist has decided to reprint under his/her own name. This is not to say that you should not try to get your company or product featured in a newspaper or magazine–you should–but do respect ethical boundaries of journalism and require the publications willing to run your story or pitch to do the same.

Beyond PR-related placements, you may also find that your audience prefers hearing information from the company itself, an independent industry expert, or maybe an Average Joe or Jane. This is the reason that some commercials for medicine feature doctors explaining the science behind the medicine while other commercials feature everyday people talking about how the medicine has helped improved their lives. Similarly, some customers are more skeptical than others with respect to any sales pitch or information campaign. There are those consumers who believe companies exist for the sole purpose of making money for themselves and the companies' shareholders whereas other consumers believe that companies do have their customers' wellbeing at heart (and an entire spectrum of consumers between those two extremes). Knowing where your selected audience falls on this continuum can inform the tone of your campaign and the ease/difficulty you are likely to face when persuading that audience to do or believe anything.

Attitude. While the Lifestyle and Education components of the FUSIONLearn™ survey provide information regarding an audience's basic background and knowledge, the Attitude section sheds light on how customers *feel* about you, your company, and what you have to offer. Indeed, the Attitude section introduces the notion of **opinions**, **preferences**, and even **judgments** about you, your competitors, and the industry in which you operate, in general.

The Attitude section is a particularly important one because, as I often say to my students, persuasion is nothing more than *shifting attitudes*. If our audience feels like video games are for little boys prior to seeing our integrated marketing campaign designed to educate them about women and gaming (Company: Nintendo; Prospective Audience: Wandering Customers; Desired Objective: Knowledge campaign to make people realize women constitute more than half of the gaming market) then an *unsuccessful* campaign would be one in which that audience feels the same way about video games, little boys, and women after seeing the campaign. A successful campaign would be one in which the attitudes of that audience shifts after experiencing our integrated marketing campaign: they now believe that women are equally as likely as little boys to play video games. It's that simple: persuasion simply involves shifting attitudes.

Two of the most useful tools with respect to capturing attitudes and, importantly, a shift in attitudes are a **perceptual map** and a **preference map**. Perceptual maps and preference maps are awesome because they capture 1) the world as customers see it (perceptual map), and 2) the world as customers wish it would be (preference map). The first step to creating a map is to ask customers what the most important attributes are about whatever it is we are hoping to understand. Say we are thinking about getting a puppy (because who doesn't love puppies?!). We poll hundreds of people and find out that the most important attribute is the puppy energy level. Some people love really energetic puppies whereas others prefer their puppies to be calm and chill. The second most important attribute winds up being size: some people prefer smaller dogs, some prefer medium-sized dogs, and others prefer large dogs the size of a small pony. We can plot these attributes on a two-dimensional coordinate plane, with energy level on the x-axis, size on the y-axis. Then, we can present customers with a list of puppy breeds and have them plot each of those breeds on the coordinate plane based on *how they perceive those puppies with respect to the two attributes*. Note: this is an important point. It's not whether the puppies are actually energetic or chill or are actually big or small—what matters is how the audience *perceives* those puppies. Perceptions matter more than reality. That is how you make a perceptual map!

Following this exercise, we can ask the audience to imagine an ideal world where they could create a puppy from scratch. What would the absolute *best* energy level be for their ideal puppy? What would the absolute *best* size be for their ideal puppy? We can then plot these ideal points on a coordinate plane. This is a preference map: what do you prefer if you were able to create a product (or, in this case, a puppy) from scratch to meet your ideal dimensions?

However, the real magic happens when you layer these two maps together. We can look to see if the idealized puppies that people have dreamed up (on the preference map) are similar to any of the actual puppies that already exist in the real world as they are perceived by customers (on the perceptual map). If people say they want a tiny dog that is super high energy, well, good news: Chihuahuas exist! If people say their ideal dog is a massive dog with very low energy, more good news: Bernese Mountain Dogs exist. But let's imagine that when we layer the maps together we get a cluster of people who say they want a medium-sized dog that is also medium-energy. Golden Retrievers are too big and too high energy. Toy Poodles are too small and too chill. So what can we do? Well, you can do what breeders around the country have done and create a hybrid dog like the Goldendoodle, a dog that incorporates the benefits of both Golden Retrievers and Poodles in a medium-sized, medium-energy dog.

Alternatively, assuming we live in a world where Goldendoodles are not an option (what a sad world that would be!), you could launch a campaign designed to change the attitudes of the audience. By showing Golden Retrievers in a campaign next to dogs that are clearly larger than them (e.g., Irish Wolfhounds, Great Danes), suddenly Golden Retrievers might be perceived as being more medium-sized than before. In another approach, we could design a campaign in which Poodles are surrounded by ultra-low energy dogs (e.g., Basset Hounds, Pugs, Bulldogs, etc.). Suddenly, Poodles look like spastic crazies high on some illegal substance and are perceived to be much higher energy. Perceptual and preference maps provide insight on where our companies, products/services, and brands fall in the marketplace relative to other companies, competing products/services, and competing brands. The magic of combining them might inspire us to create a new product, to tweak an existing product, or to design a campaign such that it shifts consumer attitudes in a way that better aligns their ideal wants with what we have to offer–all very powerful stuff based entirely on attitudes.

To help keep things simple, here's the step-by-step for both maps:

Perceptual Map

Step #1: Identify the market

Step #2: Identify the brands, products, or services competing in that market

Step #3: Ask customers to list the 5 or 10 attributes most important to them in that market

Step #4: Have participants rate each of the brands, products, or services from Step #2 on the two most important attributes listed in Step #4

Step #5: Plot the average scores from Step #4 for each brand, product, or service on a coordinate plane (x-axis: most important attribute; y-axis: second-most important attribute)

Step #6: Voilà! You made a perceptual map! Go do something nice for yourself!

Preference Map

Step #1: Using the attributes identified from Step #3 above, ask customers to dream up their ideal brand, product, or service according to their preferred levels of those two attributes

Step #2: Plot these ideal points on a separate map to layer on top of your perceptual map or simply plot them on the perceptual map you previously created

Step #3: Rejoice! Your preference map has been created!

Step #4: Now look for potential consumer clusters (i.e., lots of people sharing similar ideal choices) and "market opportunities" (i.e., consumer clusters for which no existing product is perceived to fulfill stated preferences)

Step #5: Also look for strategic insights regarding how to shift your existing product (or new product) so that it is perceived as better fulfilling the stated preferences of consumers. This may involve tweaking the product, crafting a campaign with a message designed to persuade, or developing a new product.

Because I care about you and your time, I have included the questions you need to create these maps in the FUSIONLearn™ survey. All you have to do is calculate the averages and plot the results. When you strike it rich after the maps lead you to success, just don't forget the kind, old professor who encouraged you.

Two other useful tools for assessing attitudes and developing persuasion strategies include the **Attitude Toward the Object Model (ATOM)** and the **Behavioral Intentions Model (BIM)**, which I will explain in detail next.

If you read *Urge*, my first book, then you have seen these models before. I include them here because: 1) not everyone has read *Urge*, and 2) they are extremely useful models that help us understand the market and strategize brilliant marketing plans (i.e., they are important). So for some of you, this will be a nice review; for others, this will be a brand new introduction to some powerful concepts. For those of you who have seen these models before, don't worry: I have a new surprise in store for you shortly!

The Attitude Toward the Object Model has two components: 1) the evaluation of an attribute, and 2) the belief that a target object (i.e., brand, product, service) possesses that attribute. To determine an individual's attitude toward a particular object one simply multiplies the attractiveness rating of an attribute by the metric capturing the belief that the object has that particular attribute and then sums up all these totals for each attribute to get an overall score. Mathematically, the model looks like this:

$$A_o = \sum_{i=1}^{N} (b_i)*(e_i)$$

Ahh! Equation! Don't panic. Let me illustrate with an example to help clarify. Tea is a popular drink of choice for most people when vodka isn't readily available. Three brands–Lipton, Tazo, and Harney & Sons–sell tea bags at most grocery stores throughout the United States. Let's say that, when asked which attributes were most important when it came to purchasing tea at grocery stores, customers frequently mentioned price, the variety of flavors offered, and the tea's taste. Then, on a scale from 1-10, customers rated each of the attributes with respect to how important or attractive that attribute is with respect to purchasing tea (from 1 = not at all important/attractive to 10 = extremely important/attractive). As we can see from the average of the ratings across all customers below, a tea tasting great is pretty important (…that makes sense) and having a variety of flavors from which to choose is also fairly important whereas price, while not unimportant, is also not extremely important to customers. Customers were also asked to rate the belief that each of three tea brands possessed the indicated attributes again on a scale from 1-10 (where 1 = the brand does not have this attribute at all to 10 = the brand definitely has this attribute). So, for example, Lipton is perceived as having a good price (a 9 on a scale from 1-10) but is not perceived to offer many varieties and is not perceived as having a good taste, either. Harney & Sons, on the other hand, is perceived to taste great (e.g., its Hot Cinnamon Spice tea is heaven in a cup), but the tea is perceived as being somewhat expensive and as offering fewer varieties than Tazo (but more than Lipton).

Attribute (i)	Evaluation of the Attribute (e_i)	Lipton (b_i)	Tazo (b_i)	Harney & Sons (b_i)
Good Price	6	9	6	4
Flavor variety	7	3	8	6
Great Taste	9	3	6	10
ATOM Score:		102	146	156

From these ratings we can calculate the overall attitude for each of the tea brands by multiplying the evaluation of each attribute (e_i) by the belief that a particular tea has that attribute (b_i). So, for Lipton, we would take $(6)*(9) + (7)*(3) + (9)*(3) = 102$. We would repeat this process for Tazo and Harney & Sons (their scores are listed in the table above). From these attitude scores it is clear that customers have the most favorable attitude toward Harney & Sons and the least favorable attitude toward Lipton.

The power from the ATOM approach rests in its ability to help us strategize ways to improve attitudes with respect to our brand. Pretend you are a marketing manager at Tazo. Customer attitudes toward your brand are fairly good, but they are not as high as their attitudes toward Harney & Sons, so what can you do? Well, you could design a campaign to: 1) change the attractiveness of the identified attributes, 2) change the belief that a brand possesses a particular attribute, and/or 3) add or remove attributes that come to mind beyond the three currently listed.

First, with respect to attribute attractiveness, people perceive Tazo as having a lot of variety with respect to flavor (8 out of 10) but the attractiveness of the Flavor Variety attribute is only a 7 out of 10. So one strategy is to launch a campaign emphasizing the importance of being able to choose among a vast array of tea flavors, potentially increasing that 7 to an 8, 9, or even a 10. It turns out that if Tazo were to pursue this strategy, its new overall attitude scores still would not beat out Harney & Sons, so let's consider the second approach.

If Tazo were to improve the belief that Tazo branded tea products possessed a particular attribute, it would be wise to focus on improving perceptions regarding its taste. Why? Well, there's room to grow (it scores a 6 out of 10 presently) *and* customers identify taste as being an extremely important/attractive feature of a good tea (9 out of 10). Shifting the perception up one point (to 7) does nothing to beat Harney & Sons, but shifting up just to an 8 gives Tazo the edge over its competition. Thus, Tazo would be wise to consider a campaign in which they feature real people tasting Tazo, perhaps blind taste test commercials, social media posts in which real people taste Tazo and respond, or store promotions that encourage product sampling to reinforce the belief that Tazo tea tastes delicious.

The final approach, adding or removing attributes that come to customers' minds, is another clever way to shift attitudes. Say Tazo runs a campaign that emphasizes packaging for people on the go. Tazo may have launched a new sachet that preserves flavor while transporting the tea better than traditional tea bags or other individualized packaging. When consumers factor this attribute into their attitude formation, the game changes at Tazo comes out on top as you can see:

Attribute (i)	Evaluation of the Attribute (c_i)	Lipton (b_i)	Tazo (b_i)	Harney & Sons (b_i)
Good Price	6	9	6	4
Flavor variety	7	3	8	6
Great Taste	9	3	6	10
Packaging	8	5	9	5
ATOM Score:		142	218	196

Therein lies the magic of ATOM! By knowing customers' attitudes about the important attributes and the options they are considering, we are able to design and develop strategies that can shift those attitudes to be more favorable for our company, brand, product, or service. Pause for a second and realize the value of this because it is an important idea in this chapter: data, dry and boring data, can inspire our cool, fun, and creative marketing campaign. That's sexy stuff.

The other model I mentioned, the Behavioral Intentions Model (BIM), is a bit simpler. Whereas ATOM is all about objects, attributes, and what an individual thinks about those objects/attributes, the Behavioral Intentions Model incorporates a *social* component: it's not just about what *you* think, it's what you believe *others* think, as well. We are social creatures, after all, and each of us cares about what other people think of us (whether we admit it or not). Here's what the equation looks like:

$$B \approx BI = (w_1)*(A_{behavior}) + (w_2)*(SN)$$

Mathematically speaking, BIM is simply a weighted average function:

w_1 (which is the % of attention I pay to *myself*)
*
$A_{behavior}$ (which is *my* attitude about engaging in a particular behavior)
+
w_2 (which is % of attention I pay to *others*)
*
SN (which is the "Subjective Norm" or what I think others think about engaging in a particular behavior)
=
BI (behavioral intentions or what I *intend* to do; an *approximation* of my actual behavior)
$\approx$ (approximately equal – our intentions do not always perfectly correspond to our actual behaviors)
BI (what I actually *do*, which may or may not be the same as what I intended to do)

The BIM assumes that we're either paying attention to ourselves or to other people, so those w_1 and w_2 must always add up to equal 100%. Another important thing to note: the last part, "what I think others think about engaging in a particular behavior," may or may not be equal to what other people *actually* think about engaging in that behavior. In other words, it is our *perception* of what we think other people think, not necessarily the reality.

Let's work through BIM with an example to help solidify the concept. Say that a lot of people like to eat cookies (or biscuits, if you're European) with their tea, but not everyone does. We survey a group of young British moms, aged 25-35 on a rainy London day and find out:

- They listen to themselves about 30% of the time

- They, personally, love eating cookies/biscuits with tea, rating it an 8 out of 10 (where 1= hate it, 10 = love it)

- They think other moms like themselves don't like eating cookies/biscuits with tea because it is unhealthy and, as such, believe those other moms would rate eating cookies/biscuits with tea at about a 2 out of 10 on the same scale

Using the BIM, we can develop a Behavioral Intentions Score for these London mothers. Plugging the numbers into the equation, we have $(30\%)*(8) + (70\%)*(2) = 3.8$ out of a possible 10. That's not a great score if we are in the business of selling cookies. Note: the 70% came from the fact that we know people are either paying attention to themselves or other people, so if we are told they are paying attention to themselves 30% of the time, well, they must be paying attention to others 70% of the time (100% - 30% = 70%).

Managerially, the BIM provides us with several insights about what we can do to increase the likelihood that people will eat our cookies. One strategy is to get these London moms to pay attention to themselves more (i.e., increasing 30%, which decreases 70%), which would increase the Behavioral Intentions score. Practically speaking, that campaign would say something like, "You know best for yourself; make your own decisions!" Another strategy would be to increase these moms' attitudes toward cookies. There is not much room to grow (they're already at an 8 out of 10), but a message for that kind of campaign would say something like, "You don't just like cookies with tea, you love them!" with reminders about all the deliciousness that eating cookies with tea brings. One final strategy is to increase these moms' perceptions about what *other* moms think about eating cookies with tea (i.e., increase the Subjective Norm). The message in a campaign like this would say something like, "Other moms *love* eating cookies with their tea," and show images of these other women drinking tea and enjoying cookies. That simple!

The true power of ATOM and BIM is that they provide rich data that shed light on strategic moves we can take to improve customers' attitudes and behavioral intentions. Even the messaging of our creative content can be influenced by this data, which highlights this extremely important link between research findings and creative executions that so nice exemplifies the theme of this book.

Now, for those of you already familiar with ATOM and BIM, I wanted to provide some more tools for you to use with respect to attitudes and persuasion. To do so, it is worth mentioning what is known as the **Yale Attitude Change Approach (YACA)**, which is often discussed in tandem with the **Elaboration Likelihood Model (ELM)**. YACA identified three fundamental components that influence attitude change: 1) the source of the message, 2) the message itself, and 2) the audience receiving the message. If you are a human being who has ever tired to convince anyone of anything, this should not be particularly groundbreaking. As children, when we want to convince our parents to do something, say buy us a particular toy or take us to a particular restaurant for dinner, we corral our siblings together, figure out which sibling is in the best graces with our parents, craft a carefully-worded message, and then make sure we approach our parents at the right moment (e.g., when they are in a good mood and relaxing v. on their way to work and stressed). However, researchers have (thankfully) taken a more sophisticated approach to studying this sort of intuitive approach to persuading others. In short, persuasion is a function of a source's credibility and expertise/experience, the message's evidence and appeal, and the audience's intelligence and esteem (McGuire 1968). Not surprisingly, the more credible and more experienced the source, the more persuasive the message (…duh), and the more evidence behind a message and the more appealing the message's delivery, the more persuasive the message (…also duh). However, one interesting finding pertains to the audience receiving the message. You would *think* that, after the first two variables, the trend is for high intelligence and high self-esteem. While having the intelligence to understand a message and enough self-esteem to pay attention without wallowing away in self-pity are good attributes to possess, it turns out that having too much intelligence and too much self-esteem actually impedes the persuasion process. People of lower intelligence and lower self-esteem are typically more easily persuaded (which explains the tendency for cults to prey on people who have experienced tragedies or a spate of bad luck…it may also explain Donald Trump's surprising success during the 2016 Presidential election season). So some argue that the "ideal audience" with respect to persuasion and attitude change is a moderately intelligent audience with moderate self-esteem. To express this mathematically, we have something like...

$$P = \frac{(SC)*(SX)}{3} + \frac{(ME)*(MA)}{3} + \frac{[10-(2*|5-AI|)]*[10-(2*|5-AE|)]}{3}$$

...where we can simply measure each variable on a scale from 0 to 10 (putting 5 squarely in the middle). The variables represent:

SC = Source Credibility (0 = no credibility, 10 = extremely credible)
SX = Source Expertise (0 = no expertise, 10 = ample expertise)
ME = Message Evidence (0 = no evidence, 10 = ample evidence)
MA = Message Appeal (0 = no appeal, 10 = extremely appealing)
AI = Audience Intelligence (0 = low intelligence, 10 = extremely intelligent)
AE = Audience Esteem (0 = low self-esteem, 10 = high self-esteem)
P = Persuasiveness

So by asking questions pertaining to the source, the content of the message, and the audience itself, we can gain some insight regarding how persuasive our communication is likely to be coming from a particular source, when presented in a particular way, and when communicated to a certain audience, which can be very helpful. Also, by measuring the responses in this way, our Persuasiveness (P) score should range from 1-100, with 1 representing an extremely unpersuasive approach and 100 representing an extremely persuasive approach per the YACA.

Like ATOM and BIM, YACA gives us yet another way to break persuasion and attitude change down into manageable nuggets that we can more easily fix or adjust to improve the persuasiveness of our campaign. Perhaps our attempt to persuade could be more successful if we chose a more reputable source or someone perceived to be an "expert" on the subject. Maybe our attempt to persuade needs to take into account how appealing the message seems or how stubborn the target audience is on the subject. One thing worth noting: every variable herein is a *perception* not necessarily "reality." This should come as a bit of relief with respect to the intelligence and esteem variables–we are not looking for people who walk around with "average IQs" or mediocre self-esteem. No, instead we are considering their perceived intelligence about a particular subject or their confidence regarding whatever it is we are trying to persuade them about. All of us are smart about something, but we are less certain of ourselves and less intelligent about particular subjects. For example, I can tell you a lot about marketing because I have studied and practiced it for a long time. If you try to persuade me about something in the realm of marketing, well, I am likely to be stubborn and resist this persuasion more than if you were to attempt to persuade me about something in the realm or particle physics, a subject about which I have only moderate intelligence and do not feel particularly confident about. These perceptions are fleeting, dynamic, and can be manipulated (e.g., I may feel like I know nothing about particular physics in my normal day-to-day, but pit me against a 1st grader and suddenly I fee like a particle physics genius; conversely, pit me against someone doing his Ph.D. in particle physics and I suddenly feel dumber than a box of rocks). The point is that these measurements say nothing of reality or traits but rather speak to perceptions and state-level beliefs about the world as it is in the moment. This should help you sleep more easily at night!

As I mentioned, the Elaboration Likelihood Model (ELM)is often included in discussions of YACA. I also included ELM in *Urge*, but I want to revisit it here to tie it to our current conversation on attitudes and persuasion. ELM basically proposes that there are two "routes" to persuasion: the central route and the peripheral route. The central route is more deliberate and involves thoughts, reasons, and logic. The peripheral route is more incidental and involves pretty pictures, nice music, emotions, and heuristics associated with persuasion (e.g., believing that a long argument is a better argument just because it is longer). We all engage in a bit of both central and peripheral processing whenever we engage with any persuasive stimuli, but our ability to engage in central route processing is a function of our motivation, ability, and opportunity to do so. We have to want to (e.g., have enough desire), be able to (e.g., have enough knowledge/intelligence), and be given the chance to (e.g., be provided with time and a stimulus) engage the central route. The peripheral route is a bit more automatic, which can be helpful particularly in a world where we have less and less time to pay attention to the increasing number of stimuli, but can also be dangerous (e.g., letting pictures of pretty people or emotional songs dictate our decisions when rational thought would lead to a different conclusion). When reviewing the data from the FUSIONLearn™ survey, it is helpful to know the extent to which your audience is willing to engage in central route processing (i.e., is it a topic that is motivating, that they have the ability to think about, that they have an opportunity to deliberate on) and be aware of how/whether your communication contains elements that speak to both the central and peripheral routes.

In addition to capturing specific attitudes toward our company, product/services, and/or brands, the Attitude section also includes questions designed to capture **general attitudes** customers have about us. From liking/disliking to dullness/excitement, passé/trendiness to wastefulness/good investment, we can capture consumer attitudes, in general, that may shed some light on what encourages people to purchase our wares or, equally as informative, what might be discouraging them from doing so. People often make the mistake of researching only customers who *buy* our products, but it is just as interesting and helpful to know what people who *aren't* buying your products think about you so that you might improve and reach more possible customers.

Some final questions worth asking that will permit us to test links between attitudes with important decision-making variables during our post-research collecting analysis of the data include: 1) What *thoughts* do you have about X? How important are those thoughts? 2) What *feelings* do you have about X of those listed? How strongly do you associate those feelings? 3) How likely would you be to use X? 4) How likely would you be to buy X? and 5) How much would you be willing to pay? These questions all get straight to the point of asking customers their intentions with respect to X (which could be our product, service, brand, or company) directly. Although intentions may not always equate to actual behavior, some information is better than no information. Plus, as you will see in the next chapter, when we know these endpoints and we determine which variables that affect these endpoints, we will be equipped with the information we need to make some important strategic decisions. To give you an example without spoiling the next chapter, if we find a statistical link between number of customizable features available to our customers and their willingness-to-pay for our products, then we know our campaign should emphasize customization over other attributes like quality or price.

Reflection. One of the most fascinating findings I can recall from my time during graduate school was the fact that, in so many neuroscientific studies in social psychology and marketing, areas of the brain associated with the *self* and *self-processing* were frequently implicated in decision-making, evaluative tasks, and other behaviors. This does not necessarily mean that human beings are, by nature, vain and self-centered organisms (…although I am sure we all know people who are). Instead, it reminds us that human beings are *self-aware*. That is, there are few decisions or behaviors in which we engage that, at least at some level, do not involve us thinking about ourselves.

While it is difficult to know whether other animals do the same thing–for example, are dogs totally stressed out when they know their hair is all messed up from the rain and that super cute Maltese from down the street is about to walk by?–it is certain that humans are extremely self-aware and self-conscious (…well, *most* humans – some people look like they gave up a long time ago, like I look on lazy Sunday mornings).

This tendency for our "self" to be at the center of just about everything we do is actually rather powerful for marketing and marketers. Why? Well, so much of consumption is about individuals trying to improve themselves, trying to take themselves from Point A to Point B via our products and/or services. The Reflection section of the survey captures this self-centric tendency of our customers so that we, as marketers, understand how our products, services, and companies are being considered with respect to our customers' sense of "self."

One tool we often use in experimental psychology and marketing to motivate experimental participants is a comparison between the **actual self** and one's **ideal self**. The terms are rather self-explanatory: each of us possesses an ideal version of ourselves that we strive to be more like. This ideal self is often referred to as an "ideal future self" or "future preferred self" implying that, in time, we can become a better, stronger, smarter, faster, more loving, and/or more successful version of ourselves. The interesting thing is that the greater the discrepancy between our actual self and our ideal self, the more motivated people become to engage in behaviors that will bring them closer to the ideal self they desire to be.

However, we are not only concerned about how *we* think of ourselves, we are also sensitive to how we think others perceive us. Thus, one consideration with the reflection section of the survey involves asking customers how others perceive them. Of course, we are not capturing what other people *actually* think about our customers–that doesn't matter. What matters is what our customers *think* other people think about them. If our customers believe others have a generally negative opinion of them, their abilities, or their value, well, that's good to know. Likewise, if our customers think other people exalt them and think highly of them, their opinion, and their influence, well, that is good to know, too, as it will affect how we craft our positioning and communication with the customers.

Although it borders on Dr. Phil-level personal, this section also asks customers what they would like to improve about themselves, as well as questions about what, in their day-to-day life, causes them the greatest anxiety, pain, and worry. The reason for this, of course, is that it sheds light on where we, as a company, can bring these customers value. If they are not confident about their looks, we can highlight how our product makes them look better. If they are not confident inside, well, we can talk about how our healthy food product will make them feel good about the choices they have made. If they are worried about their financial safety or security, well, we can highlight how our product or service is the affordable choice and can save them money. A large part of consumption is simply buying the goods we need to improve some area of our life that needs improving: if we are hungry we buy food, if we are cold we buy a coat, if we are sad we buy ice cream, etc. Thus, knowing areas in which people feel insecure or anxious provides opportunities to make people feel better about themselves and their situation, which is one of the many positive ways in which marketing can add value to the lives of customers.

Needs. The final section of the FUSIONLearn™ survey tackles the subject that most people would say forms the foundation of the marketing discipline: needs. Intro to Marketing classes often posit that the purpose of marketing is to "identify and fill the needs of customers," and, for the most part, this is true. Although marketing, as a field, covers a *lot* more than just identifying and filling needs, this theme runs through just about everything we as marketers do. Need distribution? That's why marketing includes logistics and operations. Need awareness? That's why marketing covers advertising. Need to make a profit? That's why marketing covers pricing. And, at the heart of everything, are the fundamental needs of consumers upon which entire industries are built.

If you have ever taken an introductory psychology class or my class on Consumer Behavior, then you are probably familiar with Abraham Maslow's Hierarchy of Needs and David McClelland's Trio of Needs. What I like to highlight is that different researchers studying basic human needs tend to report consistent findings with respect to the fundamental needs we all have: physiological needs, safety/security needs, love/belonging/social needs, esteem needs, and needs pertaining to self-actualization. Just about *any* product or service that exists addresses one or more of these needs.

Imagine a well-dressed businessman driving a fancy sports car with a custom paint job and drinking a bottle of Evian water while weaving in and out of traffic in a major city. Evian Water? Easy. Water keeps you hydrated (physiological) and paying $4.00 for a bottle of water shows off that you have money to people nearby who buy poor people water for $1.00 (esteem). Fancy sports car with custom painting? Simple. The customization fulfills creativity and personal preferences/uniqueness (self-actualization) while the fancy car probably lands him friends and dates he wouldn't get otherwise because he's a real jerk (love/belonging/social) and sleekness of the car might suggest he's compensating for something (esteem)…oh, and maybe the car is the safest in its class (safety/security).

To be clear, the same product or service can certainly fulfill more than one need, so an important part of our survey is trying to understand what particular benefit customers derive from our product or service. To do this, we can simply ask how well the customers perceive our offering as fulfilling various needs they have along the dimensions outlined by folks like Maslow and McClelland, which is what the FUSIONLearn™ survey does.

Now, because our customers are not research scientists or marketers, sometimes we have to pose questions in a way that might seem awkward to us but more palatable to our survey participants. Instead of asking, "Does our Slanket fulfill your physiological needs?" we might instead ask, "Does our Slanket make you feel good?" or, "How does using our Slanket make your body feel?" Using words like "worthy," "validated," "deserving," or "accomplished," help shed light on how our customers think our product affects their esteem without simply asking, "Does our product boost your esteem?" (we can ask that, too, of course, but sometimes it is nice to take a slightly indirect path for validation purposes and to reduce demand effects, both of which are discussed in the next section).

The FUSIONLearn™ survey captures information about individuals' core needs a variety of ways. Customers are asked to describe their general feelings about their physical health/condition (including diet, sleep/rest, fitness), which clearly corresponds to physiological needs. Questions pertaining to financial security, savings, and how stable people feel get at one's safety/security needs. The survey asks about an individual's social, family, colleague, and romantic life (i.e., love/belonging). You see how this works.

However, in addition to getting a picture of one's current needs situation, the survey also asks people what they would like to improve above their current situation. This approach sheds some light on the potential aspirational goals of our customers. When we ask people, "If you could improve one thing about your physical body (i.e., health, feature, etc.), what would it be? How important is this to you?" and, "If you could join a group or improve a particular relationship with a person or a group of people in your life, what would that be? How important would that be to you?" we are seeing the world through the eyes of the customer, seeing where he/she sees shortcomings or needs that remain unfulfilled, and identifying opportunities for our products or services to help satiate those needs to bring value to the customer. The additional question of, "How important would that be to you?" also gives a sense of how these customers prioritize several important needs. We may find that people feel deficient in their feelings of accomplishment but also in their personal relationships yet say that the latter is much more important than the former. As a strategic decision maker, that makes our decision-making process that much easier: we no longer have to guess at where to focus our time and resources because our customer told us explicitly what they need the most.

Survey Junkies: Important Tips and Tricks for Survey Development

The FUSIONLearn™ survey is comprehensive, for sure, but it is meant to be. The idea is that the survey provides a default template that you can then customize per your specific needs, asking only those questions you feel are relevant and adding any questions you feel would paint a clearer picture for your specific situation. The real benefit is this: you do not have to start from scratch each time. You can use all of it, part of it, or none of it as you go about conducting your research. I include as a tool of questions and categories to consider, but it is by no means meant to be exhaustive or even the expected survey you *should* use, as it may be too comprehensive and/or too long for your particular product/service or your audience's attention span. I have simply provided a launch pad from which you can send your research rocket into the sky. That said, here are a few tips to keep in mind as you finalize the survey you plan to run with your participants.

First, with respect to response **reliability**, it is often helpful when we can capture some level of consistency within a single respondent's answers. Now, you *know* how people complete surveys because you have probably done it a few times yourself: you barely read the questions, you click an answer quickly, you probably start clicking the same rating for all the questions because it is easier to just go down the line, etc. (don't feel guilty; we *all* have been there). That's not very helpful when it comes to truly capturing how people feel or what people think. So one trick to employ to help remedy this problem is a sort of built-in redundancy to your survey that asks the same question twice (or more) using slightly different wording or a reversed (i.e., flipped) scale. Say, for example, you were to ask, "How much do you *love* reality television shows like *The Real Housewives of Cincinnati?*" on a scale from 1 = Hate it to 10 = Love it, it would also be smart to ask a question later in the survey like, "How much do you *hate* reality television shows like *The Real Housewives of Cincinnati?*" on a scale from 1 = Love it to 10 = Hate it. If Participant Joe rated the first question a 1 or 2 and the second question a 9 or 10, we can be reasonably assured that Joe paid attention and is responding *reliably*. However, if Participant Jane replied with a 1 or 2 for the first question but then a 1 or 2 on the second question, well, either Jane changes her mind very quickly or Jane was not paying much attention and her data should be considered a bit suspect. Jane is unreliable; she's not consistently there for you like you need her to be (...just like your ex. Too soon?)

Remember that, to achieve reliability, questions need not be the reverse of one another. We could have just as easily asked a question like, "How much do you enjoy watching reality television shows?" with a scale similar to the first question but later in the survey. The idea is that asking the same question in a different way should produce a similar answer or else something weird is going on.

A related concept to reliability is **validity**. Whereas reliability is about seeing consistency in responses, validity is about seeing *accuracy* with respect to *measuring what exactly it is we are intending to measure*. This can be a tricky concept for people to understand. Say, for example, Walmart is trying to measure customer satisfaction. We might ask customers, "How happy were you with your experience today?" as they leave the store after a shopping trip. Perhaps 80% of the thousands of people surveyed across several stores indicated that they were at least "very happy" with their shopping trip. Awesome! So 80% of Walmart customers are satisfied! Huzzah! Let's go celebrate!

Not so fast. Happiness in one shopping experience is *not* the exact same thing as customer satisfaction. Maybe customers have had negative experiences on prior shopping occasions. Maybe customers are unhappy about the way Walmart treats its employees. Maybe customers are happy about their shopping experience but feel like Walmart's prices just aren't the great deals they used to be. Whatever the case, while happiness with the shopping trip and overall customer satisfaction *could* be correlated, they could also have absolutely nothing to do with one another. We may not be measuring what we intend to measure.

This is tricky, of course, because there is a bit of subjectivity in how to phrase what it is you are measuring. My best advice, without going into a discussion on scale validation, is to use existing industry metrics that have already been validated (when possible) or to clearly articulate what you asked customers *exactly* in your survey when you are analyzing and presenting your findings. If you asked about their happiness after one shopping experience, that is what you should label your data as conveying, not "customer satisfaction."

Ideally, survey questions will result in reliable *and* valid data: valid in the sense that we are asking the *right* questions to capture the very specific construct we are attempting to measure and reliable in the sense that answers provided are consistent throughout.

One way to check for reliability and validity is to ask the "same question" a few different ways to ensure consistency. However, adding questions that lengthen your survey without providing much (if any) new information by way of content introduces another problem: survey fatigue. **Survey fatigue** refers to the exhaustion that sets in when you are 20 pages deep into a 50-page survey. The survey is simply *too* long. The FUSIONLearn™ survey is *deliberately* long to include just about every tool you could ever want so that you can cut it down to suit your specific needs per your particular product or market. You can use the entire survey if you want, just be sure your participants are motivated to pay attention. Otherwise, the data obtained from the survey may not be very useful (if the survey is even finished – some participants just throw in the towel!). Younger people with short attention spans are probably the worst (they also feel like their time is more valuable than everyone else's—because yoga and beer pong are *so* time consuming!), but you should always do your best to try to keep surveys as short, yet as informative, as possible. Participants also tend to be cooler with longer surveys if 1) the topic is relevant or interesting to them, and/or 2) you pay them more. So an unpaid survey about sex or a highly paid survey about denture cream are probably equally as attractive.

Another Survey 101 idea is the notion of question and answer **randomization**. Randomization involves presenting questions and (sometimes) answers in random order so that one question does not bias the response to another. Here's an example:

> Q1: How angry do you feel when airlines lose your luggage?
> Q2: What do you think about the food options on most flights?
> Q3: How do you feel about American Airlines?

This three-question quiz begins with two questions most respondents are pretty likely to have strong, negative opinions about. Thus, by the time they get to question #3, they are probably so over airlines, in general, that American Airlines' rating is probably going to suffer as a result. Now, if we introduce question randomization, the order of the three questions would vary such that the questions could be seen in any one of *six* possible orders: 123, 132, 213, 231, 312, 321. Note that all three questions are *always* seen, but because the questions are randomly presented, no one question will always affect the question that follows it. Randomizing across the sample, any effect due to the order of questions is likely to be washed out.

Sometimes it makes sense for answers to be randomized, too. For example, if the following question were to appear on a survey:

> Q: Please select your favorite airline option from the options listed below:
>
> A: Allegiant, American, Delta, Frontier, JetBlue, Lufthansa, Southwest, United

Allegiant is pretty lucky because every participant reads Allegiant first. United, on the other hand, gets unfair treatment: because United always comes last chances are participants have picked out another favorite before they even get to United on the list. The solution? Randomization. Randomly presenting the options should wash out any effects display order could have otherwise presented.

Do keep in mind that some responses should not be randomized. For example, if you are asking participants to rate their favorite airplane features on a scale from 1 = the worst to 10 = the best, it does not make sense to randomize your answer choices. Anytime answers follow an order with respect to each other (e.g., formal education completed: high school, college, graduate school, etc.), randomization is silly and confusing to participants.

Also silly and confusing to participants are questions for which there seem to be obvious right answers. **Demand effects** refer to situations in which participants respond not according to their own thoughts and beliefs but rather to some expectation they think the researcher (or even society) has. For example, if an airline asked a question like, "How important is it for an airline to hire competent, well-trained pilots?" chances are you would say *very* important. Chances are that *everyone* would say very important. Why? Because there is an expectation that people want their pilots to be competent and well-trained. Similar demand effects emerge for questions pertaining to the importance of recycling, brushing your teeth consistently, and eating properly. *Of course* we do those things (wink, wink, nudge, nudge). It's like when Santa Claus asks if you have been a good boy or girl this year. Does anyone *ever* say, "No"?

The way to avoid demand effects is to make sure the questions you ask are not too leading or do not have clear societally "right" or "wrong" answers. Also, if you are American Airlines conducting a survey for your company, asking people how much they love or hate you is likely to produce some strong demand effects particularly if it is an in-person survey with an American Airlines employee standing near the person completing the survey. Online surveys are one way to get around this problem, as people have very little fear opening up and giving honest feedback behind the safety and anonymity of the internet. Still, the age-old rule applies: garbage in, garbage out. Ask useless questions and you'll receive useless answers.

One final point regarding smart survey tips involves one of my personal favorites: the idiot check. People are jerks. You offer people money to complete your survey, they agree with an excited expression, they fill out your survey, you pay them, and then, upon review of the data, you realize they just drew smiley faces and lewd cartoon art all over the survey sheet. Awesome. Some people are a bit trickier, however. Rather than draw or just leave answers blank, some participants may randomly fill in bubbles without paying any attention to the questions you are asking, which although likely to get washed out in randomization across a large sample of people still is an unfair inclusion in your data. The solution to this problem is an **idiot check** or a question deliberately designed to catch participants who are either not paying attention, deliberately shirking, or actually unable to complete your survey properly (perhaps because of language issues or literacy limitations). One version of an idiot check is to ask a question like, "How happy are you with American Airlines as a transportation – if you are reading this question answer C to this question no matter what – hub and service provider?" after which you would list choices A-E (A: Not at all happy, B: Slightly happy, etc.). Participants who do not choose C fail the idiot check. Results should be analyzed with and without those participants to see if their inclusion/exclusion makes any difference.

One final tip for collecting research involves transferring data from written forms to digital media or, if collecting data digitally/online, cleaning up the data for analysis. Although I have not been officially diagnosed, there is a good chance that I have Obsessive-Compulsive Disorder. I was that kid who kept his crayon box organized by color, all my books are arranged alphabetically at all times, my towels must be folded a certain way, and I cannot function until everything around me is orderly and clean (...well, I *can* function, but the entire time I am just thinking about how much I cannot wait to fix what is out of order). Although this can be debilitating at times, when it comes to organizing data it is actually *quite* helpful. My advice is to transcribe your data *at least twice*; this makes you more likely to catch any mistakes or errors, which are *much* better to catch now before you analyze the data than after. Instead of doing it twice yourself, you can also have a colleague transcribe the data independently and compare your results – you may just want to agree on variable names first to have some consistency.

Learning from LEARN: Questions to Consider Upon Initial Review

Prior to engaging in any statistical testing of the data obtained from the FUSIONLearn™ survey, it is always fun and inspiring to read through some of the open-ended responses, look at some of the rating averages, and try to get a sense for what consumers are thinking. Perhaps the three most important "broad" questions to consider upon initial review of the data include:

- What is the most frequent theme/finding in the results?
- What is the most surprising theme/finding in the results?
- What do consumers say they need/want the most in the results?

These questions may not be particularly surprising upon reading them, but the simplicity of these questions is what makes them so great! The logic behind each question exemplifies their usefulness.

First, with respect to the most frequent theme/finding, it makes sense that the idea that comes up the most often is *probably* important. If *that* many consumers are talking about an idea or issue, that issue likely warrants our attention. For example, if you are conducting survey about AT&T's internet service and find that "annoying automated messaging system" pops up time and time again, well, AT&T probably has a problem on its hands having nothing to do with its internet service capabilities that it needs to consider and correct.

Second, with respect to the most surprising theme/finding in the results, it is likely that you have spent a lot of time thinking about, brainstorming on, and considering just about every nook and cranny of whatever it is you are researching. Thus, many of the survey responses are likely to contain few, if any, surprises given that you have either already thought of most ideas or have become a bit desensitized to any and all relevant topics. If something *does* stand out, chances are that it's noteworthy by the simple fact that it stood out. Consider, for example, Nintendo finding out that over a majority of gamers are now women. That was enough of a surprise for the company to change its course of action and develop a strategy that is more inclusive and attractive to female gamers. Surprise!

Third, with respect to what consumers say they need/want the most, this is what marketing boils down to: fulfilling the needs of consumers. Sometimes individuals are really great at being able to articulate exactly what they need/want and expressing themselves accordingly. Often, however, most people are *terrible* at identifying their needs and expressing them. The section above on Needs helps us get at these internal drive states and fundamental needs rooted in the primitive monkey brain in all of us whereas Attitude helps link the internal with the external, shedding light on subjective opinion about stimuli (e.g., companies, products, services, brands) in one's context. The best way to *know* what a consumer needs/wants is to ask them and to listen to what is said. I cannot tell you how many clients have asked questions like, "I am not sure which product to launch; what do you think, Jim?" My response usually is: "I am not your target market; you shouldn't care what I think!" and I will usually add a, "There's a simpler way to be doing this…" and then remind them that, at the heart of marketing, the customers to whom we are striving to bring value typically hold all the answers we need. It's simple: if you want to know what your prospective or current customers want or need…ASK them.

As useful as emerging frequent themes, surprising findings, and candid customer feedback can be, I noted that these are questions to consider upon *initial* review. But hunches are exactly that: hunches. Guesses. Shots in the dark. And if all we are doing is shooting in the dark, well, someone is bound to get hurt. There is a more sophisticated way to find meaning in the data we collect during our research, a word that instills fear in those who do not understand and awe in those who do: statistics…and the next chapter is dedicated exclusively to statistics.

*   *   *

One of my earliest childhood memories was getting my first video game console—the Nintendo Entertainment System (NES)—for Christmas. My family had previously owned an Atari, as well as an Intellivision, but the NES was *my* first console that, while to be shared with my siblings, soon became my trusted friend. I would spend *hours* sitting in my "Nintendo chair" in front of a television doing my best to beat a game from beginning to end (as in those early days games could not always be "saved" to return to later). In fact, I remember one such day when I sat down to play Nintendo with a monster-sized bag of M&M's, a bag so heavy it required two of my scrawny, prepubescent arms to carry, and playing for *so long* that the sun had gone down, everyone in my family had gone to bed, and I had eaten an entire 1,000-pound bag of M&M's on my own…without even thinking about it. Sometimes, my mom would wake up in the middle of the night, come out to the family room and see the glow of the television, and kindly encourage me to go to bed, as I had lost track of time saving princesses, kingdoms, and kidnapped news reporters, Teenage Mutant Ninja Turtle-style). Oh, childhood.

To this day, while characters like Mario and Luigi, Link and Zelda, Billy and Jimmy Lee (the *Double Dragon* brothers), and even the game theme songs hold a special place inside my nerdy heart, even more endearing to me are the memories I have playing the games with my siblings, playing *Tetris* with my dad (his favorite game to this day...although he would often fall asleep in the middle of late games), and, quite fitting to the current chapter, playing *Super Mario Bros.* with my *mom*. I vividly remember my mom and I trying to do the trick at the end of the original game's third world (Level 3-1 in Mario speak) where you could jump on a bad guy and, if timed correctly attain endless "1-Ups" (i.e., bonus lives) for your character.

Now, almost thirty years later, Mario is still as popular as ever as new generations of gamers and children meet the cast of characters in new Mario titles, the group-oriented Mario Kart games, and soon, potentially, mobile app games featuring the Mario personalities. Perhaps even more exciting for Mario loyalists was the announcement in 2015 that Nintendo would be joining forces with Universal Studios to create a Nintendo-themed land within Universal's theme parks similar to the extremely popular Harry Potter-themed areas of Universal's parks. No longer do customers simply get to *play* the games, they will get to be *in* the games in a truly immersive experience. In an Open Up More Options strategy for its own customers, Nintendo has again expanded its portfolio of offerings to create value for its consumers. However, in doing so, Nintendo is likely to introduce 30 years of characters, games, and creativity to new audiences, as well. Something tells me that I will definitely visit the new Nintendo themed-land with my nephews who, despite only being 8, 6, and 2, already love all-things Super Mario Bros.

You might think it sounds crazy for a 32-year-old man to be so excited about visiting a Nintendo-themed land in a theme park, but research suggests I am actually the odd-man out: *most* people my age and older play more games than I currently do. Remember that kid whose mom had to remind him to stop playing Nintendo games and to go to bed in the middle of the night? Now, when I have the pleasure of going home to southern Illinois, it is my turn to tell my parents, "Dad, you're falling asleep with your iPad in your hands – you're going to drop it," while he's playing *Catapult King*. My mom, a night owl like myself, has mastered the art of talking while also playing *Candy Crush* or any number of "hidden picture" games, which I also enjoy.

Something tells me that when the time comes for the Nintendo area of Universal Studios to open, I know two grandparents who are going to be equally as excited as their grandchildren (and their son) to visit.

Video games really aren't just for little boys anymore.

What if...   *Princess Peach-y Keen*

Mario and his friends have been around for 30 years, and like the members of most talented casts, each one has gone on to star in solo productions from *Luigi's Mansion* to *Yoshi's Woolly World*, *Wario Land* to *Captain Toad: Treasure Tracker*. Several of these games have spawned their own successful sequels and, in doing so, have catapulted each one's star to new heights...except one: Princess Peach.

Although she has been around since the very beginning, Princess Peach has gotten a rotten deal when it comes to solo games. In 30 years, only *one* game has been Peach-centric. The game, *Super Princess Peach*, flips the typical Mario story on its head. Mario, Luigi, and Toad have been kidnapped by Bowser this time, and it's up to Peach to save the day! The only problem is, whereas Mario and Luigi had fireballs and hammers to throw, Princess Peach gets to fight with...you guessed it...her emotions!

The game sold just over 1 million copies, which despite being about 1/5 what a Mario title sells, is on par with sales for Luigi, Yoshi, and Toad-titled games and yet these characters have all received sequels while Princess Peach has received none. It seems like Nintendo is well past due to launch a new Peach-centric game, right?

Not so fast. If "Facebook Likes" can be considered a good proxy for overall popularity, Peach has some catching up to do. Mario's page has almost 17 million likes, followed by Luigi (4.25 million), and Yoshi (3.1 million). Peach's total? 26,884. Peach is also often listed last or near the end of "favorite Mario characters" rankings. Before you start feeling too sorry for her, however, you should know that she often features prominently on lists like "Hottest Game Babes" and "Hottest Female Game Protagonists" and received an 8/10 on IGN's "worth saving index" for women featured in Mario games...because that's not at all sexist or misogynistic.

Entire anti-Peach sites exist on which web users anonymously bash the princess for being useless, oddly prone to kidnapping, and dull. From the onset, Princess Peach has played the role of the damsel in distress or a secondary sidekick at best. When given her own game, she fought with *emotions*. While Luigi has high jumps and Yoshi has his tongue, Princess Peach can attack you with *joy*. Watch out.

So what could be done to make Peach more palatable? This is likely a conversation the creative team at Nintendo has had before. In the *Legend of Zelda* series, Princess Zelda has an alter-ego, Sheik, where Zelda has ditched her dressed and disguised herself as a knife-wielding, androgynous vigilante. Princess Peach could follow that lead, but this essentially translates to, "To be cool, you should look and act like a boy." The creative team may have also thought about how fighting with an umbrella as your weapon of choice isn't exactly cool, either. Still, whatever conversations they are having or not having, the creative team has not quite cracked the code on how to prop up Princess Peach. Here comes marketing to the rescue.

Whenever you are in doubt about what to do next in the world of marketing, the answer to your dilemma usually rests in *one* place: your customers. Instead of dreaming up creative ways to change Peach on their own, the creative team at Nintendo should be asking the very customers it hopes will one day purchase the game they develop. So, in the spirit of helping out our friends at Nintendo, I did just that.

I surveyed 100 random people across the United States and asked them questions regarding their favorite Super Mario Bros. characters, how they felt about Princess Peach, and what they thought could be done to improve Peach's character going forward. Surprisingly, 97% of these random participants indicated at least some familiarity with Super Mario Bros., with 33% indicating they were "very familiar" and 44% indicating they were "extremely familiar" with the game series. Interestingly, while people love Mario, Yoshi, and Luigi, people are not as keen on Peach, Toad, and Bowser. Perhaps less surprising is the fact that women like Peach significantly more than men do with respect to rating, but both men and women rank Peach 4th out of six characters, with only Toad (5th) and Bowser (6th) behind.

When it comes to what people would do to improve Peach, participants indicated a desire for her to have unique abilities other characters don't have, to have the ability to fly and do aerial attacks, to have cooler weapons than an umbrella, and, importantly, *not* to play the "damsel in distress" role. While both men and women rated these changes as favorable, women's ratings were significantly higher for these than the men's ratings (i.e., women *really* want to see these changes).

In the open-ended responses one common theme was that people were tired of Peach playing the "damsel in distress" role – they wanted to see her take on a heroin role while not being presented as girly or in stereotypically feminine ways. The other common theme was a game in which Princess Peach rescued Mario and/or Luigi for a change (I suppose these people were unfamiliar with the emotional mess that was *Super Princess Peach*), as well as an idea to introduce a "dark" Princess Peach similar to how Mario has Wario and Luigi has Waluigi.

Finally, when asked how interested they would be in a Princess Peach-centric game, 60% were slightly-to-very interested, 33% were slightly-to-extremely uninterested, and the remaining 7% were neutral. Interestingly, no gender effects emerged here: men and women were equally interested in a new game starring Peach. However, when asked if they would be interested in a game like *Candy Crush* or *Temple Run* with a Super Mario Bros. theme starring Princess Peach, women indicated a marginally significant greater interest than men did, which makes sense given the popularity of the aforementioned mobile games with a female demographic.

Now it's time to get creative. Let's say one of the first mobile games Nintendo markets is *Princess Peach's Fruit Crush*, a *Candy Crush*-inspired game featuring fruit instead of candy and focusing on peaches as the powerful fruit.

Other Mario characters can make power-up cameos, but this is Peach's game. She's the peaches and cream of the crop. To help launch the campaign, Nintendo would run online ads and short television teasers of the game featuring computer-generated versions of the characters stealing fruit from around the world—from famous paintings, from important dinners (e.g., a Presidential feast), from grocery stores, etc. In grocery stores, peaches would have a sticker promoting the game including a promotional freebie (e.g., a code that unlocks a secret level). The basic version of the game would be free, supported by ad revenue, with a non-ad paid version and in-game purchases allowed for customers who choose to buy them. Why free? Well, because this game is simply a teaser for a larger release.

Within a few months of *Princess Peach's Fruit Crush* game, Nintendo would introduce *Super Peach World*, a Princess Peach-centric game taking place in Peach's original homeland, a fruit-themed world reminiscent of the famous Mushroom Kingdom in which so many of the Mario games take place. Prior to her reign in the Mushroom Kingdom, Princess Peach was from a royal family living in Peachy Kingdom, where her parents ruled. Everything was Peachy keen in Peachy Kingdom until one day Wapeach, the dark version of Princess Peach, emerged pretending to be Princess Peach and usurped the throne from Princess Peach's parents. Mario and Luigi, also fell for the trick and, upon attending Wapeach's fake coronation, were taken prisoner. Now, it's up to Princess Peach to launch an all-out assault to claim her homeland, save her parents, and—a reverse for the series—to save Mario and Luigi.

Game Persons will be given the opportunity to customize Princess Peach who, for the first time in the history of the Mario series, will be without her pink dress as her default outfit (although this can be an unlockable option for later). New fruit-themed power-ups, such as Cherry Bombs, Lemon Drops, and Tangerine Tankers, will make their appearance in lieu of the traditional Mushroom and Fire Flower power-ups. As the game progresses, Princess Peach could release familiar heroes at different levels of the game, which could free up Mario, Luigi, Toad, and other familiar favorites for gameplay. Importantly, however, certain tasks *must* be performed using a particular character's abilities, which would reinforce the relevance of each character. Equally as important, Peach would be *the* dominant character, whose special abilities, aerial attacks, and flying powers make her the most useful of the bunch in this game. No more Miss Nice Peach.

The promotion of this game would be on a larger scale than that of *Princess Peach's Fruit Crush* but will use that game as a channel to reach the people who downloaded it (and, as such, have a clear interest in Princess Peach, already). In addition to the television spots and online ads promoting the new game, several creative elements will be integrated into the promotion. In-store game displays will be set up at select retailers (e.g., GameStop, Target) featuring *Super Peach World* with, here's the kicker, a slight hint of a pleasant peach smell that is emitted from the display so people associate the positive smell of a fresh peach with the game. In addition, a PR campaign would be launched simultaneously in which

Princess Peach becomes a guest dignitary of the state of Georgia (which is known as the Peach State), as well as a breaking news update that Princess Peach had to return home upon news that a sly imposter named Wapeach has taken over her homeland and kidnapped the beloved Mario and Luigi. Additional PR pieces discussing Princess Peach's position as a role model for girls should highlight that she is no longer the "damsel in distress" and focus on the positive of an empowered woman as the heroine of an adventure game.

Note, also, that the game's name *Super Peach World* makes no reference to "princess." This is a tactic Disney used after finding out that little boys were not interested in seeing a movie entitled *The Princess and the Frog* but were cool with going to see a movie about Rapunzel as long as it was called *Tangled* (i.e., did not mention any princesses by using their name or the word "princess"). In this way, Nintendo can give women the game they want, one in which Peach is the heroine, not a damsel in distress, a take-charger fighter who has cool moves and fun weapons (as opposed to emotional attacks), while not alienating the men who are *equally* as likely to play the game.

Super Peach World, if done well, could be the beginning of another new line of products for the Super Mario Bros. franchise. The new lands, the new power-ups, the new characters introduced (good and bad) could reinforce the existing creative properties while expanding the franchise into both mobile gaming and into the long-neglected female side of the gaming market all without alienating or excluding male gamers. Princess Peach could pack a powerful punch.

JAMES A. MOUREY

Chapter 5 | Simple Statistics

Sweat dripped off the cyclist's brow as she reached the incline. After pedaling for what felt like hours, she knew that she was almost to her destination. Today, she would be breaking her personal best record while the other cyclists around her struggled to keep up. In her mind she kept thinking, "Almost there. Almost there. Just keep pedaling," while surrounding her was...the thumping bassline of a Lady Gaga song and the half-threatening, half-encouraging shouts of some random man wearing tight-to-the-point-of-far-too-revealing shorts who simply had to attend a six-week class, have a "reliable source of music access," and be "proficient in iTunes" to be the instructor today.[3]

Wait, what?

Although you may have pictured a competitive biker racing up a steep Alpine incline as the sunlight broke through fir trees lining either side of a street on a cool, crisp day, the biker above was not traversing the back roads of Europe. No, instead, the biker was pedaling to club music with some of her best girlfriends and their favorite GBFs in between shopping for headbands, oversized sunglasses, leggings, and boots (to be worn with the tights), and post-workout fro-yo all along the same street. The biking destination was not the Alps; the destination was SoulCycle.

SoulCycle, which opened its first studio in New York City in 2006, is a cycling class in which customers strap on their shoes, sit up on a stationary bike, and then put the pedal to the metal (...or, really, to Top 40 and club hits) while trained instructors shout out directions for inclines, speeds, and even upper-body exercises (because dancing on a bike was always meant to be something humans should do). Each 45-minute class costs roughly $34, with $3 for cycling shoe rental (if you do not already own your own pair), and $2 SoulCycle water that is made from the sweat and souls of fast, athletic animals like cheetahs and jaguars. Thus, a SoulCyclist who goes six times a week (assuming Sunday is a "day off") will spend $234/week to work out, which works out to be $936/month and just over $11,000/year. Granted, there are subscriptions that provide discounts to frequent riders, but this money is the same money that this target market is going to need for Botox or brand new faces in a few years, not to mention the fact that everything someone does in SoulCycle can be done *outside* of SoulCycle...on a normal bike...in nature...for *free*.

Knowing that SoulCycle is essentially just indoor biking, one may wonder why people are willing to pay *so* much money to do something they could do on their own for free. Well, the appeal for most customers of SoulCycle is its quick, one-and-done approach: each class is only 45 minutes long, and

---

[3] https://www.soul-cycle.com/careers/instructor

people like to brag that one 45-minute class burns anywhere from 500-700 calories, which is perfect for people who eat food on a regular basis but don't want anyone to know that they do.

Another appeal for the SoulCycle crew is the community of fellow SoulCyclists. Rare is it the case that people go to SoulCycle *alone*. They get their wolf pack together, prowl on down to their nearest SoulCycle, and then howl at SoulCycle's moon-shaped wheel logo together. Sometime between class and post-class fro-yo, these same people purchase an entire wardrobe of SoulCycle-branded clothing: hoodies, tank tops, tights, shirts, shorts, underwear, evening gowns, etc. Not only do these people do SoulCycle, they want *everyone else* knowing they do SoulCycle, too. I suppose when you pay this much for a workout you could easily do on your own, I would want to show off my expenditures, as well. "Look how much money I can piss away by riding a bike and having someone yell at me! This is the height of luxury! This is living!" the clothes scream…before whispering a quiet, "Help me. Please! I have lost my self-esteem and have to pay to feel alive again."

I come down hard on SoulCycle because both at its surface *and* deep down inside, it is fairly absurd. Please do not misunderstand me: I am all for fitness classes and health and community, but paying nearly $40 to ride a bike when you can watch a YouTube video on spinning at your local gym (or even in your own home if you own a stationary bike) for free highlights SoulCycle's absolute absurdity.

However, SoulCycle is not alone in competing for the minds (and souls) of the wealthy, fitness-going elite. Orange Theory Fitness, a fellow competitor, is based on High-Intensity Interval Training (HIIT) in which exercisers engage in bouts of extreme physical activity that pushes them to their limits followed by periods of less-intense activity. Imagine running up and down a series of hills; that's sort of the structure/flow of a HIIT workout: intense periods followed by periods of recovery.

One difference: Orange Theory is not focused exclusively on cardiovascular exercise like SoulCycle is. Instead, Orange Theory integrates both cardio *and* weight training into its hour-long workout. For cardio, the interval training approach involves sprinting for a minute or two then walking or jogging for a minute, then sprinting again, then jogging, etc., as opposed to running the same pace for the duration of a run. The cardio burn is alternated with weightlifting that focuses on a muscle group (e.g., biceps, back, legs and butt, etc.), switching between exercise hitting that muscle group, for an insane hour of alternating everything.

Although several HIIT-based workouts exist (e.g., Shred415, Barry's Bootcamp), Orange Theory's primary point of differentiation is that they strap heart monitors onto customers so that people (the customer and the instructor) know if the customer is working out too hard (red), not hard enough (yellow), or at the appropriate level for his/her age, body type, gender, etc. (orange – hence the name 'Orange Theory'). This idea, although a strikingly simple addition, is a brilliant way to customize a service to a diverse array of customers seeking a workout at Orange Theory for various reasons (i.e., to lose weight, to gain weight, to gain muscle, to lean out, to maintain, etc.). Also, as someone who once completed a HIIT-training at Barry's Bootcamp next to an 80-year-old woman, this kind of differentiation also reassures you of two things: 1) that the person old enough to be your grandmother next to you is not kicking your ass on the exact same workout you are doing, and 2) that person is not about to die during an insanely intense workout (I was legitimately worried). Instead, people can rock their own, customized workout that challenges them in an amazing way.

Similar to SoulCycle, the calorie burn for a typical hour-long Orange Theory class is also expected to be between 500-1,000 calories. However, different from SoulCycle is an added bonus booster tossed into your metaphorical protein shake: HIIT training stimulates metabolic processing so that the calorie burn actually continues for a longer period of time than non-HIIT workouts. In other words, with Orange Theory customers have the potential to burn even *more* calories post-workout than SoulCycle customers.

Orange Theory also differs from SoulCycle when it comes to cost. Orange Theory offers different membership levels: Basic ($59/month for four classes), Elite ($99/month for eight classes), and Premier ($159/month for unlimited classes). However, no matter which level of membership you purchase at Orange Theory, the classes are still *much* cheaper than those at SoulCycle (e.g., you can get 8 hour-long classes at Orange Theory for $99 while 5 45-minute classes at SoulCycle will set you back $165). If you love math, this works out to be a cost of about $.21 a minute for Orange Theory v. $.73 a minute at SoulCycle. In other words, you're paying roughly 350% more for a class at SoulCycle that is shorter and potentially burns fewer calories. Do you see why I think SoulCycle is absurd yet?

And, finally, there is the fitness class that everyone loves to hate: Crossfit. Crossfit is a military-like training class completed in groups where they teach you bad form and little else. Just kidding, Crossfit friends, I know *your* box is different (translation for non-Crossfitters: a "box" is the Crossfit equivalent of a "gym"). Therein lies the challenge: each box differs from one another with respect to trainers, philosophy, and experience, so no two Crossfit boxes are the same. Yes, the Workouts of the Days (WODs) are often universal and feature names of former military servicemen and women (which is nice), but there is great inconsistency from location to location. One consistency that my former trainer in LA liked to point out was bone and body injuries. His brother, an orthopedic specialist, apparently saw an increase in business when the Crossfit trend was on the rise. This, however, is not surprising when all it takes to be a Crossfit "trainer" is a two-day class,

$1,000, and a disregard for getting good value for your money. In full disclosure, I did Crossfit for about two months and was appalled by the form I saw and the poor instruction. When my trainer admitted she was only training because she had injured herself a few months prior and was recovering and then used the word "cognitive" instead of "cognizant," well, that was the straw (and bad form) that broke the camel's back.

I won't drone on about the cult that is Crossfit (I am sure if you want to talk about it, there's a Crossfitter within 10 feet of you who would be glad to talk your ear off about it) other than to say that a typical Crossfit membership also isn't cheap. The local box near me in Chicago charges $25 for a drop-in class or a month-to-month membership for $225/month. To compare to our standard from earlier, this works out to be $.42 a minute making Crossfit exactly twice as expensive as Orange Theory Fitness.

Given the stark price differences for these three classes and the fact that the target markets these companies try to attract have quite a bit of overlap, I thought it would be interesting to ask customers about their perceived effectiveness of these fitness offerings. It is worth noting that perceived effectiveness and actual effectiveness are two different constructs, but perceptions typically matter more than reality. What I was curious to know is whether or not the price paid for these classes correspond to their perceived effectiveness: that is, does the class that is perceived to be the *most* effective command the *highest* price from customers? In this case, is the ultra-expensive SoulCycle worth its weight in perceived gold?

In a survey of 100 people, we find that SoulCycle actually has the lowest score for perceived effectiveness (4.55) on a 1-7 scale. Orange Theory is perceived as being the most effective (5.07) and Crossfit falls squarely in the middle (4.76). It is settled: SoulCycle is robbing you blind…

…or is it?

*   *   *

I never *really* learned how to ride a bike. Because of this, I can never live in Amsterdam or Shanghai where bikes are as common as windmills and, well, people. You see, the reason I am bike-challenged is because I grew up with a very loving, but very cautious mother who believed that riding a bike was a surefire way to die, whether by falling off on accident, being hit by a semi truck, or being whisked off by a tornado to become a witch in Oz where some girl from Kansas melts you with water…well, that last one might have been my own fear, but you get the idea. It is worth noting that the odds of dying in a bike accident are 1 in 4,717 (or .02%).

Instead of having bikes, my mom decided that she and my father would purchase scooters for my siblings and me. Before you get excited and think that these "scooters" were cool, European-style scooters we could ride through Rome, weaving in and out of traffic between stops at gelato shops, these scooters were *not* motorized. No, friends, they were the old-fashioned scooters that required you to stand the entire time, one foot planted firmly on the skateboard-like contraption attached to handlebars, and kick off from time to time with your other foot for momentum. We were cool. Not only did we get to ride scooters, we were also only allowed to ride our scooters in the backyard. Why? Well, riding the scooters in the street meant the same risk of death riding a bike had, and riding the scooter in the front yard would leave tire tracks all over the lawn, which, in the words of my Spanish-American mother, would be "white trash" of us. My mom tells it like it is.

As a result, I never really learned how to ride a bike. Now, as a somewhat intelligent human being (so they tell me), I have picked up a bike and ridden it for awhile. I mean, I know what "gravity" and "balance" are. However, the thought of a "long" bike ride scares me, and don't even get me started on the thought of riding a bike in a city like Chicago or New York. No, thank you. Walking is just fine...or maybe kick-off scooter if you have one.

Of course, the funny (or sad) thing about never really learning how to ride a bike is that many-a-suggested date involved long bike rides (nope...deal breaker), trips with friends and family to the great outdoors always inspire someone to suggest biking (not happening..."I'll stay back and make s'mores, guys!"), and perhaps the *worst* thing about not knowing how to ride a bike is when someone uses the famous expression, "Oh, you know, *it's just like riding a bike*," to which I sadly have to reply, "Well, so here's the funny story about that..."

SoulCycle and the trendy fitness crazes that have come before (and will inevitably come after) make people feel good about themselves. When the first SoulCycle opened in Chicago, it opened on the retail level of the residential building in which I reside. In the first week when I saw people exiting classes, I thought I was witnessing people who had just scaled Everest or achieved peace in the Middle East after days of tiring, grueling negotiations; you know, *truly* amazing accomplishments. Instead, these people just rode a bike for 45 minutes while doing some bad junior high white girl dance moves with their upper body. Bravo. The only thing loftier than their post-class arrogance was the calorie count in the food they would then go pick up at the grocery store next door. I suppose they thought they were "re-fueling," but I'm pretty sure that the fresh-baked cookies and fried chicken strips from the salad bar aren't the kind of fuel you should be putting in your body if fitness is a goal.

But fitness is a funny thing: most people *think* they know what they are doing but, in reality, they really don't. Some people have met with a trainer once or twice, learned a few tips or techniques, and assume that now, months or years later, they can pick up right where they left off...*it's just like riding a bike*.

You know what this reminds me of? Statistics. "What?! That was a strange leap, Jim!" you're thinking. Not at all! Most people *think* they know what they are doing when it comes to statistics but, in reality, they really don't. Similarly, some people have taken a statistics course once or twice, probably many years ago, and assume that now, years later, they are as sharp and as wise when it comes to statistics as anyone else... *it's just like riding a bike.*

The truth of the matter is that most people don't really understand statistics (or fitness, for that matter) and, here's the kicker, those same people *didn't really understand statistics when they learned it in the first place.*

The very first time I took a statistics course I was a freshman at WashU. The class, Quantitative Business Analysis (affectionately called QBA), was a two-part class (QBA I and II) taught by a man by the name of Mike Gordinier. Professor Gordinier was a pro-gun, pro-foul language, usually grumpy, call-you-out-in-the-middle-of-class kind of professor who once publicly shamed a kid for talking during class *so* bad that you could cut the tension in the room with a knife (...I don't think I took a breath for ten minutes after Gordy was finished devouring the kid). I remember being afraid of saying anything stupid in that class because I was afraid Prof. Gordinier, sick of everyone's stupidity for existing in a world with no regard for statistics, would just shoot me. Thus, it might be surprising to you that I went on to serve as a Teaching Assistant for Prof. Gordinier for the next three years, although I am still not sure he ever knew my name. Knowing Mike, he probably just always thought of me as that Italian, Greek, or some-kind-of-Hispanic TA.

What might also be surprising is that on my first exam in QBA I, I scored a 67. That's 67 out of 100. You're thinking, "And *you* went on to TA for that class?" Trust me, I was *devastated.* I had never failed an exam before in my entire life, and I was convinced that this was my first taste of that stupid warning, "Look to your left, look to your right. One of you won't be here in a year." I was *so* disappointed. I had gone to class every day. I studied. I *thought* I understood the material. But the examination was *so* hard. Almost no one finished, the questions felt tricky, and every single question was a real-world application question, not some easy textbook example that I had been practicing in preparation for the exam.

Exam in hand, I went to the weekly Friday subsection that was taught by a fellow undergraduate TA (the role I would later fulfill). My TA was a delightful, brilliant person by the name of Jill Larson. Jill, it turns out, had also been my TA for Management 100 (along with the equally brilliant, awesome, and cowboy hat-wearing Shalin Tejani), the business class every freshman at WashU is required to take the first semester of freshman year. I remember walking into the room, sad and frumpy, and opening up to Jill.

"I failed the exam, Jill! I feel awful! I'm worried I'm not going to get an A in the class now! I don't know what to do," I rambled aloud.

"Wait, what? What did you get on the exam?" Jill asked with a strangely calm tone given my dramatic plea for help.

"A 67," I replied.

"A 67?!" she replied, somewhat shocked, "Jim, you're fine."

What?! Fine?! I wasn't fine! I just got a 67 out of 100 on an exam. What did she mean, "I was fine?" I remember being simultaneously miffed that Jill seemed so nonchalant about my strife but also a bit hopeful that she might somehow be right. Before I could say anything, Jill continued.

"Jim, the mean for the exam was something like 45. You actually had one of the top scores, and because the class is curved, that means you technically got an A," Jill said.

Well, this news was refreshing and welcome news. In high school, I never had a "curve" in any class. Sure, I knew what an average was, but we never really went into standard deviations and normal distributions in my high school math classes. Despite being in AP Calculus and a proud member of the Math Team (yeah, I own it), most of the math done by kids at my high school were things like, "If I date Brian for five weeks but don't do anything with him until after three weeks, how soon will I be pregnant?" or, "If Katie has a class at 11:00am but wants to hang out at the Stoner lot until 10:30am, how fast will she have to walk if she's wearing a Grateful Dead teddy bear backpack containing 20 pounds of books?" (The answers, in case you are wondering, are 1) Trick question. She's already pregnant, and 2) What's class?).

I left the subsection in much better spirits. I remember calling home and explaining everything Jill said to me to my parents who I'm sure were also relieved (although, to be fair, my parents had already told me that, "As long as I did my best, that's all that mattered"–my parents are amazing like that). I was relieved to know that I would not be failing statistics but also confronted a somewhat disconcerting (and rather ironic) realization: for being *in* a statistics class, I sure did not understand this whole statistics game, and that needed to change...stat.

Big Data, Big Business, & Why Statistics Matter Now More Than Ever

Most people hate statistics. I know this because I live statistics every single day of my life. As an academic, statistics are an important part of my job: we test our ideas and theories quantitatively and, with the help of statistics, provide some reassurance that any findings we discover are not purely based on dumb luck or chance. Sure, there are flaws and limitations with statistics just as there are flaws and limitations with anything, but statistics provide some degree of certainty or accuracy to a largely uncertain, chaotic world...and who doesn't want that?

Statistics were also an important part of my job even back in my consulting days in Los Angeles. As the Executive Director of the research institute I started with the consultancy's creator, I had the fun of dreaming up new training modules, testing their effectiveness (using statistics), and then making decisions about which modules should stay and which modules needed to go or needed to be changed for future testing. Now, let me point out that not many "soft skills" companies engage in this kind of data-based consulting (which is why people, usually engineers and scientists, often roll their eyes when the HR person comes in to talk about "feelings"). And, quite unfortunately, when it came time to bring in a new CEO of sorts to watch the house while our owner/creator was away on book tours and speaking engagements, our team was "blessed" with a gentleman for whom an entire tome of failed leadership practices could be written (...and I was one of the fortunate ones).

Howard, we shall call him for the sake of anonymity, had a very different philosophy on the role that statistics needed to play in business. Whereas I was focused on producing modules that, when put under the microscope, stood up to rigorous statistical testing with respect to effectiveness, Howard's approach was more, "Here are our existing modules. Find science that supports what we are *already* doing. Then we will say our approaches have been scientifically supported."

Um. No. That's not how science works.

Clearly this was not going to be a match made in heaven. I could not and would not, in good conscience, market our modules as "scientifically validated" without proper testing. This meant having control groups, experimental groups, appropriate sample sizes, statistical comparisons, etc. You know...science.

Needless to say, that guy didn't last long (thankfully), but it highlighted something quite striking: executives at some of the top companies, including this gentleman who had held very high positions at well-known companies, were completely apathetic when it came to statistics. Whether it was because Howard did not understand statistics or simply did not believe in their effectiveness, he was content having our consultants *tell* our clients our approaches were rooted in sound science without that actually being true. Not me.

The scary thing, however, is that Howard is not unique. Most undergraduate and MBA programs require students to take some form of statistics. In other words, *just about everyone* who has *ever* gone to business school should know statistics. However, it is often the case that otherwise brilliant business students somehow forget what they were taught in their marketing classes or conveniently forget to use statistics in their work.

"Statistics?!" they joke, "Who needs those?!"

My response: everyone.

If/when, on the very rare occasion, these business folks decide to incorporate statistics into their decision making, they often feel like the *one* class they took back in business school will be enough to guide them. To them, picking up statistics again *is just like riding a bike.*

However, the odds of that being true are typically *not* in their favor, so the rest of this chapter is a primer on what I think are the most useful, most accessible, and most easily applicable concepts from statistics that we, as marketers, should incorporate into our day-to-day work. As data becomes even easier to collect and data sets increase exponentially, the expectation that decisions will be data-driven is also likely to increase. In an ideal world, all of us (marketers and non-marketers alike) would make more decisions that incorporate statistics or logic inspired by statistics, but baby steps…baby steps.

In the previous chapter we spent a great deal of time talking about the importance of research and data collection to smart, sound decision-making. The current chapter is an addendum to that chapter: although you can certainly glean insights from making surface-level reviews of your research findings, that kind of primitive analysis barely scratches the surface of the rich treasure trove of insights awaiting you deep down in the data. Most people are too scared to explore this side of research or want to but simply don't know how or where to get started. Although it would be impossible to teach an entire statistics course in a single chapter, I can provide a refresher of the main ideas you should know to help you get started. Once you apply these concepts a few times you will find that the process gets easier and easier, which will allow you to become even more sophisticated in your analyses, trying out new tricks and skills…dare I say it…*just like riding a bike.*

Ways and Means: A Simple Refresher on Basic Statistics

As the opening example of this chapter illustrates, simply collecting data and drawing conclusions based on simple comparisons (e.g., 5.07 > 4.55, so the first option is "better") can be dangerous. At the heart of statistics is the idea that the world is a *somewhat* predictable place. In statistics, the most frequently used number to know whether or not your findings are "significant" is our old friend the "p-value." You remember him? The little guy who tells us if our data mean anything? Modern convention says that if $p < .05$ then our finding is "significant," and if p is between .05 and .10 then our finding is "marginally significant." Anything above .10 is considered statistically "insignificant," meaning there is no real difference between whatever it is we are comparing. Another way this is often stated is that when $p < .05$ your findings are only 5% likely to be untrue (stated differently, your results are 95% likely to be true), but this, it turns out, is actually a common misconception.

Let's talk about what the p-value is in plain English and in the simplest of possible terms. A basic scientific experiment comes down to testing whether or not there is a relationship between two (or more) things–e.g., gun laws and gun deaths, calorie intake and obesity, bank account size and partner attractiveness. The default position (a.k.a., the **null hypothesis**) is that no relationship exists between anything–the world is an entirely random place. If you have an idea about how two (or more) things might be related, well, congratulations! You have a **hypothesis**! Many hypotheses follow an if/then structure: "If states have more gun ownership restrictions then deaths should go down," "If a mouse consumes more calories then it will be more obese," "If people have a bigger bank account then their partners are likely to be more attractive." You run a study between two (or more) groups varying only *one* variable (i.e., the **independent variable**: number of gun laws, number of calories, bank account size) and then compare differences in a desired **dependent variable** (i.e., the outcome: number of gun deaths, obesity rate, partner attractiveness). After running the data through a statistical program, you will get a p-value churned out in the output. All the p-value is really telling you is *the probability you would obtain the data you just collected if the null hypothesis were true.* Or, stated more simply, the likelihood of the data turning out this way if the world were truly a random place (i.e., if the null hypothesis were true). That is why a p-value that is less then .05 would be remarkable: it's saying there is less than a 5% chance that this data would appear in a world where this is no relationship between the variables being studied.

It is important to note what the p-value does *not* say: the p-value is not the probability that your hypothesis is correct given your data. People get this wrong all the time. Many modern researchers advocate for the use of confidence intervals and other metrics in lieu of p-values, but given that p-values do provide a simple measure for whether or not a real difference is likely to exist, we will keep it around as the modern statisticians debate its potential substitute.

Oh, and as for the p-value's random 5/95% cutoff? Well, that's completely arbitrary. We could just as easily require statistical significance to be $p < .01$ or $p < .08$ or $p < .1892$. Essentially, the discipline of statistics is simply acknowledging that things are not going to be certain all the time, as that's not really how the world works. However, by capturing measures like averages, standard deviations, and p-values, we can explain the world better than just guessing or conducting rudimentary analyses.

Before we talk about statistical significance, let's start this refresher with a conversation about **means** or "averages" as you likely learned in grade school. A mean is simply the sum of several individual ratings or scores divided by the total number of ratings or scores being added together. So if John, George, Paul, and Ringo each have 22, 11, 5, and 15 guitars, respectively, the average number of guitars owned by the group is 13 ((22+11+5+14) / 4). Simple, right?

Two measures related to the mean are **variance** and **standard deviation**, which, it turns out, are also related to each other mathematically (variance = standard deviation^2). Both variance and standard deviation are simply measures of how much variation exists in the data making up the mean. From our guitar example, the variance winds up being 50 and the standard deviation is 7.07106. This probably means *nothing* to you, so let me explain. Imagine there is a second group of four different people–Benny, Björn, Agnetha, and Anni-Frid–who, among them, have 14, 12, 16, and 10 guitars, respectively. The mean number of guitars owned by this group is *also* 13 ((14+12+16+10) / 4), but the variance is 6.67 and the standard deviation is 2.58. This should help us understand how these numbers are valuable. Notice how, in the first group, the number of guitars owned varies wildly from person to person, with John having 22 guitars but Paul having only 5, a difference of 17. In the second group, each member has roughly the same number of guitars, with the greatest difference between the person with the most (Agnetha) and the person with the least (Anni-Frid) being 6. Thus, variance and standard deviation are important because they tell us the *distribution* of the data points. Although these two groups have the same average number of guitars, the ownership of guitars per each individual is quite different between the two groups, more spread out in the former and more uniform in the latter.

Another way in which variance and standard deviation are useful pertains to data and its *potential* to be misleading. Now, a common criticism from some people, usually people who are bad at statistics or math, is that, "Numbers lie," "Statistics are misleading," and that, "Data can be interpreted or massaged any way you want." These people often say this because they lack the knowledge or ability to identify questionable statistics or shoddy research methods. However, data need not be manipulated to be misleading; data can be messy, mistakes can be made during data collection, and weird things sometimes happen. But if you actually know how statistics work you can spot these anomalies before making any strategic decisions based on faulty data.

Here's an example. Let's say we have a third group of people–Bono, The Edge, Adam, and Larry–and, on average, they own 13 guitars as a group. Cool. If we were making decisions, we might consider this group to be similar to the two prior groups, as the other two groups also own 13 guitars on average. However, when we look at the variance and standard deviation of guitar ownership for this third group, we see that the variance is 545.33 and the standard deviation is 23.35. What?! How could this be? These strangely high numbers suggest something is wrong: the per-person guitar ownership in this third group is *anything* but uniform. When we look at the per-person data we see that The Edge owns 48 guitars, Bono owns 2 guitars, Adam owns 2 guitars, and Larry owns 0 guitars. This averages out to a group average of 13, but clearly The Edge is dominating guitar ownership while the other three only own a couple guitars (if any). Welcome to the idea of the **outlier** or a data point that is abnormally higher or lower than the majority of the other data points.

Outliers are problematic for several reasons, not least of which is the fact that they exert undue influence on the very measures we use to make important decisions (e.g., means). If we didn't know any better, we might have treated the previous three groups the same because their means were identical. However, the mean in the third group was strongly influenced by a single outlier. Without that one data point, the third group's average becomes 1.33 guitars, not quite as many as 13 guitars. Imagine spending millions of dollars on a guitar-themed campaign for that group in which only one of the four members is a guitar enthusiast (compared to the other groups where all four members are guitar fanatics). Outliers can be due to any number of reasons: a participant errs when making a rating, a coder errs when recording the data, or someone really is just *that* peculiar. Whatever the reason, outliers do *not* give us an accurate or representative picture of the world as it could be. Instead, outliers skew the results, results that would look much different if the outliers were not present. Wouldn't it be great if we could just get rid of outliers?

Brace yourself: you can. Sort of.

Before I go into a conversation about removing outliers, we need to have a serious conversation that takes us back to our conversation on ethics at the very beginning of this book. Eliminating or removing data is *not* something you should do for fun or for the purpose of obtaining the results you were hoping to get. Not only is that unethical, it also is not at all helpful to your success. If you analyze your data and find that people do not like the product you are selling, then manipulating your data to make it look like people *do* like your product is not going to make those people any more likely to buy your product. See what I mean? That said, if an outlier (or outliers) exist, then your data may not be a true reflection of the world as it is. In this instance, it may be appropriate and justified to remove the data because you are essentially removing a mistake. However, there is a *systematic* way to remove outliers from your data. You cannot just look at the data and say, "Oh, The Edge's data point is *way* out there; I'm getting rid of him!"

One rather popular way to remove outliers was (and still is in many circles) a general rule-of-thumb in which you simply look at your data, look at data points that fall more than two deviations above or below the mean, and remove those points. If you wanted to be even *more* conservative, you could limit removal to points only more/less than *three* standard deviations away from the mean. Maybe you have heard of this?

Well, forget about it.

One (rather obvious) limitation with that rule-of-thumb is that means and standard deviations are *affected* by outliers. The third group in the previous guitar example had one person with 48 guitars, which led to a really high variance (545.33) and standard deviation (23.35). By following the old rule-of-thumb of the "Mean +/- 2 x Standard Deviation," we would have 13 +/- 2 x 23.35 = -34.6 to 59.7 is an acceptable range of data: having 48 guitars is no outlier in this case. Lest you think this is a *good* thing because it is more conservative with respect to data removal, keep in mind two things: 1) you are basing decisions off skewed data, and 2) this approach can also lead to including other outliers that should not be included.

In a dramatic example of this last point, let's consider *one* final guitar-owning group: the Duggar family. If you are unfamiliar, the Duggar family is an American family with 19 kids who, because of their superstar fertility, got their own television show because that's what American television has come to. Also, they are from Arkansas (because of course they are), the father's name is Jim Bob (because of course it is), and they have a billion children because, "Jesus told [them] to" (because of course he did). Incidentally, Jesus also told me not to watch their show, and I am thankful for that every day of my life.

So, continuing with our example…let's say each of the 19 Duggar kids were given guitars so that the might one day create a family band like the Partridge family or the von Trapp family. The guitars were distributed as follows: 1,1, 1, 1, 1, 2, 2, 2, 2, 3, 3, 3, 4, 4, 4, 5, 500, 680, 999. If you do the math, you'll see that the mean number of guitars is 116.74, the standard deviation is 283.98, which makes our range of acceptable data points (using a +/- 2 standard deviations rule) -451.22 to 684.70. For that low cutoff, well, we're not expecting *negative* guitars, so that's good news. For the high cutoff, it would seem that only 999 is considered an outlier despite the fact that 500 and 680 are *awfully* higher than most of the other data points. Why? Well, that 999 skewed the mean higher and increased the standard deviation size, which means the range of acceptable data points became much larger (despite some of the numbers really being silly…*cough* like having 19 children).

There is an alternative approach, however, one that is becoming increasingly preferred (despite the fact that the idea originated in the 1800s). Remember the concept of a **median**? Like a mean, a median is a measure of central tendency, but unlike the mean, the median is easier to determine and a lot more fun to figure out. To find a median you simply rank your data in order, count from left or right until you get to the middle of your results, and then the number in the middle (or between the two numbers if you have an even number of data points) is the median. Even monkeys can do that kind of math. (A sexier, more sophisticated way to do that is to take your sample size, add one to it, divide that sum by two, and then count to that number from the beginning or end of your data set and you'll find yourself at the middle…but only whip this out when you're *really* trying to impress someone). Unlike a mean, a median is *not* as sensitive to the value of an outlier and, as such, is often considered to be a better choice for dealing with outliers.

The alternative approach to identifying outliers involves using the **median absolute deviation** (a.k.a. MAD, the first acronym of this book that is *not* a Jim original), which provides information about the variability within a data set without being skewed by outliers. The equation is only slightly scary and looks like this:

$$MAD = b * M_i\left(\left|\,x_i - M_j*(x_j)\,\right|\right)$$

Non-math people are probably freaking out right now, but it's really not too complicated. Forget the equation–I'll take you through a step-by-step example:

Consider the Duggar data in which each of the 19 kids owns a number of guitars:
1,1, 1, 1, 1, 2, 2, 2, 2, 3, 3, 3, 4, 4, 4, 5, 500, 680, 999

Let's find the median of the original data:
(n + 1) / 2 where n = sample size, so… (19 + 1) / 2 = 10
Counting 10 from the left or right of our ordered data puts us at 3
Thus, the median is 3

Now we subtract the median from every number in our data set:
1-3, 1-3, 1-3, 1-3, 1-3, 2-3, 2-3, 2-3, 2-3, 3-3, 3-3, 3-3, 4-3, 4-3, 4-3, 5-3, 500-3, 680-3, 999-3
which gives us…
-2, -2, -2, -2, -2, -1, -1, -1, -1, 0, 0, 0, 1, 1, 1, 2, 497, 677, 996

We take the absolute value of those numbers and rank the new values in order:
0, 0, 0, 1, 1, 1, 1, 1, 1, 2, 2, 2, 2, 2, 2, 497, 677, 996

We find the "new" median of this series:
Counting 10 from the left or right of our ordered data puts us at 1
Thus, the "new" median is 1

Multiply the "new" median by the constant *b* (which = 1.4826) to obtain the MAD:
The constant *b* = 1.4826 assumes a normal distribution of data
New Mean * *b* = 1 * 1.4826 = 1.4826
So our MAD = 1.4826

Now, the penultimate step to obtain our cutoff points is the *only* area of subjectivity:
Choose a factor of 3 for a truly "conservative" test
Choose a factor of 2.5 for a "moderately conservative" test
Choose a factor of 2 for a "poorly conservative" test

My advice: it's always best to be as conservative as possible when removing outliers. You may find that it doesn't matter, that the outliers are *so* large than any level of conservativeness eliminates them, but make it a tough standard as opposed to a convenient one. So…we'll go with a factor of 3 here.

Now for the final step:
The equation for the cutoff: (Original Median) +/- (The Factor You Just Chose) * (MAD)
For our example, this gives us: 1 +/- (3)*(1.4826) = -3.4478 < x < 5.4478

The range of acceptable data from the median absolute deviation approach suggests that anything about 5.4478 is an outlier. Intuitively, this makes sense, when the majority of our data points consists of 1s, 2s, 3s, 4s, and 5s, it *is* weird to have the oddly high numbers (especially when it comes to guitar ownership). Whereas the old approach only excluded 999, the newer approach also removes 500 and 680 and, in doing so, likely provides a more accurate picture of what is really happening in the real world. Don't forget: this approach excluded these three values using the most *conservative* factor.

One final caveat for data with respect to outliers: just because a number is abnormally high or abnormally low does not *always* mean it is incorrect or an outlier. Context *does* matter. If you are looking at the ages of people in a university classroom, chances are you will get a lot of 18s, 19s, 20s, and 21s. If you see a 1,000, chances are someone either made a mistake or you have a ghost in your class. However, if you see a 52, it could be a mistake *or* it could be someone who returned to finish a college degree later in life. In short, use your brain, avoid eliminating data whenever possible, and if you have to do it make sure 1) you do it correctly using the skills I just taught you, and 2) you note that you removed outliers and present how the analyses changed with/without those outliers in the mix.

Means and medians. Variances and standard deviations. Sample sizes and outliers. There are the basics and, together, these values provide a nice summary of the data, a snapshot of what the world might be like. However, we want to go a step further than just seeing a still snapshot of the world: we want to know if what we are seeing is truly the reality, and to do that we pit means against each other, judo wrestler style, to see if one is really bigger than the other or not.

Significant Others: Why 132 May Not Be "Different" From 102

Once we know for sure that our data is accurate and free of any mistakes, coding errors, or outliers unfairly skewing the data, we can begin conducting some useful comparisons, comparisons that make life worth living. As the opening example illustrated, it seemed like people believed Orange Theory Fitness (HIIT training) to be more effective than Crossfit (injury training) which is more effective than SoulCycle (spinning). However, we discussed that trying to make predictions for an *entire* population based on just a smaller sample of that group means that there is *some* possibility that are samples' numbers will not be exactly representative of the entire group. Enter statistical testing!

When we are equipped with means, sample sizes, and standard deviations we can compare different groups and know, with fairly good certainty, that they are or are not *truly* different from one another. There's a bunch of other "fun" stuff that goes into play–assumptions regarding sample independence, distribution type, representativeness and randomness of the samples–but we are going to keep it simple in this book. My goal is to teach you skills that will be useful for you in your job right now, but if you are interested in theory and diving in a bit deeper, well, a Ph.D. may be in your future!

So let's use our fitness perceptions example to illustrate how this all works. We know that 100 people completed a survey in which they were asked to rate their perceived effectiveness of three different workouts: SoulCycle, Orange Theory Fitness, and Crossfit. Based on their responses, we obtained the following data:

	Mean Effectiveness Rating	Standard Deviation
SoulCycle	4.55	1.06
Orange Theory Fitness	5.07	1.31
Crossfit	4.76	1.29

Just looking at the means of the three fitness options suggests a clear order when it comes to perceived effectiveness: Orange Theory, Crossfit, and SoulCycle. However, remember that this is based on us asking just a handful of people (n = 100). The standard deviations suggest that there's some variability with respect to perceived effectiveness within the sample, which suggests that this variability will also be present in the larger population. If that variability is large, well, there's a *chance* that our means actually don't differ all that much (i.e., there's a lot of overlap between the possible values for the fitness options' perceived effectiveness). If the variability is very small (i.e., most ratings are very close to the mean) and the means are drastically different from one another, well, it's more likely that any difference between the means is real and is likely to remain so at the population level.

To know whether the means differ from one another, in general, we can conduct a Within-Subjects comparison (as all the values come from the same sample) to get an overall significance level of $F(2,198) = 5.58$, $p < .004$. Comparing the means in pairs, we find a significant difference between Orange Theory and SoulCycle ($F(1,99) = 12.23$, $p < .001$), which isn't particularly surprising since the difference between those two means is the largest. When we compare Orange Theory and Crossfit, we get a marginal difference ($F(1,99) = 3.24$, $p = .08$), suggesting that the difference between Orange Theory and Crossfit might actually be there but is not as strong as the difference between Orange Theory and SoulCycle. When we compare SoulCycle and Crossfit, we no significant difference ($F(1,99) = 2.07, p = .15$), which translates to, "In the minds of consumers, there is *no* perceived difference between the effectiveness of SoulCycle and Crossfit."

If you are a huge nerd like I am, here's where things can get fun: using the data, we can see if the perceptions of effectiveness vary by other factors. Say, for example, we believe that women might find SoulCycle to be *more* effective than men. We can test this. Maybe we think effectiveness perceptions vary by age (e.g., older people perceive these workouts as less effective than the trendy youngsters). Maybe there's a difference based on familiarity or based on whether people have actually *tried* these different workouts.

I shall keep you in suspense no longer. It turns out that there is no difference between men and women with respect to SoulCycle's perceived effectiveness (M_{men} = 4.48 v. M_{women} = 4.64, p = .46), Orange Theory's perceived effectiveness (in fact, the means were almost identical: M_{men} = 5.069 v. M_{women} = 5.071, p = 1.0), or even Crossfit's perceived effectiveness (M_{men} = 4.62 v. M_{women} = 4.95, p = .21). Age had no effect on perceived effectiveness of any workout option. And, not surprisingly, people who had actually tried SoulCycle thought it was more effective than people who had not (M_{Tried} = 4.91 v. $M_{NeverTried}$ = 4.36, p < .01). The same was true for Orange Theory (M_{Tried} = 5.91 v. $M_{NeverTried}$ = 4.66, p < .001) and Crossfit (M_{men} = 5.24 v. M_{women} = 4.60, p < .03).

What does this suggest from a marketing strategy perspective? Well, a few things. For starters, people, in general, perceive Orange Theory Fitness to be the most effective workout when compared to SoulCycle and Crossfit. That's a solid finding that Orange Theory could use in its marketing messages. Beyond this, we see that people do not perceive a real difference between Crossfit and SoulCycle with respect to effectiveness. Thus, if marketing managers at either company were trying to steal share from the other (i.e., selected Others' Customers as their Prospective Audience, they would need to launch a campaign that would shift these effectiveness perceptions to the point of an actual difference in the minds of customers. The lack of a gender difference in effectiveness suggests that the marketing messages need not be differentiated by gender. However, the most exciting finding of all (in my opinion) is the fact that people who have *tried* these classes perceive them as being significantly more effective than people who have not. What does this suggest? Free trials! Get people in, get them working out, get them hooked. SoulCycle offers free cycling shoes and a discounted rate for your first class–I suppose that's a start–but anything that can get people in the door, sampling the experience, and sweating is more likely to make them perceive your fitness offering as effective.

See how magical statistics can be? Just by collecting some simple data and conducting some rather straightforward comparisons, we now have some strategic ideas that can help increase value to our customers and, in doing so, value to our company. If our customers feel like our service is more effective and come engage with us more frequently, they will be healthier, more satisfied, and more loyal customers...and will fit into their pants better than ever before.

Being Anal About Analyses: The Right Kind of Test for Your Data

I am deliberately avoiding going into specifics on theory, assumptions, and other details because I want to present the simplest, most useful discussion I can for the broadest possible audience, math lovers and math haters alike. This may infuriate any statistician reading this book, but I workout a lot, so chances are good I could take out that statistician if need be (#Brofessor). Thus, we will continue with this simpler, more parsimonious explanation of stats.

For all the details we are excluding for simplicity, there is one detail definitely worth including: choosing the right kind of statistical test for your research question. It turns out that not all statistical tests are created equal and, unfortunately, cannot be applied across *all* data sets in *every* situation. If only the world were simpler! In this section, I'll take you through a few of the simple considerations you should bear in mind when determining which test is appropriate for you.

One consideration involves your sample itself. There exist two broad types of study designs: **Between Subject** designs and **Within Subject** designs. Between subject designs compare groups of people who are *different* from one another in some aspect. This could be gender, it could be that one group uses your product and the other doesn't, it could be that one group listed that they are aware of your brand and another group did not. The point is that you are comparing the same questions between two (or more) *different* groups of people. Within Subject designs, on the other hand, involve comparing data *within* the same group of people or, stated differently, comparing one piece of data someone provided with another piece of data that same person also provided. Examples of this include testing someone prior to using your product and then testing them again after. If SoulCycle asked users to rate their fitness level before working out and then again after working out and compared these two values statistically, this would be a within-subject comparison. The same is true for asking one sample to rate the effectiveness of three different fitness options on the same effectiveness scale (which we did earlier). The difference is that the data points in the within-subjects design all have one thing in common: the same person is providing all the data. This, of course, means that the data points aren't exactly "independent"–they are tied to the same person and, as such, a test needs to accommodate for this.

Another consideration involves whether your independent variables (the things you are manipulating or measuring) and your dependent variables (the outcome you are measuring) are **categorical, ordinal,** or **continuous (or interval) variables**. Categorical variables represent distinct buckets or "categories" like yes/no, male/female, Democrat/Republican/Independent/No Party. Ordinal variables are like categorical variables except the categories have some sort of order to them (e.g., highest level of school completed: high school, associate's degree, undergrad, graduate school, Ph.D.). Continuous variables represent concepts that can be measured on some scale that implies order like age, level of satisfaction, or income level as long as the interval between each possible option is the same. Certain tests are better for certain combinations of independent and dependent variables based on their type. If you have a categorical independent variable and a continuous dependent variable, well, we can do a good, ol'-fashion independent sample t-test or an ANOVA (analysis of variance) in a stats program like SPSS. If you have a continuous independent variable and a continuous dependent variable, you'll want to do a simple correlation or regression analysis. Luckily, there are algorithmic charts abound on the interwebs that will steer you in the right direction if you are not sure which test would be appropriate for your study design.

One more important reminder to include regarding the right kind of test for the right kind of study design is the right kind of *interpretation* of your results. Science works like this: you have Group A and Group B. Group A is the control group—we don't do anything special to them—they just watch our commercial for Kool-Aid that features the brand's logo for 5 seconds at the end. Group B is the experimental group—we do something special to them, but only *one* thing: we show them the same Kool-Aid commercial but when the logo appears for 5 seconds we also play a 5 second jingle. Aside from the jingle, we keep everything else the same between the two groups. What we want to know is whether or not the jingle significantly increases the effectiveness of the commercial with respect to measures like ability to recall the information in the commercial, likelihood to buy Kool-Aid, and how much people are willing to pay. If there's a significant difference between the two groups, we can be reasonably assured that the jingle *does* make a difference and can make a decision on whether or not to include it accordingly. If we want to be *real* sticklers about things we might even include a *third* condition to test whether *any* noise during that five seconds produces the same result as the jingle (i.e., it's not uniquely the jingle that is causing the difference but hearing sound, in general), but that's Honors-level work. Thus, this kind of science leads us more to **causal** reasoning: we can be somewhat certain that the presence of the jingle (or sound) during the display of the logo is what *causes* greater recall or a higher willingness to pay for whatever winds up being significantly higher.

Then there's what we call **correlation**. Correlation simply means that two variables move together but, and here's the important part, *we cannot be sure which variable causes the other one to move.* The only thing correlation reveals is that there is a relationship between two variables. For example, if we were to look at a survey of registered voters and compare their score on a continuous measure of education (e.g., number of years of formal schooling) with their level of political leanings (e.g., a continuous measure from extremely liberal to extremely conservative), which I did during the 2016 American presidential election, you might find a significant relationship between the two such that the fewer years of formal education you have the more conservative you tend to be (which is exactly what the data showed). Now, this does *not* mean that there are not highly educated Republicans; there certainly are. What it means is that, on average, the more educated you are (as measured by number of years in school) the more liberal you tend to be. However, we could flip this and say the more liberal you are the more likely you are to stay in school for a long time. We cannot be sure of which one causes the other and, furthermore, there may even be a third variable that affects *both* (e.g., perhaps parental political leaning is significantly correlated with years in school and a child's political leaning). It is wrong and dangerous to make causal statements about correlational data because the only thing correlational data tell us is that two variables are related. Incidentally, most neuroscientific data is correlational in nature (with one exception being Transcranial Magnetic Stimulation in which parts of the brain are essentially "shut off" to see how thoughts or behaviors are affected), so the next time you read a "news" story saying that X part of the brain does Y, ignore it (it's probably wrong) and just read the comics instead.

Quantitative v. Qualitative Revisited: Coding Qualitative Data

Some of you, probably the most talkative of the bunch, might be feeling a bit disheartened right about now. Why? Well, you are the kind of people who love interviews, focus groups, and other qualitative approaches to collecting data. In the previous chapter we talked about how the best insights come from an ideal blend of quantitative *and* qualitative data. I promise I am not abandoning my qualitative friends in their time of need. No, instead, I am about to build a bridge between these islands, one full of quant nerds with their pocket protectors and the other full of qualitative softies with their party platter of cheeses and planned ice breakers.

Here's the bridge: just as quantitative data can be described in everyday, meaningful language, so, too, can qualitative data be described in numbers! We tend to refer to this as **coding**, the process in which verbal responses are transformed into numbers. What you choose to code from interviews, focus groups, and other qualitative data is entirely up to you, but what follows are some common examples.

Content coding involves determining a rule of some kind, key words to look for, key content worth noting in the individual responses that can be counted and transformed into numbers. Say, for example, you are conducting a study on shopping preferences around the holidays, and you ask people about their shopping behaviors. You theorize that some people think of holiday shopping as an activity done with others (e.g., "We get in line early and we spend the entire day looking for deals.") while some people focus on themselves (e.g., "I have a hard time deciding what I want to get, but I shop for days."). As such, one way to test this is to go through the free responses and count up the number of times someone uses a collective pronoun (e.g., "we") v. a singular pronoun (e.g., "I"). Another example might be coding for positive words v. negative words, the number of times your brand or product name appears in responses (awareness), or some combination of both. If you are not yet familiar with the =COUNTIF function in Excel, I suggest you do some quick Googling. It will change your life.

Another consideration with respect to qualitative data is to capture the *length* of a response as measured by **word count** and/or **character count**. This may seem peculiar, but consider this idea from a meta level: people willing to write *more* likely have a different relationship with your company or your product than people who say nothing or who keep their answers brief. That's informative unto itself, but we can also use this information to split our samples based on how "involved" they were in providing feedback to see if any significant differences emerge for other variables of interest. Thankfully, Excel has a function for character count, as well =LEN, and a slightly more complicated one for word count (but it exists!).

Another sort of "hybrid" qualitative/quantitative approach is capturing the **response time** individuals spend on survey questions. Response time is clearly a quantitative measure, typically measured to the second or millisecond, and is easily captured using any online data-gathering resource. Typically, the more time spent on a question, the more engaged the participant is or the more thought a participant is putting into the question. This, of course, is not always true: sometimes people get distracted while completing a question, which will increase his/her response time without really meaning they were any more involved or engaged with that particular question. Most of that will get washed out in the randomization and averaging inherent in statistics, but it is something of which to be aware.

There are two major things to keep in mind with respect to all this coding business: 1) determine the rules before you start coding, and 2) have multiple coders (who are blind to the study's purpose) code the data.

For the first part, it's a good idea to have a theory or prediction going into any research study. Post hoc predictions are always a bit tricky (i.e., essentially looking at the data after it has been collected and then backwards engineering to guess what *might* be happening, if anything). That is *not* to say that some good science has not been produced from this latter approach–it just seems a little less sophisticated to some than developing a strong theory up front, articulating your predictions, and testing those predictions. The reason it's a good idea to determine the rules *before* you start coding is that it is a bit more conservative: you are cutting the shape of the hole and then seeing if the pegs fit through it or not as opposed to looking at the pegs first and then customizing a hole so that all the pegs fit the way you want them to. If you pursue the latter approach, you will likely find *something*, but whatever that something is is likely to be atheoretical and, as such, not really helpful in advancing our understanding of the world at large. It is okay to compare data based on gender, age, and other demographics after the fact and to test the relationships between variables that you may be inspired by based on the data, but the point here is to have an idea going into the study as opposed to a plan to data mine after data has been collected to figure out your theory. One disclaimer here: this approach refers primarily to true experiments–if you are collecting data about your customers for the sake of learning more about them (i.e., more descriptive than experimental), this rule can be relaxed a bit.

For the second part, coding can be a bit subjective. Words considered to be "good" or "bad" vary from person to person. People might make mistakes when counting certain words manually as opposed to using Excel (or might make a coding error in Excel that affects results). Typically, two or three coders who are blind to the study and its hypotheses (i.e., they do not know what the study is about or what predictions have been made about how various variables might be related). So, here's the rather simple solution: have separate coders code the data and then compare the data for consistency. The comparison is simply a correlation (typically denoted using what we call Cronbach's alpha: α), that we hope is high and significant, as this means our coders were fairly similar in their coding of the data. If our coders' data comes back with a low correlation, well, chances are something is off. If the data comes back highly correlated among our various coders, then we can be reasonably assured that two or three separate people using the same guidelines found pretty much the same things within the data. That's a good thing. This is another reason it is important to delineate the coding rules early and clearly: these guidelines are what your coders will use to code your data–if they are unclear or ambiguous, the chance of there being high inter-coder reliability is pretty slim.

Big Kid Analysis: Excel is for Amateurs, SPSS is for Pros

The final point I want to make about statistics and data analysis has to do with some rather useful techniques that may change your life in ways you could have never imagined! Okay, that might be overselling it just a bit, but I promise you that the following tips will change the way you analyze your data and, as a result, will produce *meaningful* marketing implications that you will put into practice.

Here's the thing: for all this talk of means comparisons and significance testing, we can step back and ask ourselves, "So what? Who cares? What does this do to help me and my business?" Fair question, right? We talked about some of the strategic insights that can be gleaned from knowing groups either differ significantly or do not, whether different variables are correlated or are not, and so on, but surely there must be something more?

There is.

In academia, it is not simply enough to show that two groups are "significantly different" from one another. If you turned in a paper saying, "People who have tried SoulCycle are more likely to say SoulCycle is effective than people who have not tried SoulCycle," the editor will promptly desk reject your paper, send it back to you, and say, "You're an idiot!" Editors are nice like that. Instead, what we concern ourselves with in academia is the *why*. *Why* are people who have tried SoulCycle more likely to say that it is effective? What is the *process*? This is critically important because once we know the process, we know what we can tweak, fix, improve, or change to achieve a particular end result.

Let me give you an example. Say we are doing a consulting project for a small mom and pop coffee shop (simply named "Mom & Pop's Delicious Coffee Shop") who wants to know whether they should bus the tables or require patrons to return their own cups and silverware and throw their own trash away. This seems like a simple, arbitrary decision, but it would be costly and time-consuming for the employees to have to continually bus tables, which may make that service more of a burden than a blessing. So our independent variable (the thing we are manipulating or changing between conditions) involves having bussing or not and our dependent variable (the outcome we want to know changes or not depending on how the independent variable is manipulated) is a measure of satisfaction. If we were looking for a simple causal relationship (a.k.a. if we were being basic), then seeing if $X \rightarrow Z$ or "bussing tables" $\rightarrow$ "higher satisfaction" would be all we need to show. However, let's take it a step further and theorize *why* or *how* bussing tables might lead to greater satisfaction. Maybe it makes customers feel they are cared about? Maybe it is just a matter of convenience? Maybe it makes the food be perceived as tasting better? So instead of $X \rightarrow Z$, now we have $X \rightarrow Y \rightarrow Z$ where Y is the mysterious "causal" link between bussing tables and satisfaction. This is what we refer to as **mediation**. In this case, Y might mediate the relationship between X and Z. Statistically, we test this model and find that there *is* a significant link from "bussing the table" to "customers feeling cared about" which, in turn, increases their "perceived level of satisfaction." The other potential mediators, convenience and food taste, are not significant. This is great news because now we know something about how bussing affects satisfaction: customers feel *cared* about. Perhaps figuring out other small touches to make customers feel cared about will also enhance satisfaction. Behold, the power of mediation.

A related concept is that of **moderation**. Whereas mediation can be thought of as answering the *how* or *why*, the path from beginning to end, moderation can be thought of as pressing **BOLD** on your keyboard or, in some instances, turning bold *off*. In other words, moderation occurs when the introduction of a new variable makes a previously documented effect stronger *or* makes that effect go away. I'll give you an example from some of my academic research. In a project I have with my colleagues Jenny Olson and Carolyn Yoon, we knew that making people feel socially excluded would lead them to seek ways to reestablish social bonds with other people. That effect had been documented for decades in different ways by researchers around the world. Our idea was that products with anthropomorphic (i.e., humanlike) features might fill that void and reduce or mitigate the need for individuals to seek out interpersonal interaction. Sure enough, we found that if socially excluded participants engaged with an anthropomorphized product following their exclusion experience, they were significantly less likely to seek out real people to engage than socially excluded people *not* given anthropomorphized products. Creepy, right? Welcome to 2016 when everything talks to you like a human (Right, Siri?).

However, we further hypothesized that this effect was likely an automatic effect happening at a level beneath conscious awareness. It was not as if people were thinking, "I'm lonely, but here's this non-living product that sort of looks like a human. I'll choose this instead!" So we wanted to see if making participants aware that the anthropomorphized product was not *actually* alive would mitigate or eliminate the ability for it to fulfill social needs. Sure enough, making the fact that the humanized product was, indeed, humanlike but *not* actually alive eliminated the effect. In other words, explicit knowledge of the anthropomorphization *moderated* the prior effect.

Moderation and mediation are important for two reasons. One, we live in a complicated world where many different variables are interconnected and affect one another. While knowing that two variables interact in some way is helpful, what is even more useful is knowing *why* one variable influences another or the process by which this happens. Another reason moderation and mediation are useful is that, once we know how variables are related and have a simplified model of the world around us, we then know how tinkering with one variable might affect other variables. The strategic implications of this idea are endless.

And my last piece of good news: these mediation and moderation processes are not too difficult to do, but I have good news and bad news. Bad news: you are going to have to graduate from the comforts of Excel. Good news: you get to try to a big-kid version of Excel known as SPSS. Within SPSS you can also add a feature called PROCESS, which was developed by Andrew Hayes, a brilliant professor at The Ohio State University. Process allows you to enter your variables into different model designs (see Andrew's website for the PROCESS macro and the related model templates) to test the relationships among variables in very, very simple ways. Now, it is very easy to get lost in the rabbit hole of testing every possible combination of variables in post-hoc survey analyses, but remember what we talked about earlier: sophisticated scientists have their theories going *into* a study. It is okay to test relationships you might dream up after the fact, but to the best of your ability, always try to be proactive and smart when it comes to your statistical testing as opposed to reactive. People will like you more for it.

Phew. That was quite the statistical review! The only other topic I thought about including (but will not for the sake of time) is a note on Bayesian statistics, a rather hot topic in recent years. Now, I could go on and tell you how Bayesian is my bae, but let's just end our statistics review with the idea of **ABCD**: always be collecting data. As you go about your day, dream up a priori predictions about how the world works, go out and test those predictions, and then update your original thinking based on what feedback you get from testing those ideas out in the world, and dream up new predictions–*that* is an effective way to incorporate statistics in your everyday life…and, even though you didn't realize it, but I actually just taught you the philosophy behind Bayesian statistics in this final paragraph. Boom. This math lab just exploded, so let's move on to more creative topics, shall we?

* * *

When I started this chapter I came down pretty hard on SoulCycle. Now, of course, you know that my eye-rolling reaction to SoulCycle and its patrons may stem largely from a deeply-rooted psychological void when it comes to my bike-riding inadequacies. This may be the very reason that I prefer fitness offerings like Orange Theory and Barry's Bootcamp to a place like SoulCycle, a bias that some might worry leads me to favor these HIIT-focused options over the spinning sensation that is SoulCycle.

However, like any good marketer, I ran a quick survey of folks representing the target market for elite fitness classes and found that, indeed, *most* people perceive Orange Theory as being a more effective fitness offering than SoulCycle and Crossfit (marginally so in the latter comparison). Biased though I may be, the numbers do not lie.

I cannot stress to you enough the *power* that statistics can bring to you and your integrated marketing campaign. A team of six people working on the same project can look at a research survey's findings and find six different "most surprising" parts, six different "most frequent" themes, and six different "strongest consumer needs." There is a bit of subjectivity in these interpretations, which can stall a team, lead to intragroup debates, and even steer a campaign in the wrong direction for the wrong reasons.

However, quantifiable data provides a more objective solution. The data can speak for themselves. And, thanks to statistics, the data can tell us what is *truly* different, what *really* stands out, and even *how* the world works with respect to the variables that matter to us, our customers, and our combined mutual value.

To be clear, any information from research is better than no information at all. Even making decisions without putting data through statistical analyses would likely be helpful and productive than not incorporating any quantifiable information into our decision-making. However, statistics help us make even better decisions and help us recognize missed opportunities, spurious relationships we believe are present (but are not), and other insights that a mere simple review of the data would not reveal.

Just as it is difficult and unwise to pick a fight with the largest guy at the local Crossfit box, it is equally as foolish to try to pick a fight with someone who not only has collected qualitative and quantitative research data but who has also put that data through statistical analyses to shed light on what that data is actually saying. Unless you, too, have analyzed the data, know the research methodology, and can speak intelligently about the findings (or lack of findings), there is going to be a very clear winner in a showdown between the person with evidence to back up his/her ideas and the person who does not.

Now is probably a good time to share with you a story that I do not share with many people: there was a time in my life that I was *scared* of going to a gym. I was no athlete growing up—I was a mathlete, the smart, nerdy kid who did band, newspaper, theatre, Model UN, etc. I was skinny and would have blown away on strong, windy days had my genetically-huge forehead not been there to hold me down. Even my freshman year at WashU when I went to the gym with a group of guys from my floor, I had *no* idea what I was doing, and I was afraid that I would make an absolute fool of myself. I never went back to the gym while at WashU.

It wasn't until years later, when I was living in Los Angeles, that I finally got up the nerve to start going to the gym. This was both the best and the worst place to start working out: the best because you *had* to (there's an ordinance that if you do not look a certain way you get kicked out of LA...kidding...sort of) and the worst because everyone is a fitness model. I am certain that I was probably still nervous and unsure of myself, but I have gone for so long now and am so comfortable with working out that it all seems like a distant blur to me. I just had to do it. I had to start somewhere, and now I don't even think twice about it.

Statistics is just like working out. You want to see results, but when you are first beginning, you don't even know where to start. You are afraid you won't know what to do. You are scared that other people are going to judge you for looking silly or making a mistake. So you just don't even try. Then, at some point, you realize the only way to improve yourself is to actually take a risk and put yourself out there and try. The first time might be a bit shaky, but over time you get the hang of it and feel more confident in your abilities. You will even come to discover that those typical beefcake gym-goers are not thinking twice about what it is you are doing; instead, they are just happy for you that you have chosen to show up. Everyone starts somewhere.

So no, statistics is *not* just like riding a bike. Statistics is like working out: it can be painful, sometimes you want to skip it, but you know that doing it is much better for you and will pay off in the long run. You will be stronger for having done it. People who don't do it will be impressed that you do. And while you may not always achieve the results that you want, you can always go back, try new techniques, and see if that leads to improvements.

It's a cycle. Not a SoulCycle...a StatsCycle.

What if... *Giving SoulCycle a Real Soul*

In an era of Facebook and Instagram, selfies are certainly a "thing." However, a special subset of selfies, the "workout selfie" (which is related to the "shirtless selfie"), is in a certain low class of its own. While I think it is certainly helpful to keep track of your fitness progress whatever your goals may be, I have never understood why *sharing* that workout picture with the world was necessary for anyone. One obvious explanation (that is probably true in most instances), is that the selfie is an esteem booster for people who need it. Some people excel at work to feel good, some people volunteer and help others to feel good...others pose in front of gym mirrors and take photos to garner "Likes" and hearts on social media.

I have seen these people in the gym. I have seen these people on Instagram. God bless 'em. But here's the thing: a *lot* of people probably work out for self-serving purposes, just not everyone feels the need to blast this information online. What if gyms and fitness companies could help these wayward, selfish, selfie-taking souls actually turn their workout into something that could benefit others, as well? What if SoulCycle actually *had* a real soul?

I did a little digging and found that SoulCycle *does* actually have a charitable component. The program, Soul Charity, claims to have raised over $2 million to support local charities since 2007 on SoulCycle's very own website (despite the fact that the page has not been updated since 2014 as of this book's writing). Here's the kicker: according to SoulCycle the way the program works is that a partnering organization has to sell bikes for the charity class, handle all the promotions, and coordinate all the RSVPs. Basically SoulCycle just lets you use their bikes and space while you do all the heavy lifting. How kind and charitable!

While I think charity of *any* kind is awesome, SoulCycle could *really* step up its charitable efforts, which 1) would allow it to play on its unique branding, specifically the word "soul," and 2) would help the rest of us change our perception about the company and the kind of annoying people who go there. Let's revamp SoulCycle's charitable strategy to fit in with its branding.

First, as a part of every new SoulCycle location opening, a certain number of stationary bikes are donated to area schools for fitness purposes. The initiative could be couched in SoulCycle's efforts to get young people thinking about how fitness can be fun while also helping achieve positive PR and awareness from adults affiliated with the schools, including parents, teachers, and people watching on the news or reading about the initiative in the local newspaper. SoulCycle also has every reason to do this because by teaching kids about the joy and fun of cycling to keep fit, they are potentially creating lifetime customers (and before anyone gets all preachy about a fitness company marketing to children in schools let's keep in mind that Coca-Cola and Pepsi have infiltrated schools *for years* with no obvious health benefits to kids, so...relax).

Second, SoulCycle should consider donating a percentage of its earnings each year to a charitable organization that is relevant to the company. Whether this is a charity organization that gives bikes to underprivileged children or to people without cars so they can get to work, an organization that fights diseases afflicting the young female demographic SoulCycle attracts, or a community of people like those needing wheel-based assistive devices for mobility, SoulCycle *can* and *should* contribute to an organization as it would most certainly bring more positive returns to the company, its customers, and so many appreciative people on the receiving end of the charitable giving.

Third, to motivate the SoulCyclists themselves, SoulCycle could consider another integrated component this time using social media. In a program called the "Share Your Soul" project, SoulCycle customers could be incentivized to go out of their way to do something good for someone else. Whether something as simple as buying a stranger's cup of coffee or even their $1,000 SoulCycle class that day or something as comprehensive as starting their own charitable organization or fundraiser for another person facing difficulty, the "Share Your Soul" initiative would be a consumer-centric, customer-created viral campaign that would both lead to people doing good in the world *and* more people finding out about SoulCycle (…not to mention the overarching goal of positioning SoulCycle in a new, positive light in the marketplace sort of akin to how people tend to feel about TOMS Shoes). Admittedly, this approach still has the potential to be a bit self-indulgent: people are talking about *themselves* doing these great projects. Still, there is no question that this kind of social media post would be much preferred to another workout selfie or shirtless selfie.

Those were just three ideas off the cuff. The team at SoulCycle's headquarters could sit down and brainstorm some ideas of how they could take very simple, cost-minded steps to truly put the "soul" into SoulCycle. Other simple ideas, like giving riders the chance to add on a $1 for a particular cause that may be timely (e.g., give a $1 for breast cancer research during October), is another simple solution. The charitable giving does not have to happen all the time, and there does not have to be any more than just *one* charitable solution, but SoulCycle is missing out on an enormous opportunity to bring value to those in need, themselves, and their current customers.

Remember that any excellent integrated marketing campaign does not just achieve some business objective using funny, entertaining, and memorable executions across a variety of media. No, an *excellent* marketing campaign does all of that *and* incorporates social responsibility, as well. Sure, SoulCycle could continue as it is, charging a small fortune for each class and laughing like a maniac while carrying its sacks of money to the bank like an old-timey rich cartoon character. Or SoulCycle could class itself up, create value for itself by creating value for others who truly need it, and, in doing so, remind its loyal customers that it is not just themselves they should be focusing on this world. Your waist size can improve. Your weight can go down. And sure, these things feel great, but few things warm the soul as much as helping other people who need it the most. With any luck, those people will pay it forward, and so on, and so on…and *that* is the kind of "soul cycle" we really need.

SYNTHESIZE

CHAPTER 6 | The Creative Spark

Taste the *feeling*.

Normally if someone said he/she were, "Tasting their feelings," I'd be worried they were either having a stroke or making bad post-breakup binge eating choices, but this particular tasting of feelings has nothing to do with health problems (…well, not directly anyway) or filling life voids with food products (…although there *is* a breaking up-inspired execution).

In early 2016, Coca-Cola announced a game-changing approach to the way it markets its products. Whereas the company used to have dedicated commercials for the different products in its portfolio (e.g., Coca-Cola, Diet Coke, Coke Zero), starting in 2016 all of the products would begin being featured in the *same* commercials. No longer would there be a separate commercial for Diet Coke or Coca-Cola Life. Instead, the company's many products would be marketed together in a new campaign entitled *Taste the Feeling*.

The *Taste the Feeling* campaign is designed to link Coca-Cola products with the emotions we all experience every day: happiness, sadness, fear, anxiety, and more. While this is not an altogether original idea, where the campaign succeeds is the nearly flawless integration of its products in between everyday, highly emotional moments as if to say, "Coca-Cola is an integral part of your daily life. It's there for the good times. It's there for the bad times."

For Coca-Cola, this shift in strategy may be coming at a good time.

Despite the persistent media coverage suggesting that soda and soft drinks are doomed as more and more people switch to healthier alternatives, the actual data on these sales are a little less straightforward. While sales for traditional "colas" have declined in the United States, global soda consumption has actually been increasing in the past decade. Similarly, within specific markets sales for some products, like Diet Coke, have also declined. However, sales for Coke Zero and Coca-Cola Life have actually increased in those same markets, suggesting that these other "healthier" alternatives are cannibalizing sales of Diet Coke.

Still, with constant media attention being paid to Coca-Cola's and even Diet Coke's alleged contribution to the growing obesity problem (pun intended), more and more consumers are becoming leery about grabbing a bottle of soda to drink, instead opting for fitness water or other bland beverages that may not taste as good but that also don't increase their waistline either.

As more customers shift from being loyal Coca-Cola drinkers to occasional soda drinkers for various health-related reasons, it would make sense for Coca-Cola to remind these Wandering Customers that their portfolio includes a wide variety of soda choices that may suit these customers' changing preferences (i.e., Open Up More Options). Coca-Cola does not have to worry about its loyal fans: they are not going anywhere regardless of what new scientific study comes out linking soda consumption to obesity or aspartame to cancer. Another group that Coca-Cola need not waste its time on are customers loyal to its fiercest competitor, Pepsi. Those customers are not switching their loyalty anytime soon. Hot Off the Press Customers are hard to find in the soda market (who has never tried soda before?), which leaves these Wandering Customers—the people who sometimes drink a Coca-Cola and who sometimes do not.

With respect to Understanding consumers, it is likely that Coca-Cola's own research would reveal stories similar to those receiving airtime in the media: people are worried that drinking too much soda is bad for them, soda is counterproductive to people's fitness and health goals, the nutritional value of soda simply is not there. Even switching to Diet Coke is something the customers are probably worried about, as more studies questioning the link between diet soda and obesity or artificial sweeteners and cancer cause concern. Still, when asked about Coca-Cola, most customers have really positive memories associated with the brand—happy feelings from childhood (an ice-cream float) or adulthood (a rum and Coke) they still link with the brand and its products.

Combining these Focus goals of Opening Up More Options to Wandering Customers with the Understanding findings that customers who *think* about Coca-Cola avoid purchasing its products but customers who *feel* the emotions associated with Coca-Cola *do* purchase Coke products, a Big Idea is born: *Taste the Feeling*.

The *Taste the Feeling* integrated campaign is designed to get prospective customers linking Coca-Cola and its many products with the emotions experienced in life. The unstated goal is to keep people from *thinking* about soda, its potential negative health effects, and all the news reports that essentially lambast soda companies and their products. Not to be *too* obvious, but the word, "Feeling," is in the very title of the campaign. The commercial spots do not list reasons or logic for drinking Coca-Cola's products. Instead, the commercials feature *very* vibrant, powerful imagery, emotionally-charged moments, and words corresponding to *feelings*. The storylines—from a couple meeting, growing, breaking up, and reconnecting to two brothers annoying one another, the older brother coming to the younger brother's rescue, and then returning to their sibling shenanigans—are emotionally-charged stories to which customers can relate. The ads mention nothing of health facts and nothing by way of "reasons" to drink Coca-Cola. No, the campaign is all about linking Coca-Cola with emotions.

In true integrated marketing form, Coca-Cola did not just create television commercials. In addition to the television spots, Coca-Cola redesigned their international website and its localized versions to feature the

Taste the Feeling campaign (see: https://tastethefeeling.coca-cola.com). Upon entering the site, users are presented with the full-length commercials and an interactive component in which the campaign's theme song begins playing, rich visuals picked from the advertisements appear, and a GIF-generator allows individuals to type how Coca-Cola makes them feel and then to share that customized GIF on a variety of social media platforms. One downside is that, as of this book's writing, Coca-Cola still has not updated its Facebook page to incorporate the Taste the Feeling campaign (in fact, its last official post is from the 2016 Super Bowl, which was nearly one month ago!). Of course, this is an integrated marketing fail, but perhaps it is reassuring to see that even the biggest and best do not always get it *perfect*.

However, one novel integrated marketing component to the Taste the Feeling campaign was Coca-Cola's commissioning of an original song to serve as the "anthem" for the campaign. The song, "Taste the Feeling," was recorded by newcomer Conrad Sewell and remixed by Avicii. Featuring lyrics like, "It feels good, in my heart, in my soul when you're right here beside me; I don't ever want this day to end; Mmm, we can watch the waves, have a Coke, and you sit here beside me; take a little of my heart again," the song is sort of a cheesy pop song that is as catchy as it is relevant to the campaign. Less than one month after being published on Coca-Cola's official YouTube page, the song has over half-a-million views and 99% of people who have rated the song have given it a thumbs up. The comments in the comment section praise the song, as well, which is likely to lead to great word-of-mouth as fans talk about and share the song on their respective social media networks. Not too shabby.

Another component of the campaign is a unique sound signature that closes out several of the new spots. The six-second audio clip includes the sound of a can being opened and a bottle top coming off a glass bottle, simultaneously, with the familiar sound of fresh, fizzing soda, a group singing "Taste the Feeling," and someone sighing a refreshing sigh.

Visually, Coca-Cola and its agency partners have done an exceptional job integrating the brand and its products in the aforementioned highly emotive situations. True to its "one brand" strategy, the commercials feature several Coca-Cola products in the same commercial and, quite importantly per integrated marketing, the animated graphic that appears at the end of each spot includes the brand logos for up to as many as four of Coca-Cola's primary soda offerings (i.e., Coke, Diet Coke, Coke Zero, and Coca-Cola Life) in the form of red, silver, black, and green bottle silhouettes. This, of course, speaks directly to the Open Up More Options Desired Objective of the campaign.

While it may be too early to tell whether or not the *Taste the Feeling* campaign is a success for Coca-Cola, the social media metrics on its official YouTube page show that each video in the campaign has a like rating of 90%

or above with each video having hundreds of thousands of views. Although *liking* a commercial may not necessarily translate to *purchasing* a bottle of Coca-Cola, one thing is for sure: people are definitely *feeling* Coke's new *Taste the Feeling* campaign…time will tell if their tastes have also changed as a result of the campaign or if Coca-Cola's flavors have gone flat.

* * *

Finally! It's here! At long last! A chapter dedicated to creativity and the "fun" part of marketing! Up to this point we have covered fundamental business objectives, marketing research, and even statistics in a book about integrated marketing strategy (?!) when most books on this topic just include a lot of pictures of print ads and say things like, "Make sure you have a lot of white space in your ad!" …racist.

Well, for those of you who prefer pretty pictures and brainstorming to hard data and strategic planning, fear no longer! We have arrived to a series of chapters that will make you feel right at home. And for those of you who prefer the more quantitative, bottom line fundamentals to creativity, well, you should be excited, too! You will learn some tricks and techniques in the next few chapters that can take even the people *most* afraid of creativity, spontaneity, and idea generation and turn them into creative forces with which to be reckoned!

Remember, my philosophy is quite simple: marketing is as much a science as it is an art. Sure, we began the book with important conversations regarding business objectives, research, and statistics, but this does *not* mean that campaigns cannot be clever or funny or aesthetically impressive–they can be and they *should* be! However, even the cleverest, funniest, and prettiest campaigns that fail to achieve their intended business objective are not very useful to a business' bottom line. This is why we begin with a conversation about Focus and Understanding before jumping into the more creative elements of Synthesis and Ideation. As you will soon learn, these comparatively "drier" components of Focus and Understanding actually fuel the energy upon which Synthesis and Ideation burn; and, together, they are the flint and steel that produce a creative spark.

In the case of this chapter's opening example, Coca-Cola had a Focus of Opening Up More Options to Wandering Customers (i.e., reminding people that it has a portfolio of several products). The company also had an Understanding that customers who *think* about the health effects of drinking soda had a negative perception of the brand and its products but customers focused on the feelings the brand and its product evoked were much more likely to consider buying a Coca-Cola product. Striking these two ideas together sparked a creative idea–Taste the Feeling–upon which an entire campaign is still being built. In the next chapter we will talk about what makes a good idea a great Big Idea, but before we get there, we need to talk about how to come up with ideas in the first place. To do that, this chapter is all about creativity, the creative process, and sparking creative ideas.

What It Means to Be Creative: Necessary and Sufficient Conditions

When people think of what it means to be creative, they often think of words like "unique" and "original" or "different." Often, people refer to artists who were "visionaries" or people who were "ahead of their time," people pushing the boundaries and experimenting in uncharted waters.

That is *sort of* correct.

While it feels good and right to say that a "creative genius" is someone who surprised the world with a brand new idea or never-before-seen concept, the evidence suggests this is not *exactly* true. We would probably agree that people like Walt Disney and Steve Jobs fall into the category of "creative types." But animated cartoons and touch-screen phones existed before Mickey Mouse and the iPhone. Walt and Steve just took what was already out there and made it even better. Artists like Kanye West and Lady Gaga, who practice the art of outlandish musical productions, are artists in their own right, but David Bowie and Elton John came first; the former duo just took the idea of performance art during musical productions and made it their own.

Of course, this is not to say that there are not artists out there who are altogether original and unique. When I was working at the marketing agency in St. Louis there was a contemporary artist who used human scabs and fingernails as his media of choice (...I know. Gross, right?). Clearly, I was not a fan, but to say that this person was neither "creative" nor an "artist" would be untrue, for art was created. My hope was that no one else had ever done this before because, well, it just sounded so nasty. But who is more creative: the people who reimagine old ideas into new concepts that work or the people who create concepts seemingly from thin air that may be outlandish and, as such, not exactly "popular?" How does one even begin to measure something as subjective and as amorphous as creativity?

Thankfully, some academics have spent their entire research careers addressing questions just like those. The verdict? Well, most modern researchers consider creativity on two core dimensions: 1) novelty, and 2) appropriateness. So it turns out that *both* approaches to creativity matter! Novelty is a function of two components—originality and uniqueness—while appropriateness includes measures of usefulness and effectiveness (Gardner 1993; Sternberg and Lubart 1999). What is interesting about this conceptualization of "creativity" is that it suggests one cannot simply be outrageous or shocking (i.e., novel) to be considered "creative." Similarly, one cannot simply rehash old ideas and expect to win the blue ribbon in a creative competition. Creativity is as much about originality and uniqueness as it is about appropriateness and effectiveness.

Knowing how creativity is assessed (i.e., the end point) is helpful when it comes to creating in the first place (i.e., the starting point). How? Well, if a creative idea is one that is deemed to be novel and appropriate for the task at hand, then our starting point should be to brainstorm ideas that are new and useful for the task at hand. Specifically, using the research on creativity, we have metrics upon which we can compare the ideas we dream up to know where they fall on the creativity spectrum. Let's review some questions to ask as we try to come up with a great Big Idea for a campaign...

Originality. *Has this exact same idea been seen before?* Original ideas typically *feel* new, but this is also the right point in time to make an important point about originality and the notion of being *too* original. We know from psychology that people like familiarity (i.e., "familiarity breeds liking"). So true is this tendency for humans to like the familiar that we are even more likely to believe *untrue* statements just because we have been exposed to them several times (this very concept forms the backbone of most politicians' campaign strategies). This phenomenon is called the illusion of truth effect and stems from what we refer to as "fluency effects" in the psych world: seeing the same stimulus at a later point in time feels more fluent than seeing a novel stimulus, and that fluency is misattributed to the statement's perceived truth.

Why do I bring this up in a conversation about originality? Well, being too original can be jarring. While this kind of surprise or contrast may be good at attracting people's attention, it may do you a disservice when it comes to general liking. I'll give you an example from my days of sketch writing. One year for Odyssey of the Mind the task was to recreate a Shakespearean story during a different time period. I remember having a very lengthy conversation about what would be the most creative solution to chat challenge. My team and I agreed early on that doing a well-known play, like *Romeo and Juliet*, would be extremely uncreative. We decided we would do a lesser-known play, *The Taming of the Shrew*, and set it during a wildly unrelated time period: the Salem Witch Trials. Taking two completely unrelated stimuli and making them fit together felt like the most creative thing we could do.

Fast forward to the competition. As we sat in the audience during one of the competing team's performance you can probably imagine the horror we experienced when they came out performing the famous witch scene from *Macbeth* during, you guessed it, the Salem Witch Trials. "Witches during a time period known for witchcraft?! That's not creative!" we tried to reason with ourselves. Here we were trying to make a square peg fit in a round hole with our skit while this group clearly took the path of least resistance in our opinion. *Everyone* knows that witch scene from *Macbeth*. We were doing *The Taming of the Shrew*! And the Salem Witch Trials? We had translated a complicated, comedic love story to a very dramatic, dark, and serious period of history. We didn't just take a story about witches and transplant it into another period concerning witches!

The result? The other team won first place, and we won second place.

We had *never* won second place at the regional competition, but thankfully this still qualified us to go to the state competition. We had to do some serious soul searching with respect to creativity and what it means to be creative. During the conversations between regional and state competition what we came to realize was that audiences like the familiar and, better yet, they like when you take the familiar and *tweak* it every so slightly to make it an original version of an old classic. While I would still argue that our version of *The Taming of the Shrew* during the Salem Witch Trials was certainly far more original than what the competition presented, the older and wiser version of me realizes that our solution was *too* original.

To fix the problem, we decided to scrap our original solution entirely and, instead, to take *Romeo and Juliet* (easily the most well-known Shakespearean play), tweak it slightly, and rework the play to incorporate the Scopes monkey trial on evolution. The judge bench and witness bench became the perfect setting for revamped balcony scene, and despite the clever originality of the skit, everything was couched in a very familiar story. We told an original tale and made the classic story of *Romeo and Juliet* our own, but we did so in a way that allowed the audience to follow along and come with us for the ride.

Thus, when it comes to originality and creativity, the sky really is *not* the limit. I hate to pooh-pooh on anyone's dreams, but this should be welcome news. You do not have to dream up something that has never been dreamed up before. Instead, imagine the ideal level of originality as an inverted-U shape (i.e., the Goldilocks approach): too little originality is not good enough, too much originality risks alienation or being misunderstood, but the right amount of originality is something that *feels* new and refreshing but still familiar enough that the audience can relate (e.g., like how Disney's *Frozen* put a twist on the familiar fairytale story).

Unique. *Could anyone else come up with this idea and use it as easily as us?* Some of the most forgettable marketing campaigns are those that, although beautifully executed, are simply not unique to the company and/or its brand. An example of one such terrible marketing campaign comes from the 2016 Super Bowl and a longtime stalwart of solid advertising: Anheuser-Busch. For whatever reason, AB thought it would be a great idea to have an advertisement playing on the idea of the 2016 election featuring comedians Seth Rogen and Amy Schumer. Aside from the low-brow, cheap humor involving the word "caucus" (which actually fits the target market), the entire election theme is completely irrelevant to Anheuser-Busch and Bud Light (unless you associate the crappy feelings people have about elections with the crappy taste of Bud Light…oooh, zing!). In a somewhat foolish move, AB decided not to include *any* commercials incorporating its famous Clydesdales or, popular in more recent years, the Golden Retriever puppy, icons that have become unique to AB and a fan favorite during the Super Bowl. The result? People universally panned the election-themed commercial; they weren't funny, they were not memorable, and they were not unique to Anheuser-Busch or Bud Light. The idea was that Bud Light was something *everyone* could agree on. You know what else is something everyone can agree on? Just about everything else: world peace, Olive Garden breadsticks, pizza for dinner, ice cream, puppies, etc. This was the first campaign the Bud Light team did with Wieden + Kennedy, the agency that took over the account from BBDO. Anheuser Busch may want to reconsider. I would be remiss if I did not offer a simple solution to fix this terrible campaign: actually having customers vote between two Bud Light-branded products – this is a subtle tweak but doing this would shift the campaign to be exclusively about the products being contested thereby making the campaign idea unique to the Bud Light brand and its products. Other companies could also pit products in its portfolio up against one another, but at least this takes the campaign from dull and generic to interactive, engaging, and specific. Simple solution, friends. Simple.

When coming up with a creative idea, part of the consideration should be whether or not the idea is unique to your brand, your company, and/or your product or service. This notion is particularly important in business because competitors copy *all the time*. If you develop an idea that is easily imitable, it is only a matter of time before your competitors do the same thing. The more unique an idea is to you, the more difficult it is for a competitor to copy that idea, in general, and the more difficult it is for your competitor to copy without seeming completely unoriginal. A good example of this in the real world would be Microsoft's stores that launched after Apple revolutionized the world of retail. Apple, renowned for its sleek, clean, all-white stores (in terms of decoration, not people – that'd be terrible) came up with an original, unique retail experience. Shortly thereafter, Microsoft decided it should get in this retail game, as well, and developed its own retail stores that looked *oddly* similar to Apple's stores. Featuring a similarly clean design and layout just with slightly more wood finishes, Microsoft's retail stores clearly looked like Apple store copycats. Score: Apple – 1, Microsoft – 0.

Again, ne'er one to critique without offering a suggestion, what could Microsoft have done to put a unique spin on its retail stores? Color. Red, green, blue, and yellow. We are all familiar with Microsoft's logo and its four colors. Why not emphasize the store windows (playing on the name) and then divide the store into four key color-coded areas: mobile, computing, gaming/software, and support? Suddenly Microsoft becomes less of an Apple copycat and more of an original company using its unique characteristics to its benefit.

So when it comes to being unique, ideas that are not easily imitable are the best, and those ideas tend to incorporate something in the DNA of your brand, your company, and/or your products/services – the very thing that makes you stand out in the minds of consumers is a great place to start.

Useful. *Is this creative idea functional and elegant?* If we wanted to develop a campaign for BMW, we could come up with an elaborate, fictitious story about a group of German cows living in the Alps who, realizing the need for better transportation for the less-intelligent creatures known as human beings, decided to create the "Ultimate Driving Moo-chine" (…see what I did there?). We could come up with an entire history: names, locations, dates. There could be stuffed animals for purchase, personal social media pages for the smart cows behind the initiative, and an app game that lets you be an Alpine cow jumping through lanes of traffic (all BMWs, of course) in the spirit of the classic game "Frogger."

That's quite an idea and a creative one by just about any standard, but is it very useful? The campaign, at least as described, really did not say much about the cars themselves, nothing about their safety features or amenities. Sure, the idea was fun and entertaining, but it does not seem very useful by way of doing what it could to sell more BMWs or to educate people about BMWs. Similarly, the idea is rather complex: a fictitious story about a community of car-creating cows? I mean, it *could* work, but it definitely requires the attentional investment of customers.

A good creative idea is one that is not simply entertaining or imaginative but one that also serves some function. That function *can* be "to entertain," but the point is that there is a difference between *imaginative* ideas and *creative* ideas. People can be as imaginative and grandiose as they want if all they are doing is telling an imaginative story, but when it comes to creativity, the academics in their ivory towers suggest that an idea needs to have a purpose and not just be puffery.

Along those same lines is the notion of "elegance." Growing up, I always just thought "elegance" referred to something that was fancy, but when I was working in California I once found myself in the office of Peter Gruber, a megastar in the Hollywood business world who had produced the original *Batman* movie from 1989 (which explained the full-size Batman suit standing upright in an enclosed glass case in his office). Our firm was hosting a retreat at Guber's home on the topic of storytelling, and a random, hodgepodge mix of storytellers had assembled to share their best practices. Admittedly, I had *no* idea who Peter was until we started working with him on the event (an aside: celebrity is completely lost on me - I once sat next to Darren Star, the creator of the wildly successful shows *Beverly Hills, 90201*, *Melrose Place*, and *Sex and the City*, for four hours at a dinner party and accidentally called him "David" the entire time. Oops.), but I always remembered Peter going on and on about this idea of "elegance." I remember thinking, "Yeah, um, look around this room and this estate; I'd say you know a thing or two about *elegance*," but Peter did not mean "fancy" elegance. The actual definition of elegance is that of "stylish restraint" or "beauty in simplicity." To be elegant does not mean to be opulent alone; no, to be elegant means to be aesthetically pleasing in your deliberate simplicity and parsimony. Thus, good creative ideas are not just functional, they are also deliberately simple by design: *is this the simplest way we can present an idea that serves a purpose?*

Effective. *Does this idea get people to do what we want them to do?* An idea can be original, unique, and even useful but if it does not succeed at motivating an intended audience to do what we want them to do, well, it does not do us much good. This can be tricky because usefulness and effectiveness seem like synonyms and, in many cases, are used as such. In this context, to be *useful* refers to the concept that an idea is functional (i.e., is tied to doing something) while being *effective* refers to the concept that an idea motivates others.

An interesting example of an idea's effectiveness is that of the Food and Drug Administration's (FDA) addition of graphic warnings to cigarette packaging in 2012. Cigarette packaging has, for many years, included the U.S. Surgeon General's warning that smoking can be harmful or detrimental to one's health. However, people were still smoking (i.e., the warning was not very effective). So, per the examples set by nations around the world, the FDA developed an idea to include graphic images showing the harmful effects of cigarette smoking (e.g., blackened lungs, cancerous growths, etc.) in an attempt to more strongly curb smoking. As expected, these graphic images had a rather pronounced effect on would-be smokers. Thus, the usefulness of the idea was its function to get people to reconsider smoking while its effectiveness was actually getting people to have an aversion to smoking and, even further, to stop smoking altogether.

The usefulness and effectiveness components of creativity are sort of a means/end symbiotic pairing. An idea is creative if it is linked to some function *and* is effective at achieving that functional end goal (while also being original and unique). If this sounds like a tall order, well, that is because it *is*. But let us keep in mind one very important point: being creative is not a binary state. In other words, it is not the case that an idea is either creative or it isn't. Creativity is a continuum. An idea that is very original, is extremely unique, serves a functional purpose, and is rather effective at achieving or producing its end goal would be deemed extremely creative. An idea that is somewhat original, kind of unique, slightly functional, and marginally effective at achieving its end goal would still be "creative," just a bit less so. And again, there is still a fair bit of subjectivity inherent in determining how original, unique, useful, and effective an idea is. At least now, however, you and your team have *some* agreed-upon metrics of how best to rate whether an idea is "creative" or not (otherwise, you're stuck with answering the question, "Is this creative on a scale from 1-not creative to 10-extremely creative?").

Now that we have an idea of what it means to be creative, the next logical question we should ask ourselves is, "Where does creativity even come from?!"

The Flash of Genius: A Treatise on the Origins of Creativity

Although we may now have a better understanding of what creativity actually is, creative inspiration is still an elusive concept. The Greeks believed that Muses, nine sisters representing poetry, music, dance, comedy, and more, graced our minds with their artistic presence, which then resulted in great masterpieces. That's sort of a nice way of saying, "Hey, Tracy! Gosh, that painting you did is beautiful! Too bad it was some Muse's idea." For the Greeks, creativity did *not* come from within; it was semi-divinely inspired.

As any artist, musician, choreographer, designer, architect, [fill in the blank with a creative profession] will tell you, sometimes creative ideas are present, bubbling over even…and sometimes, a lot of the times, they are not. Most artists will tell you that you cannot "force" inspiration, that you must "let good ideas come to you." That is a beautiful perspective, in theory, but when someone has bills to pay and deadlines to meet, well, we don't always have time to be waiting around for a creative idea to stumble its way into our brain. Yet, when trying to force that creative inspiration, many painters have been petrified upon staring at the daunting challenge of a blank canvas. Many songwriters have struggled with finding perfect combination of lyric, chord, and melody to express *exactly* what they intend to convey. And probably *all* of us have struggled with "writer's block" (or, in 2016, "typer's block"), where we sit in front of a blank computer screen, computer cursor flashing on a white faux piece of paper as taunting, "You can't think of *anything*, can you??"

With respect to "writer's block," the Greeks' use of Muses to explain creative inspiration was actually quite brilliant. You see, according to the Greeks, if you could not dream up a creative idea it wasn't because *you* were "washed up" or less talented; it could just be that the Gods were having a bad day, the Muses were on vacation, the spirits that guided creativity and inspiration were simply "out for lunch." Isn't that a convenient explanation? Try using that the next time you are on a deadline. "Oh, you know, I'm so sorry, but the Muses took this vacation for Erato's birthday, sort of a 'girls' weekend' getaway plus they had a Groupon, so…"

But if inspiration does not come from a group of magical, mythical sisters, if our brilliant ideas are not divinely inspired and directed, then where do all those ideas come from? And, if we know the source of these creative ideas, is there some way we can tap into that pool of creativity whenever we want or need to?

To answer these questions, we turn to science. You heard me right: we're going to dive into *science* to answer questions about *creativity*. It is at about *this* point of the book when some creative type starts gripping the edges of the book and furiously yelling – "But creativity is an art! Art is not science! That's why it is art! You cannot measure creativity!" Relax, Rita. There *are* scientific aspects of art (e.g., the Golden Ratio) just as there are artistic aspects of science (e.g., look at anything under a microscope), so it is worth exploring a few interesting findings with respect to creativity and inspiration. In the next several sections, I will share some of the insights from academic studies of creativity and inspiration in non-academic terms because I don't want you to fall asleep…you might be driving right now.

The Blank Canvas Myth

If you engage people in a conversation about creativity (I mean, who doesn't do that every day?), most people say things like, "Creativity means having no limits!" and, "Creativity is freedom of expression!" Intense stuff. Indeed, the cartoon version of an artist grabs a blank canvass, a huge painter's palette, and a single paintbrush before painting a beautiful masterpiece before us. Similarly, shows like *Glee* (meh!) and movies like *Pitch Perfect* (huzzah!) lead people to believe that musicians simply come up with full vocal arrangements on the spot and compete with these complex arrangements in drained pools with good acoustics on college campuses (…because that's *exactly* what we did in undergrad).

This idea that creativity just sort of emerges from nothingness and that one should strive for total freedom in order to be his/her most creative self is, somewhat surprisingly, not exactly true. In their 2005 paper "Designing the Solution: The Impact of Constraints on Consumers' Creativity," my colleagues Paige Moreau and Darren Dahl found that introducing constraints in the creative process, specifically in the form of a "toy creation" task, led to more creative solutions (as measured by novelty and appropriateness, our friends from the previous section).

Paige and Darren argued that when solutions to a problem already exist, most people will follow the "path of least resistance" and follow an existing solution if they can because humans, although wonderful creatures, are really just smart, slightly-less-lazy monkeys (…that last part is my own contribution). However, if you introduce constraints in the form of "input resource limitations" or "extra requirements," the path of least resistance solutions may no longer be viable, which means *new* solutions must be created…behold: creativity!

The way Paige and Darren manipulated "input restrictions" and "input requirements" was by randomly dividing the study's participants into one of four possible conditions based on two factors. For the first factor, input restrictions, participants were either told *they* get to choose the five shapes to incorporate into a toy they were going to design (no restriction) or that five shapes would be selected for them (restriction). For the second factor, input requirements, participants were either told *they* could choose how many of the five shapes were incorporated into the toy (no requirement) or that they had to use all five shapes (requirement). Per Paige and Darren's predictions, three independent design professionals, blind to the conditions and the experiment's purpose, rated the toys of the group who were given five shapes and forced to use all five as significantly more creative than any of the other three groups.

This is all very academic sounding, so let me use a real world example to illustrate the idea. Imagine a small pond. Two groups of students are tasked with the challenge of crossing the pond without getting wet. Group A is given rafts, canoes, kayaks, miniature boats with paddles, some lumber, plastic barrels, and rope. Group B is given some lumber, some old barrels, some rope, and a few other building materials. Neither group knows what materials the other group has. Whose transportation device is likely to be more creative?

My money is on Group B. While both groups are provided the same "building materials," chances are that, lacking any straightforward means of water transportation (i.e., a "path of least resistance") compared to Group A's boats, kayaks, etc., Group B is forced to think a *lot* harder about how to get across the pond. While the contraptions Group B builds may very well emulate traditional boats, rafts, and canoes, a lot more thought will go into their transportation devices than the level of thought going into Group A's effort. While Group A may opt to use the additional building materials as creative decorations or adornments, my hunch is that they are not going to go out of their way to use those materials to build a brand *new* way of traversing the pond.

Although this example sounds silly, it was actually a *real* class assignment in one of Dr. Sam Micklus' industrial design classes while he was a professor at Glassboro State College (now Rowan University) in New Jersey. Students were given limitations and "input constraints" in the form of scarce, odd building materials along with the additional rule that the students were "not allowed to touch the water with their bodies" (i.e., you can't get wet). The students created all sorts of odd devices, some looking more like traditional rafts and boats that successfully crossed the pond, others that looked like nothing anyone had ever seen before, some of which worked and others that did not work.

One of the devices that did *not* succeed was the work of a young man in the class. The young man, forced to think a little bit harder about how he might cross the pond given the building material constraints, realized that some of nature's critters manage to cross bodies of water without sinking and do so with very few resources, specifically their legs and their body. Those critters? Insects, of course, and specifically a water stick-bug known scientifically as a "ranatra fusca."

Now, you have probably seen a water strider at some point in your life. It turns out that water striders are an entire family of insects (Gerridae) with nicknames like water bugs, pond skaters, water skippers, and, my personal favorite, Jesus bugs (presumably because of the Biblical story where Jesus walked on water, although part of me would love to see a water bug with a beard, a white tunic, and a halo walking on water). I have a weird disgust of water bugs stemming from the occasional presence of a bug or two in our pool growing up. Water bugs are resilient little buggers: even when you scoop them out of the pool with a net, their little legs keep flailing around like a crazy person hell-bent on destroying you. In spite of their grossness, the bugs are fascinating creatures who stay afloat by distributing their light body weight evenly across their legs, legs that are long, slender, and maximize the amount of surface tension atop the water. In these simple terms, this is what keeps the bugs afloat.

Anyway, the young man decided he would create a device that emulated neither a boat nor a raft but, instead, a water bug. Using parts of an old wooden crate, a few long wooden rods, and a few other materials, the student created a human-sized water strider that he would operate by sitting in the middle.

The result? Failure…well, failure in the sense that the student did not successfully transport himself from one side of the pond to the other. The issue was that maintaining balance was difficult in the contraption the student designed. The beauty of a water bug is that they distribute their weight evenly across their legs. If that weight is uneven: splash! However, Dr. Sam pointed out how this student's original solution was the most *creative* of those constructed that day. Although the human-sized water strider failed to achieve its objective of crossing the pond, the device was more original, unique, and useful than the other transportation devices. It could have been *more* effective had the student had more time to balance out the weight of the contraption, but it still did manage to keep the student afloat for quite awhile and to make progress crossing the lake.

I should point out that Dr. Sam, the professor in charge of the class, is the genius behind the Odyssey of the Mind program I discussed earlier in the book. To this day Odyssey of the Mind rewards outstanding creative solutions, solutions that may not have *successfully* solved the problems they intended to solve but were extremely creative (i.e., original, unique, useful, and effective), as a salute to taking creative risks. The name of the award? Well, Ranatra Fusca, of course!

So that's a rather straightforward (but not altogether intuitive) idea: give people a few constraints on their inputs and add on a few extra requirements of what their solution must achieve, and you'll get more creative solutions than just giving people a blank canvass. This sometimes happens naturally: one common constraint for most creative projects is the budget. Time is often another constraint. You have no idea how much more creative I become when I have a deadline. But adding additional constraints, and/or introducing requirements that inputs be used in a certain way or achieve some additional objective, forces us to get out of our comfort zones, beyond the paths of least resistance, and into the space where creativity and creative ideas reign.

The Devil is in the Details: Abstract v. Concrete Thinking & Creativity

Construal Level Theory in the world of psychology corresponds to the idea that there exist two distinct levels of processing–abstract and concrete–wherein the former pertains to big picture, holistic approaches to thinking and the latter pertains to specific, nitty-gritty, detailed approaches to thinking. So if we were thinking about our mobile phone concretely, we might say something like, "The phone is black. The phone is rectangular. The phone makes phone calls," whereas if we were thinking about our mobile phone abstractly, we might say something like, "The phone is a good paperweight. The phone is like a modern day miniature television. The phone is like a member of my family." Notice how these latter descriptions already feel a bit more "creative" than the former, which seem fairly basic.

Research studies (Jia et al. 2009; Förster et al. 2004) have shown that people tend to respond in more creative and insightful ways across a variety of tasks when processing abstractly as opposed to concretely. Intuitively, this sort of makes sense: when people are overly concerned about the obvious (read: basic) details of something, they are less likely to concern themselves with the less-obvious characteristics and traits of a stimulus. When mired in the details, people are less likely to see things for what they *could* be because they are too stuck on seeing things as they currently are.

Wow. Let's re-read that last sentence: "When mired in the details, people are less likely to see things for what they *could* be because they are too stuck on seeing things as they currently are." If I ever become famous enough to warrant a gravestone large enough to have that quotation inscribed, please make it happen, dear reader, for this is the *secret* to unlocking creativity.

How have researches been so successful at yielding more creative responses out of some participants and not others? Well, the answer lies in the statement I just made: subtly getting people to stop thinking about basic details and getting them to process at a more holistic, abstract level. There are two equally awesome ways to get people to do this. The first, a technique used by Förster and friends (2004), involved the use of *time*. Specifically, the researchers simply asked participants to think about the future or completing a task in the future or they did not. You see, when human beings think about events occurring at some point in the distant future, we tend to automatically shift into abstract processing. As an event gets closer in time, our processing tends to become more concrete. For example, one year ago, all I thought about regarding my trip to France were vague big ideas like in which general area I would stay or big idea concepts I planned to cover for the MBA students I would be teaching. Now that the trip is just a week-and-a-half away, well, my mind is spinning with details like train tickets and departure times, clothes I need to pack (or still need to purchase), and specific in-class examples in which I plan to engage the MBA students. Time has a funny effect on the mind.

So the first way to turn up the creativity is to subtly get people thinking about the future. What might happen in a year? In five years? The interesting thing is that the future-oriented thinking doesn't even have to be about the task at hand. That is, if you are trying to come up with a creative idea for a marketing campaign, you don't have to ask, "What would this marketing campaign look like if we were designing it a year from now?" You *could* ask it that way, but you don't have to. You just have to get people shifting their mindset from the here and now to the future. The likelihood that they will be processing more abstractly increases, as does their propensity to provide creative, insightful ideas.

Another way to dial up creativity using construal level as our inspiration is through a subtle manipulation of what we refer to as "psychological distance." Psychological distance is yet another way to shift one's construal level and refers to perceived distances (whether real or simply imagined). In a clever manipulation, Jia and colleagues (2009), simply told one group of people a task had originated by students from their university studying abroad in Greece and another group that the task had originated by students from their university who were also based at the university. Interestingly, the participants in the former condition were more creative on the subsequent task because they were more likely to be processing abstractly than the latter participants. Simply invoking the notion of "distance" was enough to lead to differences in creativity. Thus, another approach to facilitating creative thinking is to subtly cue distance, whether real or imagined, physical or psychological, as this tends to produce more abstract thinking and, as a result, more creative ideas.

If I were to summarize this section, it would seem that one of the best ways to evoke creativity is to imagine a team of people addressing the same problem you are from halfway around the world 5 years from now. Kidding aside, simply thinking about the future, thinking about distance, and considering a challenge or problem from a different perspective increases the likelihood for creative ideas.

Something Feels Off: Disfluency and Creativity

In the earlier conversation on originality in this chapter, I mentioned the psychological construct of "fluency," an experience that just "feels right." Compare this to "disfluency," an experience in which something feels a bit off. Given our conversation about avoiding paths of least resistance, this would seem to suggest that a fluent experience would lead people to simply "go with the flow" whereas a disfluent experience would lead people to consider other alternatives (i.e., be more creative).

Sure enough, my research (Mourey 2015) and the work of my colleagues (Mehta et al. 2012) has found that people experiencing disfluency tend to think a bit more "outside the box" than people experiencing fluency. In our work, we find that feeling like the world around you is just a bit off (e.g., seeing images of a wedding where the wedding dress is green and the tuxedo is purple) shifts people's thinking to question the intuitive "path of least resistance" and to offer alternative solutions. Mehta and colleagues find that the presence of moderate ambient noise during a task creates disfluency and leads people to process at a more abstract level, which, in turn, leads to more creative responses on various tasks.

When it comes to putting these ideas into practice, companies have been known to hire "creativity consultants" who come in and disrupt the organization and its work processes in order to stimulate creativity. Something seemingly as silly as rearranging furniture to interrupt flow, adding "white noise" machines, and other disfluency-inducing techniques can be enough to stimulate creativity. So one way to increase your level of creativity is to find ways to change up what is expected, to create just enough of a feeling of disfluency that this uneasiness leads you down new paths. If that sounds complicated, just take a trip somewhere new. I have always found that I feel (and am) much more creative when I am traveling than when I am home. Why? Well, when you are a stranger in a new place, *everything* feels disfluent.

Fun fact: you may not have noticed this, but this particular section began with a heading that appears on a *different* page than the text that follows (pending future edits of the book, that is). That probably felt *weird* to you. It should have; it was deliberate. When my colleague Daphna Oyserman and I write papers, we are sensitive to these very subtle experiences of fluency that feel "right" or "wrong." Although this formatting decision may seem trivial, the experience of fluency or disfluency accompanying the content one reads could affect that content's effectiveness, persuasiveness, or liking, in general. The takeaway: you will never look at the world the same way again!

Creativity and the Brain: Insights from Neuroscience

With the advent of neuroscience and fMRI studies in psychology and marketing, it is not surprising that one area receiving attention through this modern methodology is the study of creativity. That's the good news. The bad news? Well, even though we are able to see into the brain better than ever before, the underlying brain processes associated with creativity are still quite elusive. Modern brain science has allowed us to rule out some old ideas regarding creativity: there is no left-brain, right-brain distinction; low arousal or inattention does not facilitate greater creativity; and there is no one specific region of the brain implicated in creative thought.

A meta-analysis of 72 experiments in 63 papers (Dietrich and Kanso 2010) found that very few clear links exist between brain regions/circuits and increased creativity. Delineating creativity into three categories–divergent thinking, artistic creativity, and insight–the authors only found that artistic creativity often correlates with areas of the brain implicated in motor function (which kind of makes sense: dancers, painters, etc.) and some associations between insight and the Anterior Cingulate Cortex and the prefrontal areas. What does this all mean? Well, it simply means there is no single area or process implicated in creativity and creative idea generation. Thus, for as much as we are learning about creativity, there still exists a shroud of mystery when it comes to creativity and the creative process.

Although it is unclear from the results of the meta-analysis, it would seem that some commonly-held beliefs about creativity may require further scrutiny. Some people believe that great ideas come when our mind is actually tired whereas others also believe that focusing on other tasks permits creative processing and idea generation to occur in the subconscious areas of our mind. I often find that some of my most creative ideas come late at night. Growing up, I also realized that most of my creative friends tended to be night owls, as well. In fact, it is sort of a psychological stereotype that creative types tend to be night owls. My theory for this late-night creative surge is that my brain, tired from being active for so long, can no longer filter the outlandish, creative ideas bubbling up from the deep recesses of my brain (that's not how the brain actually works, but it makes for a nice mental picture). Furthermore, we *do* know that the brain engages in top-down and bottom-up processing, the former a more controlled, volitional process and the latter a more automatic process. Thus, it seems reasonable that after a long day the brain's ability to fight the good fight preventing those automatic ideas from emerging would be lost, thereby allowing novel insights to enter the mind. Incidentally, I have often wondered whether or not this is the reason artists often take drugs to fuel their creative endeavors: the drug impairs their brain's ability to have top-down control over bottom-up ideas. That said, the "how-to" takeaway from this is *not* to do drugs…just to be clear. Instead, try late-night brainstorming sessions or thinking about an idea as you drift off to sleep in bed. Be sure to keep a notebook nearby to write down any idea that may come up because you *will* forget it in the morning (even if you think you won't…trust me).

Groupthink: Brainstorming Together v. Alone & Creativity

When people think of creativity or the creative idea generation process one word that almost *always* comes up is "brainstorm." Brainstorming refers to the process of developing creative ideas typically in a meeting-like format and often with other people. Just as pervasive as the use of the term "brainstorming" is the golden rule of brainstorming: *no idea is a bad idea.* That is not true, and the reason that we know that is not true is because we have all had bad ideas. Dating that special someone because they weren't your "usual type." Bad idea. Signing up for that fitness class because you think you're more likely to go if you already paid. Bad idea. Trying to be spontaneous and figuring out what you want to do when you get to your vacation destination instead of planning ahead for tickets and sightseeing. Bad idea.

Just as in life, so, too, are there definitely bad ideas in brainstorming. The reason we have that, "No idea is a bad idea," rule is because we are nice people, and we do not want to hurt anyone's feelings, especially when it comes to something as personal and as individually-specific as a new idea. However, tiptoeing around people's feelings is more likely to lead to a subpar solution compared to having an open conversation about the value of an idea, whether good or bad, in which conversation is directed to the idea itself (i.e., not a personal attack), its merits and limitations, how it can be improved upon or integrated into another idea, etc. However, rather than engage in this kind of interactive brainstorming, companies have opted for softer approaches.

Recent work in management (Paulus and Yang 2000) has found that group brainstorming, with the right structure, can be more advantageous than individual brainstorming. Advocates for individual brainstorming suggest that this is one way to help prevent "groupthink," where everyone sort of coalesces around the same idea (thereby limiting the number of creative options on the table). What the newer research suggests is that people should be encouraged to brainstorm their own creative ideas and solutions, but then the group needs to come together to give adequate attention to each *idea*, having substantive conversation about each one. Importantly, there needs to be an "incubation" period following this conversation in which the members of the group think about the ideas as they have now evolved per the group interaction. The group then reconvenes to discuss the ideas further with novel insights, additional thoughts, and perhaps even some tweaks or changes. The idea is that the final idea the group then selects will emerge as the leading idea from a wider pool of good ideas and, because of this enhanced competition of ideas, be a stronger, better, and more robust idea. It's sort of like *Survivor* but with ideas.

Creative Idea Generation: Activities for Your Next Brainstorm Session

Up to this point, I have provided you with some important considerations and a few tricks to help fuel your creative fire. These tools, alone, should benefit your idea generation process, but I am sort of known for making sure I leave people far better off than when they came in....so, at the risk of overdoing it, I am doing to give you a few more tools that I think will come in handy for you. Why? Because I like you. ☺

In some instances, these activities can be used directly to help you devise creative ideas for whatever it is you are working on, and other times the activities are a good warmup to get the brain thinking in the right creative state of mind.

Spontaneous. Odyssey of the Mind, the beloved international school program I have mentioned a few times, includes an activity we call "Spontaneous." The name comes from the fact that until the day of competition teams have *no* idea what problem awaits them. The team will simply enter a room at a designated time and be presented with a problem they must solve. Sometimes the problem is a verbal one, such as, "Name as many kinds of 'green' things as you can in 3 minutes." A group of judges will score answers as either common (e.g., "grass") or creative (e.g., "Alan *Green*span getting sick on a rollercoaster"). Other times, the problem is what we call "hands-on," such as, "Here are twenty random household items. Build a bridge that spans these two desks using only the items and that will hold as many golf balls as possible," or, "Here is a shoe. Name as many ways you can use this shoe as possible in the next 3 minutes." One never knows what to expect walking into a Spontaneous room, but that does not mean one cannot be prepared by practicing example Spontaneous problems in the weeks leading up to the competition.

One skill that comes in handy during Spontaneous is an ability to think quickly. The team is timed and must answer quickly. In some Spontaneous problems the team is given a finite set of cards and each time they say an answer, a card has to go in the basket. Once they are out of cards, the team is finished (remember when we talked about introducing constraints to stimulate creativity? Odyssey was ahead of its time).

You can find practice Spontaneous problems available for free at the state websites (Virginia: http://va.odysseyofthemind.org/weekproblemarchive.html - Tennessee: http://tnodyssey.org/spontaneous-problems/) for associations participating in Odyssey of the Mind. I will warn you, however: Spontaneous is addictive and almost always hilarious.

Beachball. I have played this word association game since I was a kid, but it is always great to get the brain primed. In fact, I still play this on long car rides just to kill time because it is such a fun challenge. The way Beachball works is to start by saying a compound word like, "Beachball," or, "Crossroad," or, "Passport." Then, the next person must say a compound word (or two-word statement) that begins with the second word in the original compound word. Confusing? Let me illustrate with an example. If the first word is, "Yearbook," the second person could say, "Bookworm," and the third person could say, "Wormhole," and so on and so on. If someone gets stuck for too long, they can start a new compound word, but the idea is to see how many rounds the group can go without stopping. Of course, part of the fun of the activity is coming up with an answer that is a bit of a stretch. Say, for example, the game begins with the word, "Rainstorm," and proceeds to, "Storm cloud" (one of those two-word statements), then, "Cloud nine," then, "Nine Lives," and then someone says something like, "LiveStrong," essentially turning "lives" into "live" to fit the charity name "Livestrong." It is sort of a rule violation, but it is exactly the spirit of divergent thinking we are trying to foster, which is part of the game.

Conducted Story. Conducted Story is a staple of short-form improvisation activities (which we will actually talk about in a later chapter), but the reason I love it is that it requires participants to be listening and thinking at the same time, which, if you think about it, is not something most people are very good at doing (especially in the workplace). The way the activity works is that one person, the conductor, stands or sits in a position where he/she can see all the other participants in the room. The group takes a suggestion for a title (it does not really matter what it is), and then the conductor starts the story by pointing to one of the participants who must start reciting a story as if he/she has known it for years. As is typically the case, many stories begin with a common, "Once upon a time…" or some other derivative intro, but almost always the stories veer into some rather wild places after that. Why? Because at any point in time the conductor will stop pointing to the person talking and will point to a new person who must pick up *exactly* where the last person left off. So, for example, if Person 1 is talking and says, "Olivia moved the old, dusty picture frame away from the wall and found a small box that was just as old and just as dusty. When she opened the box she…" but then the conductor points to a new person, then that new person must begin with something like, "…found a pair of old diamond earrings, a half-eaten piece of bread, and a mysterious letter." The goal of the story is to keep it flowing and making as much sense as possible, but the broader goal of the activity is to make people more comfortable with hearing others' ideas, being ready to give their own ideas at any point in time, and reconciling the two so that the best possible story can be told. If that sounds familiar that's because this is the same thing we try to do when brainstorming creative ideas for a marketing campaign. Nice, right?

Take It Back/Synonym. If you had a weird infatuation with the thesaurus like I did when I was a kid (weird, I know…I mean, "Bizarre, peculiar, zany, unique"), then you will appreciate this activity. Take It Back/Synonym are two different twists on the same activity. In Take It Back one person is designated as the "clapper" and, at any point in time, that person can clap when someone else is speaking at which point in time the speaking person has to "take back" whatever it is they just said and say something else. It might go something like this:

> Person 1: Amelia, thanks so much for inviting me to your birthday party!
> Person 2: Oh, Jules, it's always a pleasure to have you at any celebration or soirée!
> Person 1: That's kind of you to say! I can't wait to eat some cake!
> (Clapper claps his/her hands)
> Person 1: I can't wait to see your presents!
> (Clapper claps hands again)
> Person 1: I can't wait because the doctors have diagnosed me with this condition where I literally cannot wait for things.
> Person 2: Oh, Jules - I had no idea! That's awful! (pretends to hear something) I think I hear the doorbell, can you wait right here?
> Person 1: (infuriated) WAIT? Didn't you hear what I just said?
> Person 2: I know, I know, I'm sorry. Sometimes I can be so forgetful.
> (Clapper claps his/her hands)
> Person 2: Sometimes I can be so inconsiderate.
> (Clapper claps his/her hands again)
> Person 2: Sometimes I can be so dictator-like, but this is my day and we're going to do it my way.

That's Take It Back. The idea is that you have to be ready to think quickly on your feet and get in touch with your gut to keep the momentum up. A variation of this game is Synonym, which is essentially the same game except the new statement following a clap has to be a synonym of what was just said, either conceptually (as a phrase) or in the literal sense (a word that means the same thing as the last word spoken). So if someone were to say, "The commercial begins in a typical Starbucks with fancy faux wood paneling on the walls, the smell of coffee in the air, and people doing work," and then hear a clap they could either say, "…with comfy furniture surrounded by tall tables, the odor of caffeine creations, and customers toiling away on laptops." The idea is that whatever is said has to be a more creative, novel way to say what was just said. If the clapper wants to be a real jerk, he/she can keep clapping after each time the person speaking offers a new phrasing. After about three or four of these it becomes increasingly difficult to express the same idea in an original way, but wait a minute, that sounds familiar…part of creativity is expressing an idea in an original and unique way but still communicating the usefulness of the idea and how it is effective. Seeing the link?

These activities may sound fun to you or they may sound absurd if you are the boring kind of person who is afraid of having fun. Either way, you should try them out the next time you are trying to get into a creative frame of mind. You would be surprised at how fun *and* effective these activities can be.

FUSION and Creativity: Sparking Creative Ideas

As I mentioned at the beginning of this chapter, the FUSION model naturally captures some techniques you can use to enhance your creativity and your creative idea generation process. Although you did not realize it at the time, the selection of our Prospective Audience and our Desired Objective are not just important business strategies, they also represent constraints in the campaign generation process. In addition to creating a campaign, in general, we must also address the needs of a particular audience and incorporate a tangible business objective. Not every campaign, particularly non-integrated campaigns, require this. Thus, our Focus goals bring us one step closer to a more creative solution by being constraints in the creativity process.

Adding to the fun is our Understanding results. During Understanding, we learn a great deal about our potential customers: what they like, what they hate; what they need, what they don't need; what they pay attention to, what they ignore. Guess what? More constraints! Not only do we have additional requirements based on this information we also have input restrictions based on information about what sort of media in which we can/cannot advertise, what kind of things we can/cannot say, what sort of needs we can/cannot address. Although it is easy to see these limitations as exactly that–limiting–creative types see these findings as inspiration, creative challenges, constraints that will actually facilitate the creative idea generation process rather than impede it.

Which brings me back to my metaphor of flint and steel. Our Focus and Understanding goals are the flint and steel of our integrated marketing campaign. Once we have established our business goals and have collected information regarding the very people we hope to motivate into doing something, we are packed with exactly the tools we need to start generating some creative ideas. It's that simple. You don't have to be an artist or a visionary. You don't have to be a designer or a musician. All you have to do is strike the flint against the steel, the Focus goals with the Understanding findings, and before you know it, that creative spark will ignite a *fire*.

*   *   *

I grew up in a Coke house.

Let me clarify that: I grew up in a house where Coca-Cola was the soft drink brand of choice. Since the moment my parents let my siblings and me drink soda, Coca-Cola was *always* the brand we had in our house. In fact, I never remember having Pepsi in the house unless we were hosting a holiday party and were being accommodating for our guests.

Nowadays, I do not really drink much soda, but in the off chance I order a Diet Coke and the server asks if Diet Pepsi would be, "Alright?" I lose my $#!T. No, it would *not* be alright. That is *never* alright. If I wanted Diet Pepsi then I would have said I wanted Diet Pepsi! The only thing worse is when they don't ask you if Diet Pepsi would be okay but bring it out anyway...like I wouldn't notice the difference! In fact, the only time I ever drank Pepsi willingly is when I would spend the night at my grandma's house. Her favorite soda of choice was Pepsi (with no caffeine – detailed, I know; she was a lady who knew what she liked). Sometimes, in the middle of the night when my grandma was asleep on the couch (because she always fell asleep on her couch watching *Love Connection* with her blanket pulled up just above her mouth because she had already removed her dentures and did not want the paparazzi to see her this way), I would sneak into the kitchen, grab a caffeine-free Pepsi, and raid the cow-shaped cookie jar full of butter cookies. That was the only time Pepsi tasted good to me: when I was a petty thief starving in the middle of the night and there was literally *nothing* else to drink. So you get it: I like Coca-Cola.

For a long time, when Americans were fat and okay with it, Coca-Cola's world domination seemed never-ending. People would guzzle two-liters of soda like they were water, on hot days people would drink a can of ice cold Coca-Cola (instead of water), and people associated soda with the word "refreshing" (instead of water). Now, Americans are still fat but less okay with it. As such, Coca-Cola's never-ending domination does not seem so never-ending anymore. Sure, the company has either created new products or acquired companies touting healthier beverages, like fortified waters and all-natural drinks, but these new drinks are not the company's forte. Coca-Cola is a soda company. If people stop drinking soda altogether, well, where can Coca-Cola go from there?

The good news is that people are unlikely to stop drinking soda anytime soon. With all the media reports of shifts in consumer health preferences, alleged associations between soft drinks and obesity, between diet sodas and cancer, and any number of other stories pooh-poohing the soft drink industry, people have too many positive associations with these familiar brands and their products, Coke *and* Pepsi (...see, that's me being nice). I remember my father bringing us home "frozen Cokes" as children (which were a real treat), always having a fully-stocked fridge of Dr. Pepper during undergrad (most people had beer, mind you, but my friend Erin Harkless and I always had Dr. Pepper), and getting permission to have a soda with dinner instead of something boring and basic like water or, even worse, *milk* (milk is only meant to be consumed with chocolate). These are positive emotional memories, memories that no matter how many years I go without drinking soda will *always* be a part of me.

People change and so, too, do companies and their products. Both Coca-Cola and Pepsi have altered their main product lines to include zero-calorie versions of their beloved drinks that are not "diet," altered versions of their product to include only natural ingredients, and other slight tweaks catering to the shift in consumer preferences. This is not going to keep everyone in the market nor will it bring back those who already left, but these solutions create value for customers looking for a way to hold on to a taste they love, a way to hold on to the positive emotions and memories they have about Coca-Cola and Pepsi and let go of the adverse health effects associated with drinking soda. In short, these customers just want a way they can still, "Taste the Feeling," and now Coca-Cola allows them to do just that.

What if... *Coca-Cola's Months of Emotions*

One challenge when dreaming up an integrated marketing campaign is making sure that the excitement and energy associated with the campaign will last. As many creative types will tell you, it is difficult to know the lifespan of an idea. Comedians' jokes are not nearly as funny to them the ninth or tenth time they deliver them. Singer-songwriters' new songs lose a bit of their luster by the end of a concert tour. I cannot tell you how many times I have written and then been tempted to rewrite jokes, comedy sketches, songs, book passages (including some in this book) because something that at one point in time seemed *so* clever or original or funny simply does not feel that way anymore. In these moments I am forced to remind myself that each audience is hearing a joke or a song or an idea for the *first* time, a first time that will be just as magical and amazing as the first time I had the good fortune of being inspired to create.

Fortunately, by their very design, integrated marketing campaigns are meant to include components that continue to spice up the campaign throughout its lifetime. Certain executions are timed for particular parts of the year in a coordinated media schedule that keeps the campaign relevant, fresh, and interesting. Not every marketing campaign does this, which is why I am sure there is one television spot out there you cannot stand because you see it *all* the time, it is rarely relevant, and it just feels old and dated.

Coca-Cola's *Taste the Feeling* campaign runs the risk of having a fate similar to other campaigns that fizzled out long before they should have. The reason for this is that there's only so much time the current executions in the campaign will keep people's interest. What if, however, Coca-Cola devised a smart integrated plan that coordinated executions to drop throughout the year?

Specifically, let's say that Coca-Cola decided to keep the campaign fresh within the realm of the *Taste the Feeling* theme by associating each month out of the year with a relevant emotion: January (refreshing), February (love), March (lucky), April (springy), May (outdoorsy), June (prideful), July (freedom), August (steamy/sweltering), September (colorful), October (scared), November (thankful), December (jolly). Although the overarching *Taste the Feeling* campaign and its look/feel will still exist and dominate, the monthly highlighted emotions would be proverbial icing on the cake; a fun, simply way to keep customers engaged and interested throughout the year.

For example, in February, Coca-Cola drinkers could be asked to share stories of Coca-Cola and first dates, weddings, etc., in a viral component of the campaign. In May, Coca-Cola could present customers with some camping tips and Coca-Cola-based recipes that can be cooked on the go. Imagine Coca-Cola informing customers how Coca-Cola products can be used to marinate various meats one could cook out on a camping trip. In August, the company could engage in a PR event in which Coca-Cola misters are set up around big, humid cities that cool people down with air and water (not Coca-Cola...that would be a sticky situation) but also provide the opportunity to get an ice-cold Coca-Cola near the misters to help you cool down. Perhaps Coca-Cola could even launch temporary Coke-based slushies per portfolio flavors just for the summer. Mmm.

Coca-Cola could get even more creative in its integrated marketing campaign and work with partners to help leverage the product within particular communities. The January "refreshing" feeling might present a good time for Coca-Cola to partner with Weight Watchers or Jenny Craig and promote its Diet Coke and Coke Zero offerings as diet-friendly solutions that allow resolution-setters the chance to, "Have their Coke and eat it, too" (...get it?). Similarly, Coca-Cola could partner with Nathan's Famous, the company responsible for the annual International Hot Dog Eating Contest, as the official beverage of choice for the event. Given that the event coincides with the 4th of July holiday in the United States, Coca-Cola could even create a (potentially viral) social video that shows what happens when one combines Mentos with Diet Coke in the context of a "fireworks" theme (this same sort of soda fountain could be integrated into a New Year's pop the bubbly video).

What is nice about this additional component to the integrated marketing campaign is that it incorporates another message that is central, and rather unique, to Coca-Cola: Coca-Cola is as much a part of your celebrations throughout the year as *anything* else. Whether it is the turkey at Thanksgiving or the ham at Easter, a hot dog during the 4th of July or champagne at New Year's Eve, chances are that Coca-Cola products are also in attendance at the party. Coca-Cola has shared in all the emotional highs and lows throughout every season, something that we may sometimes take for granted.

Bigger picture, as I mentioned above, focusing on a different particular emotion each month allows the campaign to give itself a jumpstart every couple weeks without going off-campaign or requiring a great deal more effort, resources, or money. In this way, people are less likely to grow weary of the same ideas being presented over and over again. Another benefit is that if, for some reason, customers do not like a particular execution or theme, it is just a matter of weeks before a new idea comes along that the customers might like.

One final point about these time-centric executions that is extremely relevant to the modern world: by having components of the *Taste the Feeling* campaign deliberately evolving and changing the entire campaign itself feels like a more dynamic, living, and interactive campaign than one that stays the same. The reason this is more important now than at any time in history is that customers have grown to *expect* this kind of interactivity with a brand and its products. This kind of dynamism makes customers feel like they are more closely connected with the brand, and this approach also permits the brand managers and campaign coordinators to take advantage of news events, popular culture, and emerging trends in the moment, which can be an extremely powerful way to engage customers, as well as garner media/PR attention.

Indeed, this kind of campaign also whets the appetite for what is about to come next. If January is refreshing and February is love, then what might March be? April? Humans like to have cognitive closure, so why not make them *thirsty* for more (...sorry, I had to do it)?

JAMES A. MOUREY

CHAPTER 7 | A Big Idea You Can LOVE

She's a blonde bombshell.

At 5'9" with an 18" waist, 33" hips, and 36" chest, she is known around the world for her stunning looks, her poise, and her unyielding backbone.

But this beautiful dame is not just a head-turning treasure. No, in addition to her unparalleled beauty, this woman has worked as a veterinarian (she loves animals!), an astronaut (she loves space!), and even spent time in the army (she loves America!). Lest you think this catch is still swimming for fish in the sea, it turns out that she has a longtime partner who is equally as good looking, has a place in Malibu, and, although often working as a pilot, is often seen cruising around on his Harley Davidson or in a corvette with the top down (…rumor has it that he might be compensating for something missing downstairs).

By now you are either dying to meet this fascinating woman or rolling your eyes in disgust (and perhaps a bit of jealousy) for a woman who seems to have everything: good looks, great career, love, money, fame. But here's the secret: you already know her.

Barbie was introduced in 1959. As the story goes, a woman by the name of Ruth Handler (the doll's creator) noticed her daughter and other little girls playing with their paper dolls and baby dolls but ascribing adult characteristics to these dolls. The lack of an adult toy doll (…err, toy doll that is an adult) available to children meant that if little girls wanted to play "doctor" that the doctor role had to be played by either a baby or a doll made from paper. While a baby doctor sounds kind of amazing (and very *Doogie Howser*), a paper doll doctor sounds worrisome – I mean, imagine a *paper* doll doctor asking for a scalpel. That's a terrible idea.

Ruth and her family were traveling in Europe when she stumbled across a doll for adults (…not *that* kind of doll for adults – this is really tricky to write!). Strangely, although the product was a doll, it was sexualized because it was based on a comic strip character who often used her sexual prowess to get what she wanted (…but then again, who doesn't?). Ruth and her husband purchased rights to the German doll, which essentially began the birth of Barbie as we know and love her. Interesting side note: the earliest dolls had eyes that were looking off in the corner as if Barbie could not even be bothered with you. Fortunately, modern Barbie stares straight out and smiles so kids don't have to feel constantly judged.

However, in spite of her enduring popularity, Barbie has not been without her controversy. For starters, one of the most frequent criticisms of Barbie is her figure. Child advocates say that Barbie presents an unrealistic expectation of the female figure for young girls. Barbie's body shape, lack of acne or other skin blemishes, and makeup-covered face all represent some standard to which little girls learn to compare themselves at an early age. Other concerns regarding some of Barbie's professions, from secretary to stewardess, suggest her career options reinforce stereotypes about female societal roles. This, of course, is easily refuted by Nascar Driver Barbie, Football Coach Barbie, and even President Barbie in which the beloved doll holds roles typically held by men. However, as recently as 2010, Computer Engineer Barbie stirred up a controversy when her accompanying book involved her accidentally uploading a virus to a computer and needing two male friends to help fix the problem and program the game she created. Oops.

In spite of this, Barbie continues to be one of the bestselling toy items for children and has maintained its top-of-mind position in the "doll" category. In the early 2000s, Mattel was worried about the threat of the then-popular Bratz dolls. Bratz dolls, designed by a former-employee of Mattel (he claims he drew Bratz-like dolls prior to his stint at Mattel; Mattel, of course, argues otherwise), are sort of like Barbie's weird cousin who came from a broken home and may or may not have daddy issues. Whereas Barbie might appear on an episode of *Ellen* or *The Tonight Show with Jimmy Fallon*, her Bratz cousin is more likely to star in an episode of *Jerry Springer* or *Maury Povich*. The point is that Bratz dolls carried with them a certain "edge" that little girls found appealing; so appealing, in fact, that Bratz did start stealing some of Mattel's market share...no one was surprised that Bratz, with their troubled history, were also petty larcenists.

Part of the appeal of the Bratz line of dolls was that they were "truer" representations of young girls: not perfectly built, diverse, rougher around the edges, full of different personalities (although their pouty lips and huge eyes make them look a bit like the Roswell alien). Barbie was, is, and will likely continue to be more sophisticated than the Bratz dolls, and the marketers at MGA Entertainment (the company that owns Bratz) have exploited this by essentially sexualizing the dolls via their clothing (or lack thereof), which has led Bratz dolls to have their own share of controversies.

In general, it is clear that the doll market, one that primarily targets young girls (although, side note: Mattel has recently included young boys in its commercials for Barbie), is considered sacred space. In recent years, society has come down hard both on companies like Mattel, whose Barbie presents young girls with a potentially unrealistic, idealized example of what it means to be a woman, and MGA Entertainment, whose Bratz dolls have been likened to strippers, sex workers, and drug-addicted Barbies.

So if you are Mattel, how do you fight the perception that your main product plants the seeds of unrealistic expectations in the minds of young girls? How do you counter the idea that your product is doing more harm than good? In short, how do you provide evidence that your core product is fulfilling needs of young girls in a helpful, healthy way?

It turns out, many of us already *knew* the answer to that question, we just never really gave it much thought. You see, growing up, my sisters *loved* Barbie dolls. They loved them so much that when our family dog, a long-haired Chihuahua named Coco Maria Chanel (I couldn't make that up if I wanted to) decided to make one Barbie's foot her chew toy, my sister Kelly began a years-long spiteful relationship with Coco. ¡Ay Dios mío, Coco! Whereas I was busy playing with my X-Men action figures and Batman toys (...don't judge), my sisters were creating elaborate, soap opera worthy storylines starring their various Barbie dolls (including Ken, Skipper, and the rest of Barbie's friends). Occasionally, I would join them in their game of Barbie make-believe, which a little boy sometimes feels self-conscious about (Mattel is working on that). I would "man it up" by introducing Batman to Barbie despite her towering over him like a giant. We would imagine all kinds of scenarios: going on vacation, camping, family reunions, dance parties. At no point in time when playing with my superhero figurines did I feel obligated to have a super power or six-pack abs or a sleek car. While I am sure I may have subconsciously taken on male scripts and societal roles or maybe thought that the ideal male body must resemble the Superman or Aquaman toys I had, all I really remember from those days was fighting crime, my superheroes having normal lives, and how silly little Batman looked in Barbie's oversized camper.

This, of course, is the experience of *most* children when they play with dolls and figurines. While it is important to include diversity and realistic images of adult bodies and personalities when designing dolls, what matters to kids is not what the doll looks like; what matters is who the doll can *be* and, more important, who the *child* can be through the doll.

In late 2015, Mattel launched a commercial entitled "Imagine the Possibilities." The spot begins with a question: "What happens when girls are free to imagine they can be anything?" Then we see adult students sitting down in a university lecture hall. A young girl walks into the front of the room and says, "Hello, my name is Gwyneth, and I'll be your professor today, and I will be talking about the brain." The scene shifts to a veterinarian's office, a soccer stadium, an airport gate's waiting area, and a museum where a young girl is depicted in each scene working as a vet, a football coach, a very busy businesswoman, and a docent. The customers, soccer players, airline passengers, and museumgoers are caught off guard but are delighted by the sharpness, creativity, and confidence of the young girls. It is not until the end of the commercial that we see a little girl, our college professor, playing with Barbies positioned in a miniature tiered university lecture hall. Words on the screen read: "When a girl plays with Barbie, she imagines everything she can become."

Bingo.

Now, I have to admit that the first time I saw the commercial, I teared up. In fact, when rewatching the commercial to write this book, I teared up again (in the middle of Starbucks, no less). Lest you think I am the only one who appreciates this commercial, you should know that as of this book's first writing the commercial has been seen at the official Barbie YouTube site a total of 18,155,153 times. The like/dislike ratio sits at 28,965 likes to 767 dislikes, which means 97.4% of people who rated the commercial liked it. That's impressive. (You can watch the commercial here: https://youtu.be/l1vnsqbnAkk)

However, one of the most interesting tidbits about the commercial is that Barbie, herself, is only portrayed for about 12 seconds in the entirety of the 120 second spot. To restate differently: the core product being advertised in a multi-million-dollar commercial designed to focus on the product, exclusively, appears on screen for just 10% of the entire commercial. While this may sound absurd, it drives home the point: Barbie's *physical appearance* does not matter. What matters is that Barbie is a conduit for the imaginations of little girls (and boys) everywhere that allows them to live out *their* dreams. Genius. And if children becoming whatever they dream they can be doesn't make you feel good inside, well…you must be made of plastic.

*   *   *

Goose bumps. Chills. Awe.

Call it what you will, but each one of us has had experiences where something–a song, a story, a piece of art, a dance performance, a dramatic monologue, a joke, even a piece of breaking news–has elicited a physiological, visceral reaction from us that gives us chills or goose bumps. Sometimes we cannot describe it or even understand *why* we are having the reaction we are having, but it happens: we find ourselves overwhelmed by something, some stimulus in our context, that *moves* us. It is in that moment that we simply *know* that whatever it is that is causing this reaction is truly something special. It's kind of like that indescribable feeling when you experience *love* at first sight.

In the creative world, coming up with a good idea is not just important, it is the difference between survival and death. A television show that runs out of good ideas "jumps the shark," an artist who runs out of good ideas is "washed up," and a clothing designer who runs out of good ideas is "out of style." In the world of marketing, failure to come up with a good idea leaves people immobile. Companies and campaigns cannot move forward without a good idea that initiates some momentum and propels everything forward. But as you know from life and living, coming up with "good ideas" can be quite difficult. Even if you were to develop a list of ideas, how do you know which ideas are *good* ideas and which ideas are just mediocre or even bad ideas?

In the previous chapter, I reviewed some tips and tricks that tend to help people with creative idea generation, tactics that help stir the mind, body, and soul and release all the cleverness being held deep, down beneath the surface. Now that we have creative idea *generation* out of the way, we can graduate to creative idea *evaluation*. Not all ideas are created equal, and to create a successful integrated marketing campaign we need to have an outstanding Big Idea. But how do we know whether or not an idea is good enough to be a Big Idea? How do we know an idea can fuel multiple marketing executions across a variety of media platforms? And, umm, by the way, what is a Big Idea in the first place?

The Big Idea: How To Find the Spirit of an Integrated Campaign

In marketing, a **Big Idea** refers to the concept that serves as the central theme, spirit, and message of an integrated marketing campaign. The Big Idea is a "big" deal because every marketing execution across every single medium *must* have a clear relationship with the Big Idea. If we were doing DNA testing on Maury Povich, every marketing execution better have at least some of the Big Idea's DNA in its system or else we have a problem.

In the Barbie example that opened this chapter, the Big Idea is that Barbie is not just a toy to little girls, she is a conduit for every little girl's dreams, aspirations, and future. Entitled, "Imagine the possibilities," every execution should include an element of make-believe or playing pretend, a little girl thinking about playing a different role in life, and a connection between Barbie and real-world experiences of little girls. A commercial showing an animated version of Barbie having a rave at the Barbie house is not going to survive the chopping block, but a commercial featuring a little girl pretending that Barbie is a DJ and then fast-forwarding to that girl deejaying a party in Ibiza just might (...incidentally, I hear Molly from the American Girl doll collection is also really into clubbing these days).

By this point in the campaign creation process it should be the case that you and/or your team have proposed several creative ideas that *could* be potential Big Ideas, but how do you know which one should win? Although there may be several promising candidates, we hope to find the creative idea that we **LOVE** the most, an idea that is **Logical**, **One-of-a-kind**, allows for **Variations on a theme**, and is **Emotionally evocative** (or otherwise engaging). I will take you through each component so that you have a better idea of what to look for in an ideal Big Idea.

Logical. A great Big Idea should connect our Focus goals and the research findings from our Understanding step in a logical, easy-to-follow way. Say, for example, we are hired to develop a marketing campaign for IKEA. Working with the company we have established that the Focus goals include reaching out to first-time homebuyers (i.e., Hot-Off-the-Press Customers) and making these customers aware of all the various new home product essentials IKEA stocks (i.e., Open Up More Options). From the research findings, we discovered that these customers are cost-conscious, believe that IKEA is not high-quality furniture, and expect to be able to customize their choices (…oh, we are silly entitled Millennials!). A great Big Idea that logically ties all these components together might be one entitled, "Mäde in Sweden" in which the idea is to use the word, "Mäde," followed by a blank space that is filled in with words like, "…by you" to promote the customization of the products, "…to last," to promote the endurance of the product, and "…to go together" to discuss the products accompanying any individual product in the portfolio. Each execution features the familiar "Mäde _____." graphic with the words that appear in the blank, and the feeling of the campaign is an informal, almost documentary-like exposition of how IKEA has a lot of products to offer, the products can be customized, and the products will last (and have warranties to be safe). The tone will be jovial and can include statements like, "With prices this low, you've got it Mäde," or, "You can tell people you Mäde it (we won't tell them we helped)," and, "For your first home, everything should be home-Mäde," and other fun phrases incorporating the Mäde theme. The "Mäde to go together" would also translate well to a web and in-store feature where product recommendations are made for each product in the store (speaking to the Open Up More Options objective). As you can see in this example, we can logically draw connections among the Big Idea, the Focus goals, and the research findings from Understanding.

One-of-a-Kind. I touched on this idea in the chapter on creativity, but for a Big Idea to be one we can love, well, it really does need to be inimitable by other companies. In the previous example, simply adding the two dots over the "a" to create the Swedish letter ä for the "Mäde in Sweden" campaign makes that idea unique to IKEA and inimitable by its competitors (no one is going to shop at Tärget and Wälmårt), well, not to mention that the Big Idea includes the name Sweden, as well. I once had the misfortune of working on a campaign sponsored by Visit Florida, the public/private corporation responsible for boosting tourism to Florida. One of the proposed Big Ideas was a campaign titled "Visit Florida: It Just Makes Sense" in which the proposal was to emphasize the five senses and how those senses can be stimulated during a trip to Florida. Lame. Why is this lame? Because just about *any* possible company could launch the exact same campaign. Instead of Visit Florida, imagine the city of Las Vegas running a campaign called, "Visit Vegas: It Just Makes Sense" in which they talk about all the ways Vegas stimulates the senses. Easy to do, right? And therein lies the problem. A great Big Idea should be as unique as possible to the company, brand, and/or products/services it is attempting to market. My proposed idea for

Florida: "Orange Ya Glad You Chose Florida," a campaign with a Florida orange theme, with a light sense of humor, executions that all incorporated oranges and educated potential visitors (who had never been before) about the many activities and destinations that await a visitor in Florida. Georgia could do peaches. New York could do apples. My home state of Illinois could do…wait for it…corn, but no one could do oranges the way Florida can, which is why it would both stand out and be difficult for competitors to copy. This kind of distinction also helps customers remember messages insofar as they pertain to you and not to your competitors. We have all had the unfortunate experience of seeing a commercial, hearing a great deal or discount, and then, days later, having difficulty remembering which company the commercial was for. A one-of-a-kind idea that fits with your company, brand, or product/service will aid recall, which in today's cluttered media environment is definitely a plus.

Variations on a Theme. Integrated marketing campaigns consist of several components. From dynamic videos to still print ads, interactive websites to social media conversations, whatever Big Idea we choose must be able to be translated across different media or else we are going to feel quite limited when developing ideas for our creative executions. Let's say that we are developing a campaign for Beats headphones. One Big Idea could focus on the sound quality of the headphones using audio clips and an idea entitled, "Hear the Difference. Beats the Difference." This idea would play particularly well for television, online video, and web in which the audio could be manipulated to show what it sound like using devices *other* than Beats products compared to how those same clips sound with Beats audio. This, of course, is not a terrible idea, but because the Big Idea focuses so much on sound we have limited ourselves in our potential executions to only those media where sound is an option. Now let's imagine another campaign, a slightly tweaked version of our original, entitled, "Beats Makes Sound Xplode." In this campaign, we have set the audience up for an in-your-face experience. The campaign can include the same audio experiences as before, but accompanying each experience is a sound wave positioned somewhere on the screen with an X placed at the moment the audio switches from a generic headphone to Beats. Similarly, in print ads and non-audio media, we show the same X at various audio wave intersections where it is clear the sound "steps up" to a new level when Beats enter the scene. The print ad could be in black and white in the section corresponding to the generic headphones and then explode into vibrant, saturated color for the Beats section. An interactive web game could challenge listeners to "Press X" on their keyboard when they hear the audio quality of the music get better during the game. See what I'm doing here? Even though both campaigns get at the same core idea–Beats headphones have better audio quality than other headphones–the latter idea permits more executions across a variety of media as opposed to the former idea, which limited our executions to audio-specific media. Making sure our Big Idea permits variations on its theme is essentially ensuring that we will not have our hands tied when it comes to creativity. Some constraints are good, but limiting ourselves in the channels we can use to reach out to consumers is not good, so the Variations on a Theme requirement helps mitigate these potential limitations.

Emotionally Evocative. The final consideration to help us determine whether a creative idea is just a *good* idea or a great *Big* Idea involves its ability to connect with customers on an emotional level. Now, to be clear, there are some campaigns that are primarily rational and cognitive in their approach that perform rather well, but most campaigns include both rational and emotional appeals. And, let's be honest, if I were to ask you to name a great commercial or print ad you like chances are you are going to think of something that was particularly funny or sad or heartwarming (i.e., a campaign that was emotionally evocative). A good example of the use of emotional evocation as a Big Idea is Subaru's recent campaign "Love. It's what Makes a Subaru a Subaru." Now, this idea is not altogether One-of-a-Kind, as I could just as easily ask, "What makes Depend Adult Diapers Depend Adult Diapers? Love," or, "What makes Preparation H hemorrhoid cream Preparation H hemorrhoid cream? Love." However, Subaru shifted its gears away from a purely cognitive campaign, which is typical of most car companies (i.e., listing safety features, tech specs, etc.), and incorporated the feeling of "love" throughout its campaign executions. The campaign's television commercials show heartwarming relationships like a father/daughter relationship in which the daughter is driving for the first time and the father, who still sees her as a child, is reassured by Subaru's safety record. The print ads consist of letters from *real* Subaru customers talking about their love of Subaru after they walked away, unscathed, from car accidents or drove away from their wedding in a Subaru car with "Just Married" written in the rear window. Promotional sales events known as "A lot to Love" events (i.e., you can love a car "lot" full of Subaru vehicles) accompany the campaign, as well. No matter the medium, any interaction with Subaru reinforces the love-themed emotional positioning of the brand and helps tap into the hearts, as well as the minds, of consumers.

How ironic that the example we end this section on is one that features "love" as its central theme, as it turns out that the secret to knowing whether a creative idea would be a solid Big Idea is LOVE: the idea is logical, one-of-a-kind, permits variations on a theme, and is emotionally evocative. Like anything, the development of an outstanding Big Idea gets better over time with practice as these LOVE tenets start becoming second nature to you. To help get the ball rolling, let's do an example together, shall we?

Where is the Love: An Example of Big Idea Development–Tropicana

I know I give Pepsi a hard time as a Coca-Cola loyalist, but to be fair, PepsiCo is a massive company. With over a quarter-million employees and annual revenues of over $60 billion, PepsiCo is one of the largest food and beverage companies in the entire world. So even though I am still loyal to the Coca-Cola I learned to love in my youth, I still have a soft spot in my heart and an appreciation for PepsiCo, its products, and its diversified approach to business.

Included in the PepsiCo portfolio of products is (obviously) soft drinks, other beverages like Gatorade and Tropicana, and even food products via its Frito-Lay division (e.g., Doritos, Lay's, Rold Gold Pretzels, etc.). This delicious combination of products has served PepsiCo quite well over the years, but as with any food company in the past decade, PepsiCo faced challenges with respect to shifting health trends and dietary preferences. So, in 2009, PepsiCo launched Trop50, a new version of its orange juice that contained 50% less sugar and 50% fewer calories. Not bad, right?

Not all consumers liked the new product, with some claiming that Trop50 was simply, "Classic Tropicana diluted with water," and others complaining that the product's claim of "no artificial sweeteners" was not true if you consider PureVia (a mix of ingredients including rebaudioside A, a stevia extract) a chemical creation. Still, Trop50 was successful at winning back Wandering Customers who began veering away from Tropicana consumption in favor of other alternatives fitting their newer, healthier diets. Now, Trop50 comes in over six flavors and has replaced traditional orange juice as the breakfast drink of choice for many in the intended target of young-to-middle-aged women.

Let's say we were in charge of launching a new campaign for Trop50 using our FUSION model:

> **Focus.** When determining the Focus goals, the powers that be at Pepsi want us to focus our efforts on consumers still on the fence about buying Tropicana-branded products like Trop50, a group that might buy orange juice on occasion but a group that also worries about the health effects of drinking too much juice with artificial preservatives and sweeteners. From that, we know that our Prospective audience consists of Wandering Customers. In addition, we have been tasked with increasing the sales of Trop50 specifically within this selected audience. Now, Trop50 in this instance includes both the original orange juice flavor and its variants (e.g., Pomegranate Blueberry, Pineapple Mango, etc.), so we have some leeway, but the idea is to sell more Trop50-branded products more often. Thus,

from this directive we know that our Desired Objective consists of Multiplying Purchases.

Understanding. We do a bit of research using the FUSIONLearn™ survey and find a few important insights that have the potential to inspire our campaign. First, with respect to Lifestyle, we have identified the customers to be middle income consumers who "like a good deal," have a mixed opinion of shopping, and skew female, roughly 30 years old. With respect to Education, this audience knows Tropicana and they have heard of Trop50, but they are not entirely sure what exactly Trop50 is in comparison to traditional orange juice other than that it is perceived to be "healthier." They are also more likely to trust their girlfriends' thoughts and the opinions of real people than communications that come directly from a company. With respect to Attitude, the audience has generally favorable attitudes toward Tropicana and even Trop50 despite not having purchased the latter. With respect to Reflection, this particular audience was to be healthier and, quite importantly, to "hang with the prettier girls." That's an odd insight but an interesting one, nonetheless, as it suggests Trop50 has the potential to take on an aspirational positioning. Finally, with respect to Needs, most of the needs elicited from this particular audience pertained to health, beauty, and looks.

Synthesize. Taking the Focus goals of trying to increase the purchase frequency of Trop50, specifically, and to engage customers that are neither loyal nor disloyal to Tropicana but who have at least heard of Trop 50, as well as the Understanding insights regarding the emerging customer profile, their current beliefs and articulated needs, we can start brainstorming some creative ideas. One idea, the "No Way to OJ" campaign, would be the orange juice market equivalent to the "Just Say No!" campaign to drugs in which women were encouraged to just say, "No way!" to OJ. Hmm. That's not a *terrible* idea, but it does threaten to cannibalize sales of regular Tropicana. It's also not particularly original or unique to orange juice per our measures of creativity, so there's that. Another idea, "Make Him Your Main Squeeze," anthropomorphizes Trop50 as the new love in a lady's life and relies on the use

of "squeeze" to tie the campaign back to oranges. While a
bit more original and slightly more relevant to the product,
this idea might be a bit of a stretch. The campaign could
talk about the different Trop50 flavors and how there is
probably one suited to your interests and/or preferences
in a parody of *The Bachelor* or *The Bachelorette*, which would
play well to this audience per our research findings, the idea
is not particularly useful or effective at addressing the
needs this audience has with respect to health, beauty, and
appearance. Furthermore, the source of the messages in
that campaign seem to come from the company itself as
opposed to other real women. A third idea, the "Feel Nifty
With Trop50," campaign is immediately unique to Trop50,
so that's a plus, and already seems to have the potential to
evoke emotions with the use of the word "feel" right in the
campaign's title. The "Feel Nifty with Trop50" campaign
would be designed to play on the number 50 with respect
to the research insights uncovered during the
Understanding phase of the FUSION process.
Components might include a promotion where customers
get 50% off a second bottle to encourage increased
purchasing, a promotion in which 50 trips are given away
to Hawaii (the 50th state), 50 recipes to try that incorporate
Trop50's different flavors, 50 female celebrities who drink
Trop50 and their favorite ways to do so (e.g., "Melissa
McCarthy likes a Trop50 Pineapple Mango mimosa in the
morning"), the 50 Miss America contestants recording
short videos of their favorite flavors per Trop50's
sponsorship of the show, the creation of a Trop50 Fit Fan
Club for real women who have used Trop50 to lose weight,
maintain weight, have healthier biometrics, etc., to discuss
tips, tricks, and techniques for feeling "nifty" and fit.
When we pit this idea against our LOVE standard, it seems
to pass with flying colors: the "Feel Nifty with Trop50"
campaign logically connects our Focus goals with our
Understanding research insights, it is a One-of-Kind idea
unique to Trop50 thanks to the use of 50 in the campaign
executions, there are plenty of potential variations on the
theme (e.g., 50th state, 50% off, 50 recipes to try, etc.), and
the campaign is emotionally evocative (e.g., feeling nifty,
bringing women together, aspirational feelings, positive
messages, feeling healthy, etc.). Indeed, it seems like the
"Feel Nifty with Trop50" campaign has what it takes to

make the leap from solid creative idea (i.e., it is original, unique, useful, and effective) to an integrated-marketing-worthy Big Idea.

I realize that this example may make the Big Idea generation process seem a lot simpler than what you imagine it is…well, that is because it *does* make the process a lot simpler. If you were hoping for some divine inspiration or some soul-searching journey that takes you from one corner of the globe to the other in search of enlightenment, well, good luck with that. Beautiful Big Ideas sometimes *do* emerge in a flash of insight, which is an altogether wonderful experience. Sometimes lyrics pop into my mind. Sometimes a melody manages to sneak its way into my brain. But these flashes of insight do not happen all the time, and even when they do, sometimes those ideas that seem so great at first lack endurance and fizzle over time. Other times, I'll sit down at the piano, think through what I am trying to express logically with my lyrics, plunk out a few potential melodies or chords until one strikes me in a way that I *feel* it emotionally. I make sure that the song I am starting to construct is not too similar to any songs that have come before it, and I craft verses, a chorus, and a bridge that are built around a central motif or chord progression. Indeed, some of my best songs were not creative flashes of insight or inspiration but, instead, were the result of hard work, thinking, trial and error, and a bit of luck. Excellent integrated marketing campaigns, too, can emerge from fortunate flashes of insight or from deliberate consideration of creative ideas with respect to logic, one-of-a-kind, variations on their theme, and their ability to evoke emotional responses from customers. There really is no one right way to arrive at a great Big Idea. Whether it is a flash of insight or a deliberate process, the important part is arriving at an idea that will achieve business objectives, integrate your target audience, and inspire creative executions across a variety of media. Sure, this sounds like a lot–it *is* a lot–but you can do it…and I bet you even have fun in the process.

That Which We Call a Rose: The Importance of Naming a Big Idea

Naming a child seems like it would be one of the most stressful decisions a human being ever has to make. I mean, think about it: that name is going to stick with someone for the rest of his/her life. People make judgments about others all the time simply based on their name (don't even pretend like you haven't). You would think that people would take this decision very seriously given the gravitas of a name. However, this is certainly not always the case. For example, I was named after my father because he promised my mother a new furniture set that, to this day, he has yet to deliver on. Similarly, I have decided that if, one day, I lose some bet and have to have children that I will name my child Entendre. I'm hoping for twins.

The seriousness of naming a child is paralleled only by the seriousness of naming a Big Idea. When naming a Big Idea, a few important considerations include 1) making sure the name conveys the spirit of the creative idea, 2) keeping the name as short and simple as possible (…remember our conversation about elegance?), 3) using everyday words that are easily understood and accessible to most people, 4) differentiating the name from other names that may have come before, and 5) sexying the name up a bit with alliteration, rhyme, rhythm, or a pinch of cleverness. Remember our "Mäde in Sweden" IKEA example from earlier? It checks off all the boxes necessary for a reasonably good Big Idea name, even adding the umlaut over the "a" in Made to "sexy it up" a bit. The Big Idea is something that you will constantly refer back to during the creation of the rest of your campaign, so you want to make sure the name excites people in the same way that the actual idea, itself, excites people.

When you are naming your campaign, imagine you are naming your child because, in many ways, you are. You will spend a lot of time making it (or make it very quickly – everyone is different and we won't judge you either way). You will spend several months waiting for it. The day it is delivered will be one of the happiest days of your life (and also one of the most exhausting). It will keep you up late at night for weeks or months in that early phase. Eventually you will sleep more easily and just keep the monitor on it to make sure it's doing alright. It will do things that make you laugh, things that make you cry, and things that confuse you. And then, at some point, you will get rid of it and replace it with a new, better version of itself…okay, so maybe that last one is only applicable to a campaign (…but that kind of depends on the kid).

Limbo: Between Big Idea and the Ideation Process

Here's a personal question for you: have you ever had to use the restroom (say #1) *so* bad, but you were not close to a restroom? Realizing this, you pack up your belongings wherever you are and head in the direction of a bathroom nearby, whether at a public place or your own home (which I hope has a bathroom). Here's the crazy thing: you can be a two-mile walk from home and have to use the restroom, yet you manage to walk the two miles and arrive at your doorstep with zero problems. However, the moment you put your key in the door, well, suddenly *something* changes. Your ability to hold it in, to stave off the urge to tinkle, the skill to control your own body suddenly flies out the window. If you are anything like me, this is when you begin doing a funny little dance, back and forth on each leg trying to think of *anything* besides rain, waterfalls, or the fact that you have to pee. Finally, you get the door open, you race inside and throw your belongings down, run to the bathroom and do your best to prepare yourself for what you *know* will be immeasurable relief…well, assuming you made it.

I use this example to illustrate an important point: human beings get really, really excited when they are on the cusp of something grand. Generating a Big Idea is, well, a *big* deal. You see, once you have settled on a Big Idea you can launch into what is typically *the* most fun part of an integrated marketing campaign: the specific marketing executions. You get to start talking about what the commercials will be like! You get to start talking about which celebrity would be a great endorser! You get to start talking about the colors and the music and the decorations! Yes, you finally get to plan the prom.

My theory for why this occurs has to do with the brain, dopamine release, and the appetitive processes in which our excitement and anticipation overwhelm us as we get closer to satiating some need that we have. However, it is precisely because of this natural tendency to lose control when we are on the cusp of something that we must do our best to maintain some semblance of self-control during the Big Idea generation process. Before you know it, you get ahead of yourself and retreating back to where you should be becomes exponentially difficult.

It is natural to "think ahead" to the many possible specific executions of the Big Idea. Someone will inevitably ask, "What will the television spot look like?" or, "How would this translate to our social media accounts?" In fact, this is actually what the "variations on a theme" requirement of a Big Idea is all about. The tricky part is not veering *too* far down that path before selecting a Big Idea that works on all the other levels. Why? Well, one reason is that people can fall so much in love with a specific execution that the love and excitement for that particular execution creates a halo around the overall Big Idea and other proposed executions that may not really warrant a halo. Say we are developing a campaign for the fitness apparel company lululemon and trying to come up with a solid Big Idea. One idea presented is a play on the word "lemon." Someone on the team gets the idea to do a nontraditional element in which we build lululemon-ade stands in major cities like Los Angeles, Chicago, and New York with clever signs talking about what to do, "When life hands you lululemon(s)." Although clever, fun, and creative, it is unclear whether or not the Big Idea of using a "lemon" theme is going to work. The lemon Big Idea may not logically link our Focus goals and our Understanding insights. The lemon Big Idea may not evoke strong emotional responses. It might, but we just are not sure quite yet. If we spend too much time brainstorming all the cool things we can do with lemons, well, we may have a *lemon* of a campaign on our hands when all is said and done.

Although it is okay to imagine the possible executions a Big Idea might lead to, something that often trips people up is the sunk cost fallacy. One of my biggest pet peeves is when a team member says something like, "Well, we have already spent so much time talking about this execution that it would be foolish to turn back now!" Nope. Not true. Unless we, as a group, have decided on all the ideas that should have come first (e.g., the Big Idea), then nothing should wed us to specific executions or ideas for specific executions because that's not how the process works.

The point to keep in mind here is that specific executions, although important, are a smaller component of a larger whole. Specific executions will come and go throughout the lifetime of an integrated marketing campaign, but the Big Idea is around the entire duration of the campaign. A strong Big Idea should be what motivates amazing executions, not the other way around.

Earlier in this chapter we talked about how certain experiences like hearing a beautiful song, watching an incredible movie, or locking eyes with a special someone walking by can give you goose bumps. These experiences are "feel good moments" that are difficult to describe, but you know them when you feel them. In those moments, everything makes sense: you feel good, you feel like the world around you has disappeared, it is just you and whatever is eliciting this powerful reaction out of you.

Often, people believe that these experiences are the result of good fortune, the stars aligning a particular way, the world simply making it happen magically. That can happen for sure. However, even in those moments, the "magic" typically comes from an idea making such good sense, from the idea being emotionally evocative, from the idea being unique, and from the idea having remarkable relevance and breadth. We tend not to notice this because we never really analyze why these magical moments make us feel the way we do, but if you pause, take a step back, and actually *think* about why you feel the magical way you do, you will see LOVE within these experiences.

One final point about Big Ideas, LOVE, and the interaction of the two: you cannot love what you do not know. *Le Petit Prince* is one of my favorite books of all time. In the book, a fox says to the main character, "On ne connaît que les choses que l'on apprivoise." which translates literally to, "One can only know the things that one has tamed," and figuratively to, "In order to know something, one most spend time observing and getting to know it." It is easy to dismiss ideas because they do not seem to fit the LOVE criteria, but I implore you to spend time on you and your team's proposed ideas. Actually give each one a fair shake. You may find an idea a bit off-putting or unusable at first, but the more time you spend thinking about the logic of the idea, the emotional quality of an idea, how unique it is, and how it might be expressed across different media the more you might be surprised. And remember that LOVE is also in the eye of the beholder. You may not be your target audience. What seems illogical or unemotional to you may be perceived as extremely logical or extremely emotional to your target audience. Part of being a good marketer involves perspective taking.

If a great Big Idea is loved, then it is also more likely to be remembered. A great Big Idea is one that is likely to stir thoughts and emotions. A great Big Idea stands out from the crowd. A great Big Idea is one we love running into over and over again in a variety of places and contexts. A great Big Idea gives us goose bumps. A great Big Idea gives us chills. A great Big Idea fills us with awe. A great Big Idea *is* LOVE.

*   *   *

After decades of being the blonde standard of beauty people everywhere have grown to love (and sometimes hate), Barbie is finally changing with the times. As I write this book, Mattel just announced the introduction of new Barbie dolls featuring different (read: more realistic) body shapes, skin tones, and even face shapes. The idea, of course, is that these new Barbies are more representative of the girls who will play with them, as well as representative of the women they see every day: moms, teachers, doctors, etc. That Mattel made these changes following four years of declining sales has led some cynics to criticize the company for acting in its own self-interest as opposed to some greater societal good, but regardless of what prompted the "Imagine the Possibilities" campaign, the fact remains that Barbie has forever changed the way customers think about Barbie and the value it brings to young girls.

With respect to our LOVE litmus test, the "Imagine the Possibilities" campaign logically links Mattel's goal to win back the attention of Wandering Customers–who may have strayed to Bratz dolls or other "more educational" toys competing for the interest of young girls–with the goal to increase purchases of Barbie dolls (i.e., Multiply Purchases), as well as to the Understanding insights with regarding attitudes customers had about Barbie (i.e., she's an unrealistic standard to which little girls should not compare themselves but also a great conduit for young girls to live out their dreams and aspirations). The campaign is one-of-a-kind in its identification of how young girls use Barbie to "play pretend" in a way that other toys are not used. While other dolls *can* be used to this end, it is Barbie that is known for this kind of play even with respect to the use of the term "Playing Barbies" to describe this kind of pretend playing. The campaign permits variations of its theme in that one can 'imagine possibilities' in a variety of ways: little girls imagining their future, the endless possibilities of new Barbie bodies, skin colors, and face shapes, the possibilities of Barbie across a variety of media (e.g., Barbie went on a drive with Derek Zoolander and documented the day on Instagram just because Derek asked her to hang out). And, finally, the campaign packs an emotional punch in the form of tapping into nostalgia, the feelings of youth, the excitement and joy that comes along with playing pretend and allowing one's imagination to soar. Indeed, it is difficult to watch the adorable commercial of little girls working in adult jobs and speaking with such confidence, expertise, and authority without getting a bit emotional, without feeling goose bumps, without watching in awe as Mattel uncovers the secret behind the magic of Barbie, a magic that few toys could ever hope to copy.

Of course, it remains to be seen what is in store for Barbie now that Mattel has initiated so many new ideas including substantial changes to the core product itself. The "Imagine the Possibilities" campaign is just getting started and has already launched effective television commercials, clever social media posts, and countless press mentions, suggesting that this Big Idea may have even more flexibility than Barbie herself.

What if...   *Ken You Believe It?*

After reading about all the significant changes happening in the World of Barbie, you might be asking yourself one question, "What about Ken?" Barbie's beau has been around for decades and yet, despite having a chiseled physique, relatively uncommon physical proportions, and a blond-haired, blue-eyed appearance, Ken has managed to avoid any and all criticism regarding his physical appearance (which is impressive given that the guy has no balls...literally.)

With the significant changes occurring on the female doll side, it is reasonable to wonder whether or not Mattel plans to change up the male dolls, as well. Right now, Ken is only available in two shades of white guy (fair-skinned blond dude, slightly tanner brunette) and one shade of light-skinned "ethnically ambiguous" guy (he could be white, he could be Latino, he could be black, he could be some combination of all three–nobody really knows for sure). To say that the male doll options in the realm of Barbie is limited would be an understatement.

Although there have been other male characters in the Barbie universe, the focus has predominately been on the female characters. You have probably heard of Skipper, Stacie, and Midge, the first two being Barbie's most well-known sisters (there have been others, but it's as confusing as a *Game of Thrones* family tree) and the last being Barbie's best friend, but do you know Brad, Allan, Curtis, Todd, Tommy, Blaine, or Ryan? They are, or were, male dolls existing in the world of Barbie, some were even dolls of color, but they were all short-lived.

Barbie's new "Imagine the Possibilities" campaign combined with shifting societal norms presents a real opportunity for Mattel to expand its male dolls for both little girls *and* little boys. Why shouldn't boys have male dolls through whom they can imagine their dreams, futures, and aspirations? To keep consistent with the changes seen in the female doll lineup, the Ken dolls should offer a variety of body types, skin colors, face shapes, and professions, from tech nerd to surfer, nurse to teacher. Mattel could donate to activities like Boy Scouts of America or Boys to Men that help young boys achieve their aspirations.

One effective way to negate the perception that Barbies or "playing with dolls" is a girl-only activity is to candidly ask little boys questions like, "Who plays with Barbie?" or, "Who plays with toy figurines?" or, "Who plays with superheroes?" Then the same boys could be asked what they want to be when they grow up. They will probably give answers ranging from football player to doctor, astronaut to video game creator. The final round of questions will ask the boys whether Batman could be any one of those professions (or Superman or Captain America), whether Barbie could, and whether Ken could. The hope is that little boys connect with Ken upon realizing that the new Ken dolls are *just like them*; they represent the kind of guy that the little boys hope they can grow up to be like. Of course, there is always going to be one kid who really thinks he can grow up to be a superhero, but chances are boys will connect with Ken in ways they never have in the past, in a way that all parents should be comfortable nurturing. Imagine *that* possibility.

IDEATION

CHAPTER 8 | All PORTS in the Brainstorm

What is your favorite color M&M?

Do you have a favorite color? Most people do, it turns out, including yours truly (blue, in case you're looking to restock my supply of Dark Chocolate Peanut M&M's, which also just so happen to be my favorite variety).

On New Year's Eve 2003, something catastrophic happened in the world of candy: all the color disappeared from every bag of M&M's, the tasty "melts in your mouth, not in your hands" treat beloved around the world. Since the 1940s, children and adults everywhere ripped open bags of plain, peanut, peanut butter, and almond M&M's, carefully separating their favorite color from the inferior "other colors," and then devouring them in all their sugary deliciousness.

Now, anyone with working taste buds and teeth (which might be everyone except for my grandma) will tell you that M&M's all taste the same. The plain blue M&M tastes the same as the plain red M&M which tastes the same as the plain green M&M and so on and so on. These aren't Skittles we're talking about here. Still, despite each and every M&M of a particular variety tasting the same, many of us have our favorite color and consider M&M's of that color to be "special." We humans are a weird bunch…regular monkeys would just eat the M&M's, but we humans are special monkeys.

Mars, Incorporated, the parent company of M&M's, was well aware that its consumers often had a favorite color M&M, which presented an interesting challenge for the company: how do you improve or change your core product and its packaging without rubbing your consumers the wrong way? Whereas Mars' competitors were able to launch exciting new products incorporating trendy flavors and exciting new campaign ideas, Mars' hands were tied. When you are an established product, existing more or less in the same way for decades, changing up your core product can be an extremely risky venture. Updating the famous candy's colors and packaging without arousing the ire of M&M's loyalists was going to require very careful thought and planning, and the solution that emerged seemed to be the most radical of ideas possible: to update the famous colors of M&M's, Mars would have to take all the colors away first.

In a campaign taking its cues from *Charlie and the Chocolate Factory*, Mars decided that 2004 would begin with every single M&M—every size, shape, and variety—being black or white. The familiar lowercase "m" was still branded onto the hard candy shell, but absent were all the colors. No red. No blue. No green. The shapes of the varieties remained—peanut M&M's were a bit more oval, plain M&M's were their typical circular shape—but the rainbow world of M&M's had changed to a binary world of black and white.

For a product relying so much on color as a source of satisfaction and enjoyment from its consumers, zapping everyone's favorite colors from every bag of M&M's was a huge move. *Huge.* Not only did Mars take away a point of product engagement/interaction (i.e., sorting out your favorite colors even if doing so mindlessly), the company also drew attention to the taste of its products by essentially stripping the product down to its fundamentals – no more flashy colors to distract people from the taste of the sweet treats.

But Mars didn't stop there…

In what may have been one of the best examples of an Integrated Marketing Strategy campaign in history, Mars decided to apply the black and white theme to literally *every single point* of consumer contact. Here are some examples:

> **The Product.** In perhaps the most obvious execution of the Great Color Quest campaign, every M&M candy was coated in either a black or white candy shell. The black candy shell M&M's featured a white "m" while the white candy shell M&M's featured a black "m." Regardless of whether it was a bag of plain M&M's, peanut M&M's, or some other variety, *every* M&M candy was either black or white. Perhaps Mars even saved a little bit of money on food dye during the campaign ;)

> **The Packaging.** Beyond simply removing color from the product, Mars also opted to remove all color from the M&M's packaging. This move was a particularly risky one, as color plays a critical role in M&M's packaging that it does not play for the product: packaging color identifies the M&M variety. Anyone with any knowledge of M&M's and its packaging knows that the brown bag denotes plain M&M's, yellow denotes peanut M&M's, tan denotes almond M&M's, red denotes peanut butter M&M's, blue denotes pretzel M&M's, green denotes crispy M&M's, and so on. Thus, taking away color from the packaging had the potential to confuse consumers who, for the first time in the product's history, actually had to *read* the packaging to make sure they were purchasing their preferred variety of M&M's. It is rarely a good idea to introduce complexity to the purchasing process, but if Mars were to be consistent in its Integrated Marketing Strategy, then removing color from its products' packaging was exactly the right thing to do. Interestingly, this shift from color packaging to black and white packaging spurred a frenzy for long-time M&M's loyalists and collectors who began purchasing cases of M&M's *in bulk* with the belief that the black and white packaging would become collectors' items.

The TV Commercials. In what quickly became the most beloved component of the Great Color Quest campaign, Mars opted to rely on old black and white films–like *Casablanca* and *The Wizard of Oz*–to exploit its colorless campaign. The advertising agency BBDO developed a spot entitled "And You Were There" in which Dorothy, upon waking from her dream at the end of *The Wizard of Oz*, describes how she just returned from a world of color where each of the M&M's spokescandies were also present and also in color. She looks around the room at the black and white candies and laments that everything was, "a lot better," in color. The use of a classic American film central to most people's childhood tapped into a core emotional theme of the Great Color Quest: nostalgia. Just as we have happy memories of magic and wonderment *The Wizard of Oz*, including our favorite parts of the film, so, too, do we have childhood memories of M&M's, our favorite colors, our favorite flavors, our favorite memories of eating red and green M&M's at the holidays or opening the miniature bags passed out during Valentine's Day parties in grade school. Beyond tying the black and white theme of the campaign into the black and white films of days past, linking the campaign to a movie so integral to our childhood and culture tapped into nostalgic memories and emotions that truly elevated the campaign to a higher level, while also giving consumers something fun/funny to talk about. The best part? Changing every television advertisement to black and white during the campaign unscored the importance of *consistency* that is central to any Integrated Marketing Strategy.

Web and Digital Media. The Great Color Quest launched at a time before Facebook, Instagram, Twitter, and other social media tools were as pervasive as they are today. However, this did not stop Mars from integrating the Great Color Quest into its web offerings. True to form, the M&M's website was transformed to a black and white design. Instead of traditional print advertisements, Mars opted to feature a photo gallery depicting the M&M's spokescandies as famous black and white film stars: Charlie Chaplin, Ingrid Bergman and Humphrey Bogart in Casablanca, and others. In a move that was truly cutting edge for its time, Mars offered black and white e-cards featuring the spokescandies that site users could send to friends in a way that blended web and word-of-mouth marketing. The site also featured games (e.g., "Remember Color?") in which users were asked to answer questions that involved color-related answers (...they really thought this through!).

The Sponsorships. Another example of how far-reaching the Great Color Quest campaign was comes in the form of M&M's and its sponsorship of NASCAR at the time. Indeed, the black and white campaign veered its way onto the racetrack by changing car #38 driven by Elliott Sadler from a colorful car to a black and white racer. NASCAR, a sport of ever-increasing popularity with an audience loyal to the M&M's brand, provided a great opportunity for Mars to reach a key constituency in a noticeable way: whereas all the other NASCAR cars featured their typical bright colors and designs, the new version of the M&M's car stood out by being black and white, consistent with the Great Color Quest campaign and markedly different from what was expected on the racetrack in a way that commanded the audience's attention.

The Promotions. The Great Color Quest launched when the M&M's characters Red and Yellow appeared on *Dick Clark's New Years Rockin' Eve* to announce that all the color had disappeared from M&M's. The severity with which the campaign was presented contrasted sharply with an alternative approach of subtly or passively introducing the idea that color had vanished. Mars wanted people to know about the color campaign and opted to announce it in a major way deliberately at the year change, a time when mental shifts and resolutions are the themes of the day. However, accompanying the absence of color was a "hope for promise" ripped right from the hands of Willy Wonka: color *would* be coming back but would be introduced one bag at a time. Specifically, single bags of the new-and-improved, brighter colors would be gradually introduced throughout the course of the campaign. Those lucky few who happened to be the random purchasers of these color-filled bags did not receive a tour at the highly mysterious and elusive Mars factory with Forrest Mars, Jr., but, instead, received $20,000, a new 2004 Volkswagen Beetle Convertible GLS custom-colored to the color of M&M's they found, and a trip to Los Angeles for the color revealing event that concluded the campaign. The winners stretched from Wisconsin to Hawaii, from 14-years old to 40, including a young girl who, in being taught a lesson to spend her own money, purchased a winning bag, as well as an expectant mother who craved M&M's throughout her pregnancy.

Nontraditional/Guerilla Marketing. Executing a marketing campaign using television commercials, websites, and sponsorships is not a particularly unique approach to marketing. Indeed, most marketing campaigns employ some mix of television commercials, print advertisements, sponsorships, and promotional activities as fundamental components of any campaign. Every now and then, however, a company will toss in a "nontraditional" marketing execution. This word "nontraditional" is loosely defined but essentially can be considered as anything one doesn't normally think about with respect to traditional marketing channels. Although not an entirely novel idea, Mars launched a Great Color Quest Bus Tour to coincide with the months-long marketing campaign. The campaign consisted of Mars employees driving a large, black and white bus across the United States to generate awareness about the Great Color Quest campaign, which the traveling troupe did by setting up shop at major events, inviting consumers onto the bus to take pictures and, of course, eat M&M's, all while documenting these interactions in the black and white *Daily Press* newspaper published and updated on the M&M's website. A campaign bus, interactive kiosks, and engaging activities at nationwide events may be more commonplace in today's marketing world, but at the time of the Great Color Quest, Mars was engaging in truly innovative, robust activities, truly leaving no stone unturned.

The Great Color Quest consisted of other components, as well, each engaging the black and white theme in its own way. Together, all the marketing executions allowed Mars to tinker with a very sensitive characteristic of its core product–color–without the risks a quick, drastic color change overnight could have presented. The story became *less* about the shift in color, which might have irked loyalists, and *more* about an appreciation of color, in general. Mars reinforced this idea by using a very clever tagline for the marketing campaign that immediately followed the Great Color Quest campaign: Chocolate is Better in Color. Sure, the new M&M's colors might be different from what consumers were used to. Yes, the colors might be brighter than what consumers expected. But hey – remember how boring M&M's were when they were only black and white? The new colors might not be the same colors you were used to, but guess what: Chocolate *is* Better in Color.

*   *   *

By now, you probably know that I love all-things creative. If I could play piano and sing all day, I would. If I could dream up stories and write children's books all day, I would. If I could design a house from foundation to roof and then build that house, I would. I live for creativity and the brilliant ideas that somehow find their way into my brain and into the brains of other people, as I am just as excited, entertained, and bewildered by the creative masterpieces of others. In fact, I think the creative accomplishments of mankind are a big part of what makes life interesting and worth living; otherwise, we would all be sitting around staring at each other in silence all the time…that would be weird.

Truth be told, we would all probably rather be *creating* something, anything really. New ideas. New recipes. New designs. There's an interesting appeal to novelty and creative expression that feels almost instinctive and innate to human beings, something Maslow would refer to as "self-actualization," but that we, as everyday, ordinary people just think of as *freedom*. Creating makes us feel *free*.

The last chapter brought us to a Big Idea, a theme or concept that captures a key insight that should resonate with our selected Prospective Audience and motivate them to engage in our Desired Objective but does so in a way that excites, enthralls, captivates, and entertains our audience. A great Big Idea inspires us, as the folks developing the campaign, to dream; the Big Idea gets our creative juices flowing and starts the fire under our feet. It is with our brains turned on, our creativity surging, and our desire to tell a complete story that the Big Idea propels us into the development of a complete integrated marketing campaign, which, friends, is my *favorite* part of integrated marketing because, at long last, we are *creating*.

In this chapter, I take you through each of the tools available to marketers within the scope of integrated marketing. From long-established media like television and print advertisements to more modern media outlets like search engines and social media, this chapter presents each tool, discusses its upsides and downsides, and reminds that while many successful campaigns make use of several of the tools available, every campaign need not use *every* single tool *every* single time. Before we begin the discussion of each tool, however, we start with a conversation about why we would even consider using an integrated marketing approach in the first place.

Justifying an IMS Campaign Via Efficiency & Elegance

The execution of a campaign as comprehensive (and likely as expensive) as the Great Color Quest campaign begs a very important question: why do anything in the first place? M&M's is clearly a well-known, well-liked brand around the world, so why would Mars even feel the need to do anything by way of advertising for such a well-established brand?

To answer that question, a young, naïve undergraduate marketing student (i.e., yours truly), placed a phone call to Mars on March 22nd, 2004. I contacted Dagmar Welling, a Consumer Affairs Specialist at MasterfoodsUSA (the division of Mars, Incorporated, responsible for all-things M&M's). Mars is notorious for being an extremely private company and, true to form, Mr. Welling did not shed any light on the financial reasons behind the decision. Follow-up research revealed that candy and chocolate confectionary sales had dipped 2% in the year leading up to the campaign, which, while a move in the wrong direction, did not seem catastrophic. Perhaps a greater motivator was a comparison between Mars and its biggest competitor: Hershey. At that time, circa 2004, Mars enjoyed the number one spot above Hershey's in the over 100 countries in which both brands operate except for one: the United States. Even as of this book's publication, Hershey's edges Mars as the number one candy company in the United States. Thus, one potential motivation for the campaign would be to generate enough buzz and excitement for a core Mars product that would help give the company an edge over its longtime competitor.

That's fine and dandy, but then why go through such a complicated and comprehensive campaign simply to change the color of the M&M's? Couldn't Mars have simply changed the colors overnight and released new packaging simultaneously? Maybe, but consider the drama and theatrics of the two, very different approaches: 1) quietly release slightly brighter colors overnight with new packaging, or 2) take away *all* color for several months, gradually introduce new, brighter colors in a global, Willy Wonka-esque game, and segue into a new subsequent campaign extolling the merits of your central campaign theme: how chocolate is better in color. When we distill it to this simple comparison a clear winner emerges. The former approach had the potential to irritate customers and evoke feelings of betrayal and confusion whereas the latter made the drastic product shift more of a fun game of which customers could be a part.

Now it should be noted that Mars had used color and, more specifically, color changes to market M&M's before. However, in these previous campaigns, new colors were always *added* to the familiar mix, never taken away (although the winning colors often "replaced" a familiar color like brown and orange). In 1995, blue was introduced as the winner of the M&M's Color Campaign, winning over 50% of 10 million votes (besting competitors pink and purple). Not one to give up a fight so easily, purple won a follow-up campaign in 2002, this time beating aqua and pink in a voting process where over 10 million votes were cast in over 200 countries, according to Mars. Moral of the story: few people want a pink M&M outside of the Easter holiday season or a baby shower.

These prior color campaigns were effective buzz generators, but neither campaign was nearly as robust in its execution as the Great Color Quest campaign. The Great Color Quest campaign allowed M&M's to essentially *own* the idea of color and the importance of each color it offers. Even the personification of those colors in the form of the spokescandies—from the regular-Joe Red and Yellow, the neurotic Orange, the sultry Green, and sophisticated and sassy Brown—reinforces this idea that each color symbolizes something special, something unique. Now, of course, consumers can choose a custom mix of colors—ranging from hot pink to lime green—at places like M&M's World in Las Vegas or the M&M's store located in Terminal 2A at Paris-Charles de Gaulle Airport, one of the first stores of its kind.

Could a simple television commercial have announced the new colors? Sure. Even a simple press release could have been sent out alerting media outlets to the color change. That approach would have cost Mars nothing and still spread the word. However, as aforementioned, just dumping this news on the customers might have been irritating to them or even upsetting. Plus, there's a chance that customers would not have come across a commercial or a news story about the color change, which would leave them confused in the store when changes to the packaging and the product just suddenly appeared one day. Because integrated marketing campaigns reinforce a message across a variety of media, conducting an integrated campaign ensured that consumers would be well aware of the massive change M&M's were about to undertake.

Another upside to using an integrated campaign is that promotions and event marketing, two of the tools in our IMS toolkit, engage consumers in ways that few other marketing approaches do not. Thus, by developing the Great Color Quest campaign, Mars was able to integrate customer experiences into the process in a way that was more likely to stimulate their interest and get them invested in the campaign. Shortly, we will discuss four underlying educational drivers that our IMS tools should strive to fulfill, and in the case of M&M's Great Color Quest, having an integrated approach fueled customer involvement in ways few other approaches could have accomplished singularly.

As with anything in business, the decision to conduct an IMS campaign v. a one-off print ad, social media post, or press release is a tradeoff. The bigger and more robust the campaign, the more expensive the campaign is likely to be. This can pay off nicely if the campaign winds up being a success. However, if the campaign flops, well, you have an expensive mess on your hands and a lot of explaining to do to your boss. However, as we will discuss in the next chapter, several professional-quality tools needed to create a campaign are now available for free or at increasingly lower costs. This makes conducting an IMS campaign much easier from a financial standpoint (although time is also money).

Another point in favor of IMS is that, in today's world, customers and companies are connected via multiple channels–television, radio, print, internet, social media. Having isolated campaigns or unique executions across different media channels would be confusing and simply add to the clutter of an already cluttered world. IMS campaigns are really becoming the standard as companies realize that hitting customers with the same look, feel, and messaging is one of the most surefire ways to break through in a muddled marketing world.

Another pro for IMS: once a campaign has been created, it becomes surprisingly *easier* to create one-off print ads, social media posts, and press releases because the campaign, itself, provides a theme or "home base" that serves as an inspirational starting point. One amazing example of this–actually *two* great examples of this–comes from Oreo cookies. During the 2013 Super Bowl in New Orleans, the power went out. Of course, no one had any way of knowing that the power would go out during the game, but within minutes a marketing wizard at Oreo tweeted a message that included a single cookie on a black gradient background with the copy, "You can still dunk in the dark." "What?! How could they know?" you wonder, "Did Oreo deliberately make the power go out? Certainly there is some *twist* to this (Oreo pun intended)!" However, before you think that Oreo's brand managers were engaging in some sneaky shenanigans, you should know that the cookie crew responsible for Oreo's marketing had decided, over a year prior, to engage with customers *every single day* as part of their latest IMS campaign. This meant that Oreo had a dedicated team of people paying attention to what customers were talking about *every* day and replying with a clever Oreo-themed post. This is why, just months prior, Oreo also posted a Facebook post that depicted an Oreo cookie with several cream layers in the different colors of the rainbow to celebrate gay pride, which was a popular topic during the month of June. Remember that luck is simply when preparation meets opportunity. Oreo was prepared, the opportunity arose, and the company got very, very lucky: the Super Bowl tweet was retweeted over 16,000 times and captured the attention of its 80,000 followers on Twitter and 32 million followers on Facebook, as well as several of their friends…all for free.

As with most business decisions, when it comes to asking (read: convincing) yourself whether or not you should conduct a full IMS campaign, it is best to engage in a cost/benefit analysis with the understanding that a comprehensive, massive IMS campaign can be very expensive, more expensive than just a single television spot or a nearly-free social media campaign. The secret to making sure that your IMS campaign gets a green light from the powers that be is to "go lean"–to be as elegant and as efficient as possible by including the *fewest* number of campaign elements that will *maximize* the overall benefit or gain possible.

Could M&M's have included free black and white coasters mailed directly to people's homes with an order form for customized M&M's? Sure. That would have allowed them to check off the "direct marketing" checkbox of an IMS campaign. Could they have created life-sized spokescandy costumes in black and white to run around the bases at televised sporting events? Yep. Then we could check off another "Nontraditional" box and maybe even a PR or Sponsorship box depending on the nature of the arrangement. But that would be overkill–that's neither elegant nor efficient. Your boss, if you had one, would look at you like you are an idiot.

So then how do we know whether our campaign includes *just enough* elements to make it effective but not *too many* elements to make it more expensive than it needs to be? To answer that question we now turn to a conversation about the educational drivers that should be a part of every IMS campaign.

Educational Drivers: Molding the Mind Through Marketing

If you think about it, every marketing execution does *one* thing: educates customers about *something*. Whether that education is about new ways to use the same product (Multiply Purchases), additional products in a company's portfolio that could be useful for a customer (Open Up More Options), exciting ways to engage with the brand (Rally the Troops), or simply to provide information as an end unto itself (Educate), each marketing execution should be in service of one of our four Desired Objectives. Because customer education is at the heart of every good marketing campaign, we should probably have a conversation about *how* people learn in the first place. As you will come to find, different tools in the IMS toolkit are better suited for particular learning styles, and because one major point of conducting an IMS campaign is to compensate for one tool's shortcoming with another tool's assets, we need to make sure we cover our bases.

Although there are several different theories regarding how people learn, several educational researchers have developed theories based on an early idea proposing that there are essentially four **learning styles**: visual, auditory, tactile, and kinesthetic (Barbe 1979). That is not to say that people are *only* visual or *only* tactile learners. Each of us can use any or all four of the different learning styles, and it is often the case that we prefer different styles depending on the context in which we are learning. For example, when it comes to academic research, I tend to prefer visual information: I would rather see your data plotted on a pretty bar chart than to hear your means and significance levels stated aloud (that does nothing for me). However, when it comes to learning a song on piano, it is easier for me to engage in kinesthetic learning that involves feeling the piano keys beneath my fingers, the chord transitions with my hands, and the movement of my arms across the keyboard as I play the song. Visualizing the movement of my hands does nothing for me, but some pianists and musicians are quite good at visualizing their movements and their music before they even touch their instrument.

The key idea is that the elements included in any IMS campaign should cover these four learning styles. That way, regardless of an individual's preferred method of learning in a particular context, an IMS campaign covering all the bases is more likely to be successful in educating customers than a campaign relying on just one modality (e.g., visual).

Let's take a look at each of the learning styles in greater depth, and I will give you an example of how each one can be incorporated into an IMS campaign:

- **Visual:** visual learning involves the use of imagery, graphics, and drawings to help individuals understand and encode new information. Not surprisingly, visual learning tends to come in handy when subjects involve design, visuospatial relationships, and structure or order. Imagine a campaign for Bengay, the topical analgesic heat rub applied to the body to relieve minor aches, pains, and strains. Someone who has never heard of Bengay before might benefit from seeing someone applying the topical analgesic to his body in a commercial, but why stop there? Including a cartoon graphic showing how the product works could also be beneficial. Furthermore, a consistent color palette in a campaign for use within television advertisements, print ads, photos posts on social media, and–most importantly–on the product's packaging will help customers recognize the product in store, as well as recall knowledge about the product later.

- **Auditory:** auditory learning involves listening. We probably all have friends who are "good listeners," because they listen to our problems, no matter how trivial, and are *so* good at repeating what we just said as if they actually paid attention. That's the kicker: auditory learning involves paying attention to the spoken word. As such, auditory learning involves oral instruction, lectures, audio books, engaging conversations and dialogues, reading aloud, and any other learning technique that involves using sound. The interesting thing about auditory learning is that it is not just about *what* is said, it is also about *how* things are said. That is, instead of focusing only on the content of what is spoken, auditory learning involves picking up on tones, inflections, and other sound cues that are also encoded. Not surprisingly, there tends to be a link between musicianship, language-learning ability, and auditory learning. If Bengay were to factor in auditory learning, its campaign would include a voiceover during television commercials articulating the benefits and uses of the product. The campaign might also include a jingle or a sound cue that can be incorporated in online campaign elements as well as any television and radio executions. Any music used would also reinforce the product: a song that starts in a minor key but switches to a major key once we see Bengay being used or the name/product appearing on screen would be helpful. Even the sound the product makes as it is applied could matter, from the freshness "pop" sound removing the safety seal to the smooth v. crackly sound of an ointment being applied to the skin.

- **Tactile:** tactile learning involves touching. Some people learn this at an early age, like those handsy boyfriends and girlfriends that our parents warned us about during our teenage years. Unlike visual and auditory learning in which people can sit back, relax, and learn from afar, tactile learning involves being up close and personal (sometimes too up close and personal) so that individuals can *feel* a stimulus in order to learn about it. For Bengay, one way to incorporate tactile learning is to provide product samples to potential customers. What better to have people learn about Bengay via tactile learning than to have them touch it, right? Well, although that is a good idea, it is not the *only* way to engage tactile learning for Bengay. Imagine, instead, a Bengay booth at a medical tradeshow where various models of human body parts are present. Some models might be of bone joints (e.g., the knee, the elbow) whereas other models might be of muscle fibers. The models would be deliberately designed to have friction or tension just as a real human body might. Letting tradeshow attendees have a hands-on experience with these models would help them learn about how the body tenses up and why Bengay could be a good solution for relieving the pain associated with that tension.

- **Kinesthetic:** although some researchers consider the tactile and kinesthetic styles to be one and the same, others posit that tactile is *only* about touch whereas kinesthetic is about *movement* and *engagement* beyond simple touch. Whether that means full body movement or taking part in a physical experiment, the idea behind kinesthetic learning that sets it apart from tactile learning is that it is about more than just letting people touch something. In the case of Bengay, one can imagine a viral social media campaign in which the company encourages users to test the non-slippery, non-sticky nature of the ointment to assuage the fear that Bengay might leave an oily residue or make skin feel sticky after use. Whether it involves applying Bengay to objects and throwing them against a wall (to see if they stick) or applying Bengay to a plastic potholder to see if it makes the holder lose its gripping power (to see if Bengay is too slippery). Although silly, I bet the videos get a lot of views and the people making them learn a thing or two about the consistency of Bengay without even having to touch the cream itself.

I want to highlight something you may have missed just now. At no point during the four descriptions did I refer to customers as "visual learners" or "auditory learners" because that is not how it works. No one is *only* a visual learner or *only* a tactile learner. As I mentioned earlier, each of us uses *all four* of these learning styles to different degrees with some styles being more dominant in particular domains than others. At some point, we are all visual learners or auditory learners or tactile learners or kinesthetic learners. This is an important point to make because people actually refer to themselves as a "visual learner" only or an "auditory learner" only quite often. Nope. Sorry. That is not true. Although you may certainly have a preferred learning style, the fact of the matter is that we use all four of the learning styles whether we like or not.

Furthermore, it is actually dangerous and rather misleading to believe that each individual has *one* dominant learning style because that would imply that we should develop a campaign that corresponds to *one* particular style if we found out through research that our target market is "visual," for example. Researchers have consistently debunked this myth that matching instructional material to an individual's "learning style" is more effective. It isn't. In fact, what research *does* support is the idea that people tend to learn information better when it is **multi-modal**. What does multi-modal mean? Multi-modal simply means that people learn information best when it is present in several different modes: visual, auditory, tactile, *and* kinesthetic.

This brings us back to the main point of this section: any good IMS campaign will contain elements that deliver information via visual, auditory, tactile, and kinesthetic learning styles. When determining how to "go lean" with your IMS campaign, which means including only those elements that are effective at achieving your Desired Objective without going overboard or being too redundant, one consideration needs to be the ability for selected tools to educate customers across these four learning styles. Every IMS campaign should engage customers using a multi-modal learning strategy as this approach will help customers encode the content being communicated into memory and increase the likelihood of these customers engaging with our brand and products/services. So now that we know what we need to do, let's talk about the tools available to help us get the job done.

The IMS Toolkit: Building a Campaign from the Ground Up

When people teach Integrated Marketing Communications as a class, they typically begin with the conversation that we are about to have. This, of course, is funny because here we are, more than halfway through a book about integrated marketing communication, and we are *just now* having the conversation that most people start with. Hmm. What gives?

Well, here's what gives: when most people teach integrated marketing they only present students with the tools without providing any context in which (or fundamental foundation upon which) those tools can be used to build a successful marketing campaign. In other words, those classes essentially hand untrained workers a box of tools and hope that they will figure out how to use them to build something stable and great. What usually happens next is that students *do* build something, but the something that they have built is unsteady, weak, and not likely the best structure they *could* have built with a bit more guidance up front about why and what tools they should have been using to build in the first place.

This, of course, is what sets the FUSION model apart from these other approaches to teaching integrated marketing. We still cover everything that these other classes cover; we just cover a lot more, information that will help you wield those tools more adeptly and effectively than your non-FUSION counterparts.

It turns out that there are *a lot* of tools in the IMS toolkit and, thanks to technology and innovation, that toolkit just keeps getting bigger and bigger as we devise new media that connect customers and companies with one another. To help keep it all organized, you guessed it, I have a simple memory aid: PORTS.

Now, I chose PORTS because to "port" something in technological speak means to transform something, like a game or an app or a program, from one medium to another. Usually this involves a bit of tweaking so that the updated version fits the medium to which it has been translated, but the spirit and feel of the original version remains. That's essentially what we are doing when we create an IMS campaign: we have a creative Big Idea that serves as the theme for the campaign and then we "port" that idea into different media and executions that, while unique per their medium, all share a common tie that binds (whether that tie be tone, look, color, or some other unifying characteristic).

A port is also a fine wine, so if that suits your fancy, you can think of that kind of port. A port is also where a ship docks, so if you are a seafaring traveler, well, you can think of that, too. Or maybe you don't even like the idea of calling it PORTS. Good news! You can remember them by thinking of IMS as being a fun SPORT to play. Or, if you are German, you can think of the famous German toast in which people say, "PROST!" to one another before guzzling down a big stein of beer (...or a stein of port, but then that just feels like we're overdoing it at that point). Whatever helps you remember the toolkit categories and each category's respective tools is entirely up to you, but here are the categories of the IMS toolkit as I like to remember them:

- **Partnerships:**
  - o Sponsorships and Endorsements
  - o Public Relations and Press Releases
  - o Sales/Customer Service
  - o Promotions
  - o Sampling
  - o Philanthropic Initiatives
  - o Bundling and Cross-Promotional Activities
  - o Product Placement

- **Outlandish:**
  - o Guerilla Marketing
  - o Content Marketing
  - o Experiential Marketing

- **Revolutionary:**
  - o Product Innovation
  - o Packaging Redesign
  - o Pricing Shift
  - o Alternative Access

- **Traditional Media:**
  - o Television
  - o Print
  - o Radio
  - o Outdoor
  - o Indoor (POP, In-Store Displays)
  - o Internet/Website
  - o SEO/SEM
  - o Mobile
  - o Direct Marketing
  - o Tradeshows/Events

- **Social Media:**
  - o Social Networks (e.g., Facebook, Instagram, Twitter)
  - o Word-of-Mouth
  - o Forums and Message Boards (e.g., reddit)
  - o Blogs and Tumblr

Some overlap exists between the various tools–for example, YouTube could be classified both under Traditional Media (with respect to the creation of online video advertisements) and Social Media (with respect to the site's interactive comments and subscription network of users). Don't let this cause you to lose sleep at night; this categorization is an arbitrary memory device as it is. We have bigger fish to fry.

Now let's go through each category and the tools within each category in greater detail so we can learn a bit about each tool's strengths, some potential shortcomings or weaknesses, and some good examples of how the tools have been put to use in past campaigns that will (hopefully) inspire you while developing your campaigns:

Partnerships. The Partnerships category includes any IMS tool that requires engaging a partner in order to use the tool effectively. Whether the partner is another company, another organization, a human being, or even another product or service, Partnership tools require that you pair up with one or more entities in your marketing execution.

One of the best-known tools in this category is **Sponsorship and Endorsements**. A sponsorship is when a company provides money, products, services, or other assets to another organization in exchange for access to something that the receiving party has, usually customers with eyeballs. Sponsorship deals vary from detail to detail but the general theme remains the same: I will fork over some of my resources in exchange for something you have that I want so that, ideally, we both benefit from the exchange. A good example of a sponsorship is Nike sponsoring the annual Chicago Marathon. Think about it: nearly 50,000 runners being cheered on by hundreds of thousands of spectators lining the streets of Chicago. That's a lot of eyeballs that can see Nike's logo plastered on all the marathon marketing collateral. Plus, Nike could not ask for a better audience: runners! What does Nike sell: shoes! And track jackets! And running apparel! Better yet, I am sure Nike's lawyers worked out an exclusivity agreement with the marathon organizers: you will notice that *no* other athletic apparel companies sponsor the event at any level. So the marathon gets money and the caché of being affiliated with the world's dominant athletic apparel company and Nike gets unfettered access to the very people it hopes will buy its products. **Pros**: generates awareness, links your brand/company with an exciting event (e.g., concert, sporting event), permits direct engagement with target audience; **Cons:** can be expensive, might get lost in the mix of other sponsors, customers can make the link that you are paying to be at the party.

Endorsements are similar to sponsorships except that the partnership in an endorsement is typically between a company and an *individual*. In an endorsement, companies typically pay some celebrity or well-known icon an undisclosed sum of money to tell the rest of us regular people how amazing the company is and/or its products are. The French company Chanel once paid Brad Pitt, American heartthrob, to endorse its products in a campaign that most ridiculed for being a bit *too* artistic (and confusing…it was supposed to be some profound statement but felt more like a poem written by someone who knows nothing about poetry). A better example, also from Chanel, involved Audrey Tatou, the French actress, starring in a commercial directed by Jean-Pierre Jeunet (who had previously worked with Ms. Tatou in films like *Amélie*). Audrey, replacing Australian actress Nicole Kidman, became the famous face associated with the brand. Endorsements work because people attribute the positive feelings they have toward the celebrity to the product the celebrity is hawking. In an interesting reversal, clothing store Abercrombie & Fitch allegedly offered *Jersey Shore* "star" The Situation $10,000 *not* to wear their clothing because they did not want their target audience associating their brand and its products with someone like The Situation (…now, of course, Abercrombie has its own problems to deal with). **Pros:** benefitting from positive feelings toward celebrities, credibility per the celebrity agreeing to be associated with the brand, humanizing otherwise intangible services or products lacking brand personalities. **Cons:** expensive depending on the celebrity, the risk of the celebrity becoming unpopular or becoming controversial (e.g., Jared Fogel for Subway), customers knowing a celebrity is only promoting a brand because of money (e.g., Paris Hilton eating a massive burger while riding a mechanical bull for Hardee's/Carl's Jr. – everyone knows Paris Hilton only eats flavored air).

Another partnership tool is the **Press Release**. A press release is essentially a summary of some big news that a company wants the world to know. Now, you might be wondering how a company sharing information via a press release is a "partnership" tool, but keep in mind that unless a reporter, an editor, or some other contact at a media company buys into your "news," your press release is dead on arrival. When I first interned at the marketing agency in St. Louis while still a student I wrote several press releases on behalf of our clients. The process was fairly routine: we had access to various publications' upcoming editions and the topics they were planning to cover, so we would dream up some interesting hook or way that our companies' products were relevant to the stories they were looking to write, and we would either call the editor or write up a release and send it to them hoping that our due diligence would be enough to get a story placed in their publication (or, in many instances, in their news segment on television). I cannot tell you how many times stories I wrote appeared in publications almost *word for word* without any credit to me or acknowledgement that the story was written by someone getting paid to write press releases for a company. You should also know that it was about at *this* point in my life I stopped believing anything I read in the news or saw on television. **Pros:** press coverage tends to be seen as objective, more credible, and more relevant than advertisements and, at a cost of virtually nothing, is a lot cheaper, too. **Cons:** requires a lot of legwork figuring out which stories are running where, getting the attention of editors and "journalists" (I use that term loosely), no guarantee all your hard work will ever see the light of day.

Although it may not seem like it, **Sales/Customer Service** is also a partnership insofar as it involves direct engagement with customers, themselves, or middlemen who serve as a bridge between you and the end users. This element is often ignored in discussion of integrated marketing campaigns, but as we drift more and more into service-based economies, I imagine more people will start paying attention to the interactions between sales people/a company and customers. Some companies, like Zappos and Southwest Airlines, are renowned for the way their employees interact with customers. Both companies are known for having friendly, playful, and jovial qualities about them, so it is not surprising that Zappos staff members are famously friendly and Southwest employees are known for their witty senses of humor. When designing an integrated campaign, it is worth ideating on how to extend a Big Idea to the domain of sales/customer service, as even a simple gesture can go a long, long way. One way to do this is to develop training manuals for your employees who will actually interact with end customers or to co-develop comparable materials with B2B partners that may ultimately interact with end customers. **Pros:** extremely personable, not often considered (thus, a point of differentiation if you include it), inexpensive. **Cons:** humans have great variability, can be seen as shticky if it seems disingenuous.

Everyone's favorite partnership category is probably **Promotions**. Why? Because who doesn't like winning free stuff?! Promotions refer to temporary deals, savings, or benefits provided to customers either for no reason, to reward purchasing behavior, or as the result of some game of chance. Promotions are fun because they usually come in the form of games, coupons, or other deals that make customers feel like they are winning the lottery. However, the oft-quoted warning of promotions is that promoting your company, product, or service too frequently or for too long a period can create the incorrect perception that your promoted item is *always* that cheap, discounted, promoted, etc. One of my favorite promotions of all time is the McDonald's Monopoly promotion that has run in over 20 countries (including the United States, France, Germany, the United Kingdom, and Hong Kong) since 1987 (?!). As someone who tends to avoid fast food but who loves Monopoly, this game always tempts me to get a large fry, chicken McNuggets, and a large soft drink when it is running. Players get a Monopoly game board and then collect property pieces affixed to various food products at McDonald's. Some of the game pieces also include immediate rewards (e.g., free soft drink, free ice cream cone) that customers can use upon return trips to McDonald's to increase future purchases. **Pros:** promotions are often fun, game-like executions that bring joy, as well as cost savings or other benefits. **Cons:** promotions can be expensive to produce, coordinate, and execute not to mention that running too many promotions often results in shifted expectations about your products' and/or services' pricing (e.g., see Banana Republic and its constant sales or Bed, Bath, and Beyond and its continuous supply of 20% off coupons).

Following in the spirt of sales/customer service and promotions is sort of a hybrid partnership of the two: **Sampling**. If you have ever been to a membership-based warehouse like Costco or Sam's Club, then you are all-too familiar with product sampling. Sampling is exactly what it sounds like: experiencing a product for a temporary period of time so that you can determine whether or not the product or service is right for you. Enterprising college students lacking a budget would be wise to hit up the samples at their local Sam's Club or grocery store as a way to obtain a free meal of sorts, but other versions of product sampling also exist. Whereas the examples so far involve partners (e.g., grocery store employees, salespeople), other sampling practices are direct-to-consumer. Consider, for example, the late-night television infomercials that let you try a new blender, a Slanket, or a Life Alert necklace free for 30 days before having to decide whether or not you want to keep it. That's sampling. Another, more modern (and slightly trickier) approach to sampling includes offers from companies like Spotify and Amazon to sample their various media delivery services for "free" (enter your card information and you will not be charged unless you forget to cancel before the free trial period has ended). Companies know that once you have a product or service available to you it can often be very difficult to give them up, even if you did not feel particularly wild about the product/service in the first place. There is a reason the car dealership wants you to take a test drive. Once you have experienced owning a product or service, well, sometimes it can be difficult to imagine life without it. I would be in so much trouble if you could sample puppies. **Pros:** once customers have a taste of the real thing, they often want more. **Cons:** sampling can be expensive; you are giving away some of your product for free with the *hope* (but not the guarantee) that people will buy. We have all been "that person" who has taken a product sample with no intention to purchase at the grocery store, trade shows, or concerts/sporting events. That can add up for a company.

Another partnership opportunity that is often overlooked involves **Philanthropic Initiatives**. Philanthropic initiatives refer to any partnership between a company and a charitable organization that is mutually beneficial. In some instances, this involves a company contributing a portion of its earnings to the charitable cause. In other examples, this involves a company generating awareness for or providing the marketing materials for a charitable organization. Obviously the charitable organization benefits from the financial resources, publicity, and/or marketing collateral provided by the company whereas the latter benefits from the positive associations, the do-gooder image, and the increased business that it attracts as a result of being seen as a prosocial organization. Now, my mom instilled in me at a young age the idea that you do not do something for someone because you expect something in return. That is where partnering with a philanthropic organization can be difficult. Obviously, when it comes to running a business, partnerships of any kind tend to be "strategic partnerships," a mutually-beneficial game of "what's in it for me?" (WIFM). However, although philanthropic initiatives can certainly be developed with an a priori expectation of getting something in return—whether that be positive juju, increased brand awareness and attention, or preferred seating at the philanthropic organization's annual gala—this is one partnership where companies should really lead with their hearts instead of their minds. Whatever benefits accrue as a result of doing the good and right thing is simply icing on the cake; doing the right thing should be a reward in and of itself. A great example of a company engaging in many philanthropic initiatives is Pepper Construction of Chicago. The company, one of the largest construction companies in Chicago, supports several organizations including United Cerebral Palsy (for teens and adults), Toys for Tots, and the African American Contractor's Association. In addition, for the past 13 years, the company's employees participate in the annual Chicago Sun-Times Charity Trust Letters to Santa program in which Pepper employees volunteer to take 2-4 letters, write return letters, and purchase gifts for children during the holiday season. There is no immediate benefit for Pepper Construction from participating in these various philanthropic organizations nor did the company seek to help with the expectation that its efforts would result in any returns. Sometimes good business is simply that: the business of doing *good*. **Pros:** who doesn't like the warm, squishy feeling that comes with helping prosocial organizations in their mission. **Cons:** philanthropic initiatives can be tedious to organize and surprisingly difficult to coordinate; also, don't get into the business of partnering with philanthropic organizations if you are not committed for the long-haul or only doing it for the sake of publicity.

Salt and pepper. Peanut butter and jelly. Ice cream and Hershey's chocolate syrup. Some products just *go* together. As such, it is often in a company's best interest to figure out what other products/services consumers associate with the product/service they are trying to sell and to partner with the creators of those products. This, friends, is **Bundling and/or Cross-Promotional Activities**. By splitting marketing-related costs like store displays, shelf space costs, and even marketing collateral, companies can often market their products more efficiently together than they can separately. A good example of effective product bundling involves one of my favorite all-time, all-American snacks: the s'more. To create a s'more one simply needs to combine 1) a marshmallow, 2) two halves of a graham cracker, 3) a piece of chocolate, and 4) a heat source. S'mores are a staple of any campfire or bonfire, but I remember my entire world changing when my family introduced me to the idea of making s'mores in the microwave (watching the marshmallow expand is the best part). Grocery stores like Safeway have thought to bundle Kraft Jet-Puffed Marshmallows, Hershey's Chocolate Bars, and Honey Maid Graham Crackers together for years, offering customers a discount for buying all three together as opposed to purchasing each separately. Now that Nabisco is a part of Mondelēz (the company that spun off from Kraft), there seems to be a missed opportunity for Kraft, Mondelēz, and Hershey's to work together, especially from spring through fall, to bundle their products together so that people everywhere can enjoy the delicious, sticky goodness that is a s'more. **Pros:** cost-savings and efficiencies, tapping into broader audiences, increased sales associated with greater perceived benefits/uses spelled out to consumers. **Cons:** less control over your product, associations with other brands and companies that, once established, may be difficult to remove.

One final partnership tool to discuss is one that became insanely popular during the reality television craze in the early 2000s but has since been waning a bit as consumers caught on and the tool lost its effectiveness. The tool? **Product placement**. Produce placement refers to the strategic placement of a product or brand name within some entertainment medium (e.g., television show, movie, song, etc.). The product appears to be a natural part of the scene when, in reality, the presence of the product has been negotiated and paid for by the product's creator. Consider, for example, the presence of Coca-Cola branded cups on the judges' desk on *American Idol*. It is often the case that the brand or product is never mentioned explicitly, but the product/brand is clearly there. A slight variant of traditional product placement also occurs when companies provide their products for celebrities to wear, use, or include in photos and/or videos.

Outlandish. The Outlandish category is a bit of a catch-all bucket that includes marketing executions that do not quite fit into one of the other categories. Remember that the PORTS approach is simply a tool to help us keep the various components of an integrated marketing campaign organized, so do not lose sleep over whether a particular execution does or does not fit in the "outlandish" category. The idea is simply that executions within this category tend to be a bit atypical for traditional marketing campaigns but can be an important asset within an integrated marketing campaign.

The first outlandish idea to discuss is **Guerilla Marketing** (not to be confused with Gorilla marketing in which nice jungle homes are advertised by showcasing their amenities and proximity to banana restaurants). Guerilla marketing refers to off-the-wall techniques designed to capture attention, communicate ideas, or shift behaviors in major ways for little-to-no cost. The term "guerilla marketing" derives from the notion of "guerilla warfare" in which small militant groups or sects stage impromptu battles or attacks (as opposed to massive, well developed attacks rooted in strategy). In that sense, guerilla marketing is essentially using quick, quirky, and in-your-face techniques to achieve a marketing objective. Say, for example, the Chicago Shakespeare Theatre based on Navy Pier is trying to advertise their upcoming production of *The Merchant of Venice*. One guerilla approach would be to have people stationed around Navy Pier, Willis (Sears) Tower, and other touristy areas wearing the traditional Venetian masks of Carnevale (you know, the scary-looking ones from that Tom Cruise/Nicole Kidman sex romp *Eyes Wide Shut*). When tourists undoubtedly get photos with the people wearing the masks, marketing material pertaining to the production could be passed out. **Pros:** Guerilla marketing tactics tend to be quite good at attracting attention because they tend to be so off-the-wall and unexpected. **Cons:** sometimes guerilla marketing tactics can be confusing or too far removed from whatever is trying to be communicated, which can lead to failure in achieving our stated business objective.

Another outlandish tool is **Content Marketing**. I include content marketing under the outlandish category because content marketing is essentially the creation of content, content often seems rather irrelevant to the company and/or its products/services, that spurs customer interest and even loyalty to the company. One of the best examples of content marketing is the Michelin company's Michelin Guide that rates restaurants around the world. Michelin, if you are unaware, is a French company that sells *tires*. What in the world is a tire company doing creating books that rate restaurants? Well, you have to get to those restaurants somehow, right? Might as well make sure you are getting there in car with safe tires! More seriously, however, Michelin first created the guides as useful tools for motorists who wanted to know information about maps, hotels, restaurants, and other needs important to drivers. Over time the guide evolved to focus on restaurants, which, you must admit, are a lot sexier to market than tires. Another similar example of content marketing is AAA Auto Insurance putting out an annual atlas. AAA is not in the business of cartography or mapmaking, but it has produced an annual map of the United States each year since the early 1900s. Despite living in an era of GPS and automatic cars, AAA still produces these atlases for those people who like to have tangible maps at their fingertips. Although these products are at least somewhat relevant to the parent companies creating them, they need not be; they simply have to gain attention, generate some buzz, and attract customers to the core products/services the company is putting out there or generate some favorable vibes toward the brand/company itself. **Pros:** permits you to work in a domain outside your typical area of expertise to reach new customers and to keep them engaged. **Cons:** may require you to work in a domain outside your area of expertise, can be so far removed from the central company and its products/services that is fails to achieve the business objective set out for the selected audience.

The last component tool within outlandish marketing that I will include here is **Experiential Marketing**. Experiential marketing is often confused with event or event-related marketing in that they both focus on some activity at which both a company and a customer (usually several customers) are present. One distinction I like to make is that event marketing is more "passive" whereas experiential marketing is more "active." A good example of experiential marketing would be a winery that provides tours during which the various people touring the vineyard engage in part of the wine production process. The *experience* of engaging in the wine creation process likely enriches the customer experience and the overall value attributed to your company and its products/services in a way that hearing about the product or even attending an event where the wine was simply present cannot. **Pros:** increasing engagement facilitates liking and purchasing, participants are more likely to encode both the knowledge obtained by and feelings associated with the experiences. **Cons:** can be expensive to stage, open to plans going awry or people enjoying the experience but not making the connection between the experience and the business takeaway.

Revolutionary. If the category name Revolutionary sounds extreme, that's because it is. Revolutionary executions in an integrated marketing campaign involve any changes to the *core* product/service itself. More specifically, if we are going to play with *any* of the 4Ps–price, product, placement, or promotion–as a part of an integrated marketing campaign, well, that *is* revolutionary. The important thing to note here is that these changes to the integral parts of our product/service are typically *temporary*, as they are simply part of our temporary campaign. They can be permanent, as was the case with the new M&M's colors during the Great Color Quest campaign, but the idea is that the change comes as a part of the integrated marketing campaign itself. The point is that any time you are tinkering with something as important as the product, its packaging, its price, or where it can be purchased per your campaign's Big Idea, you need to proceed with caution. The returns can be explosive, but so, too, can any mistakes.

One revolutionary execution can involve a **Product Innovation** of some sort. A product innovation refers to any significant change in a product or service's attributes that make it markedly different than what it was before the campaign. Of course, M&M's decision to transform *all* of its products, regardless of flavor, into colorless, black and white candy is a rather drastic decision for a temporary campaign execution. On a relatively smaller level, the decision to include seasonal prints or transform the candy colors to just red and green during the Christmas holiday would be another example of changing the product to fit an overall Big Idea (in that example whatever

Christmas-themed campaign M&M's happens to be running). Whatever the change, any alteration to our core product or service *is* a big deal because customers really have no choice but to notice it (I mean, it's *the* product or service!). **Pros:** attention grabbing, engaging, and innovative. **Cons:** depending on the degree of the change, customers may be irked, confused; can be an expensive investment for a short-term gain.

Another revolutionary integrated marketing execution is a **Packaging Redesign**. Changing up a product's packaging is not an altogether uncommon practice. Many companies alter packaging to coincide with holidays, seasons, and other timely events (e.g., the Olympics). However, integrated marketing campaign-related packaging redesign is an entirely different beast because it represents the translation and reinforcement of the campaign's Big Idea via product packaging. A good example of this comes from Coca-Cola's shift to all-white packaging in 2011 in its campaign to draw attention to the plight of polar bears in the face of rising temperatures and the melting of icebergs due to global warming. On its surface, this packaging redesign is not a terrible idea: it is simple, relevant to the campaign, unique (polar bears are white). However, all-white print on a silver Coca-Cola can looks an awful lot like another Coca-Cola product: Diet Coke. Customers were confused when the Diet Coke they thought they had purchased actually turned out to be regular Coca-Cola and vice-versa: customers looking to purchase a regular Coca-Cola were dumbfounded when it seemed like the only Coca-Cola products available to purchase were Diet Cokes! This is an example of a nice idea gone wrong with respect to packaging redesign as a part of an integrated marketing campaign, exactly what I warned about above in my caveat regarding "revolutionary" executions (i.e., they are high risk, high reward). One solution I developed for this Coca-Cola campaign years ago was to use temperature-sensitive packaging, similar to how Coors Light's used a "cold activated bottle" that featured mountains that turned blue once the temperature started dipping below 47-degrees Fahrenheit. In the revamped Coca-Cola campaign, Coca-Cola's iconic red cans would look normal when unrefrigerated but, once cold, would start displaying the image of the iconic polar bears used in its many holiday-themed campaigns as well as a thermostat showing a simulated decreasing temperature on the side of the can. The message? Global 'warming' causes the polar bears to disappear (well, and Coca-Cola is best enjoyed when cold). This gets the Big Idea across in a way that is not confusing to consumers and keeps Coca-Cola's use of colors consistent. A simple fix but an important one. **Pros:** drastically different packaging captures attention and can be as engaging as a new product itself. **Cons:** Changing a product's packaging, even if only temporary, can be expensive. In addition, as seen in the Coca-Cola example, changing packaging as part of a campaign has the potential to create customer confusion, which can lead to decreased sales, increased dissatisfaction, or both.

One revolutionary execution that can also be thought of as a promotion of sorts is that of a **Pricing Shift**. A price promotion refers to the temporary discount of a product or service's typical price for the duration of a campaign. The reason I also include a conversation about pricing under the revolutionary section is because of the fact that using pricing as a tool within an integrated marketing campaign is perhaps one of the riskiest strategies one can pursue. Why? Well, if you deeply discount during an integrated marketing campaign you are likely to see an increase in your sales; people like cheap stuff. This can be great–more people are experiencing your product/service and may become loyal customers or repeat purchasers in the future–but it can also just be a temporary, short-term gain. Similarly, a pricing shift that leads to a buying frenzy may muddy the waters with respect to drivers of a campaign's success, as it becomes less clear whether it is simply the price driving the increased purchasing behavior or other campaign elements. Also, as aforementioned, drastic shifts in price as part of a campaign can lead customers to develop expectations regarding the price point of your product or services. When the campaign ends and the pricing returns to the original numbers, customers often lack the motivation or wherewithal to make the connection that the pricing they liked was part of a temporary campaign. Instead, they just feel like you, the big, bad corporation, have successfully screwed them over. Thus, it is wise to be very, very careful when attempting to use pricing as a tool in an integrated marketing campaign. Although temporary discounts and pricing promotions *can* be helpful in increasing sales or repeat purchases, shifts in pricing can also lead to price wars and a downward cycle that is counterproductive to your business goals. **Pros:** people like discounts and good deals. **Cons:** once cheap, always cheap; people also have biases regarding the relationship between price and quality; competitors may also be able to compete on price and may be able to out-discount you, especially if you are a smaller or newer player in the market. Plus, the other efforts of your integrated marketing campaign may be enough to get customers to buy without having to offer discounts, so you could be unknowingly selling yourself short.

Another revolutionary execution is that of **Alternative Access**. Alternative access refers to providing atypical distribution for your product or service during the run of the integrated marketing campaign. This would be like Hasbro distributing *My Little Pony* ponies at AMC movie theatres during the release of a full-length *My Little Pony* film or selling collectible ponies at places like GameStop where "bronies" (bros who like *My Little Pony*) may frequent. Typically, these toys would not be sold at movie theatres or at a place like GameStop, but if the goal is to promote the film and to take advantage of the increased buzz about and interest in the *My Little Pony* brand, then offering these additional distribution channels may make good sense in the context of the campaign. **Pros:** novelty, attention-grabbing, and relevant placement per the campaign's goals makes it more likely you will come into contact with members of your target audience. **Cons:** costly, time consuming to create, and can potentially cause confusion with respect to future expectations about where your products will be available.

Finally, the last revolutionary execution involves significant changes in the **Promotional Strategy**. To be clear, integrated marketing *is* a form of promotion (i.e., communicating persuasive messaging to a specific, intended audience). What is being referred to here is a significant shift in the way that a product or service's messaging is typically delivered in a drastically new approach. This could refer to a shift in medium, a shift in tone, or a shift in the message; the point is that the shift is directly related to the Big Idea of the integrated marketing campaign and is temporary, tied to the duration of the campaign's planned run. Consider, for example, how NBC has integrated more of its online media tools during its coverage of both the Winter and Summer Olympic Games. Although the company launched an app and featured content on its webpage and dedicated content pages specifically for the games, the execution of this promotional strategy has often felt clunky, disjointed, and not at all user friendly. Going forward, NBC would be wise to embed this shift to online coverage and content into a larger integrated marketing campaign. The television content should look and feel familiar to the design of the app which should look and feel similar to the design of the webpage. The content should be organized in the same way across the different media types, and the benefit of integrating digital media should be fully explored (e.g., live tweets appearing on the television and web coverage via the app; alerts delivered to your phone via the app that, when clicked, can take you to the corresponding video on the website or provide information on how to tune in on your television). Note, this is not how NBC normally broadcasts shows, but if part of its Big Idea involves the idea of connecting people around the world and keeping them connected to the games and other fans, this would be an important shift in promotional strategy to reinforce that Big Idea.

Traditional Media. When most people think of marketing campaigns, they typically think of the tools contained within traditional media. From television commercials to print ads, radio to online advertisements, traditional executions are the ones with which we are most familiar. Whereas ten years ago web-based marketing was considered its own special category, it has become so integral to marketing campaigns that not including it as part of the core mix of commonly-used tools seems foolish. In fact, there's a good chance you are reading this book online right now at this very moment!

The reigning champion of marketing tools, the **television** commercial, has been the head honcho for decades. Replacing radio once mankind finally figured out how to add moving pictures to sound, television shares many things in common with the medium that it usurped: a blend of entertainment and advertising, a captive audience, natural segmentation based on audience interest and preference, etc. Most television advertisements come in one of two varieties, the :30 spot and the :60 spot, with a finite amount of time to tell your story, make your pitch, direct customers to action, and stand out from all the other folks attempting to capture the attention of your selected audience. Although entire campaigns used to be anchored by and then inspired by a television execution, this is no longer the case, especially as viewers "cut the cord" and eschew cable television for video streaming services like Netflix, Hulu, and Amazon. **Pros:** despite decreasing slightly in popularity, television remains the top tool for marketers; attentive audience engaging with the medium because they *want* to; natural segmentation based on channel type (e.g., home improvement networks, cooking networks), viewing time (e.g., daytime, late-night). **Cons:** decreasing in popularity; the advent of DVR and associated practices of zipping and zapping (former: fast forwarding through commercials; latter: switching to other content to avoid having to watch advertisements); customers wise to newer techniques, such as product placement devised to compensate for skipping commercials.

One of the other most pervasive marketing tools, the **print ad**, has also undergone a few changes in recent years. Somewhat strangely, people still read magazines despite the increase of tablets and other handheld digital devices that emulate magazines and, in most cases, allow users to access the exact same content from printed magazines. Print ads are not known for their overwhelming sense of engagement, but they are fairly good at frequently exposing readers to a brand, product, or information regarding a brand/product in a manner that permits the viewer to choose how long he/she engages with the advertisement (unlike a television ad, for example, with which one spends either :30 or :60). Although print ads are still popular vehicles through which a Big Idea can be conveyed, the placement of print ads has extended from the pages of tangible magazines to digital ads that appear on websites and in digital versions of magazines and other print publications. Just as television commercials transitioned nicely to online videos, so, too, have print ads found their digital cousins. **Pros:** engagement determined by the viewer; forced to keep things short, simple, and sweet; strong visuals and other sensory experiences possible (e.g., smell, touch). **Cons:** easily ignored; not as attention-grabbing as other kinds of media; limited with respect to dynamism, ability to change over an extended period of time like a campaign's duration.

Another stalwart in the traditional media camp is **outdoor media**. Outdoor is an umbrella term that includes just about *anything* that can be found outside: billboards, bus stops, benches. Although these executions can be extremely creative (e.g., when a tourism board to a place like Florida installs heat lamps to bus stops in places like Chicago and New York City during the middle of winter), often these executions fail to attract attention because they are taken for granted. What is the last billboard you remember seeing? The last poster near a bus stop or train stop? Unless particularly clever or engaging, chances are that it is difficult for you to recall any of these executions. Outdoor media *can* be extremely effective, but it takes a really clever idea or an extremely good placement (e.g., *the* poster everyone sees upon emerging to street level from the subway) to truly capture attention. **Pros:** unexpected; the potential to be extremely creative; subtle exposure and increased familiarity, which should lead to greater liking. **Cons:** too passive; not particularly engaging; often ignored.

Just as we have outdoor media, we also have **indoor media**! Just as with outdoor media, indoor is an umbrella term for all the marketing collateral we experience near the point of purchase (POP) including point of purchase (POP) displays, in-store advertisements, and even considerations like shelf placement and endcap promotions (i.e., purchasing to have your product placed at the end of the aisle in a grocery store to gain more attention from passers-by). While I tend to think of convenience store and grocery store displays when I think of indoor media, so, too, are the fashionable videos playing in clothing stores, the fun games set up in a medical office's waiting room, the music playing in a restaurant, or even the ambient room fragrances that are wafted into certain stores to evoke a response, whether implicit or explicit, from customers. **Pros:** last-minute attempts to change people's minds; shoppers often like outsourcing their decisions to something else, even if it is in-store marketing; effective at capturing people's attention right when it matters; **Cons:** can be expensive; may not always trigger the behavior desired.

The big, bad elephant in the room must now be addressed: **internet/website** marketing. From interstitial pop-up ads to banner ads, native advertising to sponsored content, internet marketing has blown up the past 15 years and is not going away anytime soon. While pop-up ads were/are effective at gaining attention for a split second, they are often blocked quickly now and are successful at arousing anger and hatred for the rest of eternity. Banner ads are frequently ignored, and metrics like "click-through rates" (and "open rates" and "bounce rates," etc.) are still hotly debated as either effective or ineffective in determining an ad's "success," a debate not likely to be resolved anytime soon (we will talk about this later). However, the internet can be an ideal tool given that data obtained from a user's past behavior can be used to generate highly-targeted advertisements and extremely relevant messages for the user that other popular media (e.g., television, print ads) simply cannot provide. **Pros:** can generate user-relevant ads based on prior surfing habits and search data; people are spending more time here for work and entertainment purposes than ever before. **Cons:** unclear metrics for marketing success; add-ons for ad blockers now standard in most browsers; private viewing options becoming increasingly popular for customers in a post-NSA, Edward Snowden world.

Related to internet/website marketing is a specific subset of internet marketing: **Search Engine Optimization/Marketing (SEO/SEM)**. The simplest way to think about this tool is as follows: when people get online and do *not* go to a site they check regularly (e.g., gmail), they typically search for something using a major search engine like Google or Bing. When people search for something, they type in a keyword or a question that then returns relevant responses in the form of websites. The purpose of SEO/SEM is to associate your company, brand, and/or products/services with particular concepts, keywords, and questions so that you come up at the very top of the results that the search engine provides.

Another more traditional tech tool is that of **mobile** advertising. At one point in time mobile advertising actually referred to the idea of text-based advertisements. That, however, did not last long thanks to the annoyance factor of getting text messages from companies you couldn't care less about regarding promotions you also couldn't care less about. Nowadays, mobile marketing comes in the form of in-application (i.e., in-app) advertisements that appear both as simple ads in otherwise irrelevant apps or as integrated ads in extremely relevant apps. That probably sounds confusing, so let me clarify. Some companies advertise by purchasing advertising space that appears at the bottom of a screen or between levels in game-based applications. The advertisements may have nothing to do with the content of the game (e.g., "Here's an ad for Kohl's during this rousing game of Angry Birds!") or they may be somewhat related (e.g., "Here's an ad for Iams pet food during this Littlest Pet Shop game!"). That's one version. Another approach is to partner with companies like Groupon or Living Social to have your content featured within either application's current promotions. Given that people are now walking into oncoming traffic or off cliffs because their faces are buried in their phones, it is no surprise that mobile advertising of this variety has received more attention in recent years. **Pros:** there is a chance you are reading this on your phone right now; there is a chance you will check your phone at some point within the next five minutes; there is a chance you do not leave your phone more than 20 feet away from you at any point during your day. **Cons:** people do not always pay attention to mobile ads; mobile ads can be annoying and, as such, harmful to our brand; some apps permit users to pay a small fee for ad-free versions of the app, which eliminates your chances with those customers (whom you probably want because if they *were* willing to fork out more money just to get rid of a few ads, imagine what they would pay you for!).

Another popular tool in the marketing toolkit is that of **Direct Marketing**. Direct marketing refers to any marketing in which a company is in direct contact with the end user and the contact includes an explicit "call to action." Examples include infomercials ("Call now!"), catalogs ("Order now!"), and sales calls/telemarketing ("Buy now!"). One key component of direct marketing is that the results are immediately measurable; someone either bought or did not buy, and if they bought they bought X amount at $X.XX. In this way, it is easy to calculate the return-on-investment for direct marketing (e.g., "I made 100 calls in one hour and obtained 60 sales at an average of $50 per sale."). **Pros:** direct, immediate, quantifiable, and interactive. **Cons:** intrusive, off-putting, annoying, and (in some instances like telemarketing) facing legal restrictions.

And last, but not least, for traditional tools are the interactive favorites of **tradeshows and event marketing**. Tradeshows are professional gatherings of people in a particular industry (e.g., candy, food…guns), interested in a certain product (e.g., candy, food…guns), or followers of a particular hobby (e.g., candy, food…guns). Different suppliers and relevant partners purchase booth space, usually at a large convention center in a major city, and people gather, mingle, peruse the latest and greatest products and services in that market, and then go about their separate ways when all is said and done. Event marketing is *kind of* like a tradeshow in that there is an event to attend. However, unlike a tradeshow, event marketing is typically sponsored by a single company and is an event designed to showcase *that* company's product(s) and/or service(s). In either case, tradeshow or event, people like going to parties, they like looking at stuff, and they like the free samples that are usually all over the place at tradeshows and events. **Pros:** engaging, face-to-face experiences with customers; experiential; educational; usually fun, enjoyable. **Cons:** can be expensive; easy to get lost in the mix (especially at large tradeshows); conversion rate not always super high from tradeshow/event excitement to engagement at a later point in time…kind of like kids who were best friends at summer camp and promised to write but never did (cue sad music here).

Social Media. If marketing in the 1900s was the era of television, then marketing in the 2000s is the era of social media (note: not just "the era of the internet," in general, but rather "the era of *social media*"). People often act as if Facebook, Twitter, and Instagram are groundbreaking, earth-shattering creations that materialized out of thin air and will forever change the way we live our lives. Not true. Before there was Twitter, before there was Facebook, there were sites like MySpace (which *sort of* made a comeback), Friendster, and even services like AOL Instant Messenger and the Bulletin Board System (BBS) which allowed people online to connect in real time all the way back in the 1990s! And, like any popular companies and trends, once-famous social media behemoths can fall out of favor almost as quickly as they rose to power…we're looking at you, MySpace. Even as I write this book people are beginning to question the value of Twitter, Facebook is afraid that not enough teens are engaging with the site, and Instagram has become a softcore porn site for people with low self-esteem to post selfies and find validation through "likes." What were once simple **social networks** are quickly becoming forums for political conversations, customer complaints, ego boosts, bullying, knowledge/idea sharing (e.g., Pinterest), and everyday updates of the mundane (e.g., "This morning, I ate eggs," "Today, I pooped at 12:30pm and again at 2:45pm."). Also included in this mix are apps like Snapchat, which has increased its marketing game by working with Hollywood studios and consumer packaged goods companies to release exclusive content or brand-themed filters to promote particular products. Furthermore, content sites like YouTube that allow subscribers and friending also count here. YouTube is sort of the user-created television of today, so many of the same upsides describing television also describe YouTube. However, YouTube also benefits from the viral, word-of-mouth appeal common to networks, the source credibility/objectivity YouTube "stars" provide, and the fact that people often get lost in YouTube zones where they spend hours watching video after video. **Pros:** this is where people are spending more and more time and focusing most of their attention, so you must be playing in this space; rich data on searches, preferences, and network influence. **Cons:** metrics linking engagement to actual sales still poorly understood; particular sites go in and out of favor rather quickly (e.g., see live-streaming app Meerkat's rise and fall saga from SXSW 2015 to 2016).

One upside for social networks is that, in addition to being useful tools unto themselves, they are also a useful vehicle for another social marketing tool: **word-of-mouth**. Word-of-mouth refers to getting customers to talk about your company, brand, or product in a way that spreads interest, knowledge, and/or excitement. We know from our earlier conversation on source credibility that people really put a lot more faith in the source of information if that person looks like them and/or is more proximal to them. This is why you are more likely to follow your mom's advice about which kind of toilet paper you should buy as opposed to some celebrity (unless, say, that celebrity is Oprah, in which event you simply do whatever she says). Not only do we tend to trust people close to us more, there's also a social evolutionary bias at play in that because we will see those people time and time again, we expect that they will only point us in the right direction because if, for whatever reason, they would *not* do that…well…we know where to find them. Also, people like us are more likely to be perceived as having similar needs, similar preferences, and similar experiences, so we trust that whatever *they* are saying and whatever *they* believe is also good enough for us. **Pros:** perceived to be credible; adds color and personalization to marketing messages; cheap. **Cons:** people mess up messages all the time (often unintentionally); can be hard to get the conversation started authentically without making it sound forced or like a sales pitch.

Other tools in the realm of social media include **forums and message boards**. Related but different from their social network cousins, forums and message boards, like reddit, allow people to post without having to be a part of any connected network of people. While the people who read and post to particular forums or message boards may identify with that board or its community, there is no clearly defined network of searchable friends and relationships as there are with sites like Facebook, LinkedIn, and Instagram. Another attribute that sets apart forums and message boards from social networking sites is that the former are usually designed around and dedicated to a particular theme (e.g., coding, video games, motherhood, etc.) whereas the latter are simply networks of connected contacts. **Pros:** an active, engaged audience centered around a specific theme or topic; clearly-defined opinion leaders and influencers based on post frequency and/or ratings when applicable. **Cons:** difficult to market explicitly within the forum or message board per posting rules; anonymous posts and trolling can produce negative backlash for companies, products, etc.

And finally, the last tool to consider in the realm of social media is the one-mighty **blog**. Blog, short for weblog, began as an "online diary" of sorts where people poured their hearts out for the world to read. Nowadays, blogs have evolved into personal or thematic posts about someone's everyday life, career, hobby, or general musings for others to follow and to comment on should they so desire. Unlike a forum, a blog is maintained by an individual or a group of individuals around a common theme or subject. Anyone can post comments to a blog post, but the blog, itself, is controlled by an author or a group of authors working together. This is important because, unlike forums or message boards, it *is* possible to reach out to notable bloggers and talk to them about your company, brand, or product. Well-known blogging sites include WordPress.com and the Yahoo!-acquired-and-owned Tumblr, which has somehow devolved into so many porn blogs that some governments (e.g., Indonesia) have banned Tumblr altogether! Way to go, Yahoo! **Pros:** greater perceived credibility; increased ability to work with blog writers and creators to discuss your company and its products/services; loyal followings for several blogs; cheap. **Cons:** limited audience size; audience might not appreciate explicit marketing or product mentions.

So that concludes our (rather long, but informative) review of the many specific tools available to us for possible inclusion in an integrated marketing campaign. The PORTS anagram can help us remember the broad buckets in which the tools can be placed, but it also reminds us that in today's world we need not start with the "Traditional" (T) media tools. The days when a television commercial anchored our marketing campaign are *long* gone. Now, a campaign is just as likely to be anchored by a social media campaign, a press campaign, or a non-traditional guerilla campaign. In fact, it is possible for a modern integrated marketing campaign not to include any traditional marketing elements because none is needed! The game has changed.

As you can see, there are a *lot* of tools at our disposal. Per the paradox of choice, having so many choices makes designing our campaign *that* much harder! Should we just use all the tools? No. Should we just use one of the tools? Nope. The best thing to do is to brainstorm different ideas for as many tools as possible, each idea clearly inspired by our selected Big Idea, and then start piecing together the tools like a giant jigsaw puzzle so that the finished product includes a mix that: 1) incorporates different learning styles (i.e., visual, auditory, touch, kinesthetic), 2) engages customers in different ways (i.e., generates awareness, increases interests, fuels desire, and calls for action), and 3) tells a complete story reinforced by the other executions also selected for the campaign. The remainder of the chapter covers these thoughts in a bit more detail to help you start finalizing the ideas for your creative executions so they can be transformed from ideas to reality.

Of Trends & Traditions: Simple Storytelling, Styling, & Circling Back

Earlier, when brainstorming creative ideas and ultimately developing a Big Idea, I introduced a few activities that would help facilitate idea generation. At this point, we have a Big Idea; now we just have to execute that idea, which typically involves the art of storytelling.

It should go without saying that our research findings from the Understanding section of FUSION is extremely helpful when trying to come up with ideas for how to go about telling our story. We are certainly interested in the trends, entertainment, and media choices that our target customers are into because these serve as great starting points or inspiration for the stories that we will tell in our integrated marketing executions. However, in addition to the trends of the current time are some age-old, tried-and-true techniques that have withstood the test of time across all cultures and civilizations. We would be remiss not to consider these tactics as we develop our creative executions.

Storytelling. In just about every story there exists a hero (or protagonist), a villain (an antagonist), some dilemma or challenge, and, quite thankfully, a resolution. Whether David and Goliath, the Three Little Pigs and the Big Bad Wolf, or any beautiful Disney princess and her handsome prince, we know how a story is supposed to unfold. This does not mean that we cannot deviate from the traditional storyline or insert our own creative take on classic tales. If anything, by now, you should know that some of the most creative ideas tend to be original twists on familiar favorites. Instead, for each specific execution you consider, you should ask yourself the question, "What story am I trying to tell using this medium?"

For some executions, like television commercials or online videos, it is a bit easier to tell a story because we are used to seeing stories told in these formats. However, you can also tell a story using other integrated marketing tools. Consider, for example, a recent campaign by Kraft in which they changed the recipe of their iconic blue box macaroni and cheese *without telling customers*. Kraft chose to do this on purpose because when the idea of changing its recipe to remove preservatives and artificial colors was initially presented, customer backlash ensued. To avoid the negativity, Kraft decided it would secretly change the ingredients, see if anyone noticed, and then, at a later point in time, announce that the recipe had changed and then launch a campaign entitled, "It's Changed, But It Hasn't." For the big reveal, Kraft relied almost exclusively on press coverage and its social media pages (e.g., Facebook) to tell the story. In this case, the protagonists were Kraft and its mac and cheese lovers, the antagonists were the unhealthy ingredients and the health fanatics lobbing hateful words toward Kraft, the dilemma was trying to reconcile Kraft's ingredients in a world where people were loyal to the original recipe but also wanted healthier food, and the solution was a quiet transition to a new recipe with loyal Kraft lovers not noticing the difference. To be fair, some people *did* claim to notice the difference (conveniently only after Kraft announced the shift). Yet, still playing the role of the hero protagonist, Kraft had someone from its team manning the Facebook account the day of the launch, promptly responding to positive *and* negative feedback in a concerted effort to show that Kraft *cares*. Whether the new taste fits your taste buds or not, that kind of customer concern is good marketing. It kind of reminds me of how moms, who tend to know what's good for you, let you *think* you are doing what you want (i.e., eating indulgent macaroni and cheese) but then surprise you to let you know it's really *healthier* macaroni and cheese. Well played on a meta-level, Kraft.

Of course, there are specific genres of stories, as well: mysteries, romantic comedies, buddy cop stories, coming-of-age stories, love triangles, sci-fi and fantasy stories, family feel-good stories, and many more. We have seen enough movies and read enough books to know the familiar structures and formats that stories tend to follow, and a fun part of brainstorming specific execution ideas is considering the various genres and accompanying story formats that might motivate your particular executions.

In addition to knowing familiar stories and their respective structures, there are also common characters or archetypes that appear time and time again throughout tales. Whether the hero or the villain, the maternal loving character or the naïve innocent youth, the wise old mentor or the traveler seeking enlightenment through experience, the silly and rabblerousing jester or the supportive loyal sidekick, certain character types appear over and over again, which also helps with respect to the development of specific integrated marketing executions. Remember that, although you never want to be boring, you also never want to be so off-the-wall or atypical that your audience does not have a context in which to place your story or its characters. So start with an established storytelling standard or baseline and then tweak, parody, or exaggerate details to make it your own. This idea transitions us nicely into a conversation about *style*.

Styling. If you have ever watched a show like *Project Runway* or *Top Chef* or just about any creative reality television competition, then you are likely to have come across the idea of "style." Great artists tend to have a certain style, whether a painter or a musician, some sort of unique approach to their craft that allows you to associate a piece of work you have never seen before to that artist simply because it fits his/her style. What style really comes down to is *consistency in one's approach*.

Like great art, a great integrated marketing campaign should also adopt a style that is *consistent*. Indeed, one of the most consistent words that emerges in conversations about integrated marketing is exactly that: consistency. According to some folks, the most critical feature of any integrated marketing campaign is consistency. This means a consistent look, a consistent message, and a consistent feeling. Of course, as is the case with anything, there are some detractors, a few rebellious types that say, "Nay! Not true, young marketers! One may design a beautiful integrated marketing campaign that does *not* have the same look, message, or feeling throughout! Huzzah!"

As I hinted at the beginning of the book, there are very few absolutes in marketing (or in the world for that matter, but that's a more philosophical conversation for a different time and place…maybe we can go meditate on that together sometime?), so it is not surprising that there seems to be a bit of disagreement when it comes to style and consistency. However, what may help explain this apparent disagreement is a bit more knowledge on what *kinds* of consistency are possible. Although some campaigns may not look the same or sound the same on the surface, it is possible that an underlying consistency ties them together in a meaningful, integrative way.

When I was studying integrated marketing with Todd Abrams, then an adjunct professor at Washington University in St. Louis, I was taught to think of two different types of "consistency" with respect to integrated marketing: **Execution Consistency** and **Strategic Consistency**. Execution Consistency is essentially what you are probably thinking when you think of consistency in the context of IMS: similar colors, designs, messages, themes, etc. Consider, for example, Progressive Insurance. Whether a television commercial, a print advertisement, or a web pop up, there are *two* colors I expect to see every single time: white and blue. Chances are I would also see Flo, the Progressive Insurance spokesperson, wearing a headband and a Progressive Insurance smock of some sort (typically white). I would also expect there to be a jovial tone to the commercial, some family-friendly humor, and 1950's-esque background music. That's what a Progressive Insurance integrated marketing campaign execution looks like: the execution is consistent. Now, let's compare Progressive's approach with the approach taken by Geico Insurance. Geico has several, very different ads in its campaign. From a gecko to cavemen, singing guitarists to the band Europe singing "The Final Countdown," Geico's specific executions are anything but consistent with respect to specific color use, theme, or other creative choices. However, there is a strategic consistency across all commercials insofar as they contain a silly tone relevant to the audience the spot intends to capture. Whereas execution consistency focuses on keeping the details fairly consistent from execution to execution, strategic consistency focuses more on a broader level of keeping the spirit or tone of a campaign consistent from execution to execution even though the nitty-gritty details may be different. Regardless of the consistency approach taken, a campaign's various executions should *feel* like a part of the same campaign.

Circling Back. The best stories tend to be the ones that come full circle. "Once upon a time…" almost always ends with, "…happily ever after," and so, too, should the story you are telling in a marketing campaign have some sort of resolution that ties everything together. Whether this cycle happens within an individual execution (e.g., a :30 television commercial that presents a hero, a problem, and a solution all in a short amount of time) or across the lifetime of a campaign (e.g., the Great Color Quest and the search for M&M's missing colors), great campaigns, like great stories, have an end that ties together any loose ends from the campaign and provides satisfying punctuation. Even the most straightforward traditional television advertisements from the very beginning of television advertising followed a rubric of problem identification, product introduction, and initial problem solved. Consider ZzzQuil: "Sagging eyelids got you down? Feel like you're not getting enough sleep? Introducing new ZzzQuil, a non-medicinal sleep aid from the makers of DayQuil and NyQuil. With ZzzQuil you will never miss a night of sleep again! Goodbye, saggy eyes!" Simple circling back to the beginning rounds out a story and leaves very little open to (potentially incorrect) interpretation.

On Persuasion and Crafting Persuasive Messages

When telling a story through the various integrated marketing tools available to you, please do not forget the reason we are here in the first place: to change minds, to change hearts, and/or to change behaviors. Persuasion is the name of the game, and our marketing executions should be in service of getting our target customer from where they are presently to a destination where they are better off and, as a result, *we* are also better off.

Earlier in the book, in the chapter covering marketing research (Chapter 4), we discussed changing attitudes via the Attitude Toward the Object Model (ATOM), the Behavioral Intentions Model (BIM), the Yale Attitude Change Approach (YACA), and the Elaboration Likelihood Model (ELM). Persuasion, you may recall, is simply the process of shifting attitudes from a starting point to a new point. Inherent to these attitude change models are built-in suggestions for *how* to change attitudes. In the case of ATOM those approaches include 1) changing the attractiveness of the identified attributes, 2) changing the belief that a brand possesses a particular attribute, and/or 3) adding or removing attributes that come to mind. Similarly, in the case of BIM we can 1) change the amount of attention people pay to themselves v. others, 2) change the attitude people have about doing a particular behavior, and/or 3) change the attitudes people have about what they believe *others* attitudes are regarding a particular behavior. For YACA, we can 1) change the source's perceived credibility or expertise, 2) change the message's evidence or appeal, and/or 3) change the recipient's perceived intelligence or esteem with respect to our company, product, or service.

It is important to revisit these attitude change models now because we are finally talking about the tools that can be used *to do just that*! What is remarkable is just how easy it is to dream up specific marketing executions using one of these models as our guide. Consider, for example, the Las Vegas Convention and Visitors Authority (LVCVA). The LVCVA is the group responsible for developing the slogan, "What happens in Vegas, stays in Vegas." Say we have collected data on the group's target audience of young men who, for the most part, find the messaging true and appealing, do not consider themselves stubborn or too smart for their own good when it comes to weekend getaways, but are having a hard time believing in a message coming from a formal city tourism "authority" (i.e., there is some source credibility). The same research tells us that these guys tend to like people like Charlie Sheen, James Franco, and Shia LaBeouf. Aside from having terrible taste in talent, these men could benefit from a campaign spokesperson or endorser in the form of Charlie, James, Shia, or any combination of the three. Whom better to hear about the wild antics of Vegas than three bad boys who have likely had unspeakable weekends in Vegas hotel rooms? So, just like that, we have an idea for a very specific integrated marketing execution without even having to break a sweat! (Side note: Did you know that the original slogan for the famous Las Vegas campaign was actually, "What happens here, stays here?" It seems like the LVCVA was ahead of its time with respect to making sure its Big Idea was "one-of-a-kind").

Keep in mind that as you craft your specific execution ideas you should be considering how to persuade your audience per the Desired Objective established at the very beginning of the FUSION process. Employing the attitude change models will make your life even that much easier! See? It's all coming together!

Let Gestalt Guide You: The Whole > Sum of the Parts

Speaking of "coming together," as I stated at the very beginning of the book, the theory behind integrated marketing from its inception was that the combination of different marketing tools, each varying in its respective strengths and weaknesses, has the potential to create a network of interactions such that some tools' strengths compensate for other tools' weaknesses to create a campaign whose whole is greater than the sum of its individual parts. Or, to start in simpler and shorter terms, 2+2 = 5.

I think one of the simplest ways to think about integrated marketing is to think of a food recipe. Every recipe calls for ingredients. The chef has some creative leeway when it comes to which ingredients to include. Some ingredients can be replaced with substitutes. Honey can replace sugar. Cream can replace milk. Some ingredients complement one another. Sweet can complement savory. Spicy can complement cool. At the end of the process, a chef strives to find just the right balance of ingredients, not too much and not too little, to create a flavor that will appeal to the tastes of those lucky enough to taste the masterpiece.

Like a chef, you should prepare *all* your ingredients or at least consider what could be included in your recipe. Dream up ideas for the various marketing tools available to you for the integrated marketing campaign. No, not all of them will be incorporated into the final product nor should every marketing tool available to you be incorporated into your final campaign. That would be overkill, akin to a chef throwing every possible ingredient into the pot. The resulting dish would not be very delicious. Instead, think about how the various ingredient of your campaign might complement one another: combine a tool that is great at achieving awareness with another tool that is better at engaging customers; add a tool that is adept at fueling desire with another tool that is known for motivating purchase behavior. Any one tool, individually, may not get our customers from point A to point B per our Desired Objective. However, working together, the tools create a synergy that shifts customers in truly impressive ways.

To give a more concrete example, consider the interaction between traditional television advertising and modern digital marketing. One of the limitations of using a traditional medium like television is that marketing relevance can be limited. On popular shows like *Modern Family* and *Black-ish*, companies like Apple and Buick have engaged in extensive product placements to the extent that an entire episode can feel like a 30-minute commercial for a product rather than a television show. Not surprisingly, as part of their deals these companies have secured premium advertising slots as the first commercials right after the shows break into commercials (in other words, the one commercial people *might* watch by mistake, before fast forwarding, and prior to taking a food/potty break). Although this kind of campaign is good at generating awareness or even educating customers about a product, this kind of approach tends to be very expensive, feels forced, and can come across as disingenuous.

Now, contrast that approach with a digital marketing execution. Using cookies, online advertising placement knows what you have been searching for, which pages you have been visiting lately, and other data about you and your business. Say you have been searching for information regarding the new Macbook or the upcoming Apple Watch update. Perhaps your searches include queries pertaining to new cars or a particular car brand. Using this information, websites can promote relevant advertisements per your likely needs based on what you, the customer, have indicated is of interest to you lately. This is also beneficial because web-based marketing allows for greater customer engagement and interactivity. It's usually about now that people say, "Wait a minute! This feels sneaky. What about ethics?!" While I agree that people should have the right and ability to turn off data collection per their own privacy preferences, I am equally likely to agree that this kind of focused, relevant marketing can create value for customers who clearly are in need of a particular product or service. While it is important to be transparent about data collection and provide customers the ability to turn off any data collection they do not want happening, a lot of value can come from these increasingly easier ways of obtaining and storing data.

Taken together, the traditional television execution might be better at increasing awareness or introducing customers to new products whereas the digital marketing might be better at customizing advertisements to an individual's specific preferences or needs and facilitating engagement with the company and/or its brands. Either execution, separately, fails to fully engage a customer; however, together, the executions reinforce one another, bringing customers closer to the value that we hope they attain.

Some Final Thoughts…
Getting started on an integrated marketing campaign can feel a bit daunting at first, but so does *everything* you do for the first time. Thankfully, integrated marketing includes a variety of tools marketers can use to craft memorable, effective, and entertaining campaigns. I opened this chapter with the Great Color Quest campaign because I consider it to be one of the best examples of integrated marketing that I have ever seen in my many years in marketing. Mars and its agencies were *so* thorough in the execution of the black and white theme, and the variations on this theme–from black and white movies to black and white (and read all over) daily newspapers to black and white collector edition packaging–that even to this day when I mention "that time that M&M's were black and white," even non-marketers can recall

this two-month era in the 70-year history of the company. That is an *impressive* accomplishment.

In the current chapter, I both introduced you to the many tools available to you for inclusion in an integrated marketing campaign and touched on a few tips to consider as you flesh out those specific tools' executions: how people learn and retain information, what makes a good story, why style and consistency matter, and the importance of resolution.

Fusion, unlike most books on integrated marketing, is *not* simply a book about writing creative briefs, designing print ads, and talking only about the tools listed in this chapter. In fact, the reason the FUSION model begins with a conversation about business goals and research is to remind us that the reason we are creating a campaign in the first place is not simply to entertain or to win some art prize. Although the integrated marketing campaign creation process can and should be fun, creative, and artistic, it *must* be transformative with respect to our intended audience. Our campaign *must* change the way they think, the way they feel, and/or the way they behave. Any campaign that fails to do one or more of these things is simply entertainment, not marketing, which is an idea I hope sticks with you long after you finish this book.

*   *   *

Capturing attention in today's world is increasingly difficult. With so many different media choices, so many companies clamoring for attention, and so many customers creating content of their own, it's a miracle that *anything* stands out. Even when something does, fame is more fleeting than ever before, as the next-best-thing is already up-and-coming. And the cycle repeats again and again...

M&M's Great Color Quest used the tools of integrated marketing elegantly and efficiently: the black and white surprise/contrast captured customers' attention, the stories within the television, print, and web-based executions explained what was going on, and the consistency across *every possible touchpoint* with customers ensured that *no one* would fail to get the message; everyone would know the story.

Now, over a decade later, people *still* remember that campaign, *still* remember its purpose, and *still* love M&M's. Creating an integrated marketing campaign may not seem easy, but combining a compelling Big Idea, clever, synergistic executions, and steadfast consistency, like those of the Great Color Quest, makes creating an integrated marketing campaign as simple as black and white.

What if... *M&M's What's On the Inside?*

Most books on integrated marketing do a good job describing the various tools marketers can use when developing a campaign. However, one difference between those books and the current book is that the FUSION model requires a campaign to incorporate a prosocial component as part of the foundation of any campaign. Not only are concepts like Corporate Social Responsibility (CSR) and the Triple Bottom Line (TBL) becoming increasingly integral to modern business education, it also just feels really good to know that your work is doing good for the world and the people in it.

Of course, M&M's have been around since before being "socially responsible" was the cool new business trend. However, Mars managed to extend M&M's into a charitable space by helping with the introduction of Red Nose Day to North America. Red Nose Day, started in England in 1988, is a specific campaign from the organization Comic Relief to engage the media and celebrities for the purpose of raising awareness about and eradicating poverty. To do this, Mars created the #MakeMLaugh campaign in which people were encouraged to make others laugh, capture this experience, and to upload the evidence with the hashtag #MakeMLaugh. For every post with that hashtag, M&M's pledged to donate $1 to the Red Nose Day Fund (up to $250,000).

Although kind, sweet, and noble of Mars and M&M's to contribute to a worthy cause, the particular theme of the campaign does not really fit the M&M's brand. In my quest to get Mars to launch Cashew M&M's (delicious, right?), imagine a Big Idea entitled, "M&M's: It's What's Inside that Counts." The focus of the marketing campaign would be touting the many different flavors of M&M's that often take a backseat to campaigns in which colors and discussions of the different colors, the associated characters, and their different personalities take center stage. Here, the campaign would talk about peanuts, peanut butter, almond, dulce de leche, mint, pretzels, crisped rice, and–with any luck–cashews.

But more important for the campaign would be a charitable piece focusing on diversity, anti-bullying, and inclusion. If you think about it, M&M's marketing has focused, almost exclusively, on what's on the *outside*: color. In the new campaign, M&M's would focus on the rich differences within us that make us special. Mars could donate proceeds of M&M's sales to organizations that help young people focus on the value of diversity and/or to anti-bullying organizations. Interactive components could integrate the target market via customer-created videos talking about diversity, their own stories of being bullied, etc. The campaign's commercial could show diverse groups of people finding commonality in the M&M's flavors that they love with an underlying theme that it *is* what is on the inside, the human heart that is in all of us, that counts and not the differences that exist on the outside.

See? Integrating prosocial, charitable components within an integrated marketing campaign need not be a burden. In fact, it can be quite sweet, figuratively and literally.

JAMES A. MOUREY

CHAPTER 9 | Those Who Dream and Those Who Do

Hidden away in a nondescript, unassuming building located within an equally indistinguishable business park populated by even *more* inconspicuous buildings exists a secret laboratory you have probably never heard of. No, it's not Area 51, the mysterious, U.S. government-owned expanse of land thought to house evidence of an extraterrestrial alien. Area 51 is in Roswell, New Mexico, hidden far away from major cities and civilization. This secret lab, Vat19, is located smack dab in the middle of the United States in St. Louis, Missouri, right between the wealthy suburb of Town and Country (…that's *actually* the name of the suburb), a city with one of the nation's highest median incomes, and another suburb that is also nationally (and even internationally known): Ferguson, Missouri.

Perhaps the most recognizable symbol of St. Louis is the silvery, beautiful Gateway Arch that towers over the banks of the mighty Mississippi River. Known as the "Gateway to the West," people often joke that St. Louis' iconic symbol essentially tells people, "Welcome to St. Louis…now keep going west." People may joke about St. Louis and its place in American history, but you should know that it was St. Louis that brought us the ice cream cone, iced tea, *and* the hot dog….as well as the first x-ray machine, the electrical plug and accompanying wall outlets, and the first electric typewriter (…and also toasted ravioli, frozen custard, and gooey butter cakes and cookies, but that's just bragging).

With so many amazing inventions stemming from the sensational city of St. Louis, one might be curious to know what could *possibly* be coming out of this mysterious, top-secret Vat19 laboratory. Before the conspiracy theories begin, here are a few descriptions of what surveillance has revealed thus far…

- A man is seen bathing in a bathtub full of 500 pounds of a material referred to as "liquid glass" and "crystal clear putty." Prior to the experimental bath the man shaved his body hair but, having forgotten to shave under his arms, endures the pain of the liquid glass sticking to his underarm hair. As he sinks into the liquid glass, the weight of the putty makes breathing difficult. Does he make it out alive? Does he have to call in for reinforcements? Find out here: https://youtu.be/f_KAUcRBlWs (11.1 million views, 97% like rating)

- A colorful worm appears to have been exposed to radiation has grown to be 128 times larger than a typical warm, weighing in at over 3 pounds and measuring 2.5" feet long, and has taken over major waterways throughout the central United States. Protect yourself and your family by seeing the worm in action here: https://youtu.be/7RXmNRr8x7I (61.4 million views, 93% like rating)

- A German spy infiltrates a secret supply room to find a glass vessel that he then uses to smuggle wiener schnitzel, bacon and eggs, milk for a giant cookie, and other delicious edibles all while dancing to electronic dance music and wearing shades. Watch his moves here: https://youtu.be/zuDtACzKGRs (15.4 million views, 96% like rating)

Weird, right? Although "liquid glass" putty, an oversized gummy worm, and a boot-shaped beer glass probably were not on your most-wanted list prior to watching those videos, you have to admit that you are probably just a *little bit* curious about those products now. Although the products were not created in St. Louis, the company that sells the product was, as were several of the people you saw in the videos.

You see, Vat19 is not some secret government lab dreaming up new inventions; Vat19 is simply an internet-based retailer of "curiously awesome gifts" whose employees dream up hilarious, engaging videos that help spread the word about the products and the company. The creator, Jamie Salvatorie, has said that the company only stocks products that he and his team believe *they* would be overjoyed and excited to receive as gifts, whether that gift is a 30-pound gummy bear or a funny, oversized latex horse head mask you can wear to scare your neigh-bors (...see what I did there?).

Although the silly products are unique and fun to browse, the real magic behind Vat19's success has little to do with the products and *everything* to do with the funny videos introducing the products to customers around the world. Each video is dreamed up, produced, edited, and created by the team at Vat19 using equipment that anyone can buy (and afford to buy)—nicer cameras than your typical camcorder, sure, but nothing like the impossibly expensive cameras used to film Hollywood blockbusters or "professional" commercials. Once the videos have been edited and gone through the post-production process, they are uploaded (for free, mind you) to YouTube and then linked to from the company's main site. From there, the videos take on lives of their own, with millions of people from all around the world liking, sharing, and commenting on the videos. Some fans are loyal Vat19 followers while others simply stumble across the videos. The recent video of the liquid glass bathtub experiment received press mentions online and web-based news shows...all for a cost of almost *nothing*.

Impressively, Vat19 has achieved success with a team of about 20 people, total, with just a handful of those 20 serving as the creative geniuses behind the viral commercials. In full disclosure, I am a bit biased because three of them–Jon, Danny, and Gus–are friends of mine (and former employees, incidentally) from the same small town in southern Illinois where we were born and raised. To say they are great people would be an understatement– talented, humble, kind, and hilarious–so, like most people, I enjoy their videos because they are amazing, but I also enjoy their work because I am witnessing the evolution of four talented people over years of creative endeavors.

Perhaps what is most impressive and inspirational about Vat19's story is that a group of small-town friends using only their creativity, accessible hardware and software, and the power of social media have managed to bring international fame to a small, 20-person, St. Louis-based company. Millions of people have seen their videos driving traffic to their website, generating word-of-mouth about their antics, and (hopefully) driving up their sales. Despite being a small company hidden away in that nondescript, unassuming building in that indistinguishable business park, Vat19 proves that you don't need a huge brand name, a massive budget, or a world-class creative agency to be successful. No, friends, you can *do it yourself.*

*   *   *

Humans like to create. From macaroni necklaces in kindergarten that only a parent could be proud of to groundbreaking masterpieces of art, music, or literature that the entire world can treasure, the creation process fulfills a deeply-rooted desire to leave the world a bit more different than we found it. Life, itself, is a process of creation and regardless of your religious beliefs (or lack thereof) just about every holy book of every faith begins with a story of creation.

Now, imagine the scenario in which you have an idea, but you outsource that idea to another person who will then create for you. Sometimes, outsourcing the actual creation process can be quite beneficial, freeing up our time, energy, and/or resources to focus on other pressing needs or obligations. Other times, outsourcing creation means letting go of control, having to accept someone else's creative interpretation of what we want, and *extra* resources (e.g., time, money, or both) spent correcting or remedying a creation that is not at all what we intended it to be.

I suppose you could say I am a bit of a control freak. I tend to have very detailed ideas about what I want creatively and tend to work extremely hard to transform those ideas into reality. Although I am good team player, I am quite selective when it comes to choosing my team, as I need to be sure my team members are on the same page as I am creatively and with respect to work ethic. I am the first to admit when someone is an expert or more capable than I am of completing a particular task. Similarly, I do my best to be diplomatic when I know I am the right person to get a job done and involving others may impede the creation process.

This notion of dividing labor between yourself and others is often a tricky task. Many people prefer offloading various elements of the creation process to others, particularly the tasks they either do not like or simply feel are not worth their time. Other people, like myself, enjoy taking on several parts of the creation process and following a project through from beginning to end to make sure no stone has been left unturned, no detail overlooked. When you combine my preference for control with my Obsessive-Compulsive tendencies, well, you might understand how much patience I also need to have not to come across as a holy terror with respect to group projects and organizational management (…my parents raised me well, thankfully). Oftentimes, I would just love to do everything myself, but I force myself to take a step back, focus on the strengths of others, and then corral the team so that everyone can play to his/her strengths for the benefit of the entire group.

This collective creative spirit is at the heart of the current chapter. When I began this book, I realized that I was not just writing about integrated marketing in the traditional sense (i.e., not simply going over the tools of integrated marketing like every other book on the subject does). I knew I wanted to discuss the intersection of business goals and creativity with marketing, a perspective that is ignored and neglected far too often. However, what I did *not* know at first but came to realize during the writing process is that this book also covers another topic that has not received the attention it deserves: DIY Marketing. The concept of Do-It-Yourself marketing is relatively new, as the traditional marketing model was company develops creative brief, creative brief gets sent to agency, agency develops campaign, campaign runs, company either keeps or cans agency. In an era before the internet, this model was the standard. However, in recent years as data analytics became more and more popular, the traditional model was being upended and replaced by a new preference for data, for outcome measures, for actual effectiveness as evidenced by quantitative results. Accompanying this pervasiveness of data came the increasing availability of software, shared resources, and tools that fostered creative expression. We are not just talking about Microsoft Paint and basic, rudimentary forms of creative expression. No, we are talking about high-end, professional-quality tools that produce creative executions worthy of production studios and the big leagues.

Indeed, creating your own marketing executions has never been easier for amateur and professional marketers alike. This chapter is dedicated to some of the hardware, software, and tips one should keep in mind with respect to DIY marketing. In a time when unprofessional, amateur videos produced on a shoestring budget can be more likely to go viral than professional,

Hollywood-directed videos with massive budgets, it is in your best interest to familiarize yourself with some of the tools listed in this chapter, as you may find yourself using them to create the next viral sensation. For those of you outsourcing the creative development of your marketing executions to an agency or someone else, happy skimming! But for those of you willing to try your hand at this DIY marketing, well, here are tools you may want to consider on your creative question.

Sight: Print, Video, and Visual Editing Programs

Humans are visual creatures. Some researchers estimate that 90% of the brain's incoming information comes through the eyes. Thus, having some experience with visual editing programs is certainly to be useful for any marketer, especially when it comes to creating mockups of your ideas for others to see. Or, at the very least, you can create a funny meme that goes viral, become Facebook famous, and then hire someone to do all your visual creations for you!

As an avid fan and loyal user of the **Adobe Creative Suite** of products (e.g., Photoshop, Illustrator, InDesign, etc.), my default preference for creating visual stimuli is Adobe Photoshop. While you should feel free to purchase any or all of the products in Adobe's Creative Suite, I have good news for you: you don't have to! Thanks to modern technology and this crazy sharing economy idea, several companies have created their own comparable versions of **Adobe Photoshop**. One such program/site, **GIMP** (www.gimp.org), is an open source and very free program that allows users to create visual stimuli using many of the same tools the full version of Adobe Photoshop provides. From several drawing tools to various brush styles, layered projects to text inclusion, GIMP is essentially a free version of Adobe Photoshop.

If GIMP isn't your jam, another program comparable to Adobe Photoshop for graphic design is **Pixlr** (www.pixlr.com) and its portfolio of products (e.g., Pixlr, Pixlr Editor, Pixlr Express, Pixlr-o-matic). Although most of the programs are free, a few have subscription-based payment options, as well. Still, the free versions of several of the apps will provide what you will need as a DIY marketer. Whereas Pixlr, Pixlr Editor, and Pixlr Express are comparable to the typical Adobe Photoshop style and layout so commonly associated with most graphic design programs, Pixlr-o-matic tends to focus more on photography and not graphic design more generally. This, of course, is a bit ironic because Adobe's pared down version of Photoshop, known as **Adobe Photoshop Express** (www.photoshop.com), is essentially a photo editing program that lacks many of the graphic design creation tools found in the full version of Adobe Photoshop and the free versions of GIMP and Pixlr.

Beyond the magic of still photos and graphics exists the art of the motion picture. In a time when just about everyone has Vine, a YouTube channel, or Snapchat, most people are fairly good at recording video of themselves, applying a filter that makes them look better than they really look, and then sharing that video with the world. While this amateur style is often "good enough" to go viral, sometimes we want to class up our videos, and to do that we can turn to video editing software. One such video editing software, and the one I use the most simply because it is easy to use, is Apple's own **iMovie**. iMovie comes preinstalled on Apple computers and provides a very simple drag-and-drop user interface that permits the creation of videos within seconds. The program provides transitions, title screens, automatic video and audio editing, and even sound effects for your videos. Although iMovie may not be a professional-level software editing program, it does a great job and (here's the best part) comes free on Apple computers! Of course, if Apple or iMovie don't do it for you, then another free video editing program is **Jahshaka** (http://www.jahshaka.com). As a program built on the philosophy of open source (and free) programming, Jahshaka provides all the basic features needed in a video editor, as well as extra tools including a feature for 3D content.

These graphic design tools and video editors are great resources for marketers, but if even your best efforts and commitment to trying fail to produce any good results, I would suggest checking out the website **Fiverr** (www.fiverr.com). Fiverr is a website that allows people to post tasks they need performed and to pay $5 or more (in $5 increments) for each task's completion. How does this help you by way of graphics and design? Well, one of Fiverr's service categories is exactly "graphics & design," so it is fairly easy to get quality logos, print ads, and other visual marketing collateral at an extremely low price. Goodbye ad agencies; hello graphic design students trying to build your portfolios from all over the world!

Another fun visual tool that is a hybrid between still photo and video is a site called **PowToon** (www.powtoon.com). Using an interface that reminds you a bit of Microsoft's PowerPoint with a video timeline running across the bottom of the screen, PowToon lets users create animated videos that look like professional cartoon PowerPoints. More visually stunning and engaging than a traditional slideshow but not as elaborate or as "real world" as a video, Powtoon strikes a healthy balance that brings the fun of animation together with the usefulness of PowerPoint and business presentations. Although it is possible to buy monthly subscriptions to the site, chances are you are looking for "single exports," which permits you to buy an add-free version of your Powtoon for a small fee.

The final visual tool I want to include is my website maker/website host of choice: **Wix** (www.wix.com). The beauty of Wix is that it is among the first companies who simplified the user interface of website making services.

Featuring a primarily drag-and-drop menu and hundreds of extremely stylish (and professional) templates from which to choose, Wix has made the process of creating and maintaining a website ridiculously easy. I currently have about seven different websites that I created and now run, and every single one of them is operated through Wix. Although free to try and design, you'll have to pay to get rid of the wix.com tab that appears on the free version.

Sound: Music, Sound Effects, and Audio Editing Programs

As a musician and singer-songwriter, I remember recording songs via a cassette recorder back when I was a child and then slowly graduating to MIDI/computer recording and finally all the way up to using music recording software programs. Trust me when I say I had *no* idea what I was doing when I first started, but after playing around with the programs for awhile, I started figuring it out. That said, there are still countless dials and buttons that I have absolutely *zero* idea about, but learning is what makes life interesting, right?

One audio editing program that comes free with Apple products is **GarageBand**. Although marketed as a music recording program for musicians, GarageBand also features templates for podcasts, audio books, and other sound-based recording needs. As such, if you are not a musician, do not be afraid to explore GarageBand. Although the program is simple in the sense that anyone can use it, record something, and export that audio recording in a format that can be uploaded to YouTube, SoundCloud, a social media site, or a webpage, there are countless filters, sound effects, and audio adjustments one can explore within GarageBand. Speaking voices can be made to sound clearer via a vocal enhancer. Pitchy notes can be made to sound "in tune" with pitch correction (hear that, Rihanna?). Commercial narrations can have royalty-free background music added to them to spruce up the experience. In short, GarageBand is a one-stop shop for all your audio needs; it just might take some time to get used to.

Similar to GarageBand, although slightly less pretty, is the open source and 100% free **Audacity** (http://www.audacityteam.org/). Audacity describes itself as a "digital audio editor" and can be used to create mashups, edit music, record podcasts and more! A bit less glossy by way of user interface, Audacity includes tools like vocal reduction (to create a karaoke track of a song, for example), and tempo changes without affecting pitch so that audio can be shortened or lengthened to correspond to a video's length. The nice part about Audacity being open source is that it has a large community of developers, users, and fans that are available to help you should you have any questions, not to mention the fact that add-ons are constantly being created that might be useful to you and your specific audio needs.

One final audio program worth mentioning here is **Finale Notepad**. Whereas the previous two programs require no musical experience or training, Finale Notepad is actually a transcription software that provides songwriters with the tools necessary to compose and record music. Whether by dragging and dropping notes and rests into a document or by plugging in a musical keyboard and plunking out the notes in real time, musicians can transcribe their songs into a digital format that can then be saved, printed, and played back using simulated instruments. What's nice about this is that just by playing a piano or putting notes into a score one by one, an entire symphony can play back an original song that can be used as background music, a jingle, or a sound cue to accompany an integrated marketing campaign. As an added plus, song files saved as MIDI files in Notepad can be opened in GarageBand for effects ranging from reverb and echo to different instrumentation or concert hall acoustics.

Touch: Useful Hardware for DIY Marketing

As more people get into the media creation game, it is not surprising that software prices have come down (to the point of "free" in many instances, including the previous examples) and now we are seeing more hardware in the market dedicated to the creation of digital media content. Although there are several brands offering many great products, I am going to list a few with which I have had personal experience that you may want to consider.

To start off, you may not need to look much further than your own pocket for a solid video recording device. Most iPhones and Samsung phones are now equipped with high-definition cameras that can record professional-level video. Case in point, one of the hit films at the 2015 Sundance Film Festival, a movie about transgender prostitutes working in Hollywood entitled *Tangerine*, was filmed entirely on an iPhone 5S and edited using an $8 app called Filmic Pro. Filming video clips on your phone and then uploading them to an iMac or Macbook for editing via AirDrop has been one of the easiest ways for me to record/edit high quality video.

If you are going to be filming video on a mobile phone, you may also want to invest in a video stabilizer. Although many video editing software, including YouTube's built-in editor, can automatically stabilize your video, these algorithms are not perfect and can sometimes lead to quality reduction for your video. However, the range of video stabilizer is quite wide in the marketplace, with some low-end stabilizers costing as little as $40 and some more expensive options costing several hundreds of dollars. You do you, boo; just know that a stabilizer will make your video seem *that* much more professional.

One company whose brand and products have received considerable attention the past few years is GoPro. GoPro is the maker of high-resolution cameras that record video and still images. The brand made a name for itself by associating its products with extreme sports in which athletes and daredevils strapped the cameras to some part of their body and proceeded to do normal things like jump off buildings or climb a cliff without a safety harness. The GoPro portfolio varies and changes often (what feels like every day), but the thing to know about GoPro is that not all the cameras include digital displays like the ones you are likely used to and that some of the lens settings will distort pictures to look like a fisheye lens or other, slightly unexpected shapes. GoPro cameras are excellent cameras; you just have to make sure you are using them correctly.

Speaking of lenses, those of you hoping to capture some nice still images for print ad campaigns or static online ads might be considering a DSLR or a mirrorless camera. Although the prices for these cameras have come down significantly the past few years, the best ones are still pretty pricey. But…good news! Entire companies have popped up selling lenses you can clip on to your mobile phone to transform your phone's already-solid camera into an *even better* camera. Companies like OlloClip (www.olloclip.com) provide an assortment of lenses that can improve both your still photography, as well as your video recording. What did we used to do before cellphones? Seriously?

Finally, with respect to audio recording, I would recommend making three purchases: 1) a Yeti USB microphone, 2) a pop mic filter, and 3) an M-Audio Keystation keyboard. The Yeti microphone runs about $100 but will provide you with a solid quality recording microphone that is hands-down better than the microphone built in to your computer. The Yeti offers different recording settings based on your needs (e.g., bidirectional, omnidirectional, cardioid, and stereo), gain settings, and mute/volume options (not to mention all the effects that GarageBand and other audio recording programs can bring to the table). The second purchase, a pop mic filter, is to prevent hard consonant sounds from making a "popping" noise during your recording. This tends to occur when we say certain letters (e.g,. "p") and results in an odd popping sound that stands out during audio playback. Finally, for musicians and non-musicians alike, a decent MIDI keyboard will allow you to plunk out a few notes, use the keyboard as a mixing board for different GarageBand loops/sound effects, and just look cool in general when people see a keyboard next to your computer and think you are a modern day Mozart.

And that's it! With just those few devices and programs you have what it takes to film your own commercial, record your own jingle, create your own meme, and so much more!

I know, I know: easier said than done, right? Although people have different approaches when it comes to learning how to use new programs and new tools, I have found that the best way to learn is to just do it. When

I was a wee lad, I used a free trial version of Adobe Photoshop to redesign album covers for famous musical artists of the time. By the time I got my hands on the full version of Adobe Photoshop, I was comfortable and fluent with the software to the point that I began designing logos and doing marketing consulting work for small businesses. Giving yourself a small project to work on (e.g., an album cover, a podcast, a weekly video blog) is a great way to get started, as the excitement of the project can help mitigate any frustration that might otherwise be debilitating. You do not have to post the project when it is finished; that is up to you. However, just going through the creation process using these different tools and programs will help get you up to speed on how to use them.

One final tip when it comes to DIY Marketing: you are not in this alone. While some will go to ad agencies, others should consider independent mom-and-pop shops specializing in social media marketing, for example, or event marketing (e.g., By The Barkers: www.bythebarkers.com). If that option it still too expensive, you should consider outsourcing some of the work online to extremely talented design, digital media, and art students around the globe looking to take on projects so that they can build their portfolio. These options are surprisingly cheap and professional-level quality.

Finally, at a time when creative apps are free and the tools needed to produce creative projects are available at increasingly lower prices, one extremely motivated group of people who can help you is right in front of your face: *your customers*. Customer co-creation can be a source for amazing creative material produced by the very people you want to be producing for in the first place. Why not get your target customer more engaged with the campaign creation process? Who better than to tell your target market what they want to hear in the way they need to hear it than the target market itself?!

So *dream*, dream big, and never stop dreaming.

But also *do*. Do more, do it again, and, whenever possible, do it *yourself*.

*   *   *

No one knows why certain videos go viral.

Some videos are funny: like someone getting stuck in a tire swing. Some videos are sad: like a dog lying at the foot of his owner's casket and refusing to move. Some videos are pointless: like the, "Damn, Daniel," meme of 2016. And other videos are poignant: like the alarming videos calling attention to income inequality and inconceivable disparities in wealth distribution in the United States.

Countless people, from practitioners to academics alike, have attempted to identify the secret recipe to a viral video. Despite their claims, not a single one of them has figured it out. Maybe there is no "secret recipe?" Maybe a video's ability to go viral cannot be known in advance?

Whether their goal was to create viral videos from the onset or not, the team at Vat19 now has a series of successful videos in their repertoire. From funny songs to goofy gags, solid editing to professional-style film quality, who knows what it is about the Vat19 videos that makes them so appealing. Each video is unique yet each video shares the same playful vibe. After watching one video you cannot help but want to watch another, and each video's duration is just short enough to hold our attention and yet long enough to contain solid content. While the number of YouTube views, likes, and comments may not necessarily lead to actual sales, these kind of metrics are useful when it comes to measuring brand awareness or customer engagement and can help Vat19 make better strategic decisions.

Perhaps the best insights the team at Vat19 had, however, were two important trends: 1) the increasing availability of creative tools, and 2) the almost-limitless power of social media. For almost *nothing*, Vat19 is able to advertise its company, its brand, and its products to millions of people around the world without having any need for an ad agency, a digital media specialist, or a marketing research firm. Vat19 is entirely responsible for its own media success, and although the company is known for its odd, random, and quirky products, Vat19's approach to marketing may seem just as bizarre as those products now but very well may be the way of the future. Ad agencies and marketing firms beware: Big Data companies may not be your biggest competition anymore—no, the biggest competition you may face could very well be your clients, themselves.

What if...   *VAT19, DIY, and OMG, LOL!*

The creative team at Vat19 has managed to accomplish two incredible feats: 1) create and produce dozens of viral videos, and 2) amass a community of loyal fans that spans the globe…and all this on a budget that is the David to major companies' Goliath budgets. From YouTube to Twitter, the company's website to its Facebook page, the Vat19 team has really left no stone unturned with respect to getting its messaging out there consistently, using its bright orange/white branding and its goofy sense of humor everywhere you look.

So what could Vat19 possibly do to improve or supplement its fairly well-oiled oddity machine? A quick glimpse at the company's social media pages revealed comments from fans living around the world, invested community members who follow Vat19 and its content religiously. With such a loyal fan base, Vat19 has an opportunity to generate even *more* awareness not through any actions it might take but, instead, by rallying these loyal customers to create original content of their own.

Vat19 is known for its viral videos that incorporate the company's zany products. What if the company challenged its fans to a web-based competition in which the fans had to create their own Vat19-inspired video showcasing one of the Vat19 products or the *need* for a particular Vat19 product (so that way fans don't necessarily have to spend money to make their video). Using the same DIY tools mentioned throughout this chapter, Vat19 fans from around the world would create funny videos, post the videos, and encourage everyone they know to vote for their video as the "fan favorite." This format spreads the word about Vat19 to the friends and family of the company's loyal fans, which can increase awareness of the company and its products, as well as be a great way for those friends/family to know what to get their Vat19-loving buddies this year for birthdays, Christmas, getting out of prison parties, etc.

Although there can be some risks involved with letting anyone create *anything* and linking it to your brand, there can be some controls put in place to ensure brand consistency and clear rules/restrictions about the use of Vat19's name, branding, and other intellectual property. However, if done correctly and pitched as a fun, amateur, fan-based video competition, Vat19 could benefit from having its dearest fans spread the love for the company. Who better to share the passion for Vat19 and its products outside of the company than its most loyal supporters?

Another benefit from this audience engagement promotion is that it can help Vat19 find future talent that could actually be employed by the company. One of the other most popular comments appearing on Vat19's social media pages involved asking how to get a job at the company. Obviously, with videos as funny and clever as those produced by the Vat19 team, who *wouldn't* want to be a part of the team? By holding an annual customer creation promotion such as the one described herein, Vat19 would essentially have a front-row seat to some of the top digital media talent from around the world…who also happen to be advertising their company for free!

OPERATION

JAMES A. MOUREY

CHAPTER 10 | Strategies, Tactics, and War Plans

"For every action, there is an equal and opposite reaction."
-Newton's Third Law

A new Cold War has begun.

Starting in the 1950s, two adversaries on opposite sides of the Arctic Circle began their quest for global domination. Having gained the support and commitment of the citizens in their respective homelands, the adversaries began looking outward for others who would join their cause and believe in their mission and philosophy. In this quest for the minds and hearts of people around the world, the competitors began broadcasting their propaganda and, for decades, have attempted to be the dominant world power, but in war there can only be one winner. When the gloves come off and the coats go on, who will win the war?

Canada Goose or Moncler?

Relax. This "cold war" has nothing to do with nuclear weapons or political ideologies. Instead, a literal cold war has been waged among some of the world's most well-known winter coat brands including the Canadian brand Canada Goose the Italian-based Moncler.

Canada Goose, known for its very distinctive red, white, and blue Artic Circle-themed logo, is on fire lately. Despite having been in existence since 1957, Canada Goose was a relatively unknown brand outside of Canada until Bain Capital bought a majority stake in the company in 2013. Since then, sales of the brand have skyrocketed, increasing as much as 30% in a single year, a growth rate limited only by the relatively small company's production constraints. Indeed, many high-end retailers, like Saks Fifth Avenue and Neiman Marcus, have found themselves running out of Canada Goose products in the winter season as the demand outpaced the supply of coats in stores. Everyone, it seems, wants a Canada Goose coat.

This success has not gone unnoticed by Canada Goose's competition. Moncler has also seen exceptional growth in the past several years, although still not on the level of Canada Goose. Still, as the maker of fine coats that are as slim-fitting and stylish as they are warm and comfortable, Moncler is maintaining its position as the alternative brand in the consideration set along with Canada Goose.

Other players in the winter coat market, including the American company The North Face, are well aware of the increasing popularity of brands like Canada Goose and Moncler. As these fashion-forward, yet functional, winter coat creators keep eating away at The North Face's market share, the company is hinting at its response: shifting away from bulky, warm coats to slender, stylish coats of their own.

Despite being a kind, friendly Canadian company, Canada Goose is now under the direction of the folks at Bain Consulting (who can also be described as kind and friendly…and potentially other adjectives, too). In its effort to take Canada Goose to the "next level," the powers that be are well aware of the competitive threat and response posed by brands like Moncler and The North Face. Moncler, based in Milan, has the benefit of wide European distribution, higher brand awareness in luxury markets, and the country-of-origin advantages associated with being a clothing product based in Milan, Italy. The North Face, often *the* top-of-mind brand in the North American market when people are asked to name a warm, winter coat brand, also benefits from having high brand awareness, dedicated The North Face stores in major cities across the United States and in the United Kingdom.

To counter the competition, rumor has it that Canada Goose is considering launching its own brick and mortar stores throughout the United States now that the American market represents nearly 25% of its total sales and is expected to surpass the sale in its home market of Canada. In addition, just as The North Face offers clothing for all seasons (i.e., not just winter), Canada Goose is expected to develop new products that will keep the brand relevant throughout the entire year and not just during winter. Sounds like a winning plan, right?

Not so fast. Part of the appeal of brands like Canada Goose and even Moncler is that they are not as ubiquitous as The North Face. Although The North Face has long been considered a popular brand in the U.S. and the creator of warm products for winter, The North Face has also become the brand *everyone* has. People forgave the company for its bulky coats on account of the fact that those same coats kept them from freezing to death during Boston blizzards or snowstorms in Syracuse. But when Moncler and Canada Goose started sneaking into the American market, with subtler branding and slimmer fits, well, freezing Americans found coats that were functional *and* fashionable, coats that differentiated them from their The North Face-wearing friends. In other words, part of Canada Goose's success has been the fact that it is *not* as pervasive as The North Face.

This presents Canada Goose with an interesting challenge. How do you continue steady growth in a profitable marketplace when part of your appeal is that you are not *the* dominant player in the market? How fast is *too* fast to grow? How big is *too* big to be? As Canada Goose continues to ruffle the down feathers of the winter coat market, it is unclear whether The North Face falls out of favor as the default winter coat of choice in the American market and whether Canada Goose or Moncler become the new, next-best thing.

In addition, part of Canada Goose's appeal has been its association with the Arctic Circle and the researchers and filmmakers working in the Arctic Circle famous for wearing Canada Goose-branded coats to stay warm.

Whereas both The North Face and Moncler have brands that extend beyond this icy cool positioning, Canada Goose's brand is planted squarely at the North Pole. Is it possible for a brand that has rooted itself so firmly in Arctic ice to melt away from this positioning and into the warmer markets of track jackets, hoodies, and other, non-winter apparel?

And finally, given the luxury status of brands like Moncler and Canada Goose, might there already be perceptions about the *kind* of people who wear these brands? If so, are these innovators envied or deplored by follow-up early adopters? Is it possible that the brands and their exclusive positioning are a turn-off to would-be customers? As another season comes and goes, it remains to be seen which brand comes out on top, and which brand falls out of fashion.

*　　*　　*

This is the point of the campaign creation process where people finally start to see the finish line in sight. We have come an *incredibly* long way from our starting point when we established our foundational business strategy (i.e., Focus). We did a slow and steady pace through the research collection and analysis portion of the campaign (i.e., Understanding) and then sprinted through the creative brainstorming process (i.e., Synthesize). And, most recently, we plotted out the many paths on our Big Idea hike that will get us from where we are now to our final destination. But before we get too much further, there are a few final considerations we need to address. We have all seen far too many horror movies to know what happens when you *think* the protagonist is finally on his/her way to safety, when that finish line *seems* like it is finally in sight. It *never* ends well, especially if you are attractive. Because we are attractive, we need to talk about how to survive in the face of unknown dangers lurking in the shadows.

As the opening example illustrates, integrated marketing campaigns are not developed and executed in a vacuum. No. Instead, at the same time you are figuring out your business objectives, conducting your research, and designing an integrated marketing campaign, so, too, are your competitors. Although it would be lovely if our competitors just sat around all day and waited for us to do something in order to respond, that's not how the world works. Rest assured that your competitors are designing their own integrated marketing campaigns and, even worse, preparing for what to do in the event that you launch a campaign, too.

Well, bad news for your competition: you *are* launching a campaign! And your campaign is going to be better than their campaign because you read this book! Okay, so your campaign is not going to be better just *because* you read this book, it is going to be better because you *implemented the ideas and strategies* I have shared in this book. As we near the end of the campaign creation process, there are a few final strategies to consider before the campaign launches. As Newton's Third Law states, "For every action, there is an equal and opposite reaction." So now let us think not just about our plan to act but, also, our plan to *react*.

REACT: Polishing our Integrated Marketing Plan

My Principles of Finance professor at WashU once likened the field of finance to fortune telling. "Finance," he said, "Is like predicting the future!" If the future consists of rich, old white men getting richer at the expense of everyone else, then yes, finance *does* predict the future. Conversely, marketing is often said to be about the here and now, understanding current market dynamics, current buyer preferences, and current supplier information to determine how to make magic happen in a very immediate, very proximal market. Sure, we might be anticipating future trends or planning ahead with respect to our upcoming product lines or scheduled campaign, but for the most part, that's where planning for the future stops. Perhaps this is why financiers tend to have more savings but marketers tend to have more fun. #LivingForTheMoment

More germane to the current chapter, however, is the idea that marketers tend to get so wrapped up in the details of a campaign, which piece of data inspired which particular execution, how a launch must unfold, which metric is a key measure of the campaign's success, etc., that we often forget that we live in a dynamic, constantly changing world. Our friends in Finance are known for best-case scenarios, worst-case scenarios, conservative estimates, and accounting for future variability whereas those of us in marketing are often loath to consider these future possible alternatives.

Thus, in order to make sure we do not ignore these important considerations about what *might* happen in the future that could significantly affect our campaign, I have built a step into the FUSION model that requires us to think about these issues in advance should there be a series of unfortunate (or simply probable) events.

Response. Unless you are such a tiny player in your market or so niche within a particular market that your competitors do not fear the possibility of you stealing any market share from them, chances are that whatever campaign you launch is going to be met with *some* response from a competitor or multiple competitors. Remember, this is war, so if a company feels like your maneuvering is threatening to its safety and stability, you can rest assured that the company is going to do something about it.

Thus, one way to review your campaign is to ask yourself, "If I do X, what will [insert competitor's name here] be most likely to do in response?" You can play this game with just about *any* aspect of your campaign (e.g., "If I choose this Prospective Audience…," "If I launch this press release…," etc.). The purpose of the response consideration here is not to dream up counterattacks (that's its own, special section below). Instead, the purpose of thinking about likely competitive responses is to tweak your campaign prior to its launch to mitigate or eliminate those potential competitive responses or to specifically design an element of your campaign that might soften any blow resulting from a likely competitive response. Remember that we want to retain as much control over the campaign during its run as possible. Ruffling a lot of feathers and eliciting an aggressive competitive response has the potential to throw our campaign into a tailspin, so the more we can avoid that, the better.

As an example, consider the Spanish clothing company Zara. Zara is renowned in the apparel industry for creating an extremely lean production process in which its designers, textile creators, and laborers all work closely together to churn out new clothing at unprecedented rates for the apparel industry. Because of this, new clothes are delivered twice a week to most of Zara's stores, which means customers visit Zara more frequently than they visit other clothing stores that only turn over their inventory once or twice every *season*. Say that H&M, the Swedish clothing company, wants to compete with Zara's fast inventory model and, as such, centralizes its designers, textile workers, and laborers in a similar way before launching a campaign entitled, "HyperMode," a play on "quick" and "style" that incorporates H&M. Touting its newfound ability to move new apparel in and out of stores quickly, H&M would be opening itself up for a strong competitive response by Zara who could easily claim that H&M is simply playing "follow the leader." Because H&M's marketing manager read this book and thought of Zara's potential response, built into the "HyperMode" campaign is a PR piece describing how H&M achieved this just-in-time lean production model by employing vast amounts of unemployed individuals unable to get other jobs who were also facing severe poverty and an accompanying loss of self-worth and self-esteem. The "HyperMode" campaign is symbolic of getting these hard workers back on the fast track to success, providing them with much needed jobs and even an opportunity to design clothing that could potentially be sold in H&M stores. By doing this, H&M effectively tied Zara's hands with respect to complaining about their new lean production process while also adding another value-added component to its integrated marketing campaign. In this way, per our previous conversation about synergy, some marketing executions can be incorporated for the sole purpose of mitigating or preventing competitive responses to the campaign.

Editing. Before your campaign launches, before you even test market your campaign, it is prudent to give yourself a moment to collect your thoughts and to take a breather. Take a step back from the campaign and give it a quick once-over. From this semi-removed perspective, does the integrated marketing campaign live up to its stated goals? If the answer is,

"No," at this level, well, we have a problem (what did we just spend all that time doing?!). Hopefully, however, the answer is, "Yes." Awesome! Great! You probably feel like Michelangelo looking at a masterpiece sculpture!

Hold up.

Before you call it a day and send your statue to the Louvre for display, it is time to dive right back into the details, hammer and chisel in hand, to chip away at any excess, redundancy, or imperfections present in the campaign. Sometimes we are mired too much in the details of the campaign creation process that we cannot see the forest for the trees. Once we have some time to consider the campaign in its entirety, from beginning to end, from far away to close up, we may start noticing a mistake here, an illogical or inconsistent execution there, and just room for improvement in general.

Remember our earlier conversation about elegance? Elegance is the art of making a lasting impression as simply as possible. If elements of the campaign can be removed or simplified yet still leave the same lasting impression, then those elements need to be removed or simplified. Efficiency and elegance are critical: if we can produce the same output with cheaper, more effective input, then that's what we should do.

Now, some people panic when the time comes to put on one's editing hat. People have a difficult time axing ideas because ideas are so tied to our ego, particularly creative ideas. However, one of the most beloved creative icons in the world, Tina Fey, once said that being a great producer is more about stifling creativity than it is about creating it. Not every idea can or should see the light of day in an integrated marketing campaign. We should hope that we have more than enough ideas with which to work and then have the tricky job of paring down to only the *best* ideas. It is a tough job trying to figure out what should stay and what needs to get cut, but sometimes it is the most important job there is. A simpler, effective campaign is *always* better than a more complex, effective campaign.

Aftermath. Whereas editing involves fine-tuning and simplifying your campaign before it goes live, dealing with the aftermath involves the plan of action in place for once a campaign has ended. All good things must come to an end, and exceptional marketers both know this and have a transition plan in place that will tide a company over from one campaign to the next even if there is a lull between the campaigns. The three questions to consider when contemplating the aftermath of an integrated marketing campaign are: 1) where does this campaign leave you?, 2) what's your most likely next step if this campaign is successful?, and 3) what's your most likely next step if this campaign is not successful?

If you play it right, considering the Aftermath of your integrated marketing campaign can actually inspire the next Big Idea for the subsequent campaign. As one particularly effective example, the M&M's Great Color Quest campaign led directly into the Chocolate is Better in Color campaign.

The beauty of this sequence was that, regardless of whether or not the Great Color Quest campaign was successful or a total failure, the return to color would have been embraced by audiences in either situation. A well-received campaign that involved robbing M&M's of their color only to return brighter colors to them later would segue nicely into a Chocolate is Better in Color theme while an angry, "How dare they take away *my* colors?" reaction would suggest a similar level of excitement and anticipation for a follow-up campaign in which the colors were restored.

It is worth noting this kind of seamless transition is not always possible, but thinking through the potential aftermath of a campaign is a useful exercise that can often inspire Big Ideas worth considering for the future. Furthermore, in the event that your integrated marketing campaign winds up not being successful despite careful design, contingency plans, and test marketing, it is wise to consider the aftermath of this scenario in advance so marketing momentum is not further stalled as you try to figure out what went wrong. Even campaigns that seem perfect on paper may not always play out as perfectly as we would hope in the real world, so it is best to think through all possible outcomes and have a plan of action ready in each case.

Counterattacks. Not to be confused with the Response consideration above, counterattacks refer to a sequence in which our competitor attacks us, either directly or indirectly, and then we stage a counterattack. Whereas Response refers to us thinking through our competitors' hypothetical reactions to our campaign and then adjusting the campaign accordingly, Counterattacks refers to *actual* reactions or provocations from our competitors that require a response from us. Another distinction is that Response takes place before our campaign even launches whereas Counterattacks take place during the campaign's run.

If this all sounds very warlike and gorilla chest-beating, that's because it is. As I said earlier, our competitors are not going to ignore us or our campaign to capture customers in the market that we all have some stake in. If we can anticipate those responses and mitigate them as much as possible before the campaign even launches (i.e., the Response consideration above), that's great, but we have to be ready for whatever surprises may come along during the course of the campaign.

When thinking about immediate responses to competitive threats, some integrated marketing tools are better than others. Press releases, social network posts, and even web-based videos can be a great way to respond to whatever it is our competitor has lobbed our way. Whatever tool is used, a broader strategy should also be considered in determining your response. Do you want to engage in a back-and-forth war of words or content with your competitor(s)? Probably not. Do you want to determine a counterattack that effectively ceases your competitor's threat while also shielding you from further attacks? You bet.

A great example of a counterattack strategy is one of my favorite marketing case examples of all time. Before several new competitors came along, rental car companies Hertz and Avis occupied the number one and number two spot in the rental car market, respectively. Hertz launched a campaign in the mid-1950s that touted its position as *the* dominant player in the rental car market. Clearly, Hertz did not spend adequate time thinking about the potential *Response* from Avis, as Avis followed up the Hertz campaign with one of the cleverest campaigns in marketing history, essentially saying, "Because we are #2, we try *harder.*" Bam. This was a direct attack on Hertz, so you know what that meant: *Counterattack*! Hertz came back with, "For years Avis has been telling you Hertz is No. 1. Now we're going to tell you why." Touché! While these attacks and counterattacks continued over the decades, Enterprise slowly snuck in to usurp the top spot in the rental car market and did so by steering clear of the Hertz/Avis fracas. Indeed, Enterprise's slogan is the customer-focused, "Pick Enterprise. We'll pick you up." as opposed to a competitive version of the same slogan, "Pick on Enterprise. We'll $%ck you up."

Timeline. All's well that ends well. You should know going into it that your integrated marketing campaign is going to have good days and bad days. Some of your executions are going to meet their numbers, and some are not. Some days you will be pleased with your campaign's performance; other days you will not be pleased. Campaigns tend to have a natural ebb and flow to them, spiking around certain executions and waning in the interim.

However, some of the attention your campaign receives (or does not receive) is actually up to you. Three scheduling strategies often discussed with respect to marketing campaigns and timing include continuous, flighting, and pulsing strategies. A **continuous strategy** refers to a campaign that has executions running constantly throughout the entire run of the campaign. This, of course, can be expensive if a campaign is extremely comprehensive but may be necessary depending on the nature of the good or service you are selling (i.e., is it a product that is sold all year long, like toilet paper or laundry detergent). A **flighting strategy** refers to campaigns marked by periods of extreme activity separated by periods of no (or almost no) activity. Campaigns of this kind typically involve seasonal products (e.g., a campaign for Hallmark stores around certain holidays) where it simply does not make sense to spend money promoting the products when customers would not at all consider purchasing them. The final strategy, the **pulsing strategy**, is a hybrid of the continuous and flighting strategy in which *some* marketing is *always* taking place throughout the duration of a campaign but certain periods see an uptick in campaign activity based on seasonality, company sales goals, and other objectives that make cranking up the campaign's volume a necessity. Of course, there is no one right strategy, as scheduling depends on the particular market, the business objective, the level of competition, and a variety of other factors. The takeaway is that one needs to realize that the value of an integrated marketing campaign comes not just from the content of the campaign itself but how and *when* that content is presented throughout the duration of the campaign.

Furthermore, because synergy is at the heart of any integrated marketing campaign, one final consideration when reviewing a campaign is how the different marketing executions can build on each other throughout the timeline of the campaign. A campaign could begin with brief television commercials that just list a web address and an upcoming date in the future to generate buzz, excitement, and intrigue. A social media campaign can launch to get customers talking about what might be revealed on the listed date. Then, on the big day, the website can reveal a new product and a printable coupon for in-store redemption that week only to drive traffic at a particular time of year. It may sound intense and it may seem like overkill, but scheduling the *when* of a campaign, how it unfolds, and the overall timeline is just as important as the *what*, *how*, and *why* we have covered up to this point.

Lastly, one final consideration with respect to timeline involves any major milestones along the way. Although we should always be collecting data on the performance of the campaign and its integrated executions, it is wise to set specific milestones throughout the campaign to assess the campaign's overall trajectory. This will allow us the opportunity to know what is working, what is not working, and whether any adjustments we have made have remedied the underlying problem by the next milestone check in. If we don't bother setting milestones then, before we know it, a campaign that had several highs and lows either hits its mark or doesn't, and we are none the wiser as to how we arrived at our final destination or when we could (and should) have tweaked things along the way.

*   *   *

The double-edged sword of Canada Goose's exceptional success is that it has both captured the attention and awe of prospective customers around the world, as well as the ire and revenge of competitors like Moncler and The North Face. Whereas prior to its success the company had free reign to dream big with little regard for competitive response and counterattacks–after all, how threatening could a tiny Canadian company few people have ever heard of be?–now every move the company makes will be anticipated, responded to, and even preempted by the competition. Canada Goose's coats may feature the company's famous, iconic logo on their sleeve, but now they also have a metaphorical target on their back. Going forward, Canada Goose will not only have to build well-crafted integrated marketing campaigns, but it will also have to be prepared to *react* to whatever fury that campaign may elicit from its competitors. The earlier Canada Goose can plan for these potential responses, the better.

And with that, it's finally time to launch! Well...*almost*. Just like buying a new winter coat, there's one last thing we must do with our campaign: try it on for size.

What if...   *Moncler for All Seasons*

With Canada Goose's intentions to expand its product portfolio to include spring and summer coats in addition to its ultra-warm winter coats, Moncler should be thinking of a competitive response to this potential move. As it turns out, Moncler's portfolio already includes what it refers to as "Ultralight Down Jackets," lighter versions of the company's stylish, warm coats to be worn during warm days. Still, looking at these products compared to the winter coats for which Moncler is predominantly known, these coats seem fitting for very cold summer or spring nights, as they still look as if they belong in a winter wardrobe.

Although its non-winter products may not be perfectly suited for warmer spring and summer weather, Moncler is a simple tweak or two away from amending its non-winter offerings throughout the entire year and, if wise, could stage a preemptive attack against Canada Goose using its own weapon against it. You see, Canada Goose has tied its brand to the Arctic Circle. I mean, Canada Goose's very logo *is* the Arctic Circle. This bodes well for Canada Goose during winter, but associating the Arctic Circle with summer might be a leap (unless the company manages to communicate the idea of keeping people "cool" or "Arctic chilled"). Moncler, on the other hand, has the distinct advantage of being based in Milan, Italy, a country that has the icy cold Alps in its northern region and the balmy, warm Mediterranean climate down its spine and at its southern tip. Whereas Canada Goose used its location to gain a foothold in the luxury winter coat market, Moncler can use *its* location to solidify a dominant position in both the winter coat and summer jacket markets.

In the "Moncler All Year" ("Moncler Tutto L'Anno") campaign, Moncler should communicate two key ideas: 1) it knows how to keep you warm in winter (Alps) and cool in summer (Mediterranean), and 2) it is the most fashionable of all the coat options. Relying on its Italian roots as a country-of-origin boost, the campaign's executions should depict Italian themes conveyed using a luxurious, fashionable style throughout as if watching a runway show or a commercial for a designer fragrance. In doing so, Moncler reinforces both its luxurious position in the marketplace as well as its ability to dominate brands like Canada Goose when it comes to fashion and weather-appropriate clothing expertise.

By striking first, Moncler can make Canada Goose look like a copycat imitator, which it can easily do given that it already has a spring/summer line. If Canada Goose releases a campaign for all-year clothing sooner than Moncler, then the latter's competitive response could be to highlight its exquisite exclusivity all year long, as doing so would indirectly jab at Canada Goose's increasingly wide market adoption potentially diminishing the brand's exclusive appeal. Of course, if Moncler wants to really go after the jugular, it can take subtle digs at Canada's lack of fashion via paid endorsements and the inclusion of luxurious supermodels, men and women, in various campaign executions. The Canadians may have nice, warm coats, but the Italians have beautiful coats worn by beautiful people all year long, tutto l'anno.

JAMES A. MOUREY

CHAPTER 11 | The Magical Art of Trying It Out: Test Marketing

Live from New York, it's Saturday night!

For over 40 years those words have opened what has become one of the longest-running television shows in American history: *Saturday Night Live*. A live hour-and-a-half comedy show that blends satirical sketches, musical performances, and a humorous take on the news, *Saturday Night Live* has provided countless performers with a stage to make generations of Americans laugh. Whether during the purely jovial times, such as Tina Fey's knockout performance as Sarah Palin or Andy Samberg and Justin Timberlake's "Dick in a Box" hit song, to the far somber times, such as the first shows after the September 11, 2001, terrorist attacks in the United States or the November 13, 2015, terrorist attacks in Paris, *Saturday Night Live* is an American tradition. *Everyone* in America knows about *Saturday Night Live*.

One question that is worth asking is a fairly simple one: how does a television show manage to last *that* long? Very few television shows last more than a handful of seasons, even the most popular of shows. And comedy, like so many aspects of society, changes over time. Indeed, even with *Saturday Night Live* one common criticism that often arises is that a particular season's cast was "the best" and the show "went downhill" after that season. And yet the show still anchors Saturday evening television, perhaps one of the timeslots possible, and pulls admirable ratings for a show in its fourth decade.

So what's the secret? How can a live comedy show *know*, with some amount of certainty, that its jokes are going to "land" with the audience?

Easy: market testing.

Prior to each live recording of *Saturday Night Live* at 11:30pm (EST), the cast performs a dress rehearsal at 8:00pm. Even before that dress rehearsal, the writers, cast, and often the guest host of that week have spent days writing, editing, re-writing, re-editing, reading through, and perfecting the sketches and jokes for that week's episode. Right up to the show itself, the producers (headed by the show's fearless leader Lorne Michaels) are making game time decisions as to which sketches will make the show and which ones will not. Indeed, a sketch that received huge laughs from the audience during dress rehearsal is likely to air during the live recording, whereas sketches that fall flat during the dress rehearsal are often cut and lost to the comedy abyss forever.

Market testing is not an altogether unfamiliar concept in television entertainment. Indeed, one of the classic stories in Hollywood is the tale about *Seinfeld's* pilot episode. After conducting a nationwide test of the pilot, the research findings suggested the show would be dead on arrival. Almost no one tested said they wanted to see more episodes of the show, and most people said they did not care very much for the show's characters. Ouch. Note, this *one* example is still cited as a reason not to trust data in Hollywood because, you know, using *one* data point to make your argument is always a good idea (#sarcasm).

But testing an entire television show is different from testing individual jokes or gags. However, it is worth noting that several of *Saturday Night Live*'s performers hail from a few key destinations: improv comedy institutions like Second City, iO, and the Groundlings, as well as the stand-up comedy circuit.

Second City is as much a part of Chicago as Wrigley Field or Willis (Sears) Tower. Known for being the training ground of comedy greats like Dan Aykroyd, Julia Louis-Dreyfus, Chris Farley, Tina Fey, Stephen Colbert, Steve Carell, Amy Poehler, and countless others, Second City's point of differentiation in the improv comedy world of Chicago is that it is focused on sketch comedy as opposed to purely improv. Basically, the philosophy at Second City is that improv, although splendid and wondrous unto itself, is often best at inspiring sketches that will be written out, edited, debated, and then eventually performed. At any point in time there is always a sketch show being performed in Second City's Mainstage Theatre, as well as another (equally as funny) show being performed in Second City's ETC Theatre right next door. Having lived in Chicago for several years, there are few "stereotypically touristy" things I will do in Chicago when friends and family come visit, but one thing I will *always* do, *always*, is take people to see a show at Second City. Why? Because Second City *never* disappoints; the shows are always hilarious.

Hmm, this sounds familiar. *Saturday Night Live* has managed to remain relevant and funny (for the most part...I'm looking squarely at you with a disapproving face, Colin Jost, Michael Che, and Leslie Jones) for over 40 years. In 2019, Second City will be celebrating its 60th birthday...60th! How in the world can a comedy theatre manage to stay so popular for so long in the face of changing media, greater competition both in the city and online, and shifting comedic tastes?

Easy: market testing.

The not-so-secret secret at Second City is that a lot of the material used in the stage shows has been tried out on test audiences. Oftentimes those test audiences are current students at the Second City Training Center. Just about any night of the week at Second City are performances featuring current students, writers, actors and actresses, and even training center instructors. From jam sessions to standing shows, there is always *something* going on at Second City, and the creative vibe reverberating throughout the building is constant. It is during some of these shows in the venue's smaller theatres that new material is tested, with the audience reaction being a gauge for what a real audience is likely to find funny. The fact that these test audiences are usually sober means that this market test is probably even *more* conservative than it needs to be; drunk people laugh at anything.

Of course, stand-up comedians are also known for trying out new material. If you have ever seen the same stand-up comedian perform twice, chances are he/she recycles a few of the same jokes, especially if you go to see the comedian multiple times in rapid succession. Every now and then a comedian will introduce a new joke into his/her set to see how it tests with audiences. If the joke lands, the joke might be integrated into the set; if the joke doesn't land, well, better to know now before you record the filmed special for HBO or Netflix.

Few thrills are greater than testing out new comedy material that lands. However, one must be prepared to lob a joke at the audience that just falls flat. Rather than hearing laughter, sometimes all you hear are crickets chirping. Whether you are a seasoned professional or an amateur just getting started, not every joke is going to land. It could be something about the joke, it could be something about you and your delivery, or it could be something about the audience or the context, but rare is it the case that every joke lands every time. The secret is trying to find the jokes that *tend to* land most often and keep them around while saying farewell to the jokes that miss every single time. That last part can be really difficult, especially if you find a joke particularly funny or spent a lot of time crafting what you believe is a perfectly fine joke. But remember: the audience did not pay to come see you deliver a joke and laugh at yourself; they came to see you deliver jokes that will make *them* laugh.

Many people are afraid of attempting to be funny because they are scared to death of facing the silence of an unamused audience. It *is* awkward. While some people are okay with sketch comedy or even stand-up, both of which can be written prior to performing, those same people are petrified of improvisational comedy, comedy that you make up on the spot. In improvisational comedy the performers get a suggestion from the audience and then take that suggestion and come up with a performance in real time. It is the apex of creative thinking and performance, literally operating on *no* script to impress an audience with different tastes, different preferences, and different sensitivities. In those moments of improvisation, one has to take a "read" of the audience, all while creating content and constantly reassessing the read of the audience to tweak the performance to align with what the audience seems to want. It is not easy, but it is exhilarating.

Do you know what else improvisation is? Marketing.

You are gaining an understanding of an audience, providing the audience the content you think it wants/needs, assessing how well what you are providing meets or exceeds the needs of the audience, and then changing up what you are putting out to meet the audience's wants/needs even better. And here is the crazy thing: as marketing becomes more and more "in the moment" with nearly instantaneous data collection, the ability to think on the fly like an improviser is going to become even more important.

Marketing tends to attract funny, creative types (and, no, I am not just saying that because I want to include myself in that group...although I am also totally okay being categorized accordingly) compared to other business disciplines like Human Resources (the emotional types...sorry if that upsets you; we can talk about your feelings later), Finance (the greedy types...just kidding! Love you, finance people!), and Accounting (the strict types...that's just how it is), which is why it is not at all surprising that Marketers tend to be great improvisers.

As a Marketer, every day of your life is like a real, live comedy show. You never know what surprises your customers are going to have in store for you or what budgetary constraints or curveballs your management and clients are going to toss your way. You just have to keep one eye on your audience and one eye on your work all while trying to deliver the best possible value you can deliver with your eyes crossed. This kind of monitoring, market testing, and tweaking is what separates good marketers from great marketers, funny people from hilarious people, and shows lasting just one season from shows lasting decades.

This is *your* show. Live from [insert your company here]: It's Marketing!

*   *   *

Nothing is certain in this world.

And uncertainty, it turns out, is extremely frightening to most people. In the realm of integrated marketing campaign development, reputations, careers, and big money are on the line, so any hint of uncertainty or unknown outcomes can be truly nerve-racking. This, of course, is why some companies often go to great lengths to test new ideas and initiatives prior to rolling them out in their entirety. Yet, as our chapter on statistics reminded us, even the richest data set analyzed every possible way can only yield suggestions as to what the world *might* be like, not the world as it will definitely be.

This is cold comfort, but remember: some data is better than no data, which is why test marketing is such a critical part of the integrated marketing process. Major companies, like JCPenney, have famously failed when launching new marketing initiatives (see: Fair and Square Pricing) simply because they, "Didn't have time to test market," their new initiatives. Big mistake.

Although test marketing can be expensive and excessive test marketing can lead to delayed rollouts, missed first-mover opportunities, and soaring costs, *not* doing a test market can be even costlier. This chapter is dedicated to tips and tricks you can use to engage in a bit of test marketing so that you can adjust your integrated marketing campaign *one final time* before its unveiling.

"ABCD" Revisited: The Before, During, and After of Data

Earlier, in the chapter on statistics, I mentioned that one of our guiding principles in the world of marketing research is a simple acronym–**ABCD**–which stands for, "Always be collecting data!" Just as we conducted an extensive research survey and collected data *before* we developed our integrated marketing campaign, so, too, can we collect data now that our campaign has *actually been created*. Think about it this way: the pre-campaign data informed our strategic decisions when designing the campaign. Now, before the campaign launches, we have an opportunity to reach out to the very audience we are trying to persuade to test whether our ideas are likely to be effective in causing the kinds of change and momentum we hope to see. And guess what? We will collect even more data once the campaign official launches, both during its run and at its conclusion! Always be collecting data.

Of course, one hesitation people have with respect to test marketing involves the costs associated with doing so. There are two considerations one must make here: 1) what is the most cost-efficient way we can conduct a fair test market of our campaign?, and 2) is the cost associated with the test market bigger or worse than the potential costs we would incur if all or part of the campaign fails? The first question suggests an important idea: it may be possible to conduct test marketing more cheaply than simply trying to run the campaign on a smaller scale or in a test market (which is what many people first think of when they hear "test market"). The second question provides you with a persuasive argument to any naysayers who think the campaign should just launch as it is because of a market test's costs. If spending a little bit of money now helps prevent potentially substantial losses at a later point in time (and potentially promote gains), well, that sounds like less of a "cost" and more of an *investment*. So maybe when you talk about your plans to engage in market testing you should actively use the word "investment" (e.g., "How much do we want to invest in our market test?") as opposed to "cost" or "expense."

The Right Questions to Ask: Awareness, Liking, Intentions, and WTP

Saturday Night Live and Second City measure the success of their content in laughter, but marketing campaigns require different metrics of success. There is no "standard list" of questions to ask when it comes to the effectiveness of a marketing campaign or its various components. If there were, well, life would be *much* easier and the return on marketing investment (ROMI) would not remain such an elusive, oft-debated topic!

Although there is no "standard list," there are a few output variables that show up often enough that we may want consider using them in our market testing:

- **Awareness:** Remember that the goal of some integrated marketing campaigns is not explicitly to sell more of a particular product or service but, instead, can simply be to increase awareness of a brand or a product. Thus, one question we may want to include pertains to a pre-exposure and post-exposure measure of awareness. This can be done by assessing awareness, explicitly, or a related concept like familiarity with or recognition of the product/brand. Presumably people who are aware of a product will also feel that it is familiar and should be able to recognize it when prompted with a list of brand/product names, logos, or images.

- **Liking:** This may seem like a no-brainer, but it certainly makes sense to gauge whether or not our marketing campaign and its individual executions increase liking among our target audience. While not moving the needle on liking may not decrease the likelihood of someone purchasing our product, drastically shifting one's liking of our product in a positive direction is something we should note, and whatever execution is most effective at causing this kind of change should be flagged for consideration of future iterations and takes on the same idea.

- **Purchase Intentions:** Knowing whether or not our campaign and its executions shift an audience's intentions to purchase is essential if increasing sales is our desired objective. Keep in mind that one's intentions and actual behaviors are not perfectly correlated but they *are* correlated. If we have designed an elaborate campaign for a Big Idea that explicitly promotes increasing purchases and have reinforced that campaign with specific executions (e.g., promotional price discounts, increased in-store sampling) that encourage increased purchases, well, we better see people in our test market saying they intend to purchase more of our product. Otherwise, whatever it is we *think* we have done to change the minds, hearts, and behaviors of the audience has not actually achieved our objective, and we need to go back to the drawing board.

- **Knowledge:** Teaching an audience about our company and our products/services can be an important part of any campaign. Many commercials list reasons why their product can improve a customer's life and, in doing so, add value. The central route of the Elaboration Likelihood Model is all about using rational appeals to persuade an audience. However, if those messages fail to connect with the audience then all that education has been for naught. To test a customer's knowledge about our company, a particular brand, or our product/service, we can do a pre- and post-exposure assessment where we ask people content-related questions pertaining to whatever we are marketing, expose them to information we want them to learn, and then test their ability to recall that information in a follow-up test after a short delay. Avoid telling the test market participants that the focus of the survey is testing their recall, as we do not want them actively trying to remember the information; we want it to be as natural as possible so that our results can speak to external validity (i.e., the idea that our findings in a controlled lab or research setting will externalize to the real world where there are many other distractions and stimuli competing for the attention of our audience). It is also wise to embed questions pertaining to an individual's perceived knowledge about our company, brand, and/or product/services in the mix so we can assess their perceived intelligence and confidence regarding this information before and after our test.

- **Willingness-to-Pay:** One final variable captures how valuable our company and our products/services are to customers and can give us a bit of an idea of the pricing structure we may want to use, the price elasticity of our products/services, and other information. Willingness-to-Pay can be asked in a way that captures the general willingness to pay money for our product and also in a way that elicits a specific dollar-amount valuation of our product in the minds of customers. This latter element is what allows us to know where customers see us playing in the marketplace with respect to price, and the variability within this number may suggest the window within which we can consider adjusting our price without arousing any ire from prospective customers. Similarly, these values can alert us to "just noticeable differences" (JNDs) that help us strategize ideal price points for discounts that would be noticed/appreciated by customers (as well as premium price points that would actually make our product seem more exclusive). Although these kinds of decisions would certainly require more thoughtful deliberation and planning before launching, the data collected as part of a test market can help point us in the right direction. Furthermore, vast differences between liking a product or purchasing intentions and willingness to pay can inspire future strategies that help customers realize our value or the investment they are making (or can help us set up payment plans or other payment-related initiatives to help bridge the gap between liking/intentions and willingness-to-pay).

So, those are a few of the standard questions I would include in a test market. Of course, you can always include other questions like, "How likely are you to talk about this product with friends and family?" or, "Which emotion(s) best describe how you are feeling right now? (check all that apply)" as these questions can shed some light on factors like a campaign/execution's word-of-mouth potential and ability to evoke emotions, respectively. Just remember that we cannot ask *every* possible question: the survey would get too long and the responses would not be as helpful as our participants begin suffering from survey fatigue. The trick is to prioritize the questions you ask based on the Focus priorities of the campaign. If the goal is to Educate Hot-Off-the-Press customers, find customers brand new to the market and assess how much they know initially and how much they learn after engaging with all or part of your campaign. If the goal is to Multiply Purchases from Wandering Customers, find customers who admit that they sometimes buy from you but also from your competitors and see if exposure to your campaign increases their stated intentions to purchase more from you or increases their willingness-to-pay for the products they buy from you on occasion. See how it all fits together?

Now, the specific way you ask questions that capture the output variables above may depend on your market, your research resources, and the design of your survey. Whenever possible try to capture data using a quantifiable method so we can more easily compare pre- and post-exposure, take out any subjectivity in interpretation of what the respondents meant, and can obtain measureable differences per any tweaks we make to the campaign. Qualitative data is also good to capture, as this permits open, honest feedback from the very people from whom we want to hear. Just don't put the test market participants through too much work because if they start feeling like you are taking advantage of their time without compensating them accordingly, this frustration could be let out in the form of lower ratings, apathy, or other forms of release that adversely affect the quality of our market testing data.

Comparing Apples to Apples: Considering Comparison Combinations

Although integrated marketing, by definition, involves putting together executions that reinforce one another and create an overall campaign synergy, this does not mean that we *must* test a campaign in its entirety in our market test. While doing so can be advantageous (i.e., it allows us to see that synergy in action), it can also be quite cumbersome to test an *entire* campaign within the same test market. The decision is up to you whether you prefer engaging in a **holistic** test market, in which the entire campaign is tested as a holistic entity by comparing it to another possible campaign (or to doing nothing at all), or a **piecemeal** test market, in which specific executions are compared to other alternative executions (or to doing nothing at all). The important thing to keep in mind is that your holistic campaign will result in synergies that may not show up in a piecemeal comparison. If a specific execution is designed to serve a specific function on its own, say increasing awareness, then we cannot expect testing that execution to show much movement on purchase intentions and/or willingness-to-pay. If that execution is supplemented by a different execution that has a generally weak ability to gain awareness but a strength in driving purchase intentions and willing-to-pay, then the synergy should show up when these executions come together in the full campaign. When testing the latter execution (i.e., the one that drives purchase intentions and willingness-to-pay separately), the shift in intentions or WTP may not be as strong as it may be when it is bolstered by the inclusion of the other execution (i.e., the one designed to drive awareness). So do not lose hope if the numbers do not move as drastically as you would hope when testing the executions separately; as long as they are moving in the right direction the hope is that they will only get even better when the entire campaign is presented at once.

When it comes to the design of your test marketing initiatives, keep good science in mind. Although it might be tempting to compare an execution or your entire campaign to nothing (i.e., simply expose people to an execution or to the campaign and see how they change), this leaves some room for guessing. It could be the case that engaging customers in *any* way shifts whatever it is we are measuring. While it may be more work to come up with "dummy campaigns" or "dummy executions" for the purpose of test marketing comparisons, doing so can actually make your market research that much better! Say, for example, Toyota is considering hiring a celebrity to serve as the spokesperson for their Prius brand. The company's goal is to get young, Hot-Off-the-Press Customers who are considering purchasing a car for the first time. As such, the company considers younger celebrities that this audience has indicated liking: Justin Bieber, Selena Gomez, and Taylor Swift. In a test market, we may want to propose the celebrity endorsement idea but shift out the celebrity so that one version includes Justin Bieber or Taylor Swift, another version includes a celebrity like Julia Roberts or Tom Cruise, another version includes an Average Joe/Jane, and yet another version includes no celebrity at all. What we may find is that there is *no difference* whether we use one of the celebrities the audience indicated they like and using any other random celebrity, but that having a spokesperson, in general, is what matters. Not only is this informative, it also saves us a lot of money (i.e., now we can pay a struggling actor/actress in LA as opposed to someone like the Biebs or Swift who would command a far higher price point than someone just trying to pay the rent in WeHo).

Another important consideration for comparisons and for test marketing, in general, is that there is a huge difference between *telling* someone what you are going to do and *showing* them what you are going to do. In every class I teach I go to great lengths to convey a very simple idea that is as useful in life as it is in marketing: **don't just tell someone, *show* someone**. Many times, whether to cut costs or to save time, people conduct marketing tests that *tell* participants what is going to be done rather than show them. While filming an entire commercial only to do a test market and to find out that the idea is hated anyway *is* wasteful, but so is describing what a commercial might look like in terms so vague that 200 participants dream up 200 different commercials in their minds and then rate the one *they* imagined. The solution to this problem is to do your absolute best to create mock-ups that best represent the final product of what your proposed campaign will look and feel like. This certainly takes more effort than simply describing what you intend to do but far less effort than actually creating the full campaign itself. The goal is to provide participants with executions that are *as close to the real executions* as possible in the most affordable way possible. This usually means storyboards for commercials, mock-ups for print ads and website redesigns/engagements, simulated events/experiences, and more. The closer you come to providing your participants with the *actual* executions you plan to deliver the better their feedback will be able to help you rate your *actual* campaign and its success likelihood.

That said, there will be times that test marketing executions and your actual campaign executions are so far removed from one another that using insights gleaned from the former may be questionable, at best, when it comes to making decisions about the latter. Still, do not let this deter you from using market testing whenever possible and to uncover insights wherever you can. Remember our saying: some data is better than no data. Data suggests that this is always true.

Final Thoughts on Testing: Wrapping Up the Research (…For Now)

When testing your marketing campaign, it is simply not possible to run your entire campaign to your entire audience. For starters, that would be prohibitively expensive. And second, even if you *could* test market in this way, then your entire audience will have been exposed to your campaign prior to its full launch, which would certainly impact your campaign's perceived novelty and innovativeness. We haven't spent all this time building up a campaign to let the surprise slip prior to the big party, right?

Most companies have access to their loyal customers and even to customers falling into one of our other categories: Wandering Customers, Hot-Off-The-Press Customers, and (the most difficult one) Others' Customers. That is helpful when it comes to finding people interested in participating in a test market. However, another useful place to find potential test market participants is right at your fingertips: online. Potential participants can be recruited through your website or social media pages and can self-identify as to the kind of customer they are within the context of your test marketing survey itself (e.g., "Which option best describes your relationship with Starbucks?" a) Never been before, b) I go to Starbucks on occasion but also frequent other coffee shops, c) I used to go to Starbucks but now only go to a different coffee shop (please indicate which one), d) I typically only go to Starbucks for my coffee needs).

Another great source of participants are survey panels (which can get expensive) and sites like Amazon's Mechanical Turk (MTurk) in which people agree to complete tasks and/or short surveys in exchange for financial compensation. When using these options do be sure to keep compensation commensurate with the expectations you have of the participants (e.g., do not pay them $.05 to complete an involved, hour-long survey; similarly do not pay them $20 to complete a survey that should take only a minute or two), as a disconnect between compensation and level of commitment can skew the results obtained.

Market testing is at the heart of the marketing discipline itself: in order to know what is likely to work or not we should not be the ones making that determination; our *customers* should! It is often the case that marketing executions we particularly enjoy as the creators and designers of the campaign *may not be* the executions that the target audience loves or even likes. The goal of any campaign is not to make *ourselves* happy or to sell products to *ourselves*; the goal involves changing the thoughts, feelings, or behaviors of the *target audience*. Thus, the opinion of our target audience is worth its weight in gold...our opinion is only worth its opinion in silver or bronze, at best, when compared to the opinion of our customers.

Sometimes a market test confirms that our campaign and its executions achieve the goals we designed them to achieve. Huzzah! Do a little victory dance to celebrate! Other times, we may find that our executions and even the entire campaign do almost nothing to achieve the objectives we had in place at the heart of the campaign. We may find that comparing our executions to doing nothing or to doing something (anything) else results in no significant difference or change. Don't despair! You see, this is both good news and bad news. The good news is that an alternative campaign (or doing nothing) might be (or certainly is) cheaper and, as such, will produce a greater return on investment. The bad news is that our campaign already took a lot of time to dream up and was just plain ol' cool. Still, as painful as it would be to find out that our proposed integrated marketing campaign would fare no better than any other willy-nilly campaign or doing absolutely nothing, it is better to know now before we spend loads of money launching the campaign than during or after the campaign's run when that money cannot be recovered.

Test marketing is *smart* marketing. Test marketing may not get it right every single time, but every dollar it saves us, every additional sale it inspires, and every new customer it turns on to our brand adds up. Being able to base your strategic decisions on research and numbers as opposed to "what feels right" or a "hunch" is what brings "science" to the art and science that is marketing. Although it may not be perfect every single time, test marketing will help you sleep more easily at night knowing what works well and what does not work…but will soon.

*   *   *

Most kids have sports heroes.

Other kids have a favorite singer or band or celebrity crush.

I was not that kid. I was different.

For me, my favorite "famous people" were people like Wayne and Garth and Mary Katherine Gallagher. The people I enjoyed watching on television were the Spartan Cheerleaders and Debbie Downer. Some people watched or listened to baseball games or football games religiously. I never missed an episode of *Saturday Night Live*, not one, since I started watching as a child. To this day my Aunt Lynne calls or texts me if some SNL-related special is on television. Some people drop everything they are doing when a "breaking news" alert comes on television; I stop everything I am doing when the Weekend Update segment appears on *Saturday Night Live*. Some people have favorite authors or favorite novelists. I also have favorite writers, but mine include people like Tina Fey, Kay Cannon, and John Mulaney, smart, sophisticated writers who remind us that everyday life is funny if we choose to see the humor around us.

In late 2015, when facing criticism for a joke in her show *Unbreakable Kimmy Schmidt*, Tina Fey once said, "My new goal is not to explain jokes. I feel like we put so much effort into writing and crafting everything, [the jokes] need to speak for themselves." John Mulaney, upon being complemented for his eloquence and joke structure on a recent late night talk show, described the amount of work he also puts into crafting and writing his jokes…and here you thought these famous funny peoples' jokes just materialized out of thin air! If even the funniest people in the world spend time testing their jokes, the very least we can do as marketers is test the work we create in our job, as well.

When I was a kid writing sketches for Odyssey of the Mind, my test audience was often my parents, my family, my team, and my teammate Maureen's mom, Linda Cassin. Linda would sometimes sit in on meetings as any good parent does both to chaperone and also to support our creative work. Linda also had a very, very distinct snort when she laughed—that's how I knew I struck comedy gold. One year, just being my usual silly self, I started doing impersonations of celebrities of that time including quite a compelling impression of actress/talk show hostess Ricki Lake. Linda *died* laughing. We had absolutely *zero* reason to incorporate Ricki Lake into our skit, a sketch about a little old woman whose dogs found out she was a bank robber (...trust me, it makes sense if you watch it), but we managed to work in a breaking news segment on the television that interrupted Ricki Lake's talk show, a popular talk show at the time. It *killed* with the audience every single time.

Whatever it is you do, whatever it is you are trying to test: find your Linda Cassin. Find some consistent metric that signals that you are heading in the right direction or the wrong direction. Find some standard to which you can compare your work. Find the right colleague, the right friend, the right target audience with whom you can test your creations to see how they fare.

Just like that moment right before stepping out on stage in front of an audience or in front of a microphone, when launching an integrated marketing campaign there will always be *some* butterflies. You will always wonder whether or not your efforts will land with the audience, whether your efforts will pay off, whether you could have done more. Of course, we could ask those questions and wonder those thoughts in perpetuity. Thankfully, test marketing will take away a lot of the second-guessing and a lot of the fear that comes with uncertainty. Before you know it, all the weeks of rehearsing, designing, and creating have brought us to the point of no return: it's show time.

So go ahead and break a leg out there. I'll be waiting right here in the wings when you get back (...you know, like a crazy pageant mom).

What if... *SNL's Virtual Update Desk*

For decades *Saturday Night Live* (or SNL as it is frequently called) could only capture the attention of its audience *once* a week for just an hour-and-a-half for a few months out of the year. Yet somehow in spirit of this rather limited engagement, SNL has managed to become one of the longest-running shows in history.

Whereas many modern television shows have taken full advantage of the new ways technology facilitates interaction between customers and creators, SNL has done just an okay job translating the show to modern media, an effort that has been minimal, at best. Sure, web surfers can watch SNL clips at the show's Facebook page, at the NBC (Comcast/Universal/whatever they are calling it today) website, and through partner sites like Hulu, but that's about it. The show's Facebook page sees comments in real time from viewers, but no one responds on the show's behalf, making any interaction essentially one-sided and, as such, kind of pointless.

What if the show ramped up its online presence with a more engaging viewer experience? Despite having loyal viewers (like myself), the show has done very little to build a brand community around SNL, yet there is value to be obtained from bringing these comedy fans together. One simple way to do this would be to launch an interactive feature known as the Virtual Weekend Update desk that allows SNL fans the opportunity to post Weekend Update-style jokes to a page and then to "like" those jokes so that the funniest jokes float their way to the top of the page. The Weekend Update hosts could even integrate the winning joke within the show's live segment on Saturday night (within reason, of course).

Now, one concern with this idea is that the user-generated content may impede or limit the jokes of the writing team at SNL. While I like to think that professional writers could come up with enough material for this not to be a problem, there is an alternative solution. Instead of doing jokes inspired by the news per the typical Weekend Update format, the show could launch a variation of the original idea known as the ~~Weekend~~ Status Update Desk, where SNL fans share their funny *status updates* from social media and the community selects the funniest by number of "likes." Either approach would provide the audience with more comedy, greater engagement with the show, and a reason to return to an SNL-branded page, which means more eyeballs on the brand (and ads sold on the page).

Thus, in a simple integration to SNL's media presence, viewers engage with the show like never before but in a way they have come to expect. Lest you think viewers might not participate, consider that other late night shows have developed their own interactive engagements to much success: Jimmy Fallon (an SNL-alum) issues #Hashtag challenges (e.g., #WorstGiftEver,

#MisheardLyrics, #MomTexts) and shares audience tweets on his show. Jimmy Kimmel asks his viewers to video themselves telling their children they ate all their Halloween candy. Although these videos are more involved (and result in psychological damage), viewers eagerly participate and fans love watching them. Integrated marketing tools allow us to connect with customers like never before, but don't forget that these relationships go *both* ways: sometimes you have to write the joke, sometimes you just get to laugh.

NET EFFECT

JAMES A. MOUREY

CHAPTER 12 | Metrics That Matter

Hur säger man "comeback" på svenska?

Absolut Vodka, one of the world's best-known spirit brands, has seen better days...err...better nights (it is a nightlife drink, after all). Despite being the world's second-largest vodka seller by sales volume, a distant second behind global leader Smirnoff (which has 230% more sales volume), Absolut has faced declining demand for vodka in major spirits markets like the United States as consumer preferences shift to alternatives like tequila and bourbon. In the U.S. market in particular customers have embraced craft brews and the rich origin stories of their favorite bourbons (e.g., "Renegade Jim Bob accidentally discovered his brew on a Kentucky farm after throwing out some old corn, malted barley, and rye after a scorching day working the fields. Weeks later, thirsty and too far from water, Jim Bob decided to taste his creation, and that's how Jim Bob's Blazing Bourbon was born. Drink up.") Pernod Ricard SA, the French company that owns the Absolut brand, has explicitly expressed concern about Absolut's performance in the U.S. market, and Absolut's recent marketing campaigns imply both a lack of direction and an uncertainty about what to do with the brand next.

This is a bit surprising for Absolut, a vodka brand that dominated the spirits industry for *decades*. Even non-drinkers know the brand's iconic advertisements, artist-designed works of art that were as beautiful as they were effective at generating awareness for the vodka brand. Started in 1980 in coordination with ad agency TBWA, the ads all had a similar style: the famous silhouette of the Absolut bottle integrated into a clever design that incorporated the theme or context of the ad. This campaign, the very same campaign, ran for roughly 25 years. That's a *long* time for a campaign to run! When it finally came to an end, the reasoning for the cessation of the campaign was simply that, "All good things must end." While this might be true, Absolut also had a bit of a problem on its hands: after connecting with customers in a very specific way for 25 years, how do you reinvent yourself? Worse yet: how do you reinvent yourself when your product category is slowly dying out?

To counter the shifting preferences of consumers, the solution Absolut and its fellow vodka creators devised was to expand their product lines to include a greater variety of flavors. Unlike bourbon and scotch, which are consumed as they are, most casual drinkers consume vodka in mixed cocktails. Thus, adding flavor to vodka seemed like a good way to spark renewed interest in the spirit. At first, Absolut introduced flavors like Absolut Raspberri, Absolut Äpple, Absolut Gräpe, which proved to be successful with customers. However, as the aged tastes of various whiskeys and craft alcoholic beverages began taking hold of the market, suddenly fruity variants of vodka were no longer as appealing.

Rather than consider the shifting customer preferences, vodka companies leaned into what had worked in the past and began doing more of the same: greater flavor varieties. This time the flavors were more of the variety one might see as Ben and Jerry's ice cream flavors or the fragrances attributed to smelly markers. Smirnoff launched new flavors like Whipped Cream and Fluffed Marshmallow (which, incidentally, were both of my nicknames in college...kidding). Not to be outdone, Pernod Ricard SA launched *an entire line* of eccentric flavors under the brand Oddka. Featuring flavors like "Fresh Cut Grass, "Apple Pie," "Salty Caramel Popcorn," and "Wasabi." However, while successful at garnering some media attention, this grand experiment in exotic flavors did not go particularly well for the vodka companies. This time around customers were *not* looking for additional flavor choices; they were looking for something else, but Absolut and its competitors were not quite able to put their finger on just what.

In 2013, Absolut opted to lean into another one of its prior successful ideas: linking alcohol and artistry. In what was known as the "Transform Today" campaign, Absolut partnered with visual artists and linked to these artists' respective personal sites and artistic creations. You remember that campaign, don't you? Oh wait, you don't? Well, don't feel bad; no one else remembers it either. After the "Transform Today" campaign failed to really transform anything, especially consumer interest, Absolut changed course...slightly. In 2014 and 2015, Absolut veered away from transforming "today" and chose to focus, instead, on the night with a campaign entitled "Absolut Nights." Given that vodka is primarily consumed at night and typically at bars, clubs, and other comparable venues, the focus on night made *a lot* more sense than a campaign about transforming "today." However, Absolut did not forego its dedication to all-things artsy, as the theme of the Absolut Nights campaign involved partnering with four artists (...again), but this time the artists would be transforming the nightlife experience in various ways.

The Absolut Nights campaign featured four videos each showcasing a different artist transforming something about the night life experience in a major world city: Berlin, New York, Johannesburg, and Sao Paolo. For example, in Sao Paolo the audience became characters and part of an unfolding show. In Johannesburg, the dance floor changed to interact with audience movement to create a pyrotechnic extravaganza. In New York, the iconic Absolut bottle was superimposed on the New York City skyline from a Brooklyn waterfront party. In Sao Paolo, partygoers took on new personalities and characters to "be someone else for one night." And in Berlin, 3D-printed disco ball-inspired outfits (that looked like wearable versions of Spaceship Earth at Disney World's Epcot) shot out lasers at some point in a futuristic fashion show.

Keeping in the spirit of a truly integrated marketing campaign, Absolut also integrated a musical component by featuring the debut of a new song "Welcome to My Life" by the band Empire of the Sun. With respect to promotions, the Absolut Nights campaign included a chance for customers to win a three-day, two-night trip to California. to be a part of a future Absolut Nights event (which, apparently, did not make the cut for the video campaign). In addition, Absolut created a limited edition bottle to celebrate the campaign. The bottle, Absolut Spark, was illuminated from the bottom and allowed owners to light up the canvas of their night out. In fact, the idea across all the executions was that night, itself, is a canvas and Absolut is there to help make art. Mmm, ok.

While some people might appreciate the artistry of the campaign, one thing is certain: it is *not* an easy campaign to understand without some involvement on behalf of the viewers, and guess whose attention is in short supply? Everyone's. People cannot even go to the bathroom without taking their phone to check their Facebook and Instagram these days. Unlike the elegant artsy-alcohol ads for which Absolut was revered for over two decades, the Absolut Nights campaign was complex, probably *too* complex. In addition, whereas the static print ads of the past could be viewed passively and were likely to be encountered incidentally by customers, the Absolut Nights campaign required customers to search for the content, singular moments that, even combined with the three other executions within the campaign, really did not do an exceptional job of conveying the Big Idea that the night is a canvas and Absolut is the artist.

Further evidence suggesting that Absolut was stumbling drunk in the dark with its marketing efforts was the creation and subsequent launch of Absolut Elyx, the "world's first handcrafted luxury vodka." Distilled in copper stills, Elyx is Absolut's attempt to fight back against whiskey companies and other craft creations stealing Absolut's market share. At a price point of $50, Absolut Elyx is decidedly luxurious, as regular Absolut is positioned as the mid-market price point of $20, with Grey Goose selling at a "premium" market price of $30 a bottle and Smirnoff selling as cheaply as $13.99. The belief was that consumers, ever more sophisticated in their alcohol preferences, would be willing to pay a premium for vodka if that vodka were handcrafted like their favorite craft beverages and had interesting backstories. Given that Elyx was a new product, having a cool, lengthy history was going to be tough, so the company decided to tout the fact that the beverage was distilled in a copper still dating back to the 1920s. Nicely played, Absolut. And to give it an even more interesting story, the company created the Elyx House, an actual residence in which the interior design looks both classically aged and modern, striking the sort of tone Absolut likely hoped to strike with Elyx itself. And adding a bit of shtick to the campaign, Absolut Elyx is known to be served in trademark copper pineapples, pineapples that also appear along the bookshelves at the Elyx House.

Of course, the nearly simultaneous executions of these campaigns, one an attempt to jolt a classic brand back to life and the other an attempt to extend the same famous brand into a new space, both with respect to a new price point and a new audience, highlight that Absolut was not quite sure which way to go to revive its struggling sales. Should they focus on the club crowd or the classic cocktail crowd? Should the company's marketing campaigns emphasize art or history...or art history? Does it make more sense to encourage more repeat purchasing of Absolut's products or fewer but more premium purchases of the company's higher-end offerings?

As Absolut continues on its quest to court an increasingly sophisticated crowd of alcohol drinkers, one thing is for sure: keeping tabs on what works and what doesn't work may be the difference between regaining the positive market prospects the brand once had or losing customers to the increasing competition from other spirits...the difference between being drunk on success or just a sloppy drunk.

*   *   *

Human beings like to drink...a lot. If you like statistics, then you will appreciate that nearly a quarter of the population routinely admits to binge drinking within the prior month. If you do not like statistics, then all you have to do to get an idea of the prevalence of alcohol consumption is to go to your nearest bar, club, or tavern (if you live in the rural parts) and people watch. You will likely see people imbibing in their alcoholic beverages of choice no matter the day of the week nor the time of day. In fact, as I write this, I am sitting at my neighborhood Starbucks, which recently began serving wine during the evening, watching some young guy stumble up to the counter to order *more* wine despite already being drunk...oh, by the way, it's *Monday* night.

In what very well may be a chicken v. egg conundrum, it is unclear whether it is man's thirst for alcohol or the effective marketing of alcohol companies that causes the other. Indeed, marketing campaigns for alcohol brands like Absolut, Anheuser-Busch, Heineken, and Guinness are among some of the cleverest and best-executed integrated marketing campaigns that exist.

With both alcohol's popularity and the effectiveness of most alcohol campaigns, you might be wondering why I have waited until the very last chapter to talk, in detail, about an alcohol brand's integrated marketing strategy. Well, to answer that question I have always believed that when it comes to writing you should "write what you know." You see, I am *not* a drinker. It probably has something to do with some innate need to be in control (calling Dr. Freud), the worry that I will be a mean drunk, or (most likely) the fact that my personality is generally pretty positive and outlandish anyway, so people likely assume I am already drunk or just completely crazy. However, now that we're besties, I'll let you in on a little secret: writing a book in just a few weeks while simultaneously teaching, helping to coordinate a non-profit organization's annual events, planning to spend a month teaching abroad, and wrapping up multiple research projects has *finally* pushed me to the bottle…in fact, I am drunk right now…just kidding…or am I?

Whether you are a lover of fine wines, like my Aunt Laura, or a naïve non-drinker, like yours truly, you should know this: alcohol companies know *a lot* about you. Part of the reason alcohol companies have such successful marketing campaigns is that they do a great deal of research before, during, and after a campaign. Up front, alcohol companies do a great job establishing *whom* exactly their customers are and what needs they have that are currently unfulfilled. During the campaign, the companies monitor sales very closely to know what is working, what is not working, and what needs to be tweaked. After the campaign, yet another round of data is discussed to learn from the recently-concluded campaign before launching into the next one. You may have noticed during your lifetime that alcohol advertising is among *the* most prevalent of any marketing. And thanks to steep competition in the industry, competition that has only increased with the advent of independent craft alcohol producers, these companies *have* to be good at marketing to survive. If they mess up, even just once, there are *plenty* of alternative products in the market from which customers can choose especially if the goal is just to get hammered…any alcohol can do that for you!

As we wind down our campaign and the Fusion model, it is time to see how effective the latter has been at achieving the goals and objectives of the campaign. In the previous chapter, we talked about testing a campaign *prior* to its launch. In this final chapter, we will talk about testing a campaign both *during* its run and *after* the campaign has concluded. Let's wrap this campaign up, shall we?

Fulfilling Focus: Reviewing PA, DO From the Very Beginning

At the very beginning of the book I said that the reason *any* marketing campaign exists is to *do something*. Typically, this "something" involves changing customer thoughts, feelings, and/or behaviors. However, the FUSION model required us to think through more specific *business* goals right at the onset of the campaign creation process, and it is to those fundamental objectives we will first turn to assess the success of our campaign.

Specifically, the Focus component of the FUSION model required us to select a Prospective Audience and a Desired Objective for that audience to complete. The philosophy underlying both of these constructs is that a marketing campaign, no matter how funny, clever, or creative, should be designed to achieve business objectives at its heart. Given this motivation, one of the first metrics we want to capture is how well we attracted the attention of our Prospective Audience. Did we manage to get our campaign in front of them? Did they pay attention to the campaign? How much did they engage with our campaign? The other metric we hope to capture is a measurement of the Desired Objective. If we chose to have the campaign increase purchasing behavior (i.e. Multiply Purchases), then we should see customers buying more of our product (either at once on the same shopping trip or at different times but more frequently). If we chose to have the campaign educate, then we should see that members of our Prospective Audience have learned, retained, and can recall the educational information we have included as part of the campaign. A Rally the Troops objective should see more engagement on our social media pages, more retweets, more recommendations/referrals, etc.

Thus, metrics that must be included in the post-campaign review are figures associated with our Prospective Audience, our Desired Objective, and the interaction between the two. If we see significant movement in the desired direction per our initially stated goals and objectives, well, we know we have done something right! However, even if none of these initial goals is met, do not panic, and do not throw the baby out with the bathwater. There still may be parts of your campaign that worked, and knowing what worked (and what did not) could be useful for subsequent campaigns going forward.

Marketing Metrics Reviewed: Standard KPIs for ROMI because WTF

Beyond the Focus goal/objective success check critical to the FUSION model there are also countless generic marketing metrics that pop up all over the place all the time. These metrics, typically referred to as Key Performance Indicators (KPI), claim to measure *the* most critical data a marketer needs to know. While some KPIs are useful and helpful with respect to determining ways to save on costs and/or to market more efficiently, others just sound fancy so people like to throw them out at business meetings and cocktail hours to sound smart and fancy. Here, I will introduce you to five of the most common marketing KPIs that people discuss so 1) you are aware of them, know what they are, and can speak intelligently about them, and 2) you can decide whether or not you want to include them in your campaign analysis.

Churn. Churn refers to the number of customers who *leave* in a specific period of time (e.g., one year, a financial quarter, during the campaign, etc.). Although it seems silly to be keeping track of how many customers are *leaving* from the comfort and safety of our embrace, it is important to keep in mind that our bias tends to be to focus on gaining, earning, and adding when it is just as plausible/likely that our campaign may turn some consumers off to what we are providing. Although I like to focus on the positive, too, churn can be a useful way to know if the integrated marketing campaign is causing any unforeseen or unpredicted harm or damage. To calculate churn, simply divide the number of folks who left in a particular time period by the total number of customers at the initial starting point of that same time period.

Customer Lifetime Value. Customer Lifetime Value (CLV) has always been one of my favorite marketing metrics because of the idea it represents: what is the value of a particular customer not just today, not just in the short-term, but for the entire involvement of that person during their relationship with our company. Sweet, right? Several different approaches to calculate CLV exist including the rather simple Average Revenue Per User approach (where you simply divide the total revenue earned from a particular customer by the number of months that customer has been with you) to the more complex Cohort Analysis (where you group customers based on shared behaviors, which can shed light of potential variability per external or contextual factors the Average Revenue Per User approach does not capture). Although all customers matter, customers with high CLV should be prioritized if ever forced to allocate limited resources.

Cost of Customer Acquisition. Attracting customers can be costly, and part of any marketing campaign involves striking a balance between spending enough money to acquire new customers without spending more than we should. Cost of Customer Acquisition (or Customer Acquisition Cost) refers to how much money is spent, on average, to acquire a new customer. Obviously we would like to keep this cost relatively low. To calculate this value, we simply take the per-person cost of a marketing execution, multiply that by the number of people we reached out to, and then divide that total by the number of customers who took us up on our offer. The way to improve this ratio is to either increase the conversion (or "take rate") of people who take us up on our offer, to reduce the cost of the execution, or to reduce the size of the audience we reach out to (that will help reduce total cost).

Bounce Rate. Internet metrics are fairly terrible. As I mentioned earlier, people still debate as to whether a click-through rate even matters, so this area is still one ripe for refinement. Consider, for example, how some sites have become well known for their "clickbait" which lures surfers with titillating titles or images so they will click on the link only to provide less-than-exciting content on the other side. Another common trick is to make a "Top 10" or "Top 100" list that requires surfers to click an arrow to proceed to each subsequent number with each page featuring another ad. This increases the exposure to each respective ad but, chances are, the web surfer is paying zero attention to whatever is being advertised and is not at all likely to click on the ad unless it is an accident. It is the worst. However, one metric that *is* certainly useful is the notion of the Bounce Rate. A Bounce Rate measures how quickly visitors to your website move along instead of sticking around and checking on your page for awhile. Thus, the reason a Bounce Rate is helpful in the world of digital marketing is that if customers bounce too quickly they may very well miss all the other amazing online experiences we have in store for them. To calculate a Bounce Rate one simply needs to divide the number of people who come and visit just one page (or leave the site within a designated time frame usually on the order of seconds) by the total number of visitors.

Satisfaction. Often called the "secret weapon" or "holy grail" of marketing loyalty, Satisfaction has been shown to predict future sales quite well, which sort of makes sense: if they're happy and you know it, just keep doing whatever it is you're doing. Although there are countless ways to measure satisfaction, and several people have made a link between satisfaction and future customer value, someone finally named the idea, registered the trademark, and turned a simple idea into an entire business. The Net Promoter Score®, was introduced by Fred Reichheld in a 2003 *Harvard Business Review* article. The metric is essentially one question–"How likely is it that you would recommend our company/product/service to a friend or colleague?"–typically measured on a 10-point scale. In Reichheld's version, people scoring 6 or less are "detractors," people scoring 9 or 10 are "promoters," and the in-betweeners are labeled "passives" (sort of sounds like Scientology, right?). After reading our chapter on statistics, we should know better than to place a lot of value on a *single* question attempting to measure anything. Here, too, we can be skeptical. While it is certainly good to know if a customer is likely to recommend our company, product, or service and this information *may* be predictive of likely future engagement with that customer, it is *one* measurement. Plus, what is with the arbitrary cutoffs? I guarantee that a score of 8 for a company in an industry with a lot of comparable alternatives (e.g., the restaurant industry) is *not* the same as an 8 for a company in an industry with very few comparable alternatives (e.g., energy companies). "But Jim, this metric was in an HBR article entitled *One*

Number You Need to Grow!" you're thinking, "Don't we need that number to grow?!" Not necessarily. Collecting it does not hurt, but let's not put too much stock in something that only *potentially* tells *part* of a story. Satisfaction *is* an important metric to include, but please don't believe that this is the *only* number you need to grow. It is not, and if you only consider this number when evaluating your campaign, quite ironically, you will *not* be satisfied.

Return on Marketing Investment. Finally, to use standard metrics to assess your integrated marketing campaign, one easy calculation to run is to divide the total revenues earned during the duration of the campaign by the total expenses for the campaign. This comparison leaves us with a benefit/cost ratio that can be increased by bolstering the benefit, minimizing costs associated with the campaign, and/or both. Quantifying marketing is probably among the most difficult business challenges and, consequently, is often the reason executives without a marketing background have very little hesitation when it comes to pulling the plug on a marketing budget in favor of divisions with clearer cause-and-effect metrics (...you know, boring disciplines like accounting or finance). Keeping this bias in mind, it is our job as marketers to quantify as much of what we do as possible to show, empirically, the value that we bring to the table.

Fusion Metrics: Revisiting Some Old Friends Who May Have Moved

The previous metrics are among the most commonly seen in the marketing discipline. However, please do not be misled into believing that just because a marketing metric is used by multiple organizations or has reared its head in marketing assessments over time that the metric is relevant or even an accurate tool to assess the success of our campaign. Different industries, different products, and different media require different metrics. You would not measure volume with a measuring cup, would you? Nor would you measure weight with a ruler. Just as we used different metrics in other parts of life, so, too, must we be cognizant of the fit and appropriateness of various metrics for our particular campaign and its specific executions.

In the context of this book and the FUSION model, we captured a lot of interesting data when we conducted research during the Understanding segment of our show. Throughout the book I have repeated that the purpose of any integrated marketing campaign should be to change the thoughts, feelings, and/or behaviors of our intended audience. Not surprisingly, the metrics we captured in our early research actually corresponded to these three categories: thoughts, feelings, and behaviors. With this in mind, now that the campaign has concluded we can capture these metrics again to what, if anything, has changed and if that movement was indeed significant.

Affect. Affect is the fancy psychology word describing anything and everything to do with feelings and emotions. Thus, when reviewing our campaign to look for changes in affect, we are curious as to whether or not our campaign has elicited new feelings from consumers (e.g., they once felt lost but now feel found, felt blind but now can see), strengthened the feelings that they feel (e.g., "I used to like Jif Peanut Butter, but now I love it!"), created emotional connections where there were no such connections before, and shifted preferences for our company, brand, or product/services, in general (e.g., "I cannot quite put it into words, but I really just *feel* like I like X!"). If the campaign's executions are particularly emotive we will expect a lot of movement on the feeling measures. However, even thought-provoking commercials or commercials listing lots of reasons for people to buy your product or service can make people *feel* more secure.

Behavior. Capturing changes in behavior is probably the "go-to" metric for most marketers because it includes one, very important behavior: purchasing. Of course, keeping track of the change in purchasing behavior is definitely a good idea. However, it is also a good idea to record changes with respect to *how* people are purchasing or *what* they are purchasing. One example that is directly related to our Open Up More Options objective involves looking at whether the basket of goods being purchase consists of various items throughout a company's portfolio of offerings as opposed to just one or two items. Similarly, it would be useful to know if our customers' purchasing behavior has shifted up to premium offerings, down to discounted or low-end offerings, or is exhibiting some other kind of interesting difference per the goal of our campaign. Another important metric to consider here is referrals and recommendations. How likely are people to talk about us, our produts/services, and even our campaign after they have seen it? This will give us an idea of how successful our campaign was at generating new potential customers and facilitating word-of-mouth.

Cognition. In the spirit of sexy psych words, cognition has anything and everything to do with thoughts, thinking, logic, and rationality. Here, we want to know how our campaign shifted thoughts, awareness, attribute importance/beliefs, and general knowledge about our company, our products/services, and our campaign. This is all the "heady" stuff. Quite importantly, our attitude models from before–ATOM, BIM, YACA–would be great metrics to include if they were captured in the Understanding research collection. Recreating Perceptual and Preference maps based on this new data would *also* be advantageous, as you could literally *see* the movement that was the result of your campaign on a two-dimensional space. Part of the reason marketing has been so difficult to quantify is because people simply do not know where to begin with respect to what data to capture and, once known, how to capture said data. Using the attitude change models, the questions capturing awareness, and the knowledge pre- and post-campaign provide us with hard data that can support our campaign's effectiveness. If our campaign was designed with the explicit goal to make people believe that simulated fruit-flavor accuracy is *the* most important attribute in the fruity candy product category, well, then we better see movement on the importance of that attribute in our ATOM. Likewise, if the goal was to make the Incase computer bag brand top of mind when it comes to handheld bags, well, our post-campaign analysis better see participants listing Incase when asked to list all the handheld bag companies they can.

In short, numbers need not scare you. If anything there are few things more exciting than finding out that your campaign, the project you toiled over for hours, days, weeks, and even months, did *exactly* what you wanted it to! And, guess what, even if it *didn't* do exactly what you wanted it to, now you know what needs to be improved for next time—there's no guesswork, no wondering, no mystery. You are free to include the "standard marketing metrics" like the ones I listed earlier, but the most important thing you can do is this: measure a key variable of interest prior to your campaign, measure that same key variable (using the same methodology) after that campaign, and then compare the two. If you see movement, you have done your job well; if you see a significant difference, you have done your job *very* well. If you see the room spinning, shooting stars, and endless freedom before you, well, you might be drunk (…on Fusion love), and it's time to call it a day. ☺

*　　*　　*

Most vodka is about 80 proof, which means that 40% of the beverage is straight up alcohol. Interestingly, the places that tend to be famous for their vodka include chilly realms like Russia, Sweden, Norway, Finland, Iceland and other northern European countries. In fact, this area is sometimes referred to as the "vodka belt," which goes well with your gin tunic and your hoop beer-rings (…I know, I know, but the book is almost finished).

The fact that alcohol freezes at a lower temperature than water is quite useful in this freezing cold part of the world where other alcoholic beverages might not be able to stand the harsh winter months. Yet, in order to expand their markets and their business, vodka producers from these nations have extended their products to vodka-lovers around the world, from club kids to the classy cocktail types, the cheap Smirnoff sippers to the Absolut Elyx fans and their top-shelf tastes. Now that customer preferences are shifting to alcoholic beverages with elaborate backstories and more refined ingredients, Absolut and its competitors are pushed to understand even the smallest of differences in the needs, wants, and preferences of the customers in the alcohol market.

Absolut believes it has found a solution in Absolut Elyx, the vodka in whiskey's clothing that caters to a more sophisticated vodka drinker who appreciates a restored wood and antique copper-lined condo over a modern, slick club with a thumping bassline and unfortunate fashion choices. The Absolut Elyx customer will not mind spending more for a premium experience, purchasing a bottle that is over twice as expensive as typical Absolut vodka.

What remains to be seen now, however, is whether Absolut Elyx has what it takes to be the preferred beverage of choice when these high-class comrades kick it for a night on the town. Will Absolut Elyx be the beverage of choice served in their VIP-area ice bucket or will Bourbon be the booze to imbibe? Either way, Absolut Elyx is destined for an ice bucket challenge of its own.

And, just like that, we are back where we started.

What if... *Mixing It Up with Absolut*

The alcohol industry provides a great context for understanding Millennials, that special group of consumers born between 1980 and 2000 (myself included). You see, Millennials are known for being picky: they know what they want, they have peculiar tastes, they do *not* like waiting, they grew up in a culture of immediate gratification, and they exhibit this odd preference for the underdog, the anti-establishment sort that is likely what gave rise to all-things Hipster. The increasing preference for independent brews and craft beers, as well as a growing demand for bourbon and other whiskeys, hints at these Millennial preferences, people more impressed by reclaimed wood than modern designs and by vintage clothing as opposed to the latest styles off the runways of Paris and Milan.

So how does a company like Absolut make itself relevant for these consumers in a time when heavy-handed marketing seems to be a huge turnoff to this group? Content marketing. You can recall from the previous chapter on IMS tools that content marketing refers to marketing executions that are typically out of the wheelhouse or domain of what a company is typically in the business of doing (e.g., the Michelin Guide restaurant guide from tire-producer Michelin) but that can directly or indirectly benefit the company behind the content.

Imagine a television show on Bravo (or Food Network on an equally DIY-centric station or, better yet for this target, on Netflix or YouTube) entitled, "Master Mixologist" in which the best cocktail chefs from around the world compete in a weekly competition to create the winning cocktail for a given theme. Perhaps the first season could take place in New York City so that one week might require the mixologists to create a drink inspired by artwork after visiting a museum like the MET, another week may see drinks inspired by Broadway shows, another week may be inspired by the different boroughs of New York, while another week could see drinks inspired by the different ethnic neighborhoods within Manhattan, etc. At no point would Absolut be mentioned explicitly or even implicitly (à la product placement). The goal of the show would be to interest viewers in elegant cocktails, some of which will likely incorporate vodka, to generate renewed interest in the artistry of cocktails.

Mixed in with the competitive aspect of the show would be the history of the spirits used in the beverages, as we know Millennials appreciate history. This would give many brands the opportunity to connect with this target audience with respect to origin and history, not just bourbons. Furthermore, this level of sophistication about how different spirits pair with various flavors takes cocktails to a classier level, a more refined kind of drinking that differentiates the spirits from the club/partier scene.

While any alcohol companies sponsoring the show may mitigate any benefits the subtlety of content marketing provides, there is an opportunity for *other* relevant companies to sponsor the show to everyone's mutual benefit. Consider, for example, juice companies (e.g., Tropicana) or potential mixers (e.g., Red Bull) sponsoring the show. These companies also stand to benefit from an increase in the preference for classy cocktails.

The biggest benefit from this sort of marketing campaign is that it includes countless opportunities for customer engagement. The competitive aspect of the show rallies the at-home audience behind particular contestants, particularly if the contestants are chosen strategically to represent key demographics or geographic areas (e.g., Los Angeles, Miami, Las Vegas, London, Rio, Paris, etc.), which should ignite conversations online about the competition itself. Furthermore, viewers are likely to have their own ideas for cocktails, ways to improve or change what was presented on the show, which then facilitates even *more* conversation about the various brands of spirits. Once the show establishes itself and a loyal audience, the campaign could also include either a competition for viewers or simply a place for viewers to share their own recipes. At this point it would make sense for the show to launch its own cocktail recipe book and other intellectual property featuring the show's branding, the winners, and even event-related opportunities at the bars and restaurants the contestants call home.

Because Absolut owns the show, its success in generating advertising dollars and increasing the demand for all spirits across the board would be a victory for the brand and its parent company. Although there may be some criticism about the use of alcohol in a reality-based competition, the counterargument is that the show presents alcohol consumption in an artistic, sophisticated light, which contrasts sharply with the typically seedy portrayals of alcohol consumption on shows like *The Real Housewives of [Anywhere]*. With this new appreciation of alcohol consumption, it is possible that people actually drink fewer drinks but value them more than if simply drinking beer or other alcoholic beverages.

Later, once the show has established a decent audience and has produced a few winning mixologists, Absolut can work with those individuals to produce new products within its portfolio that are designed by and/or inspired by these winners and sold under the Absolut brand name. In this way, Absolut can tie these new products to the rich histories of the mixologists, their backgrounds, their unique tastes and preferences, the creation process of their particular vodka product. This approach taps into the appreciation the target audience has for the history of the spirits they drink in an even more engaging way than hearing about old stories pertaining to a brewery. In this version, customers get to *live* the history and origin story of their favorite alcohol artists as opposed to being passive listeners, which should resonate well with Millennials.

And the best part? Given Absolut's well-established relationship between alcohol and art, the sophisticated approach taken by *Master Mixologist*, which includes scores based on taste, creativity, *and* artistic appearance is as brand consistent as possible. Absolut can leverage this unique connection to all-things artistic in a way that no other alcohol company really can (i.e., the *same* show created by Smirnoff or Anheuser-Busch simply lacks the same level of sophistication that Absolut brings to the table). Furthermore, as my dear friend, Robert Andersson (a content marketing specialist and a Swede) would probably suggest, the show's format could be licensed to international markets so that Absolut Vodka will be a drink of choice all over the world once more. I suppose we can all drink to that!

EPILOGUE | Keep the Energy Going

You made it!

After reading page after page, tip after tip, example after example, you are finally at the end of *Fusion*! For those of you who were creating an integrated marketing campaign while simultaneously reading the book, I sincerely hope that *something* I have said (hopefully several things) has helped you create a better campaign or has led you to consider an idea you may not have otherwise considered. For those of you who simply read the book to get an understanding of the FUSION model and now plan to embark on an integrated marketing campaign creation process, Godspeed and good luck! I will be here, in book form, should you need me, and I hope that you now know which section of the book to which you can refer should you get stuck or need some pointers.

For all of you, campaign creators and soon-to-be campaign creators alike, I thought it would be useful to summarize the *entire* book and the FUSION model in the pages that follow so that, going forward, you can refer to this chapter first to help get you going on future campaigns. Then, if a particular section or concept is unclear or seems murky in your memory, all you have to do is refer back to that specific section of the book to jog your memory! I am all about making life simpler, more fun, and more productive, so consider this my parting gift to you, dear friend, now that our time together is drawing to a close. I sure hope it's helpful!

– THE FUSION MODEL: A Summary –

FOCUS | What is the business goal we are trying to achieve?
   -Prospective Audience: Who presents us with an opportunity to create value?
      -W: Wandering Customers: customers who are loyal to no one
      -H: Hot-of-the-Press Customers: customers brand new to the market
      -O: Others' Customers: customers loyal to other companies
      -M: My Customers: customers loyal to our company

   -Desired Objective (DO): What do we want these customers to do?
      -M: Multiply purcbases: increase frequency or amount of purchasing
      -O: Open Up More Options: expand purchases in portfolio, premium, etc.
      -R: Rally the troops: motivate the customers to engage on your behalf
      -E: Educate: teach, inform, and convey knowledge to the customers

UNDERSTANDING | What do we know about our prospective customer(s)?
   -L: Lifestyle: What are the customers' demographics, personality, media habits?
   -E: Education: How much do the customers know/not know about us?
   -A: Attitudes: What are the current attitudes, perceptions, and preferences re: us?
   -R: Reflection: How do customers see themselves? Actual v. ideal self?
   -N: Needs: What needs of the customers remain unfulfilled?

SYNTHESIZE | Which creative idea should become the Big Idea?**

-Fuse the Focus goals with the Understanding insights to spark creativity
-A Big Idea is a creative idea that you can LOVE:
    -L: Logically connects our business objectives with our research insights
    -O: One-of-a-Kind; other companies could not also use the same idea
    -V: Variations on a theme allow for executions across different media
    -E: Emotionally evocative or engaging to increase appeal and recall

IDEATION | How can we translate the Big Idea into specific executions?

-Develop a campaign emphasizing *consistency* and *energy* using:
    -Partnerships: sponsorships, PR, promotions, philanthropic initiatives
    -Outlandish: guerilla marketing, content marketing, experiential marketing
    -Revolutionary: product innovation, packaging redesign, pricing shift
    -Traditional Media: television, print ads, radio, internet/website, events
    -Social Media: social networks, word-of-mouth, forums and message boards

OPERATIONS | How can we prepare for the unexpected, fine tune, and test?

-Before the campaign launches, there are a few final considerations:
    -Response: anticipating competitive response to preempt problems
    -Editing: locating holes, eliminating redundancy, striving for elegance
    -Aftermath: considering the transition between this campaign and the next
    -Counterattacks: dealing with provocations or reactions from competitors
    -Timeline: determining efficient media spend, execution amount, synergy

NET EFFECT | How do we know if our campaign has been successful?

-Traditional Measures:
    -Churn
    -Customer Lifetime Value
    -Cost of Customer Acquisition
    -Bounce
    -Satisfaction
-Fusion Measures:
    -Prospective Audience: increased awareness, attention, or engagement
    -Desired Objective: buying more, buying diverse, more active, smarter
    -Change in Affect: feeling type/strength, emotional connection, preferences
    -Change in Behavior: purchasing frequency/portfolio, premium, referrals
    -Change in Cognition: consideration, awareness, attribute importance

Lest you think we forgot about one central component to the FUSION model's approach to integrated marketing, rest assured there is one final question we must always ask ourselves at the end of *every* campaign: how did this campaign make our customers' lives *better*? This creation of value is at the heart of marketing and should be at the heart of everything we do. If you can honestly say how your customers' lives are better as a result of your integrated marketing campaign's success, well, you will have singlehandedly shown why marketing is *not* evil and can, in fact, bring a lot of good into this world.

Although Fusion refers to the synergy that comes from all the various parts of an integrated marketing campaign reinforcing one another, compensating for the weaknesses of some and bolstering the strengths of others, Fusion also refers to the synergy that comes from a company and its customers coming together in the marketplace. When firms become too focused on profits and customers become cynical about the motivations of companies, these two groups do not come together; they drift apart. This artificial distance makes it easier for companies to ignore the needs of consumers and easier for consumers to ignore the ways in which a company's products and services could benefit them.

One final issue I wanted to bring up before we bid each other farewell: although the emphases and examples throughout this book focused on B2C (i.e., business to consumer) campaigns, keep in mind that much of marketing consists of B2B (i.e., business to business) communication. It is often the case that the audience you want to persuade is *not* an individual shopping in your store or on your website but, instead, is another company or organization. The good news is that the FUSION model still applies. Some slight tweaks regarding tools/executions to consider or how best to conduct research and obtain data may need to be considered, but the spirit of the model remains the same. After all, the decision makers within those organizations are humans…for now, anyway. #TheFuture #Robots

*   *   *

I used to be a shy kid.

I know, I know…if you know me, that is probably impossible to believe, but it is true. I was always comfortable and creative around my family, but that was because they loved me. I had nothing to be afraid of. No idea was, "Too stupid," no idea was, "Not good enough," no idea was, "Impossible."

Then came the real world.

For whatever reason, people have a great time putting each other down, criticizing each other's ideas without helping or suggesting alternative solutions, and prioritizing their self-interests over everything else. For an observant child like myself, that was intimidating. For a creative child like myself, that was frightening. Why would I put myself out there in the real world if people were only going to poke fun at my ideas or, even worse, at me?

One day, I was calling around searching for a hard-to-find game in the *Carmen Sandiego* computer game series, specifically *"Where in Europe is Carmen Sandiego?"* I wanted this game so much I could taste it, and it tasted like Italian pasta and fresh-baked French croissants. I *loved* Europe, the homeland of my people, America's best friends, the origin of ABBA and

The Beatles! I had just about every other game in the *Carmen Sandiego* collection, and I was going to track this game down! My parents promised that if I could find it they would take me to get it.

I called stores for *hours*. The mental picture you have is probably a modern, nerdy-looking kid on a cellphone. No. This was pre-cellphone. I actually had our a huge phone book, a cordless phone (which was very high-tech at the time), and a notepad/pencil to scratch off all the numbers of places I had tried with no success.

I got to the point where I thought I had tried *every* store in town: Venture, Kmart, Babbage's (these store names should date this story). Nothing. Finally, with exhaustion setting in and sadness filling my heart, poor, little pre-pubescent Jim, scrawny and with the voice of a delicate angel, made one *final* call to Walmart that went something like this:

Me: Where in Europe is Carmen Sandiego?

Walmart lady: What?

Me: (louder and more clearly) Where in Europe is Carmen Sandiego?

(click ... she hung up ... "She must have dropped the phone!" I thought...so I called back)

Me: Where in Europe is Carmen Sandiego?

Walmart lady: (angrily) Ma'am, this is a place of business!

Ouch. The Walmart lady mistook my pre-puberty wispy falsetto as a female voice. Of course, at the same moment I was realizing that Walmart lady (whom I can only assumed was probably named something like Gladys or Verna) thought I was a woman, I also realized that at no point during our call did I say, "Hello!" or, "I have a question for you," or, "I'm looking for a computer game." No, I just answered the phone with, "Where in Europe is Carmen Sandiego?" No wonder she thought I was some prank calling nut job!

Thankfully, I had an opportunity to explain myself, "Oh, I'm sorry. I meant to say that I am looking for a computer game. Can you connect me to someone in electronics?" which prompted Gladys/Verna to say, "One second, ma'am," (again!) her sassy attitude still somehow seeping through the phone. Turns out, Walmart didn't even have the game. I was having a terrific day.

If you are wondering if I ever tracked down *Where in Europe is Carmen Sandiego?* you will be glad to know that I did. Not only that, but I also captured Carmen Sandiego in Europe *and* my voice *finally* changed...but only after I spent months self-consciously answering the phone in an artificially low, gruff voice. It was around that same time that we received a phone call from Mrs. Joanne Rompel asking my mom if I would be interested in joining Odyssey of the Mind (I probably heard the phone ring but didn't answer it, you know, on account of my voice), this international program for creative gifted kids. In a single phone call, this shy, nerdy kid with a huge forehead, a weird obsession with *Saturday Night Live* and *Carmen Sandiego*, and a love of all-things international began his confidence-building creative journey, a path that has taken him around the world and landed him right here, with you, right now.

I am still chasing Carmen Sandiego because Carmen Sandiego *is* creativity. They are both elusive, they are both alluring, but if you try hard enough and stay committed, you will *always* catch them…and even have a little fun in the process.

So, what are you waiting for? Go get 'em!

Hey, you –

This is that awkward part at the end of a date when one of us goes in for the kiss not exactly sure whether or not the other person is "feeling it" and plans to reciprocate. "I had a really nice time tonight," one of you says. "Yeah, me, too," says the other. They lock eyes, the world around them disppears, and, in that moment, they just *know*. So I just wanted to let you know: 1) I had a really nice time tonight, and I hope you did, too, 2) Maybe there was something in here that you liked, something that will make your life better, something that will make your job easier, or at least something that made you smile, and finally, if #1 and #2 are true and you're not doing anything later then 3) let's make out...

...just kidding, but I did love our time together and hope we can do it again sometime.

Keep the positive energy flowing with Fusion,

-Jim

- REFERENCES -

ALS Association (2015), "ALS Ice Bucket Challenge to Return this August," ALS Association, http://www.alsa.org/news/media/press-releases/als-ice-bucket-challenge.html?referrer=https://www.google.com/

Barbe, Walter Burke; Swassing, Raymond H.; Milone, Michael N. (1979). Teaching through modality strengths: concepts and practices. Columbus, Ohio: Zaner-Bloser

Dietrich, Arne, and Riam Kanso (2010), "A Review of EEG, ERP, and Neuroimaging Studies of Creativity and Insight," *Psychological Bulletin*, 136 (5), 822-848.

Förster, Jens, Friedman, R.S., and Nira Liberman (2004), "Temporal Construal Effects on Abstract and Concrete Thinking: Consequences for Insight and Creative Cognition," *Journal of Personality and Social Psychology*, 87 (2), 177-189.

Gardner, Howard. Creating Minds: An Anatomy of Creativity Seen Through the Lives of Freud, Einstein, Picasso, Stravinsky, Eliot, Graham, and Gandhi. New York: BasicBooks, 1993. Print.

Gilbert, Ben (2016), "Nintendo's Wii U is a Tremendous Flop, as Explained in One Chart from Nintendo," *Tech Insider*, http://www.techinsider.io/nintendos-wii-u-is-a-major-flop-2016-1

Hudson, Laura (2014), "Nintendo's New Key to Creativity: More Women," *Wired*, http://www.wired.com/2014/03/animal-crossing-director/

Internet Advertising Bureau UK (2014), "More Women Now Play Video Games Than Men," http://www.iabuk.net/about/press/archive/more-women-now-play-video-games-than-men

Jia, Lile, Hirt, Edward R., and Samuel C. Karpen (2009), "Lessons From a Faraway Land: The Effect of Spatial Distance on Creative Cognition," *Journal of Experimental Social Psychology*, 45, 1127–1131.

McGuire, W. J. (1968). Personality and attitude change: An information-processing theory. In A. G. Greenwood, T. C. Print

Mehta, Ravi, Zhu, Rui (Juliet), and Amar Cheema (2012), "Is Noise Always Bad? Exploring the Effects of Ambient Noise on Creative Cognition," *Journal of Consumer Research*, December, 784-799.

Moreau, C. Page and Darren W. Dahl (2005), "Designing the Solution: The Impact of Constraints on Consumers' Creativity," *Journal of Consumer Research*, 32 (1), 13-22.

Mourey, James A., Lam, Ben C.P., and Daphna Oyserman (2015), "Consequences of Cultural Fluency, *Social Cognition*, 33 (4), 308-344.

Paulus, Paul B. and Huei-Chuan Yang (2000), "Idea Generation in Groups: A Basis for Creativity in Organizations," *Organizational Behavior and Human Decision Processes*, 82 (1), 76-87.

Sternberg, R. J., & Lubart, T. I. (1993). Investing in creativity. *Psychological Inquiry*, 4(3), 229-232.

ABOUT THE AUTHOR

James (Jim) Alvarez Mourey, Ph.D., was born to a Gypsy tribe in the streets of Paris before retreating to the bell tower of Notre...wait, wait...wrong bio. Jim Mourey was born on a rainy March 23, 1983, in the town of Belleville, Illinois, a city known for having the longest "Main Street" in the world (9.2 miles)... bring your friends! He attended Abraham Lincoln School, West Jr. High, and Belleville West High School where he was Class President, Lead Actor in a Musical, Leading Delegate in the Model United Nations, Editor-in-Chief of the Newspaper, and a proud member of the marching band, symphonic band, jazz band, *and* the Maroon Majic (with a "j") show choir...also, for whatever reason, he was single all of those years. Jim studied business at Washington University in St. Louis, balancing his academic pursuits with the all-male a cappella group The Stereotypes, talking about feelings while eating ice cream in the common room (RA'ing), and coordinating weekly alcohol-free alternative programming for the campus community...yep, still single. During this time, Jim began working for a marketing firm specializing in luxury brands in St. Louis while also providing independent creative marketing services for small businesses in the St. Louis area. Jim's next move was to the University of Michigan where he completed his Ph.D. in marketing while keeping one foot in the real (and warmer) world of Los Angeles, serving as the co-creator and Executive Director of a marketing/management consultancy's research division.   Academia ultimately won Jim over, and now he works as an Assistant Professor of Marketing at DePaul University in Chicago where he teaches Consumer Behavior to undergraduate business and MBA students, coordinates his Modern Marketing Lab research group, advises the DePaul Marketing Consulting Group (DMCG), and teaches incoming freshmen a course on improvisational comedy that visits Second City, iO, The Annoyance Theatre, and ComedySportz. He is also the creator and producer of the podcast *It's a Brand New Day* and the web series *Street Walkers*, two projects he is proud to assemble alongside some of the funniest, brightest students. In addition to *Fusion*, Jim is the author of *Urge* (a marketing book about consumer psychology), as well as two children's books: *Butters the Fly* and *Rabbit with a Habit* (thankfully not a drug-related habit). When not busy working, writing, singing, exotic dancing, or creating, Jim spends his time living in a real-life sitcom. He once sat at a table for 15 minutes talking to a stranger he thought was someone else, farted *repeatedly* during a conference call when he was certain he muted his phone earlier in the conversation (...he had not), and awkwardly ruined a courter's flirtatious attempts to woo him by explaining the secret to whiter teeth for five minutes without pausing (hint: drink through straws). He loves his family, long runs along Lake Michigan, breakfast for dinner, and Tina Fey ... and (*leans in and whispers*) don't tell *anyone* this, but sometimes he *is* the guy ringing the bells at Notre Dame.

www.jimmourey.com

www.ingramcontent.com/pod-product-compliance
Lightning Source LLC
Chambersburg PA
CBHW021550210326
41599CB00010B/390